Security, Rights and Law

This book examines how the Israeli High Court of Justice (HCJ) has interpreted and applied international law principles in adjudicating petitions filed by Palestinians. The research focuses on HCJ judgments that have been rendered since the outbreak of the *Second Intifada* (2000) in relation to petitions challenging the legality of measures implemented by various Israeli governments and military authorities for the professed need of enhancing the security of Israeli settlements and settlers in the occupied West Bank. It discusses to what extent the HCJ provides a venue for an effective domestic remedy for alleged violations of the Palestinians' internationally protected rights. It further analyses the judgments of the Court seeking to demonstrate why it appears to show a preference for invoking principles of Israeli administrative and constitutional law, thereby promoting the domestic rather than international Rule of Law. Although the jurisprudence of the HCJ has often been hailed as that of an 'activist' court, the analysis of petitions adjudicated by the Court between 2000 and 2014 illustrates why its approach is ill-suited to a situation of prolonged military occupation. Finally, the book evaluates what impact the Court's adjudication, reasoning and interpretation has on the normative coherence of the international law of belligerent occupation.

Rouba Al-Salem graduated with a PhD in international law from Université de Montréal. She has previously worked in human rights legal research, advocacy and training as it relates to the Middle East, both at the NGO and UN levels.

Security, Rights and Law

The Israeli High Court of Justice and Israeli Settlements in the Occupied West Bank

Rouba Al-Salem

Routledge
Taylor & Francis Group
LONDON AND NEW YORK

First published 2019
by Routledge
2 Park Square, Milton Park, Abingdon, Oxon OX14 4RN

and by Routledge
52 Vanderbilt Avenue, New York, NY 10017

First issued in paperback 2020

Routledge is an imprint of the Taylor & Francis Group, an informa business

British Library Cataloguing-in-Publication Data
A catalogue record for this book is available from the British Library

Library of Congress Cataloging-in-Publication Data
Names: Såalim, Rubåa, author.
Title: Security, rights and law : the Israeli High Court of Justice and the Israeli settlements in the occupied West Bank / by Rouba Al-Salem.
Description: Abingdon, Oxon ; New York, NY : Routledge, 2019. | Series: Comparative constitutionalism in Muslim majority states | Based on author's thesis (doctoral – Universitâe de Montrâeal, 2016) issued under title: What 'Security', whose 'Rights' and which 'Law'? : the Israeli High Court of Justice and the Israeli settlements in the occupied West Bank. | Includes bibliographical references and index.
Identifiers: LCCN 2018040845| ISBN 9781138095106 (hbk) | ISBN 9781351602280 (adobe) | ISBN 9781351602266 (mobipocket) | ISBN 9781351602273 (epub)
Subjects: LCSH: Land use–Law and legislation–West Bank–Cases. | Squatter settlements–West Bank–Cases. | Israel. Bet ha-mishpaòt ha-gavoha le-tsedeòk. | Israelis–Legal status, laws, etc.–West Bank–Cases. | Palestinian Arabs–Civil rights–Israel–Cases.
Classification: LCC KMM806.6 S25 2019 | DDC 346.569404/40956942–dc23
LC record available at https://lccn.loc.gov/2018040845

ISBN 13: 978-0-367-66332-2 (pbk)
ISBN 13: 978-1-138-09510-6 (hbk)

Typeset in Galliard
by Wearset Ltd, Boldon, Tyne and Wear

In memory of my father and for my mother both of whom taught me that peace and justice come hand in hand.

In dedication to the Israeli and Palestinian human rights activists and lawyers and their relentless struggle towards greater accountability, dignity, and fundamental rights for the victims of this conflict.

Contents

Preface

This book is the outcome of a fascinating research journey, which I began as a PhD student at the Faculty of Law, Université de Montréal. However, my interest in the issue began much earlier, when I lived and worked in the field of human rights in the occupied West Bank. During that time, one of the things that struck me the most was the heated, and often emotional, reactions and debate that the adjudication by the Israeli High Court of Justice (HCJ) of petitions by Palestinians was capable of generating (every time) between and among colleagues working at various Palestinian and Israeli human rights organizations. One particular point to which the different lawyers and civil society organizations kept reverting on a constant basis, concerns the continued usefulness (and wisdom) of litigating on behalf of Palestinians in front of the HCJ. My recollection of these discussions, long after they had taken place, is responsible for generating the writing that has resulted in this book.

In many ways, a judicial process provides petitioners with an important opportunity to tell 'their story' and express their narrative. Hence, one desired goal of this book is to provide an in-depth overview of the competing narratives of the parties and to demonstrate the powerful way in which the HCJ's adjudication has affected the lives of millions of Palestinians living under military rule and has legalized measures in an occupied territory not just on the micro-level (i.e. the particular petition) but also the macro-level. Often highly succinct case summaries of HCJ judgments do not provide an overview of how the impact of a given policy on petitioners at the micro-level has implications on the macro-level. Where possible, this book has sought to provide more context and details in an effort to shed light on this important aspect.

Acknowledgements

Since this book is based on my doctoral thesis, I wish to extend my sincere appreciation to my former research director at the Université de Montréal (UdeM), Professor Stéphane Beaulac, for his impeccable supervision of my PhD journey, and invaluable support. My profound gratitude also goes to my co-research director Professor Anne-Marie La Rosa, who provided much needed guidance, fascinating conversations and legal expertise throughout.

This research would not have been possible without the devoted time, incredible energy and assistance of Avichay Sharon who relentlessly translated many of the decisions that were only available in English and without whom interviews with some of the lawyers would not have featured as the backbone of this book.

In addition, I want to thank the Fonds Québécois de la Recherche sur la Société et la Culture (FQRSC) for its generous doctoral research scholarship, which allowed me to immerse myself into this fascinating field. In addition, I thank the Faculty of Law and the Faculté des Études Supérieures et Postdoctorales at UdeM for their generous scholarship opportunities that have enabled me to complete every phase of my doctoral thesis, as well as the Center for Human Rights and Legal Pluralism at McGill University's Faculty of Law and its director Professor François Crépeau, for allowing me to exchange and debate ideas and to finalize this book during the last few months of my enjoyable postdoctoral Steinberg Fellowship in International Migration Law and Policy (2017–2018).

My deep-felt gratitude also goes to Attorneys Michael Sfard, Netta Amar, Nasrat Dakwar, Quamar Mishriqi, and an Israeli lawyer wishing to remain anonymous, for the precious time and important insights that they afforded me as interviewees. I equally want to extend heartfelt gratitude to Raja Shehadeh, Charles Shamas, and Ram Rahat for the valuable analysis that they offered me throughout their interviews. This is in addition to Dror Etkes, Michaela Rahat and an Israeli attorney (wishing to remain anonymous) for their helpful written feedback in response to my many questions. I remain humbled by all of these individuals' commitment, their sense of purpose, their strong convictions and their courage. I am also thankful for the opportunity to raise questions and seek feedback from Orna Ben-Naftali, Sharon Weill, Aeyal Gross, Valentina Azarov,

Suzie Navot, Aviv Tatarsky, Alon Cohen-Lifshitz, Richard Falk, Meera Shah and Bruno Demeyere. I also remain indebted to my friend Jacinthe Assaad and to Jess Aimie White with proofreading and editing of the doctoral thesis on which this book is based, as well as to Alison Kirk, Chloe James, Jen Hinchliffe and others at Routledge for the valuable input, feedback and follow up that guaranteed that this book saw the light of day. Last but not least, I wish to express gratefulness to my family and friends, especially to my husband, Wael, my daughter, Fairouz, and my mother, Randa, for their never-faltering love, and their unwavering love, encouragement and patience.

Rouba Al-Salem

Abbreviations

ACRI	Association for Civil Rights in Israel
Adalah	The Legal Center for Arab Minority Rights in Israel
Adh Genève	Geneva Academy for International Humanitarian Law
AI	Amnesty International
AIC	Alternative Information Center
Al-Haq	Law in the Service of Man
Al-Quds	The word 'Jerusalem' in Arabic
ARIJ	Applied Research Institute-Jerusalem
BBC	British Broadcasting Corporation
BDS	Boycott Divestment and Sanctions
Beit Mishpat	Hebrew name for the Israeli Supreme Court
Bimkom	Planners for Planning Rights in Israel
B'Tselem	The Israeli Information Center for Human Rights in the Occupied Territories
CA	Civil Administration
CAT	Convention against Torture
CEDAW	Convention on the Elimination of Discrimination against Women
CERD	Convention on the Elimination of Racial Discrimination
CHR	Commission on HR
COGAT	Coordination of Government Activities in the Territories
CPS	Council for Peace and Security
CRC	Convention on the Rights of the Child
DCO	District Coordination Office
DIAKONIA	Name of a Swedish faith-based organization
DoP	Declaration of Principles between Israel and the PLO of 1993
Dunum	A metric measure for land (4 dunums = 1 acre)
EC	European Commission
ECHR	European Court on Human Rights
ECOSOC	Economic and Social Council
EJ	East Jerusalem
Eretz Israel	'Greater Israel' in Hebrew

ESCR	Economic Social and Cultural Rights
EU	European Union
FIDH	International Federation for Human Rights
FMEP	Foundation for Middle East Peace
FQRSC	Fonds Québécois de la Recherche sur la Société et la Culture
GA	General Assembly
Hamoked	Center for the Defense of the Individual
HCJ	High Court of Justice
HEPG	Humanitarian and Emergency Policy Group
HPCR	Program on Humanitarian Policy and Conflict Research
HRC	Human Rights Council
HR Committee	Human Rights Committee
HRW	Human Rights Watch
ICAHD	Israeli Committee against House Demolitions
ICC	International Criminal Court
ICCPR	International Covenant on Civil and Political Rights
ICESCR	International Covenant on Economic Social and Cultural Rights
ICG	International Crisis Group
ICJ	International Court of Justice
ICRC	International Committee of the Red Cross
ICTR	International Criminal Tribunal for Rwanda
ICTY	International Criminal Tribunal for the Former Yugoslavia
ID	Identification Document
IDF	Israeli Defense Forces
IDI	Israel Democracy Institute
IHL	International Humanitarian Law
IHR law	International Human Rights Law
ILA	International Law Association
ILC	International Law Commission
Inter-Am Ct HR	Inter-American Court on Human Rights
Intifada	The word 'Uprising' in Arabic
Ir Amim	Hebrew Equivalent to 'City of Nations' or 'City of People'
JIIS	Jerusalem Institute for Israel Studies
JM	Israeli self-declared Jerusalem Municipality (includes annexed EJ)
JMB	Israeli self-declared Jerusalem Municipal Border
'Judea and Samaria'	Official Israeli phrase for the West Bank excluding Jerusalem
Knesset	Name in Hebrew for Israel's Parliament
LACC	Local Aid Coordination Committee
Machsom Watch	Women against the Wall and for Human Rights
MC	Military Commander
MO	Military Order
MoD	Ministry of Defense – Israel
MoFA	Ministry of Foreign Affairs – Israel

MoI	Ministry of Interior – Israel
MoJ	Ministry of Justice – Israel
NAD	Negotiations Affairs Department – PLO
NGO	Non-Governmental Organization
NIS	New Israeli Shekel (currency)
OCHA	Office for the Coordination of Humanitarian Assistance
OHCHR	Office of the High Commissioner for Human Rights
oPt	Occupied Palestinian Territory
Otef Yerushalaim	'Jerusalem Hugger' in Hebrew
PA	Palestinian Authority
PCBS	Palestinian Central Bureau of Statistics
PCIJ	Permanent Court of International Justice
PLO	Palestine Liberation Organization
PSR	Palestinian Center for Policy and Survey Research
RHR	*Rabbis for Human Rights*
RoL	Rule of Law
SC	Security Council
SSZ	Special Security Zone
TIPH	Temporary International Presence in Hebron
Tfisah lohmatit	The phrase 'Belligerent Possession' in Hebrew
UdeM	Université de Montréal
UDHR	Universal Declaration of Human Rights
UK	United Kingdom
UN	United Nations
UNCTAD	United Nations Conference on Trade and Development
UNICEF	UN Children's Fund
UNISPAL	United Nations Information System on the Question of Palestine
UNRWA	United Nations Relief and Working Agency
US	United States
USD	United States Dollar (currency)
USMEP	United States Middle East Project
VAT	Value Added Tax
WB	World Bank
West Bank	The territory west of the River Jordan that was occupied by Israel in 1967, including Israeli-annexed East Jerusalem
'West Bank'	The same as above but without East Jerusalem
WHO	World Health Organization
WWII	World War II
WZO	World Zionist Organization
Yachad	Together for Israel
Yerushalaym	The word 'Jerusalem' in Hebrew
Yesh Din	Volunteers for Human Rights
Yishuv	The Hebrew word for Jewish community and Zionist political institutions in Mandatory Palestine before 1948

Interviewees

Interviews

Amar-Shiff, Netta (24 August 2014, Jerusalem)
Attorney *A-04* (23 July 2014, Jerusalem)
Dakwar, Nasrat (7 July 2014, Jerusalem)
Mishriqi, Quamar (26 June 2014, Jerusalem)
Sfard, Michael (10 July 2014, Tel Aviv) (21 October 2014, Tel Aviv) via Skype
Shamas, Charles (21 November 2014) via Skype
Shehateh, Raja (2 October 2014) via Skype

Written responses

Attorney *A03-B* (10 July 2014)
Etkes, Dror (1 February 2015)
Mishriqi, Quamar (13 September 2015)
Rahat, Michaela (22 March 2015)

Introduction

This book is about the Israeli Supreme Court and how, in its capacity as the High Court of Justice (HCJ),[1] it has adjudicated petitions by Palestinians seeking to challenge the legality of measures that have been implemented by Israeli military and government authorities for the alleged security of Israeli settlements and settlers in the occupied West Bank. In particular, the analysis focuses on the Court's judgments that were rendered after the outbreak of the *Second Intifada* (Uprising) in 2000.

Beginning in 1967, Israel's occupation of the West Bank represents the longest military occupation in modern history.[2] In the absence of a written constitution, the HCJ, the highest judicial body of the Israeli legal system, has played an activist role in advancing the state of human rights in Israel.[3] The HCJ's adjudication of petitions from the occupied territories represented the first time in modern history when the highest judicial authority of an Occupying Power established jurisdiction over appeals from an occupied territory that were challenging the legality of actions by military authorities.[4] As early as the 1970s, the HCJ's judicial decisions also began to underscore that international humanitarian law (IHL) and in particular the international law of belligerent

1 Article 15(c) of the Basic Law: *The Judiciary*, online: *Knesset* http://knesset.gov.il/laws/special/eng/BasicLawTheJudiciary.pdf.

2 International Committee of the Red Cross (ICRC), 'Contemporary Challenges to IHL-Occupation: Overview', (11 June 2012), online: ICRC www.icrc.org/en/document/occupation.

3 'Judicial activism' has been referred to as the willingness of judges to actively review and, if need be, criticize and intervene in the decisions and actions of the executive, including those that affect fundamental rights. Amos Guiora and Erin M. Page, 'Going Toe to Toe: President Barak's and Chief Justice Rehnquist's Theory of Judicial Activism', (2005–2006) 29:1 Hastings Int'l and Comparative Law Review 51.

4 Eshter Rosalind Cohen, 'Justice for Occupied Territory? The Israeli High Court of Justice Paradigm', (1985) 24 Colum J Transnat'l L 471; (337/71) [1972] *Christian Society for the Holy Places v. Minister of Defense* (1972) 2 Isr YB Hum Rts 354 [*Christian Society* Judgment].

occupation (which is a branch thereof),[5] must guide the actions of Israel's military and executive authorities in the occupied territory and vis-à-vis its Palestinian civilian population. Over the years, the HCJ has also invoked international human rights (IHR) law, particularly the International Covenant on Civil and Political Rights (ICCPR), to which Israel is a State Party.

This book seeks to contribute to the understanding of the elements that have shaped the HCJ's interpretation of relevant rules and principles of the international law of belligerent occupation, in its adjudication of petitions by Palestinians following the outbreak of the *Second Intifada* in 2000, by focusing on two objectives: the first one, is to analyze the extent to which the HCJ has provided Palestinian petitioners, who are alleging violations of their rights as enshrined in and protected under this body of law, with a domestic venue for effective judicial remedy.[6] Towards this objective, the analysis focuses strictly on the HCJ judgments that were rendered in relation to security-based measures implemented in the West Bank for the alleged benefit of Israeli settlements and settlers. This would best highlight the challenges that the highest domestic court of the Occupying Power faces when adjudicating competing rights and interests outside the borders of the state's national territory, in an occupied territory.

Israeli authorities have also invoked the close physical proximity between Israeli settlers and the Palestinians living in the same territory to justify the

5 Peter Maurer, 'Challenges to International Humanitarian Law: Israel's Occupation Policies', (Winter 2012) 94: 888 Int'l Rev Red Cross 1503. Provisions regulating this state of affairs can be found in the *Convention (IV) respecting the Laws and Customs of War on Land and its Annex: Regulation concerning the Laws and Customs of War on Land and its Annex: Regulations concerning the Laws and Customs of War on Land*, 18 October 1907, Cons TS No 25, 277 (entered into force 26 January 1910) [Hague Regulations 1907], the Fourth Geneva Convention, *Geneva Convention (IV) Relative to the Protection of Civilian Persons in Time of War (12 August 1949)*, 75:973 UNT 287 (entered into force 21 October 1950) [Fourth Geneva Convention] and *Protocol Additional to the Geneva Conventions of 12 August 1949, and relating to the Protection of Victims of International Armed Conflicts (1977)* 1125 UNTS 3 (entered into force 7 December 1978) [First Additional Protocol].

6 The definition of reparation for an international wrongful act has been developed primarily in relation to states. *Case Concerning the Factory of Chorzów (Germany v. Poland)* (1928), Permanent Court of International Justice (PCIJ) (Ser A) No. 17 at 47. In the *Wall* Advisory Opinion, the ICJ underscored the idea that reparations can be owned by states 'to all natural or legal persons concerned'. *Legal Consequences of the Construction of a Wall in the Occupied Palestinian Territory* [2004] ICJ Rep 136 at para 152 [ICJ *Wall* Advisory Opinion]. Remedies for gross violations of IHL and IHR law include the victim's right to the following: equal and effective access to justice; adequate, effective and prompt reparation for harm suffered and access to relevant information concerning violations and reparation mechanisms. Reparation for harm suffered can come in many forms, including restitution, compensation, rehabilitation, satisfaction and guarantees of non-repetition. Principles 11 and 21 of the *Basic Principles and Guidelines on the Right to a Remedy and Reparation for Victims of Gross Violations of International Human Rights Law and Serious Violations of International Humanitarian Law*, Annex to GA Res 60/147, UNGAOR, 60th Sess, Supp No. 49, UN Doc A/RES/60/47 (16 December 2005) at para 8, online: Office of the High Commissioner for Human Rights (OHCHR) www.ohchr.org/EN/ProfessionalInterest/Pages/RemedyAndReparation.aspx [thereafter UN Guidelines].

implementation of a wide spectrum of administrative, legislative and military actions against the latter on the grounds of the vital security needs of the former. Many of these measures were challenged by Palestinians in front of the HCJ, the major ones of which will be examined in this book. One of them is the Wall, which authorities began constructing in 2002. Another measure is the designation of much of the land that is trapped between the Green Line and the Wall as a Seam Zone and the imposition of an associated permit regime to govern the entry and exit of Palestinians to and from that zone. A subsequent measure is the special security zones (SSZs) which Israeli authorities have established around settlements and to which Palestinians have no or limited access. Palestinians have also challenged the implementation of movement restrictions (particularly checkpoints and the requirement of holding a permit) on Palestinians commuting between different towns and villages inside the West Bank, or between the West Bank and annexed East Jerusalem (EJ) for the alleged purpose of ensuring the safety of Israeli citizens. Lastly, the book examines the HCJ's adjudication of petitions challenging the construction of parts of the Wall in and around *de jure* annexed EJ.

International law and its interpretation have been instrumental in shaping the discourse of the protagonists, including before the HCJ. While domestic courts tend to defer to the expertise of military authorities in times of security risks, HCJ enthusiasts have argued the Court is different, having demonstrated an increased willingness to question the rationale of these decisions, and to declare illegal a number of measures initiated by the executive branch.[7] However, there are others who have underscored that, if one were to exclude out-of-court settlements as a form of achieving redress,[8] petitions filed on behalf of Palestinians to the HCJ would still enjoy a low chance of getting upheld, particularly when challenging the legality of security-based measures.[9]

Much of the discussion surrounding the Court's adjudication of petitions by Palestinians has analysed whether, and the extent to which, the HCJ's interpretation of the general principles and rules of international law has been conducted in

7 Menachem Hofnung and Keren Weinshall Margel, 'Judicial Setbacks, Material Gains: Terror Litigation at the Israeli High Court of Justice', 7:4 J Empirical Leg Stud (November 2010) 664.

8 Yoav Dotan, 'Judicial Rhetoric, Government Lawyers, and Human Rights: The Case of the Israeli High Court of Justice during the Intifada', (1999) 33:2 Law and Soc'y Rev 319.

9 From 1967 to 1986, the HCJ has accepted only 1 per cent of petitions. Ronen Shamir, 'Landmark Cases and the Reproduction of Legitimacy: The Case of Israel's High Court of Justice', (1990) 24 Law and Soc'y Rev 781. Other data regarding HCJ judgments rendered until 2005 generate the same statistics, with the exception of the Oslo peace process years, during which accepted petitions reached 3 per cent. See Orna Ben-Naftali, 'PathoLAWgical Occupation: Normalizing the Exceptional Case of the Occupied Palestinian Territory and Other Legal Pathologies', in Orna Ben-Naftali, *International Humanitarian Law and International Human Rights Law*, ed (Oxford: Oxford University Press, 2011) 129 at 130 (footnote 8). Another study of judgment from August 1990 to August 2005 noted that out of 439 petitions, only 4.6 per cent were upheld. Guy Davidov and Amnon Reichman, 'Prolonged Armed Conflict and Diminished Deference to the Military: Lessons from Israel', (Fall 2010) 35:4 Law & Soc Inquiry 919.

a manner that reflects a willingness and an ability to enforce international law.[10] Here too, there are those who underscore that the HCJ's invocation of international law in its adjudication reflects a staunch commitment by it to providing Palestinian victims, alleging the violation of their internationally protected human rights, with a domestic venue for judicial remedy[11] as a way of enforcing international law. Others have argued that the Court's interpretation of basic tenets of international law leaves much to be desired.

This underscores that further inquiries into the HCJ's interpretation of international law is crucial for several reasons. First, the Court has viewed its role as that of a domestic court seeking to balance competing rights and interests: sometimes those interests are of the military authorities against the rights/interests of the Palestinians civilian population, other times it is the rights and interests of Israelis citizens (mostly Israeli settlers) against the rights of the Palestinians. Second, given that Palestinians live in a territory that is militarily controlled by a State of which they are not nationals, their rights are first and foremost enshrined and protected by the rules and principles of the international law of belligerent occupation, most notably as found in the Fourth Geneva Convention and the Hague Regulations. Their rights are also protected by IHR law, which remains applicable in times of occupation. Hence, the HCJ's judicial interpretation of relevant international legal principles and rules has a crucial influence on the manner and extent to which judges can effectively enforce international norms at the domestic level.[12] Third, Palestinians are not Israeli citizens. Consequently, Israeli Basic Laws do not apply *de jure* to them, while applying to Israeli settlers living in the same territory. This has limited the relevance of Israeli constitutionally protected rights to them and has made their applicability in large part contingent on the Court's determination of this issue.

To offer a theoretical framework for the analysis, the book's point of departure is that some domestic courts and their application of international law can contribute to the promotion of the Rule of Law (RoL) not only at the domestic level, but also at the international level (i.e. the international RoL).[13] In this regard, the book considers that the RoL has both a formal/procedural (thin) aspect and a

10 Article 17 of the Rome Statute of the International Criminal Court (ICC), 2187 UNTS 90/37 ILM 1002, and James R. Crawford and Thomas D. Grant, 'Local Remedies, Exhaustion of', in (May 2009) in Rüdiger Wolfrum ed, *Max Planck Encyclopedia of Public International Law* (Oxford University Press, 2008), online edition: http://opil.ouplaw.com/home/epil. The reference to 'unable' refers to the structural deficiencies of a Court while 'unwilling' refers to its functional shortcomings. Yuval Shany, 'An Old House with New Bricks or a New House of Old Vards? On National Courts, the International Rule of Law and the Power of Legal Imagination', (2012) 4 Jerusalem Rev Leg Stud 50.

11 Elke Schwager, 'Reparation for Individual Victims of Armed Conflict', in Robert Kolb and Gloria Gaggioli, eds, *Research Handbook on Human Rights and Humanitarian Law* (Cheltenham: Edward Elgar, 2013) 628.

12 Harold Koh 'Why do Nations Obey International Law', (1977) 106 Yale L J 2599.

13 André Nollkaemper, *National Courts and the International Rule of Law* (Oxford: Oxford University Press, 2011) at 7–8.

substantive (thick) aspect,[14] a distinction that applies to its presence at both the domestic and the international level. Given the wide reach of these courts, their interpretation of international law is affecting a greater number of rights holders than do the international courts.[15] Moreover, their robust effect[16] allows them in turn to harness their domestic RoL authority for the purpose of requiring governments to abide by their international legal commitments.[17]

The developments in IHL and IHR law constitute a significant contribution to the substantive aspects of international law. Today, many of their principles, norms and rules are phrased in the legalist transnational language of 'right and wrong',[18] and humane treatment,[19] a notion that underpins both implicitly and explicitly, many of the constraints on state conduct that can be found in IHL and in IHR law.[20] They also reflect the desire of mankind to provide a minimum threshold of human dignity, including in situations of conflict[21] and occupation, particularly by underscoring the need to balance between two opposing forces: military necessity on the one hand, and the wellbeing of the individual on the other.[22] Within this paradigm, international criminal enforcement has given a prominent role to international and domestic courts in advancing some of the core international RoL goals, including ending global violence, promoting minimum standards of human rights and dignity,[23] and ensuring that the international legal system remains effective, coherent and just.[24]

But access to court can only be a meaningful avenue for contributing to the thicker aspects of the international RoL if it can provide an effective remedy for

14 A continuum runs from 'thin' to 'thick': the thin or formal conception includes elements such as RoL as a formal legality, while the thick version refers to individual rights or matters of dignity and justice. Monica P. Moyo, 'Note: The International Rule of Law: An Analysis', (2014) 23 Minn J Int'l L 79.

15 André Nollkaemper, *National Courts and the International Rule of Law*, *supra* note 13.

16 This is due to the greater accessibility of national courts to individual claimants, their sensitivity to local culture and politics, and their stronger claim for domestic social legitimacy. Yuval Shany, 'An Old House with New Bricks', *supra* note 10.

17 André Nollkaemper, *National Courts and the International Rule of Law*, *supra* note 13.

18 Ruti Teitel, 'Humanity's Law: A New Interpretive Lens on the International Sphere', (2008–2009) 77 Fordham L Rev 667.

19 Salvatore F. Nicolosi, 'The Law of Military Occupation and the Role of De Jure and De Facto Sovereignty', (2011) 31 Polish YB Int'l L165.

20 Ruti Teitel, 'Humanity's Law: A New Interpretive Lens', *supra* note 18.

21 Peter Maurer, 'Challenges to International Humanitarian Law', *supra* note 5. One example found in IHL is the Marten's Clause in the *1907 Hague Convention Respecting the Laws and Customs of War*, see *supra* note 5. It reflects existing customary international law, *supra* note 5. *Legality of the Threat or Use of Nuclear Weapons, Advisory Opinion*, [1996] *ICJ Rep* 226 at paras 78 and 84.

22 Michael N. Schmitt, 'Military Necessity and Humanity in International Humanitarian Law: Preserving the Delicate Balance', (2010) 50:4 Va J Int'l L 795.

23 The merger between IHL and IHR law and the language of criminal justice has caused a shift away from states as the dominant subject of international law to include non-state actors. Ruti Teitel, 'Humanity's Law: Rule of Law for the New Global Politics', *supra* note 18.

24 Eyal Benvenisti, 'Comment on the Systemic Vision of National Courts as Part of an International Rule of Law', (2012) 4 Jerusalem Rev Leg Stud 42.

violations to individuals.[25] This is because remedy implies not only a procedural aspect to it but also a substantive one that focuses on the relief afforded to victims of an alleged violation.[26] Under IHL and IHR law, the right of victims of human rights violations to equal and effective access to judicial remedy has become well established.[27] In the case of IHL, there is also a clear duty upon the High Contracting Parties to the Fourth Geneva Convention to enact legislation at the domestic level to provide effective penal sanctions, to investigate and prosecute persons who have committed or ordered the commission of serious violations of IHL, and to suppress all acts that are contrary to its provisions.[28] It is also echoed by the UN Guidelines on Remedy, which have underscored that the right of victims to remedies for these violations includes equal and effective access to justice as well as adequate, effective and prompt reparation for harm suffered.[29]

Given that national courts such as the HCJ use domestic law as their normative system of reference,[30] the Court applies a 'domestic' prism of interpretation to what are essentially international legal issues. Nowhere is the impact of a 'domestic' lens through which the Court views the issues more apparent than in the way in which it has adjudicated petitions challenging the legality of 'unauthorized outposts'. While international law does not draw a distinction between outposts and other Israeli settlements (thereby considering all of them illegal under international law), only the former are illegal under Israeli administrative law. Even though the petitions filed by Palestinians with regards to these outposts did not challenge a security-related measure, and do not contain any international law-related arguments, Chapter 5 in this book has been devoted to the HCJ's adjudication of these petitions. This is because they offer a useful contrast to the Court's adjudication of other settlement-related issues and highlights how it adopts a position that is more in favour of the Palestinian petitioners when the issues at stake are rooted in Israeli law.

25 Sharon Weill, *The Role of National Courts in Applying International Humanitarian Law* (Oxford: Oxford University Press, 2014).

26 This includes restitution where possible and compensation where it is not. Dinah Shelton, *Remedies in International Human Rights Law* 2d ed (Oxford: Oxford University Press, 2006).

27 In IHL, the Hague Convention IV and the First Additional Protocol are said to stipulate a right of compensation for states only. Under IHR law, the individual has been increasingly recognized as a bearer of right under international law. André Nollkaemper, 'Concurrence between Individual Responsibility and State Responsibility in International Law', (July 2003) 52:3 ICLQ 615. It is also provided for under articles 68 and 75 of the Rome Statute, *supra* note 12.

28 Article 4 of the UN Guidelines, *supra* note 6. Actions by states include the enactment of legislation to provide for effective penal sanctions, articles 49, 50, 129 and 146 of the Fourth Geneva Convention, *supra* note 5. Sharon Weill, *The Role of National* Courts, *supra* note 25 at 20–25.

29 Reparation can come in many forms, including restitution, compensation, rehabilitation, satisfaction, and guarantees of non-repetition. Principle 11 and 21 of the UN Guidelines, *supra* note 6.

30 Andreas Paulus, 'National Courts and the International Rule of Law: Remarks on the Book by André Nollkaemper', (2012) 4:1 Jrslm Rev Legal Stud 5.

The second purpose of this book is to offer a reflection on the impact that the HCJ's interpretation has had on the normative foundation of the international law of belligerent occupation as a whole. This is important for the following reasons. First, for any legal system to enjoy normative coherence, it must emanate from, or be explainable by, a set of consistent principles and rules.[31] Given the significant role that domestic courts play in interpreting the former,[32] they shoulder the responsibility to invoke norms and values of international law in a way that preserves the coherence and well-functioning of the body of rules and principles that have been developed. At the same time, supreme courts, including the HCJ, are domestic courts which are entrusted with developing and maintaining the normative coherence of their legal orders by consistently reflecting the fundamental values of their legal systems in their adjudication and through their approach towards domestic and international law.[33]

Towards this objective, and as a way of framing the discussion, the book borrows a very useful theoretical construct developed by Israeli scholar Orna Ben-Naftali. In her attempt to understand whether and to what extent, Israeli policies and measures have allegedly violated the normative framework of the international law of belligerent occupation, she examined the consequences of these policies on what she identifies as the three normative pillars[34] underlying this body of law[35] and which are: that the occupation is temporary;[36] that it is a form of 'trust',[37] and that it does not bestow sovereignty.[38]

The decision to import this construct to frame the discussions in this book is based on several considerations. The first one is to offer a useful means for understanding the main normative threads running through the many rules and general principles of this body of law and serving to maintain its coherence and logic. Second, while Ben-Naftali uses it to assess the impact that the Israeli policies have on the normative framework, she does not use it to examine the consequences that the HCJ's adjudication of petitions, and its interpretation of international law, have for the normative coherence of this body of law. This is because a domestic interpretation of international law that results in weakening the normative coherence of the former is serious:

31 J. M. Balkin, 'Understanding Legal Understanding: The Legal Subject and the Problem of Legal Coherence', (1993) 103:1 Yale LJ 105.

32 Anthea Roberts, 'Comparative International Law? The Role of National Courts in Creating and Enforcing International Law', (January 2011) 60 ICLQ 57.

33 Guy Harpaz, 'When does a Court Systematically Deviate from its Own Principles? The Adjudication by the Israeli Supreme Court of House Demolitions in the Occupied Palestinian Territories', (2015) 28 Leiden J Int'l L 31.

34 Stephen D. Krasner, 'Structural Causes and Regime Consequences: Regimes as Intervening Variables', (1982) 36:2 Int'l Org. 185.

35 Orna Ben-Naftali, 'PathoLAWgical Occupation', *supra* note 9.

36 Lassa Oppenheim, 'The Legal Relations between an Occupier and the Inhabitants', (1917) 33 Law Q Rev 363.

37 Arnold Wilson, 'The Laws of War in Occupied Territory', (1932) 18 Transactions of the Grotius Society 17.

38 Arnold D. McNair, 'Municipal Effects of Belligerent Occupation', (1941) Law Q Rev 33.

> Law itself becomes infected, and is likely to operate in a manner that will defy the normative purpose on both an individual and systematic level: its application to individual cases (through judicial review) would typically entail a dynamic interpretation designed to advance the interest of the Occupying Power at the expense of the occupied people and it will contribute to and facilitate the formation of an environment (indicative of a state policy) of tolerance towards systematic violations of human rights.[39]

Third, this book seeks to contribute to the existing debate as to whether or not Israel's control of the West Bank, and in light of its policies therein,[40] can still be qualified (legally speaking) as an occupation. Fourth, given that litigation (especially in a common-law system) often creates the basic legal norms themselves,[41] the analysis underscores the fact that decisions by courts constitute an important secondary source of international law.[42] In the case of the HCJ, its judicial strategy has often established its legal reasoning regarding a certain principle and then asserted the principle as a legitimate legal precedent.[43] Hence, and in the absence of any significant case law by the domestic court of other Occupying Powers, the judgments rendered by the HCJ constitute a primary source of material for evaluating the application of the legal rules of the law for belligerent occupation.[44] At the same time, it has been suggested that the interpretation by the HCJ may not necessarily reflect the one 'that is supported by international authorities'.[45] However, given that in the Israeli case there are, to date, no international courts of compulsory jurisdiction available to act as a corrective mechanism, there is concern that there is no judicial venue the decision of which can offset some of the pressure on the HCJ to accommodate state/national interests,[46] at the expense of the international RoL.

Making sense of the HCJ's judicial process: a typology

To offer a roadmap, the book proposes a typology of principles and practices, including factors and methods of interpretation that systematically affect how the HCJ has established facts, interpreted 'the law' and chosen the remedy.[47]

39 Orna Ben-Naftali, 'PathoLAWgical Occupation', *supra* note 9.

40 Ibid.

41 Lawrence Friedman, 'Litigation and Society', (1989) 17 Annu Rev Sociol 25.

42 Article 38(1)(d) of the *Statute of the International Court of Justice*, 26 June 1945, UNTS 1945 No. 993 [ICJ Statute].

43 Patricia Woods, 'The Ideational Foundations of Israel's "Constitutional Revolution"', (December 2009) 62:4 Pol Res Q 811.

44 Vaois Koutroulis, 'The Application of International Humanitarian Law and International Human Rights Law in Situations of Prolonged Occupation', (2012) 94: 885 Int'l Rev Red Cross 165.

45 Daphne Barak-Erez, 'The International Law of Human Rights and Constitutional Law: A Case Study for an Expanding Dialogue', (2004) 2 Int'l J. Const. L 611.

46 Yuval Shany, 'An Old House with a New Brick', *supra* note 10.

47 Any normative application of the law will inevitably lead to, or entail political choices made during the entire judicial process. Duncan Kennedy, *A Critique of Adjudication: Fin de Siècle* (Cambridge, MA: Harvard University Press, 1997).

The book adopts the position that, when interpreting (a process that is central to adjudication), courts exercise discretion in the meaning that is given to the terms that they are interpreting, and that the meaning that they give to these terms within the context of a specific dispute is a political choice.[48] The making of a political choice takes place on three levels: that of establishing facts; on the level of interpreting the law; and on the level of choosing the remedy.

On the level of establishing facts, the typology has identified one element, namely the deference afforded by the HCJ to Israeli government and military authorities. The deference by national courts is particularly high when called upon to review government actions and decisions in times of emergencies and security threats.[49] On the level of interpreting 'the law', the book identifies a further six elements (elements 2–7). One of them (element 2) is the HCJ's position regarding the applicability of relevant IHL and IHR law treaties and conventions. Another one (element 3) is the meaning that the HCJ has afforded to key principles, rules and notions of the international law of belligerent occupation as well as to relevant general principles and rules of IHR law. Two reasons justify including this element. First, the interpretations by domestic courts of international law play a central role in determining 'what happens to legal rules when they are out in the world'.[50] Second, in law, definitions are invoked for a normative purpose, namely 'to determine when certain rules apply, which has special legal effects'.[51] Element 4 is how the HCJ has invoked domestic forms of judicial interpretation,[52] most notably when balancing between the competing interests.[53] Element 5 concerns the primacy granted by the HCJ to the domestic legislation, when it contradicts international law. Element 6 is the avoidance doctrines such as the non-justiciability of political questions,[54] and element 7 is one that indirectly influences the HCJ's adjudication of these petitions. This is the relationship of the HCJ with other branches of government and with the general public.[55] On the level of the remedy chosen, the typology's eighth and last element is the overall success rate of the petitions and the type of remedy chosen by the Court.

48 Sharon Weill, *The Role of National Courts*, *supra* note 25 at 16.

49 Emanuel Gross, 'Democracy in the War against Terrorism: The Israeli Experience', (2002) 35 Loy LA L Rev 1161.

50 Robert Howse and Ruti Teitel, 'Beyond Compliance: Rethinking why International Law Really Matters', (May 2010) 1:2 Global Pol'y 127 at 135.

51 Marco Sassòli, 'The Concept of Security in International Law Relating to Armed Conflicts', in Cecilia M. Bailliet, ed, *Security: A Multidisciplinary Normative Approach* (Boston, MA: Martinus Nijhoff, 2009) 7 at 21.

52 Aharon Barak, *Judicial Discretion* (New Haven, CT: Yale University Press, 1987) at 125–126.

53 Alon Harel, 'Skeptical Reflections on Justice Aharon Barak's Optimism', (2006) 39 Isr LR 261.

54 Tara Leigh Grove, 'The Lost History of the Political Question Doctrine', (December 2015) 90:6 NYL Rev 1908.

55 James L. Gibson, Gregory A. Caldeira and Vanessa Band, 'On the Legitimacy of National High Courts', 92:2 Am Polit Sci Rev (2 June 1998) 343.

Structure of the book

Chapter 1 provides an overview of the legal and political landscape governing the Israeli occupation of the West Bank, and reviews the HCJ's role in promoting and protecting human rights therein. It situates this overview within an international/domestic RoL framework, and fleshes out the main elements of the typology as they specifically relate to the HCJ.

Chapter 2 examines the decisions that have been rendered in relation to the construction of the Wall in the West Bank (excluding EJ), the creation of the Seam Zone and the demarcation of SSZs around settlements. It also discusses the ramifications that the Court's approach has had for the first identified principle underlying the normative framework of the law for the belligerent occupation, namely that occupation is inherently temporary. Chapter 3 analyses judicial decisions on petitions that challenge the legality of measures restricting the movement of Palestinians inside the West Bank and its implications for the second normative principle, that occupation is a form of 'trust'. Chapter 4 sheds light on the Court's adjudication of petitions that have challenged the legality of the construction of the Wall in and around Jerusalem (including EJ) and the consequences that this has had on upholding the third normative principle, that occupation does not bestow sovereignty. Chapter 5 examines the Court's adjudication of some key petitions challenging the legality of 'unauthorized outposts' as a way of highlighting significant differences in the Court's approach when there is no security component at stake. The book terminates with a conclusion.

1 Adjudicating human rights and security in occupied territory

The legal and political context

> I have come to the opinion that this professional viewpoint of the chief of the general staff would not, in and of itself, have led to the decision to establish the Elon Moreh community if it were not for another reason [...] namely, the fervent desire of Gush Emunim members to settle in the heart of the Land of Israel [...].[1]
>
> – Moshe Landau Vice President at the HCJ

Introduction

Few conflicts in the world elicit as much debate as the Palestinian–Israeli conflict.[2] In June 1967, following a six-day war between Israel and neighbouring Arab States, the former occupied the West Bank, including East Jerusalem (EJ) and the Gaza Strip,[3] thereby bringing its Palestinian inhabitants under Israeli rule.[4] Shortly thereafter, Israeli authorities established a military government in those territories, to 'assume responsibility for security and maintenance of public order in the Area'.[5]

1 (HCJ 390/79) [1979] *Azat Muhammad Mustafa Dweikat et al. v. Government of Israel et al.* at 16, unofficial English translation, online: *Hamoked* www.hamoked.org/files/2010/1670_eng.pdf [*Elon Moreh* Judgment].

2 Ilan Pappé and Jamil Hilal, eds, *Across the Wall: Narratives of Israeli–Palestinian History* (London: I.B. Tauris, 2010) at 2.

3 Thereafter, Occupied Palestinian Territory (oPt). From 1948 to 1967, Jordan administered the West Bank, while Egypt controlled the Gaza Strip. The West Bank was officially annexed by Jordan in 1950. *Encyclopedia of Public International Law*, vol 2, 'Israel: Status Territory and Occupied Territories' by Peter Manlanczuk (Netherlands: Elsevier Science, 2013) 1468.

4 United Nations Conference on Trade and Development (UNCTAD), 'Population and Demographic Developments in the West Bank and Gaza Strip until 1990', UN Doc UNCTAD/ECDC/SEU/1 (1994), online: UNCTAD http://unctad.org/en/docs/poecdcseud1.en.pdf. By 2016, there was a total of 2.94 million living in the West Bank, Palestinian Central Bureau of Statistics (PCBS), online: PCBS www.pcbs.gov.ps/Portals/_Rainbow/Documents/gover_e.htm. All links in this chapter last accessed on 30 May 2018.

5 *Proclamation concerning the Takeover of Administration by the [Israeli Defense Forces] IDF (No. 1) (5727–1967)* cited in Joel Singer, 'The Establishment of a Civil Administration in the Areas Administered by Israel', (1982) 12 Isr YB Hum Rts 259.

Headed by the Military Commander (MC) of the 'Area', authorities issued a military order (MO) which invested in this government all powers of the government, legislation, appointment and administration in relation to the occupied Palestinian territory (oPt), or its population.[6] All powers not considered to be of a civil nature (i.e. those strictly military and security related) were retained by that MC.[7] Since then, this administration has promulgated thousands of primary security legislations (i.e. MOs and secondary legislations).[8] These were to prevail over all other laws that are in effect in the oPt even when the former did not explicitly abrogate the latter.[9] At the time of the beginning of Israel's occupation, these local laws included Ottoman laws, British Defence (Emergency) Regulations (1945) and Jordanian law (in the West Bank).[10] In 1981, a Civil Administration (CA) was created by way of an MO to administer the 'civil affairs' of the 'local population'.[11]

Under international law, Israel's control of these territories is governed by the laws of belligerent occupation.[12] Part of international humanitarian law (IHL),[13] this body of law is codified in legal instruments such as the Hague Regulations (1907),[14]

6 *Proclamation concerning the Administration of Rule and Justice (West Bank Region) (No. 2) (5727–1967)* cited in Meir Shamgar, ed, *Military Government in the Territories Administered by Israel 1967–1980: The Legal Aspects*, vol 1 (Jerusalem: Hebrew University, 1982).

7 Jonathan Kuttab and Raja Shehadeh, *Civil Administration in the Occupied West Bank: Analysis of Israeli Military Government Order No. 947* (Ramallah: *Al-Haq*, 1982) at 25–26. It also established a military court system. Yaron Butovsky, 'Law of Belligerent Occupation: Israeli Practice and Judicial Decisions Affecting the West Bank', (1983) Can YB Int'l Law 217.

8 More than 2,600 civil and penal military orders (MOs) have since been promulgated. Uri Shoham, 'The Principle of Legality and the Israeli Military Government in the Territories', (1996) 153 Mil L Rev 245.

9 Section 8(A) of *Order concerning Interpretation (West Bank Region) (No 1301. 5727–1967) (Amendment 5728)* cited in The Israeli Center for Human Rights in the Occupied Territories (*B'Tselem*), 'On the Way to Annexation: Human Rights Violations resulting from the Establishment and Expansion of the Ma'aleh Adumim Settlement', Information Sheet (July 1999), online: *B'Tselem* www.btselem.org/sites/default/files/sites/default/files2/on_the_way_to_annexation.pdf.

10 These include, for example, the *Emergency Defense (Temporary Provisions) Regulations of 1945.* Uri Shoham, 'The Principle of Legality', *supra* note 8.

11 The CA was created as a sub-division of the military government to run civil affairs. MO *concerning the Establishment of the Civil Administration (Judea and Samaria) (No. 947) 5742–1981* printed in Jonathan Kuttab and Raja Shehadeh, *Civil Administration in the Occupied West Bank*, *supra* note 7.

12 Gerhard von Glahn, *The Occupation of Enemy Territory: A Commentary on the Law and Practice of Belligerent Occupation* (Minneapolis, MN: University of Minnesota Press, 1957) at 27.

13 Cherif Bassiouni, 'The Normative Framework of International Humanitarian Law: Overlap Gaps and Ambiguities', (1998) 8 Transnat'l L and Contemp Probs 199.

14 *Convention (IV) respecting the Laws and Customs of War on Land and its Annex: Regulation concerning the Laws and Customs of War on Land and its Annex: Regulations concerning the Laws and Customs of War on Land*, 18 October 1907, Cons TS No 25, 277 (entered into force 26 January 1910) [Hague Regulations]. In a situation of occupation, it is particularly Section III (articles 42–56), which is applicable. Georg Schwarzenberger, 'The Law of Belligerent Occupation: Basic Issues', (1960) 30 Nordisk Tidisskrift for Int'l Ret 10.

the Fourth Geneva Convention (1949)[15] and the Additional Protocol to the Geneva Conventions (1977).[16] The *de jure* applicability of the Fourth Geneva Convention to the oPt has consistently been upheld by the UN General Assembly (GA) and the Security Council (SC).[17] It has also been reaffirmed by the International Court of Justice (ICJ) in its *Wall* Advisory Opinion of 2004,[18] and by the Conference of the Red Cross and Red Crescent and the International Committee of the Red Cross (ICRC).[19]

Situations of occupation and armed conflict are also governed by international human rights (IHR) law.[20] In this regard, it is important to recall that the extra-territorial applicability of IHR-related treaties and conventions to the oPt (signed and ratified by Israel) has also been upheld by the ICJ[21]

15 *Geneva Convention (IV) Relative to the Protection of Civilian Persons in Time of War (12 August 1949)*, 75:973 UNT 287 (entered into force 21 October 1950) [Fourth Geneva Convention].

16 *Protocol Additional to the Geneva Conventions of 12 August 1949, and relating to the Protection of Victims of International Armed Conflicts (1977)* 1125 UNTS 3 (entered into force 7 December 1978) [First Additional Protocol]. Israel is not a State Party to the Protocol. Certain provisions are also reflective of customary international law. *Legality of the Threat or Use of Nuclear Weapons*, Advisory Opinion, [1996] ICJ Rep 226 at para 84 [ICJ *Nuclear Weapons* Advisory Opinion]. These include the distinction between civilians and combatants and the definition of who constitutes a combatant and a civilian. ICRC, *Customary IHL Database*, online: ICRC Customary Law Database www.icrc.org/customary-ihl/eng/docs/home.

17 For example, *Applicability of the Geneva Convention relative to the Protection of Civilian Persons in Time of War, of 12 August 1949, to the Occupied Palestinian Territory, including Jerusalem, and the Other Occupied Arab Territories*, GA Res 56/60, UNGAOR, 56th Sess, UN Doc A/RES/56/60 (10 December 2001), online: United Nations Information System on the Question of Palestine (UNISPAL) https://unispal.un.org/DPA/DPR/unispal.nsf/0/765529CE2510ABC685256B7200556EFA and UN SC Res 1544 (2004), UN Doc S/RES/1544 (2004) (19 May 2004), online: UN www.un.org/en/ga/search/view_doc.asp?symbol=S/RES/1578(2004).

18 *Legal Consequences of the Construction of a Wall in the Occupied Palestinian Territory* [2004] ICJ Rep 136 at para 101 [ICJ *Wall* Advisory Opinion].

19 ICRC, 'Conference of High Contracting Parties to the Fourth Geneva Convention: Statement by the International Committee of the Red Cross', 5 December 2001, online: ICRC www.icrc.org/eng/resources/documents/article/other/5fldpj.htm [ICRC Statement 2001].

20 For example, ICJ *Nuclear Weapons* Advisory Opinion, *supra* note 16 at para 25; *Armed Activities on the Territory of the Congo* (*Democratic Republic of the Congo v. Uganda*), Judgment, [2005] ICJ Rep 168 at para 216 [ICJ *Armed Activities in the Congo* Judgment]. See also Francoise Hampson, 'Other Areas of Customary Law in Relation to the Study' in Elisabeth Wilmshurst and Susan Breau eds, *Perspectives on the ICRC Study on Customary Humanitarian Law* (Cambridge: Cambridge University Press, 2007) 50.

21 ICJ *Wall* Advisory Opinion, *supra* note 18 at paras 109–113.

and by various UN treaty-monitoring bodies.[22] This is in addition to the Palestinians' right to self-determination, a right that has gained steady recognition from the international community over the years.[23]

Although in a situation of armed conflict IHL remains the *lex specialis*,[24] the latter should be understood as a principle that aids in the interpretation of concrete rules, and not one of solving conflicts between normative orders *in abstracto*.[25] In other words, derogation from IHR law should not take place in its entirety.[26] Adopting this approach gives weight to the notion that 'both spheres of [IHL and of IHR] law are complimentary, not mutually exclusive'.[27] Many fundamental rules

22 The applicability of IHL in a situation of armed conflict 'does not preclude the application of the Covenant, including article 4 which covers situations of public emergency, which threaten the life of the nation', nor does it 'preclude accountability of State parties under Article 2 paragraph 1 of the Covenant for actions of their authorities outside their own territories', 'including in Occupied Territories'. Human Rights (HR) Committee, *Concluding Observations: Israel*, 63rd Sess UN Doc. CCPR/C/79/Add.93 (18 August 1998) at para 4, online: UNISPAL https://unispal.un.org/DPA/DPR/unispal.nsf/0/335F22D5AC5A04FC85256CC50057BE8C [HR Committee Concluding Observations 1998]. Other examples include HR Committee, *Concluding Observations: Israel*, 78th Sess, UN Doc CCPR/CO/78/ISR (5 August 2003) at para 10, online: UNISPAL https://unispal.un.org/DPA/DPR/unispal.nsf/eed216406b50bf6485256ce10072f637/2e5a21a17aeb0c0285256d7f004f4d61?OpenDocument; HR Committee, *Concluding on the Fourth Periodic Report Israel*, 112th Sess, UN Doc CCPR/C/ISR/CO/4 (21 November 2014) at para 5, online: UNISPAL https://unispal.un.org/DPA/DPR/unispal.nsf/9a798adbf322aff38525617b006d88d7/724da0c48e837f0a85257d9a0070d766?OpenDocument&Highlight=0,CCPR%2FC%2FISR%2FCO%2F4; and UN Committee on Economic, Social and Cultural Rights (ESCR Committee), *Consideration of Reports Submitted by States Parties under Articles 16 and 17 of the Covenant: Concluding Observations of the Committee on Economic, Social and Cultural Rights: Israel*, 30th Sess, UN Doc E/C.12/1/Add.90 (23 May 2003) at para 15, online: UNISPAL https://unispal.un.org/DPA/DPR/unispal.nsf/0/778E860C0DDB295C85256D39005059C5.

23 ICJ *Wall* Advisory Opinion, *supra* note 18 at paras 115 and 118. See also *Importance of the Universal Realization of the Right of Peoples to Self-Determination and of the Speedy granting of Independence to Colonial Countries and Peoples for the Effective Guarantee and Observance of Human Rights*, GA 37/43, UNGAOR, UN Doc A/RES/37/43 (3 December 1982), online: UN www.un.org/documents/ga/res/37/a37r043.htm; *Status of Palestine in the United Nations* GA Res 67/19, UNGAOR 67th Sess, Item 37, UN Doc A/RES/67/ (4 December 2012), online: UN www.un.org/en/ga/search/view_doc.asp?symbol=A/RES/67/19.

24 ICJ, *Nuclear Weapons* Advisory Opinion, *supra* note 16 at para 25 and para 106.

25 UN HR Committee, *General Comment 31, Nature of the General Legal Obligation on States Parties to the Covenant*, UN Doc CCPR/C/21/Rev.1/Add.13 (2004) at para 11; ICJ *Armed Activities in the Congo* Judgment, *supra* note 20 at para 180 and Marko Milenovic, 'A Norm Conflict Perspective on the Relationship between International Humanitarian Law and Human Rights Law', (2010) 14:3 J Confl and Sec L 459.

26 Tristan Ferraro, ed, 'Expert Meeting: Occupation and Other Forms of Administration of Foreign Territory', Report, online: ICRC www.icrc.org/eng/assets/files/publications/icrc-002-4094.pdf.

27 Cordula Droege, 'Elective Affinities: Human Rights and Humanitarian Law', (2008) 90:871 Int'l Rev Red Cross 501 at 524.

and principles[28] of IHL[29] and of IHR law[30] are reflective of international customary law.[31] In the case of the international law on the use of force (*jus ad bellum*),[32] following the outbreak of the *Second Intifada* in 2000, Israeli authorities have invoked the right of self-defence to justify the resort to certain security-based measures.[33] While the HCJ has accepted the government's position,[34] it does not directly address the relevance of the *jus ad bellum* framework in its adjudication of the petitions examined here. At the same time, the belief that the measures are essentially in self-defence has been internalized by the Court, thereby influencing its judicial logic and approach to these petitions.

28 Rüdiger Wolfrum, 'General International Law Principles, Rules, and Standards', (December 2010) in Rüdiger Wolfrum, ed, *Max Planck Encyclopedia of Public International Law* (Oxford University Press, 2008), online edition: http://opil.ouplaw.com/home/epil.

29 ICJ *Nuclear Weapons* Advisory Opinion, *supra* note 16 at paras 79 and 83. See also *Case concerning the Barcelona Traction, Light and Power Company Ltd. (Belgium v. Spain)*, Judgment, ICJ Rep 1970 3 at paras 33 and 34 [ICJ *Barcelona Traction* Judgment]; Common Articles 1 and 3 of the Four Geneva Conventions, *supra* note 15; *Case concerning Military and Paramilitary Activities in and against Nicaragua (Nicaragua v. United States)*, Judgment on Merits, [1986] ICJ Rep (1986) at para 218, [ICJ *Nicaragua* Judgment].

30 ICJ *Armed Activities in the Congo* Judgment, *supra* note 20 at para 64; Hurst Hannum, 'The Status of the Universal Declaration of Human Rights in National and International Law', (1995–1996) 25:1 and 2 Ga J Int'l and Comp L 287. The self-determination of people has also evolved into a principle of *jus cogens. Declaration on Principles of International law concerning Friendly Relations and Cooperation amongst States in Accordance with the Charter of the UN*, GA Res 2625, UNGAOR, UN Doc. A/8028 (1970) [GA Declaration concerning Friendly Relations]; *Legal Consequences for States of the Continued Presence of South Africa in Namibia (South West Africa) notwithstanding Security Council Resolution 276 (1970)*, Advisory Opinion, [1971] ICJ Rep 16 at para 31 [ICJ *South West Africa* Advisory Opinion]; *East Timor Case* (*Portugal v. Australia*) Judgment, [1995] ICJ Rep 90; *Wall* Advisory Opinion, *supra* note 18 at paras 159–199. At the same time, it has usually been raised in conjunction with the principle of territorial integrity of existing sovereign states. As a concept it does not include the right of secession from existing states. Malcolm Shaw, *International Law*, 5th ed (Cambridge: Cambridge University Press, 2004) at 230–233.

31 Article 53 of the *Vienna Convention on the Law of Treaties*, 23 May 1969, 1155 UNTS 331 [Vienna Convention on the Law of Treaties]. For a definition of *jus cogens*, see ICJ, *Nuclear Weapons* Advisory Opinion, *supra* note 16 at para 79.

32 Article 2(4) of the *Charter of the United Nations*, 26 June 1945 Can TS 1945 No. 7 [UN Charter]. The prohibition on the use of force and the principle of non-annexation are principles of customary law. ICJ *Nicaragua* Judgment, *supra* note 29 at para 190 and ICJ *South West Africa* Advisory Opinion, *supra* note 30 at paras 70 and 87. A state asserting the right to exercise self-defence within the territory of another state must demonstrate that its 'necessity [is] instant, overwhelming, and [is] leaving no choice of means, and no moment for deliberation'. Daniel Webster, 'Correspondence between Great Britain and the United States, respecting the Arrest and Imprisonment of Mr. McLeod, for the Destruction of the Steamboat Caroline – April 24 1841', (1857) 29 British and Foreign State Papers 1129; Christopher Greenwood, 'The Caroline', (April 2009) in Rüdiger Wolfrum, ed, *Max Planck Encyclopedia of Public International Law* (Oxford University Press, 2008), online: Max Planck http://opil.ouplaw.com/home/epil.

33 Throughout, the term 'Wall' will be used except when quoting and analysing relevant judgments of the HCJ in which case the term 'fence' will be used.

34 (HCJ 7015/02) [2002] *Ajuri et al. v. IDF Commander in the West Bank et al.* at paras 3 and 41, official English translation, online: HCJ http://elyon1.court.gov.il/files_eng/02/150/070/A15/02070150.a15.pdf [*Ajuri* Judgment].

Not long after 1967, Israeli government authorities began building and expanding Jewish communities (settlements)[35] beyond the Green Line,[36] inside the West Bank, a territory which Israeli authorities referred to as 'Judea and Samaria'.[37] Settlement activity also took place in EJ, which Israel annexed *de jure* in 1980.[38] In 1993, the Oslo peace process between the Palestine Liberation Organization (PLO) and Israel was launched,[39] during which settlement-related activities continued.[40] In 2005, Israel dismantled its settlements and withdrew both its military forces and all of its settler population from the Gaza

35 John Quigley, 'Living in Legal Limbo: Israel's Settlers in Occupied Palestinian Territory', (1998) 10 Pace Int'l L Rev 1 at 5. See also Hagit Ofran and Noa Galili 'West Bank Settlements – Facts and Figures', (June 2009), online: *Peace Now* http://peacenow.org.il/en/west-bank-settlements-facts-and-figures [West Bank Settlements – Facts and Figures 2009].

36 The ICJ accepts it as delimiting the dividing line between Israel and the oPt. ICJ *Wall* Advisory Opinion, *supra* note 18, *Separate Declaration of Judge Buergenthal* at para 6, online: ICJ www.icj-cij.org/files/case-related/131/131-20040709-ADV-01-05-EN.pdf [Declaration – Judge Buergenthal].

37 Israel Ministry of Foreign Affairs (MoFA), 'FM Avigdor Lieberman addresses Diplomatic Corps on Independence Day', (6 May 2014), online: MoFA http://mfa.gov.il/MFA/PressRoom/2014/Pages/FM-Avigdor-Liberman-addresses-the-Diplomatic-Corps-on-Independence-Day-6-May-2014.aspx.

38 Basic Law: *Jerusalem: Capital of Israel*, unofficial English translation, online: *Knesset* www.knesset.gov.il/laws/special/eng/basic10_eng.htm.

39 In 1993, the Declaration of Principles (DoP) was signed to outline a framework of 'interim' self-government for the Palestinians. By virtue of this agreement Israeli forces subsequently redeployed from the oPt, but did not abolish the military government therein. 'Declaration of Principles on Interim Self-Government Arrangements', (1993) 32 ILM 1527; 'Israel – Palestine Liberation Organization: Interim Agreement on the West Bank and the Gaza Strip with Selected Annexes', (1997) 36 ILM 551[Oslo Accord, 1995]. Under these agreements, the West Bank was divided into different areas and shades of control: Area A (comprising 18 per cent of the territory), would encompass urban Palestinian areas under the full control of a Palestinian Authority (PA); Area B (making up 22 per cent), consisting mostly of Palestinian rural area under PA control, while Israeli military authorities retain security control therein. In the remaining area, constituting 60 per cent, also known as Area C, Israel retains control over the following: security matters, all land-related civil matters (such as land zoning and planning), transit roads between PA-controlled areas, the West Bank's borders with Jordan and the settlements. These are managed by the CA. See *B'Tselem*, 'Acting the Landlord: Israel's Policy in Area C, the West Bank', Report (2013), online: *B'Tselem* www.btselem.org/sites/default/files/sites/default/files2/201306_area_c_report_eng.pdf.

40 Israel maintains that the provision within the Oslo Accords, which states that 'neither side takes any unilateral measures to change the legal status of these areas', was not meant to prohibit settlement activity. MoFA, 'Israeli Settlements and International Law', (30 November 2015), online: MoFA http://mfa.gov.il/MFA/AboutIsrael/State/Law/Pages/Israeli%20Settlements%20and%20International%20Law.aspx. For the Palestinians, the Israeli decision to continue with settlement building was like '[t]wo people negotiating over a pizza, while at the same time one of them is eating the same pizza slice by slice'. Quoted by *Americans for Peace Now*, 'Settlements 101', Video, online: *YouTube* www.youtube.com/watch?v=plwRFcIEQQcandfeature=player_embedded. During the 1990s, the number of Israeli settlers in the West Bank grew from 78,000 to nearly 200,000. Karen Tenenbaum and Ehud Eiran, 'Israeli Settlement Activity in the West Bank and Gaza Strip: A Brief History', (April 2005) 21:2 Negotiation J 171.

Strip.[41] However, settlement construction and expansion continued in the West Bank. By the end of 2015, the territory housed 127 government-sanctioned settlements in which an estimated 588,000 Israeli settlers still reside.[42] From those, an estimated 205,220 Israeli settlers live in 15 settlements in annexed EJ,[43] while approximately 382,000 live in the rest of the West Bank.[44] In addition, there is an estimated 100 'unauthorized outposts', a term which refers to Israeli settlements that were built in violation of Israeli administrative requirements.[45]

Much of the construction and expansion of settlements in the West Bank has taken place with the active political and economic support of successive Israeli governments.[46] An examination of the 2009–2010 government budgets indicates that an estimated one billion New Israeli Shekel (NIS), that is, approximately 265 million USD, were earmarked for settlements each year.[47] In past years, the price of the settlements is estimated to have reached approximately

41 In 2006, Israel dismantled an estimated 25 settlements. Approximately 9,000 Israeli settlers were removed from the Gaza Strip and from two settlements in the northern West Bank. MOFA, 'Israel's Disengagement Plan: 2005', online: MoFA www.mfa.gov.il/MFA/Facts+About+Israel/Israel+in+Maps/Israels+Disengagement+Plan-+2005.htm [thereafter Disengagement Plan].

42 *B'Tselem*, 'Statistics on Settlements and Settler Population', (updated 11 May 2017), online: *B'Tselem* www.btselem.org/settlements/statistics.

43 Ibid. These figures are for the end of the year 2014 and were provided by the Jerusalem Institute for Israel Studies (JIIS).

44 *B'Tselem*, 'Statistics on Settlements and Settler Population', (updated 11 May 2017), online: *B'Tselem* www.btselem.org/settlements/statistics. These figures are for end of the year 2015 and were provided by Israel's Central Bureau of Statistics.

45 They were also built without having met the required planning and building criteria under Israeli administrative law or having obtained all formal government-related authorizations. MoFA, Prime Minister's Office, 'Summary of the Opinion Concerning Unauthorized Outposts', (10 March 2005), online: MoFA www.mfa.gov.il/mfa/aboutisrael/state/law/pages/summary%20of%20opinion%20concerning%20unauthorized%20outposts%20-%20talya%20sason%20adv.aspx [Sasson Report]. The outposts have been set up with the knowledge, encouragement and tacit agreement of senior political levels. See 'The Levy Commission, "Report on the Legal Status of Building in Judea and Samaria", Conclusions and Recommendations, Jerusalem 9 July 2012', (Autumn 2012) 42: 1 J Palest. Stud 179 at 180 [Levy Commission Report 2012].

46 'These specific measures include building infrastructure; encouraging Jewish migrants to Israel to move to settlements; sponsoring economic activities; supporting settlements through public services delivery and development projects; and seizing Palestinian land, some privately owned'. UN Human Rights Council (HR Council), *Report of the Independent International Fact-finding Mission to Investigate the Implications of the Israeli Settlements on the Civil, Political, Economic, Social and Cultural Rights of the Palestinian People throughout the Occupied Palestinian Territory, including East Jerusalem*, HRC 22nd Sess, UN Doc A/HRC/22/63 (7 February 2013) at para 20, online: OHCHR www.ohchr.org/Documents/HRBodies/HRCouncil/RegularSession/Session22/A-HRC-22-63_en.pdf [UN Fact-finding Mission on Settlements Report 2013].

47 This figure includes only special budget items that have been allocated towards the settlements and not general budget items. Most budget items are broken down according to subject items and not by geographical location. *Peace Now*, 'The Price of Settlements in the 2009 and 2010 Budget Proposal', Special Report (June 2009), online: *Peace Now* http://peacenow.org.il/wp-content/uploads/2009/06/Price_of_Settlements_June2009.pdf.

2.5 billion NIS/year (i.e. an estimated 662.5 million USD).[48] This is in addition to various government subsidies and incentives designed to encourage Jewish migrants to Israel to move to these settlements and to boost their economic development.[49] During the past decade, the annual growth rate of the Israeli settler population in the oPt has stood at a yearly average of 5.3 per cent (excluding EJ) in contrast to 1.8 per cent by the Israeli population as a whole.[50] Today, most settlements are no longer temporary constructs, but have developed into full-fledged small or medium-sized towns with sophisticated highways and 'bypass' roads to link settlements to each other, as well as to Israel proper, and with the necessary infrastructure to accommodate them.[51]

The illegality under international law of the construction of settlements by Israeli authorities has featured in resolutions by the UN SC,[52] the ICJ,[53] the UN GA[54] and the Conference of the Red Cross and the ICRC.[55] One of the most commonly invoked provisions of this Convention has been article 49(6), which stipulates that '[t]he Occupying Power shall not deport or transfer parts of its own civilian population into the territory it occupies'.[56] State practice establishes this rule as a norm of customary international law applicable in international armed conflicts.[57] Moreover, as a legal memo by a former legal advisor to the Israeli Ministry of Foreign Affairs had underscored, this prohibition is categorical

48 *Peace Now*, 'The Price of Settlements in the 2009 and 2010 Budget Proposal', Special Report (June 2009), online: *Peace Now* http://peacenow.org.il/wp-content/uploads/2009/06/Price_of_Settlements_June2009.pdf.

49 UN Fact-finding Mission on Settlements Report 2013, *supra* note 46 at para 21.

50 Hagit Ofran and Noa Galili, 'West Bank Settlements – Facts and Figures 2009', *supra* note 35.

51 OCHA-oPt 'The Humanitarian Impact on Palestinians of Israeli Settlements and Other Infrastructure in the West Bank', (July 2007), online: OCHA-oPt www.ochaopt.org/content/humanitarian-impact-palestinians-israeli-settlements-and-other-infrastructure-west-bank.

52 For example, UN SC Resolution 2334, 7853th Sess, UN Doc S/RES/2334 (2016) (23 December 2016), online: UN www.un.org/webcast/pdfs/SRES2334-2016.pdf.

53 Article 49(6) 'prohibits not only deportations or forced transfers of population such as those carried out during the Second World War, but also any measures taken by an Occupying Power in order to organize or encourage transfers of parts of its own population into the occupied territory'. ICJ *Wall* Opinion, *supra* note 18 at para 120.

54 For example, *Israeli Settlements in the Occupied Palestinian Territory, including East Jerusalem and Occupied Syrian Golan* GA Res 67/120, UNGAOR, 67th sess, Agenda item 3, UN Doc A/RES/67/120 (14 January 2013), online: UNISPAL https://unispal.un.org/DPA/DPR/unispal.nsf/0/A87AB64E58B5F54785257AF60067435D.

55 ICRC Statement 2001, *supra* note 19.

56 Article 49(6) of the Fourth Geneva Convention, *supra* note 15. The negotiating history of the Convention suggests that only minor changes were made to article 49(6), which entailed changing the word 'civil' to 'civilian' in the text that was then adopted without a dissenting vote. W.T. Mallison, Jr. and S.V. Mallison, 'A Juridical Analysis of the Israeli Settlements in the Occupied Territories', (1998/1999) 10:1 Pal YB Int'l L 1 at 18.

57 Rule 130 and Rule 144 in Jean-Marie Henckaerts and Louise Doswald-Beck, eds, Customary International Humanitarian Law (Cambridge: Cambridge University Press, 2005) at 462–463, online: ICRC www.icrc.org/eng/assets/files/other/customary-international-humanitarian-law-i-icrc-eng.pdf [ICRC Customary Law Study].

and not conditional upon motives for the transfer or its objectives.[58] The Rome Statute of the International Criminal Court (ICC) also defines 'the transfer directly or indirectly by the Occupying Power of parts of its own civilian population into the territory it occupies' as a war crime,[59] which gives rise to individual criminal responsibility and to state responsibility.[60] In addition, the transfer by an occupant of its civilian population into the occupied territory has been expressly listed as a grave breach of international law by article 85(4)(a) of the First Additional Protocol to the Geneva Conventions.[61] UN bodies, International, Palestinian and Israeli human rights organizations as well as scholars refer to the 'associated regime' of physical and non-physical infrastructures and processes that have been put in place by Israeli authorities to enable and support the establishment, expansion and maintenance of these residential communities.[62] This includes the requisitioning of Palestinian privately held land.

Provisions of the Fourth Geneva Convention have also been invoked in relation to alleged violations of international law resulting from the construction and/or expansion of settlements or as a result of security-based measures implemented for the purported benefit of these settlements and their inhabitants.[63] These include article 53 of the Fourth Geneva Convention, prohibiting the destruction of private property 'except where such destruction is rendered absolutely necessary by military operations'.[64] In the case of the Hague Regulations, they deal with the use of private and public property, the violation of which has been invoked in relation to various settlement-related policies. These include: article 43, outlining the responsibility of the Occupying Power to restore and

58 Theodor Meron, 'The West Bank and International Humanitarian Law on the Eve of the Fiftieth Anniversary of the Six-Day War', (April 2017) 11:2 AJIL 357.

59 Article 8(2)(b)(viii) of the Rome Statute of the International Criminal Court (ICC), 2187 UNTS 90/37 ILM 1002. It is also a grave breach under article 85(4)(a) of the First Additional Protocol, *supra* note 16.

60 The conduct shall be considered an act of the State if it was conducted by an organ that exercises legislative, executive, judicial or any other functions. *Draft Articles on Responsibility of States for Internationally Wrongful Acts*, UNGAOR, 56th Sess, Supp No. 10, UN Doc (A/56/10), at article 4, online: International Law Commission (ILC) http://legal.un.org/ilc/ [Draft Articles on State Responsibility].

61 Article 85(4)(a) of the 1977 First Additional Protocol, *supra* note 16.

62 UN Fact-find Mission on Settlements Report 2013, *supra* note 46 at paras 36 and 96. On a useful definition of regime, see Stephen D. Krasner, 'Structural Causes and Regime Consequences: Regimes as Intervening Variables', (1982) 36:2 Int'l Org. 185.

63 HRC, *Report of the Special Rapporteur on the Situation of Human Rights in the Palestinian Territories Occupied since 1967, John Dugard*, 4th Sess, UN Doc A/HRC/4/17 (29 January 2007) at para 8, online: OHCHR https://documents-dds-ny.un.org/doc/UNDOC/GEN/G07/105/44/PDF/G0710544.pdf?OpenElement.

64 Article 53 of the Fourth Geneva Convention, *supra* note 15. Extensive destruction and appropriation of property 'not justified by military necessity and carried out unlawfully and wantonly', is listed as a grave breach of the Fourth Geneva Convention. See article 147 of the Fourth Geneva Convention, *supra* note 15.

ensure public order and safety;[65] article 46, concerning the prohibition on the confiscation of private property; article 52, concerning the requisitioning of property and services;[66] and article 55, concerning the administration of public property.[67] Israeli authorities have also invoked article 23(g) of these Regulations in relation to certain measures that were implemented in connection with the settlements (such as the Wall's construction),[68] following the outbreak of the *Second Intifada* in September 2000.

This *Second Intifada* came in response to the breakdown of the peace talks between Palestinians and Israel and to ongoing settlement activity.[69] Acts of violence, including suicide attacks by Palestinians, took place against Israelis living in both Israel and the oPt. Shortly thereafter, the Israeli Advocate General announced that the situation in the oPt qualified as an 'armed conflict short of war'.[70] Since then, the situation in the West Bank has been treated as such,[71] a qualification that has been criticized by scholars and the human rights community.[72] All actions carried out by the military therein were henceforth to be treated as combat actions.[73] Israeli military authorities

65 Article 43 of the Hague Regulations, *supra* note 14.

66 Under article 52 of the Hague Regulations, an occupant is not allowed to requisition private property 'except for the needs of the army of occupation'. See Hague Regulations, *supra* note 14.

67 Article 55 of the Hague Regulations, *supra* note 14.

68 Article 23(g) of the Hague Regulations stipulates that it is forbidden '[t]o destroy or seize the enemy's property, unless such destruction or seizure be imperatively demanded by the necessities of war'. Hague Regulations, *supra* note 14. Since Israel exercises effective control over the West Bank, the law of belligerent occupation which includes only Section III of the Regulations applies. Article 23(g) belongs to Section II, which is part of IHL that is applicable during hostilities. ICJ *Wall* Advisory Opinion, *supra* note 18 at paras 124 and 132. The Court's failure to elaborate on this point was criticized by Judge Higgins. See ICJ *Wall* Advisory Opinion, *supra* note 18, *Separate Opinion of Judge Higgins*, online: ICJ www.icj-cij.org/files/case-related/131/131-20040709-ADV-01-02-EN.pdf [Separate Opinion-Judge Higgins].

69 Ahmed Samih Khalidi and Christophe Jacquet, 'Le conflict israélo-palestinien: retour vers le future', (2002) 3 Politique Etrangère 60.

70 UN GA, *Letter dated 4 November 2002 from the Permanent Representative of Israel to the United Nations addressed to the Secretary-General*, UNGA 57th Sess, UN Doc. A/C.4/57/4 (6 November 2002) at para 5, online: UNISPAL https://unispal.un.org/DPA/DPR/unispal.nsf/0/B1099239DEA7D8C185256C6F005899A7. Consequently, only one regime was deemed applicable, namely that of IHL as the *lex specialis*. Orna Ben-Naftali and Yuval Shany, 'Living in Denial: The Application of Human Rights in the Occupied Territories', (2003–2004) 37 Isr LR 17 at 33.

71 Iain Scobbie, 'Prolonged Occupation and Article 6(3) of the Fourth Geneva Convention: Why the International Court Got It Wrong Substantively and Procedurally', Blog of the European Journal of International Law: EJIL Talk (16 June 2015), online: EJIL Talk www.ejiltalk.org/prolonged-occupation-and-article-63-of-the-fourth-geneva-convention-why-the-international-court-got-it-wrong-substantively-and-procedurally/.

72 *B'Tselem*, 'Void of Responsibility: Israeli Military Police not to Investigate Killings of Palestinians by Soldiers', Report (September 2010) at 14, online: *B'Tselem* www.btselem.org/download/201009_void_of_responsibility_eng.pdf.

73 (HCJ 9594/03) *B'Tselem et al. v. the Judge Advocate General* cited in *B'Tselem*, 'Void of Responsibility', *supra* note 72.

also stepped up the implementation of security-based measures against the Palestinian civilian population.[74]

The HCJ and the rule of law

The Israeli Supreme Court sits at the head of Israel's court system.[75] In addition to acting as an appellate court, the Supreme Court, as the HCJ, rules as a court of first instance, primarily in matters that relate to the legality of decisions by government authorities, including bodies and persons performing public functions under the law.[76] Today, it consists of 15 members (justices), with one of them acting as the President of the Court.[77] Appeals to the HCJ are made by means of a petition.[78]

Israel perceives itself as a country that it is founded on principles such as democracy,[79] the separation of power,[80] and the rule of law (RoL).[81] The concepts of 'law-abiding' and of 'democracy' attach significance to the notion of the RoL,[82]

74 *Report of the UN Human Rights Inquiry Commission Established Pursuant to Commission resolution S-5/1 of 19 October 2000*, UN CHR, 57th Sess, UN Doc E/CN.4/2001/121 (16 March 2001) at paras 34–38, online: OHCHR https://unispal.un.org/DPA/DPR/unispal.nsf/0/4A5FCB3241D55A7885256A1E006E75AD [UN Commission of Inquiry Report 2000].

75 The Basic Law: *The Judiciary* (5748–1984). See unofficial English translation of the law, online: the *Knesset* http://knesset.gov.il/laws/special/eng/BasicLawTheJudiciary.pdf.

76 The State of Israel, 'The Judicial Authority: The Supreme Court', online: HCJ http://elyon1.court.gov.il/eng/system/index.html.

77 'The Judicial Authority: The Judges', online: HCJ http://elyon1.court.gov.il/eng/system/index.html.

78 In the first stage of the deliberation, a HCJ justice decides whether there is a *prima facie* basis for the petition. If this is the case, he/she issues an *order nisi*. After the substantial deliberation on the petition, the HCJ either turns this order into an absolute order, thereby requiring the authority against which the order was issued to comply with the order, or the petition is rejected. Israeli *Knesset*, 'The Israeli High Court of Justice', online: *Knesset* https://knesset.gov.il/lexicon/eng/bagatz_eng.htm.

79 For a discussion on whether the self-declared 'Jewish State' remains in principle compatible with democracy, see Ilan Peleg, 'Jewish-Palestinian Relations in Israel: From Hegemony to Equality', (Spring 2004) 17:3 Int J of Pol Cul & Soc'y 415 at 432; Oren Yiftachel, 'Ethnocracy: The Judicialization of Israel/Palestine', (September 1999) 6:3 Constellations 364.

80 Gretchen Helmke and Frances Rosenbluth, 'Regimes and Rule of Law: Judicial Independence in Comparative Perspective', (2009) 12 Ann Rev of Pol Sc 345. The three branches of Israel's government are the legislature (*Knesset*), the executive, and the judiciary. Eli Salzberger 'A Positive Analysis of the Doctrine of Separation of Powers, or: Why do we have an Independent Judiciary?', (December 1993) 13:4 Int'l Rev L and Econ 349.

81 (HCJ 73/53) [1953] *Kol Ha'am Company Limited v. Minister of Interior*, official English translation, online: HCJ http://elyon1.court.gov.il/files_eng/53/730/000/Z01/53000730.z01.htm. Reprinted in *Selected Judgments of the Supreme Court of Israel*, at 90 (1962 [*Kol Ha'am* Judgment]. See also Horacio Spector, 'Judicial Review, Rights, and Democracy', (July 2003) 22:3–4 Law and Phil 285.

82 There are three aspects to this concept. The first one is 'the absolute supremacy or predominance of regular law as opposed to the influence of arbitrary power'. The second one is 'equality before the law or the equal subjection of all classes to the ordinary law of the land administered by ordinary courts'. The third one is that the RoL entails that 'the law of the constitution [...] [is] not the source but the consequence of the rights of individuals, as defined and enforced by the courts'. Albert Van Dicey, *An Introduction to the Study of the Law of the Constitution*, 10th ed (London: Macmillan, 1959) at 188, 193 and 195–196.

expressed in both its formal[83] and substantive[84] aspects. The self- perception as a 'law-abiding' 'defensive democracy'[85] proved particularly instrumental during the early years of the occupation: at the time, Israeli authorities sought to base their actions and procedures of control in the oPt on an extensive web of legal rules and procedures.[86] Shortly after 1967, government authorities expressed a readiness to recognize the *de jure* applicability of the Fourth Geneva Convention to the oPt.[87] Although this MO was repealed shortly after, it has been argued that Israel's continued commitment to the RoL is reflected in the authorities' willingness to ensure that the conduct of its military in the occupied territory conforms with the provisions of the Hague Regulations.[88] They have

83 The RoL does not amount to the recognition of some minimal substantive rights and freedoms for individuals. Rather, it underscores that if and when a society wants to protect individual rights, the best way to do so is by using the British common-law technique. Albert Van Dicey, *supra* note 82. See also Stéphane Beaulac, 'The Rule of Law in International Law Today', in Gianluigi Palombella and Neil Walker, eds, *Relocating the Rule of Law* (Portland, OR: Hart, 2009) 197 at 198. The formal aspects of the RoL evaluate the way in which the law was promulgated, but do not judge the actual content of the law. Eight conditions must be met for the formal aspects of the RoL to be made possible: that there is a system of rules; that rules are promulgated and published; that there is no retroactive application of rules; that rules are clear and intelligible; that rules are not contradictory; that they are practicable; that rules are consistent over time and that official actions are congruent with declared rules. Lon Fuller, *The Morality of Law*, 2d ed (New Haven, CT: Yale University Press, 1969).

84 This conception does not reject the idea that the RoL has formal elements. However, it insists that the RoL must display certain substantive commitments. Dworkin argued that 'the rules in the book' must capture and enforce moral rights. This is because legal rights flow naturally from moral rights, a notion that emerges from the idea that citizens have moral rights, enacted by a representative legislature, and which courts enforce, vis-à-vis each other or against the state as a whole. Ronald Dworkin, *A Matter of Principle* (Cambridge, MA: Harvard University Press, 1985); David Kairys, 'Searching for the Rule of Law', (2003) 36 Suffolk UL Rev 307. Courts should therefore be deciding legal questions according to the 'best theory of justice'. This requires judges to base their decisions on principles. Legislators, on the other hand are more competent to implement policies. This kind of judicial review, Dworkin argued, restrains the pursuit of a policy within the bounds of what is consistent with equal concern and respect for all citizens. Paul Craig, 'Formal and Substantive Conceptions of the Rule of Law: An Analytical Framework', (Autumn 1977) 3 Pub L 467.

85 Orna Ben-Naftali, 'PathoLAWgical Occupation: Normalizing the Exceptional Case of the Occupied Palestinian Territory and Other Legal Pathologies', in Orna Ben-Naftali, *International Humanitarian Law and International Human Rights Law*, ed (Oxford: Oxford University Press, 2011) 129.

86 Eyal Benvenisti, *The International Law of Occupation*, 2nd ed (Princeton, NJ: Princeton University Press, 2004).

87 *Proclamation Concerning the Entry into Force of the Order concerning Security Provisions (West Bank Area) (No. 3), 5727–1967.* In addition to these proclamations, the MC published another proclamation and several MOs establishing criminal law and a system of military courts. The *Order concerning the Establishment of Military Courts (West Bank Area) (No 3) 1967, 7 June 1967*, states 'the [Israeli] military court [...] must apply the provisions of the [Fourth] Geneva Convention with respect to judicial procedures [...]', cited in ICJ *Wall* Advisory Opinion, *supra* note 18 at para 93.

88 On the grounds that they reflect customary international law.

also declared that they would remain bound by the 'humanitarian provisions' of the Fourth Geneva Convention.[89]

Therefore, while the HCJ's competence to exercise extra-territorial jurisdiction over acts by Israeli authorities beyond Israel proper was not self-evident at first,[90] it was not questioned.[91] Shortly after 1967, the Court declared that it enjoyed legal jurisdiction over petitions from the oPt, which challenged the legality of actions and decisions by Israeli military authorities.[92] By the early 1980s, the Court referred to its jurisdiction over these petitions as an established fact.[93] Since then, the HCJ has consolidated its judicial review over the actions of the MC and its official functionaries.[94] As it were, the Court emphasized that it does not recognize 'institutional non-justiciability' as a ground for abstaining from the review of a petition 'where recognition of it might prevent the examination of impingement upon human rights'.[95] This was possible because of the Court's policy of 'judicial activism'.[96] Spearheaded by the former

89 Meir Shamgar, 'The Observance of International Law in the Administered Territories', (1997) 1 Isr YB Hum Rts 262.

90 'The Supreme Court of Israel is not an International forum ... [I]t is not self-evident that the Court's power of review extends to actions carried out by the military in areas that are not part of Israeli sovereign territory and in which the Israeli legal system does not apply'. David Kretzmer, *The Occupation of Justice: The Supreme Court of Israel and the Occupied Territories* (Albany, NY: SUNY Press, 2002), at 19.

91 In its first published judgment regarding the oPt, the Court did not address the issue of jurisdiction. In a latter case, the HCJ noted that the State had not challenged the Court's jurisdiction on the matter. (HCJ 256/72) [1972] *Electric Corporation for Jerusalem District LTD v. Minister of Defense* 5 Isr YB Hum Rts 381 at 383 [*Electric Corporation* Judgment – Summary].

92 David Kretzmer, 'The Law of Belligerent Occupation in the Supreme Court of Israel', (Spring 2012) 94:855 Int'l Rev Red Cross 207.

93 (HCJ 69/81) [1981] *Bassil Abu Aita et al. v. Regional Commander of Judea and Samaria et al.*, official English translation, online: HCJ http://elyon1.court.gov.il/files_eng/81/690/000/Z01/81000690.z01.pdf [*Abu Aita* Judgment].

94 (HCJ 796/02) [2006] *Public Committee against Torture et al. v. Government of Israel et al.* at para 55, unofficial English translation, online: Center for the Defence of the Individual – *Hamoked* http://elyon1.court.gov.il/files_eng/02/690/007/a34/02007690.a34.pdf [*Torture* 2002 – Judgment]; (HCJ 302/72) *Sheikh Suleiman Abu Hilu v. Government of Israel*, English summary found in (1975) 5 Isr YB Hum Rts 384 at 385–386 [*Hilu* Judgment – Summary]; (HCJ 393/82) [1983] *Jam'iat Iskan case, al-Ma'almoun al-Tha'auniya al-Mahduda al-Masuliya, Cooperative Association Legally registered at the Judea and Samaria Area Headquarters v. Commander of IDF Forces in the Area of Judea and Samaria et al.* at paras 32–34, unofficial English translation, online: *Hamoked* www.hamoked.org/items/160_eng.pdf [*Iskan* Judgment].

95 *Torture 2002* Judgment, *supra* note 94 at para 50. However, up until the 1970s, the Court had adopted a narrow definition of standing, justiciability and review. Yoav Dotan, 'Judicial Accountability in Israel: The High Court of Justice and the Phenomenon of Judicial Hyper-activism', (2002) Isr Aff 87.

96 Sharon Weill, *The Role of National Courts in Applying International Humanitarian Law* (Oxford: Oxford University Press, 2014) at 197. The role gained prominence under the leadership of former Presiding Justice Aharon Barak. Martin Edelman, 'Israel', in C. Neal Tate and Torbjörn Vallinder, eds, *The Global Expansion of Judicial Power* (New York: New York University Press, 1995) 403.

Chief Justice Aharon Barak,[97] it was used to promote human rights both inside Israel proper and in the oPt.[98] This remained the case following the outbreak of the *First* and *Second Intifada*, during which the HCJ continued to review the legality of security-based measures by the military.[99]

Four trends have influenced the Court's perception of the purpose of its own judicial oversight. The first is the individual rights tradition that gained prominence following the wave of constitutionalism that gripped Europe and other Western style liberal democracies in the post WWII era,[100] and which resulted in the 'judicialization of politics'.[101] The second is the increased interaction between national, international and regional courts, all of which contributed to a phenomenon of 'judicial globalization'.[102] Today, the HCJ views itself as part of a community of likeminded independent institutions,[103] sharing similar values, principles and normative sources.[104] These have encouraged the Court to internalize the need to uphold the substantive aspects of democracy.[105] Consequently, and in the absence of a written constitution in Israel,[106] the HCJ has emphasized the legitimacy of extra-statutory sources of law (such as Israel's *Declaration of Independence*,[107] IHR

97 Barak briefly occupied the position of Israel's Attorney General (1975–1978), before serving as a judge on the bench of the HCJ from 1978–2006. 'Professor Aharon Barak', online: The Hebrew University of Jerusalem-Faculty of Law https://en.law.huji.ac.il/people/aharon-barak.

98 Eli Salzberger, 'Judicial Activism in Israel', in Brice Dickson, ed, *Judicial Activism in Common Law Supreme Courts* (New York: Oxford University Press, 2007) 217. Some have even referred to it as a form of 'judicial hyper-activism'. Yoav Dotan, 'Judicial Accountability in Israel', *supra* note 95.

99 Eyal Benvenisti, *The International Law of Occupation*, *supra* note 86. (HCJ 3451/02) [2002] *Almandi v. Minister of Defense*, online: HCJ http://elyon1.court.gov.il/files_eng/02/510/034/a06/02034510.a06.pdf [*Almandi* Judgment]. (HCJ 5100/94) [1999] *Public Committee against Torture et al. v. Government of Israel et al.*, at para 39, official English translation, online: HCJ http://elyon1.court.gov.il/files_eng/94/000/051/a09/94051000.a09.pdf [*Torture 1994* Judgment]; *Ajuri* Judgment, *supra* note 34 at para 41.

100 Ruti Teitel, 'For Humanity', (June 2004) 3:2 Hum Rts 225.

101 C. Neal Tate, 'Why the Expansion of Judicial Power?', in C. Neal Tate and Torbjörn Vallinder, eds, *The Global Expansion of Judicial Power* (New York: New York University Press, 1995) at 27. (HCJ 910/86) [1988] *Yehuda Ressler et al. v. Minister of Defense*, at 28, online: HCJ http://elyon1.court.gov.il/files_eng/86/100/009/Z01/86009100.z01.pdf [*Ressler* Judgment].

102 Anne-Marie Slaughter, 'Judicial Globalization', (2000) 40 VA J Int'l L 1103.

103 Anne-Marie Slaughter, 'A Typology of Transjudicial Communication', (1994–1995) 29 U Rich L Rev 99.

104 Karen Eltis, 'The Democratic Legitimacy of the 'International Criminal Justice Model': The Unilateral Reach of Foreign Domestic Law and the Promise of Transnational Constitutional Conversation', in Christopher P.M. Waters, ed, *British and Canadian Perspectives on International Law* (Netherlands: Martinus Nijhoff, 2006) 349 at 355.

105 Aharon Barak, 'The Role of a Supreme Court in a Democracy and the Fight against Terrorism', (2003–2004) 58 U Miami L Rev 125.

106 Guy Carmi, 'A Constitutional Court in the Absence of a Formal Constitution? On the Ramifications of Appointing the Israeli Supreme Court as the Only Tribunal for Judicial Review', (2005–2006) 21 Conn J Int'l L 67.

107 Prior to the promulgation of Israel's Basic Laws (1992) Israel's *Declaration of Independence* offered guiding principles of a bill of rights. MoFA, 'Declaration of Establishment of State of Israel', (14 May 1948), online: Israeli MoFA www.mfa.gov.il/mfa/foreignpolicy/peace/guide/pages/declaration%20of%20establishment%20of%20state%20of%20israel.aspx [*Declaration of Independence*].

legal norms and the spirit of Jewish law) to promote a rights-based jurisprudence.[108] Towards this objective, the HCJ strengthened its judicial review over the actions and legislation from other branches of government[109] and expanded the types of issues that it deemed justiciable.[110] It also liberalized the notion of public standing interest.[111] This has allowed interest groups to challenge the legality of the actions by military authorities in the oPt regardless of whether or not they represent a particular individual whose interest has been, or could be, affected by a particular policy.[112]

The third trend is the concern that the HCJ has seemingly expressed for upholding the formal and substantial aspects of the domestic RoL. In this regard, the Court's resort to Israeli administrative law, and its decision to consider it part of the standards that it uses for assessing the actions of Israeli administrative authorities in the occupied territories, including the military,[113] can be interpreted as a commitment to promoting the formal aspects of the RoL. Over the years, the HCJ has underscored that an administrative organ must exercise the discretion granted to it by statute for the purpose specified in that legislation, specifically after weighing all the relevant considerations.[114] Authorities have also been required to strike a proper balance between the liberty of the individual and the needs of the public.[115]

To determine whether authorities have upheld these standards, the HCJ has in its rulings invoked the proportionality test that is grounded in Israeli administrative law. This requires an administrative authority seeking to impose a measure that infringes on the interests of individuals to satisfy three cumulative conditions or sub-tests. The first is that the means employed by the administrative body must

108 *Kol Ha'am* Judgment, *supra* note 81. Patricia Woods, 'The Ideational Foundations of Israel's "Constitutional Revolution"', (December 2009) 62:4 Pol Res Q 811.

109 In the 1960s, the court established its right of de facto judicial supervision of the constitutionality of primary legislation. See (HCJ 98/69) [1969] *Bergmann v. Minister of Finance and State Comptroller*, Official English translation, online: HCJ http://elyon1.court.gov.il/files_eng/69/980/000/Z01/69000980.z01.pdf [*Bergmann* Judgment].

110 The Court has distinguished between normative non-justiciability, that is, 'whether legal standards exist for the determination of the dispute before the court', and institutional justiciability, which relates to 'whether the court is the appropriate institution to decide a dispute, or whether perhaps it is appropriate that the dispute be decided by a different institution, such as the legislative or executive branches', *Ressler* Judgment, *supra* note 101 at 46–47. The Court has rejected arguments of normative non-justiciability. *Torture* 2002 – Judgment, *supra* note 94 at para 48.

111 The requirement of standing was first dropped by the Court in the 1980s. *Ressler* Judgment, *supra* note 101 at 46. Shoshana Netanyahu, 'The Supreme Court of Israel – A Safeguard of the Rule of Law', (1993) 5:1 Pace int'l L Rev 1.

112 Galit Raguan, 'Adjudicating Armed Conflict in Domestic Courts: The Experience of Israel's Supreme Court', (2010) 13 YB Int'l Human L 61.

113 *Iskan* Judgment, *supra* note 94. Eyal Benvenisti 'Introduction to Israeli Administrative Law', (1996) 2:2 Euro Pub L 194.

114 Eyal Benvenisti, 'Introduction to Israeli Administrative Law', *supra* note 113.

115 (HCJ 3278/02) [2002] *Hamoked et al. v. Commander of the IDF Forces in the West Bank* at para 23, online: HCJ http://elyon1.court.gov.il/Files_ENG/02/780/032/A06/02032780.A06.HTM [*Hamoked 2002* Judgment]. See also *Abu Aita* Judgment, *supra* note 93; *Ajuri* Judgment, *supra* note 34.

rationally lead to the realization of the objective (the 'rational means' test). The second is that the means employed by the administrative body must injure the individual to the least extent possible ('least injurious means' test). The third requires that the damage that was caused to the individual by the administrative body (to achieve its objectives) be of proper proportion to the gain brought about by those means ('proportionality in the narrow sense' test). All three sub-tests must be satisfied before an administrative measure is deemed proportionate.[116]

Other principles that were emphasized by the HCJ throughout its adjudication include: good faith, substantial and procedural fairness, as well as due process of law.[117] It also held that an administrative authority (including the military) must use its discretion in a reasonable and fair manner. This, in the Court's view, remains the case even if the rights that are infringed on are not vested rights and, therefore, are not protected under constitutional law.[118] The approach has been hailed as a success in that it allows petitioners to overcome evidentiary problems and the Court to review the legality of measures even in situations where authorities had allegedly not resorted to irrelevant considerations.[119]

In the 1990s, the *Knesset* enacted the Basic Law: *Human Dignity and Liberty*[120] and Basic Law: *Freedom of Occupation*,[121] a development that was greeted as bringing about a 'constitutional revolution'.[122] Here, and despite the fact that the Basic Law: *Human Dignity and Liberty* promulgated lacked specific entrenchment provisions,[123] this and the latter Basic Law were used by the HCJ to strengthen constitutional protections as a way of consolidating the more substantive aspects of the domestic RoL. In the case of the Basic Law: *Human*

116 Talia Einhorn, 'Israel' in Diana Shelton, ed, *International Law and Domestic Legal Systems* (Oxford: Oxford University Press, 2011) 288.

117 Uri Shoham, 'The Principle of Legality', *supra* note 8. See also discussion in (HCJ 2056/04) [2004] *Beit Sourik Village Council v. Government of Israel* (2005), official English translation, online: https://supremedecisions.court.gov.il/Home/Download?path=EnglishVerdicts\04\560\020\A28&fileName=04020560_a28.txt&type=4 [*Beit Sourik* Judgment].

118 Daphne Barak-Erez, 'Israeli Administrative Law at the Crossroads: Between the English Model and the American Model', (2007) 40:1 Isr LR 56.

119 Eyal Benvenisti, 'Introduction to Israeli Administrative Law', *supra* note 113.

120 The law protects rights such as the preservation of life, body and dignity and the protection of property, of liberty and freedom. It also protects the right to leave Israel and for Israeli citizens to enter it, as well as the right to privacy and intimacy. Basic Law: *Human Dignity and Liberty* (Isr), online: *Knesset* website as amended by Basic Law: *Human Dignity and Liberty – Amendment*, 1994, online: *Knesset* http://knesset.gov.il/laws/special/eng/BasicLawLiberty.pdf [Basic Law: *Human Dignity and Liberty*].

121 The latter Basic Law protects the freedom to occupation. Basic Law: *Freedom of Occupation*, 1992 as repealed by Basic Law: *Freedom of Occupation*, online: *Knesset* http://knesset.gov.il/laws/special/eng/BasicLawOccupation.pdf.

122 Consequently, these 'rights became constitutionally protected and were accorded *supra*-legislative constitutional status'. (C.A. 6821/93) [1995] *United Mizrahi Bank Ltd. v. Migdal Cooperative Village et al.* at para 94, official English translation, online: HCJ http://elyon1.court.gov.il/files_eng/93/210/068/z01/93068210.z01.pdf [*Mizrahi Bank* Judgment]. David Kretzmer, 'The New Basic Laws on Human Rights: A Mini-Revolution in Israeli Constitutional Law', (1992) 2 Isr LR 238.

123 Guy Carmi, 'A Constitutional Court in the Absence of a Formal Constitution', *supra* note 106.

Dignity and Liberty, the Court used it to argue that Israeli courts were entitled to strike down any ordinary legislation that did not meet the criteria of its limitation clause (section 8).[124] This took place even though the Basic Law lacked any specific entrenchment provisions.[125]

With the adoption of these Basic Laws, the HCJ's approach to proportionality (originating in Israeli administrative law) was imported into Israeli constitutional law, to form part of the Court's strategy of adjudicating the constitutionality of Israeli legislation.[126] This constitutional assessment was carried out in two steps. The first step was to examine whether a constitutionally protected right had been infringed on for the sake of a legitimate purpose – that is, one that is consistent with the values of Israel as a 'Jewish' and 'democratic' state. The second step involved the need to assess whether or not the right's infringement' exceeded what was necessary. It is with regards to the second step, that the proportionality doctrine and its three sub-tests were employed by the Court to determine the following: that there is a rational connection between the appropriate goal and the means utilized by the law; that the objective cannot be achieved by means that are less restrictive of the constitutional rights; and that a proportionate balance exists between the social benefit of realizing the appropriate goal and the harm caused to the right.[127]

A fourth trend is the Court's desire to contribute to an international RoL,[128] a concept that also has formal[129] and substantive features.[130] In this regard, the

124 This section reads that '[t]here shall be no violation of rights under this Basic Law except by a law befitting the values of the State of Israel, enacted for a proper purpose, and to an extent no greater than is required or by such a law enacted with explicit authorization therein'. Article 8 of the Basic Law: *Human Dignity and Liberty*, *supra* note 120. Article 4 of the Basic Law: *Freedom of Occupation*, *supra* note 121 contains similarly worded phrasing.

125 Yoav Dotan, 'Constitutional Adjudication and Political Accountability: Comparative Analysis and the Peculiarity of Israel', in Gideon Sapir, Daphne Barak-Erez and Aharon Barak, eds, *Israeli Constitutional Law in the Making* (Portland, OR: Hart, 2013) 91. However, 'a statute incompatible with the conditions of the limitation clause does not have the power to infringe a protected right', *Mizrahi Bank* Judgment, *supra* note 122 at para 44.

126 Mordechai Kremnitzer, 'Constitutional Proportionality: (Appropriate Guidelines)', in Gideon Sapir, Daphne Barak-Erez and Aharon Barak, eds, *Israeli Constitutional Law in the Making* (Portland, OR: Hart, 2013) 225.

127 Aharon Barak, 'Proportionality and Principled Balancing', (April 2010) 4:1 L & Ethics of Hum Rts 1.

128 Although the RoL describes the state of affairs at a domestic national level, it can also be externalized onto the international legal plane. Stéphane Beaulac, 'The Rule of Law in International Law Today', *supra* note 83 at 204.

129 Three elements of the more formal version of this concept may be found in international law. The first element is the existence of a principled legal normativity on the international plane that is sufficiently developed. The second element is the idea that legal norms apply equally to all of its subjects (the states). Hence, every state can play a role in determining the formation of international customary law through their practice and their *opinion juris* and participate equally in the creation of this international normativity. The third element is that normativity on the international plane can be adjudicatively enforced, at least through the ICJ. Stéphane Beaulac, *supra* note 83. Mattias Kumm, 'International Law in National Courts: The International Rule of Law and the Limits of the Internationalist Model', (2003–2004) 44 VA J Int'l L 19 at 22.

130 Simon Chesterman, 'An International Rule of Law?', (Spring 2008) 56 (2) AJIL 331 at 361.

HCJ has demonstrated a keen interest in invoking international rules and principles as a means of contributing to the promotion of this notion. In the case of the formal aspects, courts promote it by allowing the disposition of international claims and by reviewing the legality of national acts with regards to international obligations as a way of ensuring rule conformity.[131] In terms of the substantive level ('thick' aspect) of the international RoL, courts can contribute to this through their interpretation, determination and development of international legal principles and rules.[132]

The HCJ's commitment to promoting this aspect has been demonstrated, in the first place, by its willingness to entertain petitions by Palestinians from the occupied territory.[133] The second way is by upholding in its judgments the conclusion that Israel's control of the West Bank qualifies as an occupation[134] and that therefore, the MC's authority must be assessed against provisions of the international law of belligerent occupation,[135] particularly the Hague Regulations and the Fourth Geneva Convention.[136]

Israel follows the common-law tradition, which distinguishes between customary international law and treaty law.[137] Hence, and following the dualist logic, an international treaty to which Israel is a State Party is not legally binding domestically and could not serve in and of itself as a basis for individual claims in its domestic courts, unless it has been incorporated into its domestic law through specific Israeli legislation.[138] In the case of treaties which Israel considers to be reflective of customary international law (i.e. declarative treaties), they can and have been applied directly in its domestic courts without the need for such legislation. However, this takes place so long as those treaties are not inconsistent with domestic rules that have been enacted by statute or which have been declared as final by national courts and tribunals.[139]

Government authorities have accepted that the Hague Regulations reflect customary international law and that they apply to the conduct of Israeli military

131 Andreas Paulus, 'National Courts and the International Rule of Law – Remarks on the Book by André Nollkaemper', (2012) 4 Jerusalem Rev Leg Stud 5.
132 Ibid.
133 Sharon Weill, *The Role of National Court*, *supra* note 96.
134 *Abu Aita* Judgment, *supra* note 93; (HCJ 606/78) *Ayub et al. v. Minister of Defense et al.*, English summary in (1979) 9 Isr YB Hum Rts 337 [*Beit El* Judgment – Summary]; *Iskan* Judgment, *supra* note 94 at para 10; *Ajuri* Judgment, *supra* note 34 at para 13.
135 *Elon Moreh* Judgment, *supra* note 1 at 11.
136 *Torture 2002* Judgment, *supra* note 94 at para 17.
137 Eyal Benvenisti, 'The Attitude of the Supreme Court of Israel towards the Implementation of the International Law of Human Rights', in Benedetto Conforti and Francesco Francioni, eds, *Enforcing International Human Rights in Domestic Courts* (Netherlands: Kluwer Law International, 1997) 207.
138 Ibid.
139 However, subsidiary legislation cannot derogate from international custom, unless a statute authorizes such derogation. Eyal Benvenisti, *supra* note 137.

and government authorities in the oPt.[140] However, regarding the *de jure* applicability of the Fourth Geneva Convention to the oPt, Israeli authorities were initially willing to consider it applicable. However, shortly after 1967, this position was reversed. Ever since, they have firmly rejected its *de jure* applicability. In support of their position, they have argued that the Fourth Geneva Convention is a constitutive treaty and therefore, not automatically incorporable into Israeli law without enforcing legislation.[141] Moreover, claims by Jordan to hold a legitimate title to the West Bank (pre-1967) has consistently been contested by them. Hence, they argue, this territory cannot be considered as the territory of the High Contracting Party to the Fourth Geneva Convention, as stipulated under article 2 of that Convention.[142] They also argue that by virtue of the Oslo Accords, the situation in the West Bank (and the Gaza Strip) can no longer be qualified as a military occupation,[143] particularly as far as 'Area A' is concerned.[144]

The official Israeli position in relation to article 49(6) of the Fourth Geneva Convention is also worth mentioning. According to a recently updated memorandum by the Israel Ministry of Foreign Affairs (MoFA):

> The provisions of Article 49(6) regarding forced population transfer to occupied sovereign territory should not be seen as prohibiting the voluntary return of [Jewish] individuals to the towns and villages from which they, or their ancestors, had been forcibly ousted. Nor does it prohibit the movement of individuals to land which was not under the legitimate sovereignty of any state and which is not subject to private ownership.[145]

140 *Beit El* Judgment – Summary, *supra* note 134. Nissim Bar-Yaacov, 'The Applicability of the Law of War to Judea and Samaria (the West Bank) and to the Gaza Strip', (1990) 24 Isr LR 485.

141 Israel ratified the Fourth Geneva Convention on 6 July 1951. However, to date it has not been incorporated into domestic legislation. Ruth Lapidoth 'The Expulsion of Civilians from Areas Which Came Under Israeli Control in 1967', (1991) 2 EJIL 97.

142 UN GA 'Annex I: Summary Legal Position of the Government of Israel', in *Report of the Secretary-General prepared pursuant to General Assembly Resolution ES-10/13*, UNGAOR, 10th Emer Sess, Agenda Item 5, UN Doc A/ES-10/248 (24 November 2003) at para 3, online: UNISPAL https://unispal.un.org/DPA/DPR/unispal.nsf/0/A5A017029C05606B85256DEC00626057. This position was first espoused by Professor Yehuda Blum, who argued that since Jordan's annexation of the West Bank had not been recognized by the international community, by occupying this territory, Israel did not oust a legitimate 'sovereign'. Yehuda Blum, 'The Missing Reversioner: Reflections on the Status of Judea and Samaria', (1968) 3 Isr LR 279 at 294.

143 UN ECOSOC, *Report of the Special Rapporteur of the Commission on Human Rights, Mr. John Dugard, on the Situation of Human Rights in the Palestinian Territories Occupied by Israel since 1967*, UN ESC, 58th Sess UN Doc E/CN.4/2002/32 (6 March 2002) at para 9, online: UN https://documents-dds-ny.un.org/doc/UNDOC/GEN/G02/112/69/PDF/G0211269.pdf?OpenElement.

144 *Statement of the Israeli Ambassador at the UN General Assembly*, reprinted in UN GA, Verbatim Records, UNGA 55th Sess, 68th plenary meeting, UN Doc A/55/PV.68 at 32, online: UN https://documents-dds-ny.un.org/doc/UNDOC/GEN/N00/755/23/PDF/N0075523.pdf?OpenElement.

145 Israeli MoFA, 'Israeli Settlements and International Law', *supra* note 40.

Interestingly, the conclusions of the Israeli government-appointed Levy Commission, which was set up in 2012 to examine the legality of the whole settlement enterprise in the West Bank, also stressed that 'the provisions of the 1949 Fourth Geneva Convention, regarding transfer of populations, cannot be considered to be applicable and were never intended to apply to the type of settlement activity carried out by Israel in Judea and Samaria'.[146]

As for the applicability of IHR-related treaties, Israeli authorities have denied the extra-territorial application of human rights obligations arising from IHR conventions to which it is a State Party. These include the International Covenant on Civil and Political Rights (ICCPR), the International Covenant on Economic, Social and Cultural Rights (ICESCR), the Convention on the Elimination of Racial Discrimination (CERD) and the Convention on the Elimination of Discrimination against Women (CEDAW).[147] After the signing of the Oslo Accords, Israel also maintained that, by virtue of these agreements, '[i]t lacks actual authority and responsibility in terms of civil or military control over the territory'.[148]

With regards to the more substantive aspects of the international RoL, the HCJ's adjudication of the legality of the actions of the Israeli military authorities in the oPt[149] have regularly underscored well-established principles of IHL, such as the principles of proportionality[150] and of military

146 Levy Commission Report, *supra* note 45 at 179–180; *B'Tselem*, 'Levy Committee Report: Where are the Palestinians?', (11 July 2012), online: *B'Tselem* http://m.btselem.org/setllements/20120711_levy_committee_report.

147 Orna Ben-Naftali and Yuval Shany, 'Living in Denial', *supra* note 70 at 33. UN HR Committee, *Summary Record of the 2717th Meeting*, UN Doc CCPR/C/SR.2717 (20 January 2011) at para 19. For a similar position in front of other UN treaty bodies, see UN CERD Committee, *Consideration of Reports, Comments and Information submitted by State Parties under Article 9 of the Convention: Seventh, Eighth and Ninth Report of Israel, Summary Record of the 1250th Meeting*, 52nd sess, UN Doc CERD/C/SR.1250 (9 March 1998) at para 7, online: UNISPAL https://unispal.un.org/DPA/DPR/unispal.nsf/0/89C006EAF4E7FCF585256DEA007480FE [CERD Committee Government Report 1998]. See also UN CAT Committee, *Written replies by the Government of Israel to the list of issues (CAT/C/ISR/Q/4) to be taken up in connection with the Consideration of the Fourth Periodic Report of Israel (CAT/C/ISR/4)*, 42nd sess, UN Doc CAT/C/ISR/Q/4/Add.1 (20 August 2010) at para 7, online: UNISPAL https://unispal.un.org/DPA/DPR/unispal.nsf/0/EF0C32774B4D44B0852577BD004E9595; UN ESCR Committee, *Consideration of Reports submitted by State Parties under Articles 16 and 17 of the Covenant: Initial Report of Israel*, UN Doc E/C.12/1/Add.27 (4 December 1998) at para 8, online: UNISPAL https://unispal.un.org/DPA/DPR/unispal.nsf/0/9867A375D6CD299985256D390052CA33.

148 HRC Concluding Observations 1998, *supra* note 22 at para 21. See also CERD Committee Government Report 1998, *supra* note 147 at paras 24 and 25.

149 David Kretzmer, 'The Law of Belligerent Occupation in the Supreme Court of Israel', *supra* note 92.

150 Under IHL, this principle seeks to ensure that an attack does not cause 'incidental loss of civilian life, injury to civilians, damage to civilian objects, or a combination thereof, which would be excessive in relation to the concrete and direct military advantage anticipated'. Article 51(5)(b) of the First Additional Protocol, *supra* note 16.

necessity.[151] Since the 1990s, the Court has also made references to IHR norms, some of which are customary international law or can be found in international treaties and conventions to which Israel is a State Party.[152]

One reason for the Court's interest in promoting the international RoL is the paradigm shift experienced by the international legal order, in which the reach of IHL, and its merger with IHR law, has resulted in a discourse that is framed in universal human rights language (i.e. 'humanity law').[153] This new regime has affected not only the process of international law making, its subject and structure, but also its core values.[154] In this regard, an active transnational legal process has facilitated the 'internalization' of global norms of 'humanity' by domestic legal systems[155] and their judicial branches.[156] Other reasons forcing the HCJ to pay more attention to the development of international legal norms[157] includes the rise of supra national tribunals[158] as well as of courts of third-party jurisdictions.[159] The complementarity between domestic and foreign courts in their exercise of jurisdiction over alleged international crimes[160] has also been highlighted as another element encouraging the HCJ to expand the limits of justiciability[161] as a way of adjudicating issues that draw interests for the launch of legal proceedings against senior Israeli officials in foreign and international courts.[162]

151 In IHL, for a measure to qualify as a military necessity, it must fulfil the following criteria: That it was taken primarily for the attainment of some specific military purpose; that it was required for the attainment of that purpose; that the purpose for which the measure was deployed was in conformity with IHL and that the measure itself was also otherwise in conformity with the law. Nobuo Hayashi, 'Requirements of Military Necessity in International Humanitarian Law and International Criminal Law', (10 March 2010) 28:1 BU Int'l LJ 39.

152 Among the sources that have been cited in the past for establishing certain rights, are the UDHR, the ICCPR and the ICESCR. However, judicial recourse to them has varied in frequency and scope. Daphne Barak-Erez, 'The International Law of Human Rights and Constitutional Law: A Case Study for an Expanding Dialogue', (2004) 2 Int'l J. Const. L 611.

153 Ruti Teitel, 'Humanity's Law: Rule of Law for the New Global Politics', (2001) 35 Cornell Int'l LJ 355.

154 Ibid.

155 Harold Koh, 'How is International Human Rights Law Enforced?', (1998–1999) 74 Indiana L J 1397 at 1399.

156 Amichai Cohen and Stuart A. Cohen, 'Israel and International Humanitarian Law: Between the Neo-Liberalism of State Security and the "Soft Power" of Legal Acceptability', 16:2 Israel Studies (Summer 2011) 1 at 14.

157 Anne Marie Slaughter, 'A Typology of Transjudicial Communication', *supra* note 103.

158 Antonio Cassese, 'On the Current Trends towards Criminal Prosecution and Punishment of Grave Breaches of International Humanitarian Law', (1998) 9 EJIL 2.

159 Ruti Teitel, 'For Humanity', *supra* note 100.

160 This includes war crimes. For an enumeration and/or definition of these crimes, see articles 6–8 of the Rome Statute, *supra* note 59.

161 Orna Ben-Naftali, 'A Judgment in the Shadow of International Criminal Law', (2007) 5 J Int'l Crim Justice 322.

162 Yuval Shany, 'Decade in Review: The Convergence of Israeli and International Law', (30 January 2010) Israel Democracy Institute (IDI), online: IDI https://en.idi.org.il/articles/10224.

The HCJ's adjudication of petitions challenging the legality of settlement-related security-based measures: a typology

Once a petition has been filed, the HCJ examines whether or not it has the authority to intervene. If it establishes that it does have this authority, it reviews the merits of the case.[163]

At the level of establishing facts

The first element of the typology is the deference afforded by domestic courts, such as the HCJ, to government and military authorities, on the ground that decision-making falls to the elected and expert branches. In the case of the HCJ, the Court has special procedures regarding evidence and which are based on equity of law. Consequently, both parties to a case are expected to provide accurate and full information when submitting their testimonies in the form of written affidavits.[164] However, the Court has no fact-finding machinery of its own, a fact that confines it to the information it receives from parties to a case. Hence, the burden of proof – that the authority failed to act in a reasonable manner – rests on the petitioner.[165] The Court only intervenes in the decision of military authorities if it can be proved that they have exceeded these margins.[166] While this approach applies to all the cases before the HCJ, this has had a significant impact on the manner in which petitions filed by Palestinians are decided[167] as it has made it difficult for them to challenge the security-based rationale allegedly spearheading the measure, including for the construction of settlements.[168]

163 Menachem Hofnung and Keren Weinshall Margel, 'Judicial Setbacks, Material Gains: Terror Litigation at the Israeli High Court of Justice', (November 2010) 7:4 J Empirical Leg Stud 664.

164 There is no cross-examination. See Orna Kohn, 'Going to the Occupier's Court: Seeking Legal Remedy from the Israeli High Court of Justice for IHL Violations in the OPT', Paper presented at *Al-Haq* Conference 21–24 May 2005, copy with author.

165 Talia Einhorn, 'Israel', *supra* note 116. Reiterating a conclusion, it has made in a judgment related to Israel proper (HCJ 6396/96) [1999] *Zakin v. The Mayor of Beer Sheva*, the Court emphasized that '[i]ndeed, an administrative authority seeking to enforce the law enjoys, like any administrative authority, the presumption of validity [...]. It stands to reason that only in rare cases said presumption will be refuted and selective enforcement substantiated'. (HCJ 5290/14) [2014] *Qawasmeh et al. v. Military Commander of the West Bank Area*, at para 30, online: *Hamoked* www.hamoked.org/files/2014/1158616_eng.pdf.

166 Eyal Benvenisti, 'Introduction to Israeli Administrative Law', *supra* note 113.

167 Orna Kohn, 'Going to the Occupier's Court', *supra* note 164.

168 In the landmark case of *Elon Moreh*, the Court received conflicting expert opinions, one from the serving Chief of the General Staff regarding the security of the 'Area', and the other one from the former Chief of the General Staff. It decided that

> [i]n matters of security, when the petitioner relies on the opinion of a security expert and the respondent relies on the opinion of the person who is both an expert and the person in charge of the state of security in the state, it is natural that special weight is given to the opinion of latter.
>
> *Elon Moreh* Judgment, *supra* note 1 at 26

However, the Court only upheld the petition, because the Israeli Minister of Defense himself had contradicted the information provided by the Chief of the General Staff, stating that the decision to confiscate a Palestinian privately owned plot of land for the construction of the settlement was indeed for security reasons. *Elon Moreh* Judgment, *supra* note 1 at 24.

At the level of interpreting the law

On this level, the second element of the typology is the Court's position versus the applicability of the Hague Regulations and the Fourth Geneva Convention. In analysing the HCJ-related judgments, references will be made to the HCJ's position vis-à-vis the applicability of IHR law treaties and conventions, in cases where the applicability of these conventions has been raised by the petitioners and hence has also been addressed by the Court. In terms of IHL-related treaties, the Court has in the past confirmed that the Hague Regulations are indeed declarative of customary international law.[169] At the same time, it has pointed out that the MC is only restricted by rules of customary international law as long as there is no contradiction between those rules and domestic statutory law.[170] This point is highly relevant to the manner in which the Court has adjudicated the legality of extending Israeli laws, jurisdiction and administration to EJ. In the case of the Fourth Geneva Convention, the Court has refused to accept the idea that it has attained customary law status.[171] Traditionally, it has also refrained from addressing the Convention's *de jure* applicability to the oPt.[172] In other instances, the HCJ has emphasized that, since the Israeli government has declared that it would apply the Convention's 'humanitarian provisions', whether or not it actually applies the Convention *de jure*, is a non-issue.[173] As for the relevance of article 49(6) of the Convention, the Court has in the past argued that the article does not reflect customary international law.[174]

In terms of the applicability of IHR law treaties, following the outbreak of the *Second Intifada* the Court qualified the situation in the oPt to be an armed conflict and determined that IHL is the *lex specialis*,[175] to be supplemented by IHR law whenever there was a lacuna.[176] More recently, the Court has included

169 *Beit El* Judgment – Summary, *supra* note 134. Consequently, they have been deemed part of Israeli domestic law, without the need for an act of transformation (by a statute) to make it binding at the domestic level. Uri Shoham, 'The Principle of Legality', *supra* note 8.

170 (HCJ 351/80) [1980] *Jerusalem District Electricity Company Ltd. v. Minister of Energy and Infrastructure et al.*, English summary in (1981) 11 Isr YB Hum Rts 354 [*Jerusalem District Electricity Company* Judgment – Summary].

171 (HCJ 785/87) [1988] *Affo et al. v. Commander of the IDF et al.*, official English translation, online: HCJ http://elyon1.court.gov.il/files_eng/87/850/007/Z01/87007850.z01.pdf [*Affo* Judgment]; *Beit El* Judgment – Summary, *supra* note 134. For an argument to the contrary, see Theodor Meron, 'The Geneva Conventions as Customary Law', (1987) 81 AJIL 348.

172 Daphne Barak-Erez, 'Israel: The Security Barrier – Between International Law, Constitutional Law and Domestic Judicial Review', (July 2006) 4:3 Int J Const L 540. In the beginning the Court preferred to leave for further review the question of whether the humanitarian provisions of the Convention do apply. See *Iskan* Judgment, *supra* note 94 at para 11.

173 *Ajuri* Judgment, *supra* note 34 at para 364; *Hamoked 2002* Judgment, *supra* note 115. However, the Israeli government has never clarified which provisions it considers humanitarian. Adam Roberts, 'What is Military Occupation', (1984) 55 Brit YB Int'l L 249.

174 *Elon Moreh* Judgment, *supra* note 1 and *Beit El* Judgment – Summary, *supra* note 134. David Kretzmer, 'The Law of Belligerent Occupation', *supra* note 92.

175 *Torture 1994* Judgment, *supra* note 94 at para 18.

176 Ibid.

IHR law treaties (such as the UDHR and the ICCPR) as part of the overall normative framework deemed relevant to its adjudication.[177] However, it has stopped short of ruling on the *de jure* applicability of IHR treaties to the occupied West Bank.[178] Instead, where the Court has referred to IHR law it has been invoked as a source that can help in the interpretation of domestic law[179] (i.e. persuasive authority).[180]

The third element of the typology is the meaning that the HCJ affords to the key principles, rules and notions of the international law of belligerent occupation as well as to the general principles of IHR law. One such notion is the 'military necessity' exception found in specific provisions of the Hague Regulations and the Fourth Geneva Convention. These include article 23(g) of the Hague Regulations,[181] and article 53 of the Fourth Geneva Conventions,[182] and to which the Court refers when examining the legality of land requisition orders by military authorities for the purpose of constructing the Wall. However, while it remains true that under IHL, security concerns give States, including occupying powers, a wide discretion in implementing security-based measures, IHL stipulates that this may only take place in exceptional cases and in good faith.[183] Thus while IHL exempts a measure from abiding by certain rules of conduct that it prescribes, these exceptions must be interpreted in a restrictive manner.[184] Where the goal is itself illegitimate – then whatever measures are adopted in pursuit of that goal are also illegal.[185]

Another relevant IHL-related notion is the duty of the occupying power to abide by article 43 of the Hague Regulations, and which outlines the legitimate considerations that can lawfully guide the actions of the MC in the occupied territory. These are: to restore and maintain public order and civil life, including public welfare in the occupied territory, and to respect the laws in force in the occupied territory 'unless absolutely prevented'.[186]

177 Yuval Shany and Orna Ben-Naftali, 'Living in Denial', *supra* note 70.

178 *Hamoked* 2002 Judgment, *supra* note 115 at paras 23–25. See also (HCJ 5591/02) [2002] *Yassin et al. v. The Commander of the Kziot Detention Facility et al.* at para 11, unofficial English translation, online: *Hamoked* www.hamoked.org/items/6600_eng.pdf.

179 Orna Ben-Naftali and Yuval Shany, 'Living in Denial', *supra* note 70.

180 Patrick Glenn, 'Persuasive Authority', (1987) 32:2 McGill LJ (1987) 261.

181 Article 23(g) of the Hague Regulations, *supra* note 14.

182 Article 53 of the Fourth Geneva Conventions, *supra* note 15.

183 Marco Sassòli, 'The Concept of Security in International Law Relating to Armed Conflicts', in Cecilia M. Bailliet, ed, *Security: A Multidisciplinary Normative Approach* (Boston, MA: Martinus Nijhoff, 2009) 7.

184 Marco Pertile, '"Legal Consequences of the Construction of a Wall in the Occupied Palestinian Territory": A Missed Opportunity for International Law?', (2004) 14:1 Italian YB Int'l L 121 at 136.

185 Nobuo Hayashi, 'Requirements of Military Necessity', *supra* note 151.

186 Article 43 of Hague Regulations, *supra* note 14. This provision is reflective of customary international law. *Wall* Advisory Opinion *supra* note 18 at paras 89 and 124. It has also been recognized as customary by the HCJ. (HCJ 606/78) *Ayub et al. v. Minister of Defense et al.*, English summary in (1979) 9 Isr YB Hum Rts 337.

A third key IHL-related notion is the concept of 'local population' whose interests must be taken into consideration under the aforementioned article 43. Here, a common assumption has been that the term 'local population' in those regulations refers to the 'protected persons' and the original inhabitants of the occupied territory.[187] Furthermore, the Fourth Geneva Convention's emphasis on the rights of the 'protected persons', and the prohibition on the transfer by the Occupying Power of its own civilian population into the occupied territory, when read in tandem with the restrictions on that Power's authority as spelled out in the Regulations, suggests that the law of belligerent occupation must be interpreted as prioritizing the rights of those who are simultaneously living under occupation, yet are not nationals of the Occupying Power.[188]

This leads to the fourth element of the typology, which is the manner in which the Court has balanced between the competing interests.[189] Towards this objective, the justices have relied on the proportionality analysis as grounded either in Israeli administrative or constitutional law. In this regard, the Court has usually conducted the assessment as part of a wider evaluation of the extent to which the MC has adequately balanced between the different considerations that must be taken into account when seeking 'to restore, and ensure, as far as possible, public order and safety' (as stipulated by article 43 of the Hague Regulations).[190]

Following the outbreak of the *Second Intifada* in 2000, many HCJ judgments examined whether the actions by Israeli military authorities in the oPt were both necessary and proportional. In the case of the judgments reviewed here, the Court begins by emphasizing the relevance of the IHL-based principle of proportionality and that it constitutes part of the standards used to assess the extent to which the MC has successfully balanced between the different considerations that can legitimately guide his actions under article 43. However, depending on whose rights and interests are at stake, the Court has then oscillated between grounding the proportionality analysis in either Israeli administrative law or in Israeli constitutional law. In cases when the interest to be balanced is the security needs/assessment of Israeli authorities against the interests/rights of the Palestinians, the Court has grounded its proportionality analysis in Israeli administrative law. In other cases, particularly those involving a clash of interests and rights of Israeli settlers and of Palestinians, the HCJ has invoked a proportionality analysis that is grounded in Israeli constitutional law.

A number of features render this approach unsuitable to the Israeli–Palestinian context. The first feature is that the Court has upheld the applicability of the

187 Noam Lubell, 'Human Rights Obligations in Military Occupation', (Spring 2012) 94: 885 Int'l Rev Red Cross 317 at 333.

188 Aeyal Gross 'Human Proportions: Are Human Rights the Emperor's New Clothes of the International Law of Occupation?', (2007) 18:1 EJIL 1.

189 Alon Harel, 'Skeptical Reflections on Justice Aharon Barak's Optimism', (2006) 39 Isr LR 261. Erwin Chemerinsky, 'Recognizing Reality of Judicial Constitutional Decision-making', (2006) 86 BUL Rev 1069.

190 David Kretzmer, 'The Law of Belligerent Occupation', *supra* note 92.

Basic Laws, not only to Israeli (non-citizens) residing in Israel proper,[191] but also *in personae* to Israeli citizens residing in the oPt.[192] At the same time, its justices have refused to rule on the *de jure* applicability of these Basic Laws to Palestinians living in the same territory.[193] The second aspect is that the right to equality is not a right that has been listed in the Basic Law: *Human Dignity and Liberty* as a constitutionally protected right.[194] Third, the purpose of the aforementioned Basic Law is 'to protect human dignity and liberty in order to establish in the Basic Law the values of the State of Israel as a Jewish, and democratic state',[195] two values with which the Palestinians of the occupied West Bank cannot affiliate.

The typology's fifth element is the primacy granted by the HCJ to the domestic legislation, if and when it contradicts international law. This is relevant to the manner in which the Court has invoked the Israeli Basic Law: *Jerusalem: Capital of Israel* when adjudicating the legality of the construction of the Wall in and around EJ.

191 Section 6 of Basic Law: *Human Dignity and Liberty*, *supra* note 120 and section 3 of Basic Law: *Freedom of Occupation*, *supra* note 121. The only right limited to Israeli nationals is that of entering Israel from abroad. See footnote 25 of Daphne Barak-Erez, 'Israel: The Security Barrier', *supra* note 172 at 551.

192 (HCJ 1661/05) [2005] *Gaza Coast Regional Council v. Knesset*, unofficial English translation of extracts by Avichay Sharon (December 2013), on file with author.

193 In a 2006 ruling regarding the legality of an amendment to the *Citizenship and Entry into Israel Law (Temporary Order) Law, 2003*, the Court refrained from examining whether the Basic Laws were applicable to the Palestinian residents of the oPt. (HCJ 7052/03) [2006] *Adalah et al. v. Minister of Interior et al.*, official English translation, online: HCJ http://elyon1.court.gov.il/files_eng/03/520/070/a47/03070520.a47.pdf. Daphne Barak-Erez, 'Israel: Citizenship and Immigration Law in the Vise of Security, Nationality and Human Rights', (2008) 6:1 Int'l J Const L 184–192.

194 David Kretzmer 'The New Basic Laws on Human Rights', *supra* note 122. A 1994 amendment to this Basic Law underscored that the principles enunciated in Israel's *Declaration of Independence*, including equality, are part of the values protected by the Basic Laws. Since then, numerous HCJ judgments demonstrated an increased willingness on its behalf to apply the equality principle and to interpret ordinary laws in accordance with this principle. Christopher McCrudden, 'Human Dignity and Judicial Interpretation of Human Rights', (2008) 19:4 EJIL 655. However, 'an extended bench of the Supreme Court has not recognized the principle of equality as a "constitutional right" in any written decision to date'. See 'Historical Background: The Palestinian Minority in the Israeli Legal System', online: *Adalah* https://archive.is/VllVw#selection-493.1008-493.1947.

195 Article 1 of the Basic Law: *Human Dignity and Liberty*, *supra* note 120 (also referred to as the 'purpose' section). This was criticized for shifting the balance of power between the values of liberalism and Judaism. Menachem Mautner, *Law and Culture of Israel* (Oxford: Oxford University Press, 2011). It was also criticized for attributing to the State values that are embedded in the State rather than society. Don Avnon, 'The Israeli Basic Laws' (Potentially) Fatal Flaw', (1998) 32 Isr LR 535. To date, at least 11 of those Basic Laws also express a similar desire to preserve the 'Jewish character' of the State. In November 2015, the Israeli cabinet approved the Basic Law: *Israel as the Nation State of the Jewish People*, seeking to constitutionally determine the identity of the State of Israel as the nation state of the Jewish people. Moran Azulay, 'Government Passes Controversial Jewish Nationhood Bill', *Ynet* News (23 November 2014).

The sixth element of the typology is the invocation of the political question doctrine. Except in instances in which petitions have challenged settlement construction on the ground that it has led to the alleged illegal expropriation of Palestinian privately held property,[196] the Court has generally maintained that there is no need to rule on the legality of settlements under international law.[197] At other times, it has argued that the legality of the settlement construction is a political question and therefore non-justiciable.[198]

The seventh element is the Court's relationship with other branches of government,[199] and the perception of the Court by the Israeli general public.[200] While not an element that directly affects the HCJ's adjudication, the relationship that the judicial branch enjoys with the other branches of government has a crucial impact on the former's adjudication and scope of powers.[201] In the Israeli case, the HCJ's review of the actions of the military authorities has not been well received in many quarters of the Israeli population.[202] In fact, the HCJ's public standing has witnessed a considerable decline, and is particularly low among the right wing and religious segments of the Israeli public.[203]

Much of the criticism by the *Knesset* and the Israeli public has centred on the HCJ's activist nature and the fact that the court has intervened in matters of policy. The criticism has gained momentum, in light of the HCJ's decision to strike as unconstitutional a number of state-led policies, including on 'unauthorized outposts'.[204] Given that in Israel the executive branch is the one which decides whether or not to ratify most treaties, with the *Knesset* enjoying only a limited involvement in formalizing commitments to international laws, there is a concern that the HCJ's judicial activism leaves the Court in charge of applying

196 *Beit El* Judgment – Summary, *supra* note 134, which was cited in *Torture 2002* Judgment, *supra* note 94 at para 50. *Elon Moreh* Judgment, *supra* note 1.

197 *Elon Moreh* Judgment, *supra* note 1.

198 (HCJ 448/91) [1993] *Gavriel Bargil et al. v. Government of Israel et al.* printed in (1992) 4 Isr LR 158. Yoav Dotan, 'Judicial Rhetoric, Government Lawyers, and Human Rights: The Case of the Israeli High Court of Justice during the Intifada', (1999) 33:2 Law and Soc'y Rev 319.

199 Yoav Dotan, 'Judicial Review and Political Accountability: The Case of the High Court of Justice in Israel', (1998) 32:3 Isr L R 448.

200 Eyal Benvenisti, 'Comments on the Systemic Vision of National Courts as Parts of an International Rule of Law', (2012) 4 Jerusalem Rev. Leg. Stud. 42.

201 Stephen Goldstein, 'Protection of Human Rights by Judges: The Israeli Experience', (Fall 1993) 38 Saint Louis ULJ 605.

202 David Kretzmer, 'The Law of Belligerent Occupation in the Supreme Court of Israel', *supra* note 92.

203 While the multi-year average of trust by the Israeli public in the HCJ stands at 60 per cent, this represents a 20 per cent decline from that enjoyed by the Court in previous generations. In addition, only an estimated 42 per cent of the right-wing and the religious Zionist segments of the Israeli public have confidence in this Court. Yedidia Z. Stern, 'What these Conservative Supreme Court Justices Won't Do', *Times of Israel* (6 March 2017).

204 Yonah Jeremy Bob, 'Analysis: Shaked v. Supreme Court – Who Will Win the War to Shape the Court's Future?' *Jerusalem Post* (4 November 2016).

international law without the enactment of significant public debate.[205] A third ground for criticism directed at the Court, is that it is a 'bastion of unapologetic liberalism',[206] and therefore not representative enough of Israeli society.[207]

At the level of the chosen remedy

On this level, the eighth and final element of the typology is the overall success rate of these petitions, and the kind of substantive redress granted. While there has been a steady decline in the number of petitions by Palestinians to be flatly rejected by the HCJ due to favourable dismissals,[208] given that petitioning the Court is a very expensive endeavour for many Palestinians, and that only a limited number arrive at exercising their right to appeal a decision, whether or not petitions are upheld, is an important indication about the extent of effective judicial remedy that the HCJ affords them.

205 Yuval Shany, 'Decade in Review', *supra* note 162.
206 Shmuel Rosner, 'How Israel Got Its Supreme Court Right', *New York Times* (9 March 2017).
207 Ibid.
208 Guy Davidov and Amnon Reichman, 'Prolonged Armed Conflict and Diminished Deference to the Military: Lessons from Israel', (Fall 2010) 35:4 Law & Soc Inquiry 919.

2 The HCJ's examination of security-related measures challenging the occupation's temporary nature requirement

> This Court has emphasized time and time again that the authority of the military commander is inherently temporary, as belligerent occupation is inherently temporary.[1]
>
> – Justice Aaron Barak, Chief Justice at the HCJ

Introduction

One of the most fundamental principles underlying the normative foundation of the international law of belligerent occupation is that occupation is temporary.[2] The late nineteenth century definition of occupation presumes it is a short-term provisional state of affairs during which the efforts that are made to maintain the status quo[3] must be managed in a way that brings about a return to normality.[4] Once it has come to an end, inhabitants of the occupied territory are to resume their enjoyment of the rights and liberties that were recognized under their own domestic legal systems.[5]

International humanitarian law (IHL) provides guidelines for when a situation amounts to an occupation. The Hague Regulations stipulate that a 'territory is considered occupied when it is actually placed under the authority of the hostile army. The occupation extends only to the territory where such

1 (HCJ 2056/04) [2004] *Beit Sourik Village Council v. Government of Israel* (2005) 35 Isr LR 83 at para 27, official English translation, online: HCJ https://supremedecisions.court.gov.il/Home/Download?path=EnglishVerdicts\04\560\020\A28&fileName=04020560_a28.txt&type=4 [*Beit Sourik* Judgment]. This petition was upheld partially by the HCJ.

2 Eyal Benvenisti, 'Origins of the Concept of Belligerent Occupation', (2008) 26:3 LHR 621.

3 Eyal Benvenisti, *The International Law of Occupation* (Princeton, NJ: Princeton University Press, 2004).

4 Orna Ben-Naftali, '"A La Recherche du Temps Perdu": Rethinking Article 6 of the Fourth Geneva Convention in the Light of the Legal Consequences of the Construction of a Wall in the Occupied Palestinian Territory Advisory Opinion', (2011) 38 Isr LR 211.

5 David Kretzmer, 'The Law of Belligerent Occupation as a System of Control: Dressing up Exploitation in Respectable Garb', in Daniel Bar-Tal and Itzhak Schnell, eds, *The Impacts of Lasting Occupation: Lessons from Israeli Society* (New York: Oxford University Press, 2013) 31.

authority has been established and can be exercised'.[6] In other words, once a State has established its authority over a given territory of another state and has demonstrated the ability to exercise that authority,[7] the situation qualifies as an occupation.[8] This triggers the applicability of the aforementioned body of law, including the Hague Regulations and the Fourth Geneva Convention.[9] These laws apply as soon as this occupation begins and cease to apply when the occupation itself ends.[10]

Whether a situation qualifies as occupation is a question of fact.[11] Traditionally, the presence of foreign forces was considered to be the way in which control over a foreign territory is established and exercised, thereby giving the Occupying Power the capability and obligation to administer the territory and its population. However, even where a foreign power exercises indirect overall effective control over a foreign territory, it could still be considered an occupant and would have to remain bound by the law of belligerent occupation.[12]

Given that the law of belligerent occupation emphasizes the temporary nature of the occupant's authority over a given territory,[13] which flows from its de facto control of that territory,[14] it is distinguishable from annexation,

6 Article 42 of *Convention (IV) respecting the Laws and Customs of War on Land and its Annex: Regulation concerning the Laws and Customs of War on Land, 18 October 1907*, Cons TS No 25, 277 (entered into force 26 January 1910) [Hague Regulations].

7 Yoram Dinstein, *The International Law of Belligerent Occupation* (Cambridge: Cambridge University Press, 2009) at 42.

8 *Case concerning Armed Activities on the Territory of the Congo (Democratic Republic of the Congo v. Uganda)* Judgment, [2005] ICJ Rep 168 at para 310.

9 Article 2 of the *Geneva Convention (IV) Relative to the Protection of Civilian Persons in Time of War* (12 August 1949) 75:973 UNTS, 287 (entered into force 21 October 1950) [Fourth Geneva Convention]. See also International Tribunal for the Former Yugoslavia (ICTY), *Prosecutor v. Mladen Naletilic and Vinko Martinovic*, IT-98-34-Trial Chamber (31 March 2003) at para 217, online: (ICTY) www.icty.org/x/cases/naletilic_martinovic/tjug/en/nal-tj030331-e.pdf [thereafter *Naletilic* Judgment]. All links in this chapter last accessed on 31 May 2018.

10 David Alonzo-Maizlish, 'When does it End? Problems in the Law of Occupation', in Roberta Arnold and Pierre-Antoine Hildebrand, eds, *International Humanitarian Law and the 21st Century Conflicts: Changes and Challenges* (Lausanne: Editions Interuniversitaires Suisses, 2005) 97 at 98.

11 'US States Military Tribunal at Nuremberg, Trial of Wilhelm List and Others', in Marco Sassòli and Antoine A. Bouvier, eds, *How Does Law Protect in War?* (Geneva: ICRC, 1999) at 679.

12 *DIAKONIA*-International Humanitarian Law Resource Center, 'Occupation', (11 December 2013), online: *DIAKONIA* www.diakonia.se/en/IHL/The-Law/International-Humanitarian-Law-1/issues-addressed-by-ihl-2/Occupation/?_t_id=1B2M2Y8AsgTpgAmY7PhCfg%3d%3d&_t_q=Occupation&_t_tags=language%3aen%2csiteid%3adfed4c1a-bbd8-450f-954a-02cff1abcc09&_t_ip=24.201.7.109&_t_hit.id=Diakonia_Web_Models_Pages_ArticlePage/_f5911847-6f4f-4f5c-91f4-35ab4c4eebe2_en&_t_hit.pos=1.

13 It is 'a transitional period following invasion and preceding the agreement on the cessation of the hostilities', *Naletilic* Judgment, *supra* note 9 at para 214.

14 Michael Bothe, 'Beginning and End of Occupation', in ICRC, *Current Challenges to the Law of Occupation, Proceedings of the Bruges Colloquium 20–21 October 2005*, published in Dr. Marc Vuijlsteke and Floricica Olteanu, eds, (Autumn 2006) 34 Collegium 26, online: www.coleurope.eu/research/publications/collegium.

'whereby the Occupying Power acquires all or part of the occupied territory and incorporates it into its own territory'.[15] This is due to the fact that occupation does not bring about any lawful acquisition or transfer of rights for sovereignty to the occupant.[16] It continues only until an end to the armed conflict is achieved between the parties, whereby the territory is returned based on the terms of a peace treaty.[17]

A number of obligations flow from the temporary nature of the occupation as reflected in the provisions of the Hague Regulations and the Fourth Geneva Convention.[18] The first is that the Occupying Power exercises its authority over the occupied territory, only by virtue of its effective control, for the duration of the occupation.[19] Second, although the occupant must establish a direct system of administration over the territory it controls,[20] any modifications of the existing order in the occupied territory by the former must also remain minimal.[21] Third, the action of the Occupying Power in that territory is limited by international law to balancing between its own security-based needs and those of the occupied population.[22] As the HCJ elaborated, for the actions of the Military Commander (MC) in the occupied territory to be lawful under international law, they can be guided by only two considerations:

> Ensuring security interests in the area on one hand and safeguarding the interests of the civilian population on the other. Both are directed towards

15 Jean S. Pictet, ed, *Commentary: IV Geneva Convention Relative to the Protection of Civilian Persons in Time of War* reprinted (Geneva: ICRC, 1994) at 275 [*Pictet* Commentary].

16 Ibid.

17 Allan Gerson, 'War, Conquered Territory and Military Occupation in the Contemporary International Legal System', (1977) 18 Harv Int'l LJ 525. ICTY *Prosecutor v. Dusko Tadić*, IT-94-1-AR72, Appeals Chamber (2 October 1995) at para 70, online: ICTY www.icty.org/x/cases/tadic/acdec/en/51002.htm.

18 Article 43 of the Hague Regulations restricts the occupant's ability to change laws in force in the occupied territory. Hague Regulations, *supra* note 6. In the case of the Fourth Geneva Convention, examples include article 47 underlining the non-recognition of annexation, article 49(6) prohibiting the transfer of the civilian population of the Occupying Power into the occupied territory, and article 64, which stipulates that the status of judges and public officials shall not be changed. Fourth Geneva Convention, *supra* note 9. Orna Ben-Naftali, 'PathoLAWgical Occupation: Normalizing the Exceptional Case of the Occupied Palestinian Territory and Other Legal Pathologies', in Orna Ben-Naftali, ed, *International Humanitarian Law and International Human Rights Law* (Oxford: Oxford University Press, 2011) 129.

19 Lassa Oppenheim, 'The Legal Relations between an Occupying Power and the Inhabitants', (1917) 33 Law Q Rev 249.

20 Yoram Dinstein, *The International Law of Belligerent Occupation*, *supra* note 6. Even where the occupant fails to establish such an administration, this does not relieve it of its duties under the law of occupation. Eyal Benvenisti, *The International Law of Occupation*, *supra* note 3 at 5.

21 Adam Roberts, 'Transformative Military Occupation: Applying the Laws of War and Human Rights', (July 2006) 100:3 AJIL 580 at 582.

22 Eli Nathan, 'Israel Civil Jurisdiction in the Administered Territories', (1983) 13 Isr YB Hum Rts. 90.

> the area. […] Military necessities are their military needs and not the needs of national security in the broader sense.[23]

Fourth, this underscores that the measures that the Occupying Power can implement in the occupied territory are limited, that they must be taken in good faith and must not violate jus strictum norms of IHL.[24] This requires the Occupying Power to ensure that its policies and practices in the occupied territory, irrespective of whether they are proportionate responses to their immediate provocation, are not driven by illegitimate or unreasonable purposes (such as annexation).[25] In addition, IHL provisions providing for exceptions of military necessity must be interpreted in a manner that does not render the safeguards enshrined in IHL treaties meaningless.[26]

Fifth, a temporary occupation implies that the situation has an end. This is not one and the same as an indefinite occupation.[27] To assume that the two terms are interchangeable, risks rendering meaningless the interests that the law of belligerent occupation is designed to protect and which, other than the occupant's own security-related needs are: the interests of the occupied population in regaining control over their lives and in exercising their right to self-determination; the interests of the international system, in promoting sovereign equality between States.[28] And while none of the legal instruments of the law of belligerent occupation clearly specify the criteria for the end of the occupation,[29] article 6(3) of the Fourth Geneva Convention underscores that the prevailing

23 (HCJ 393/82) *Jam'iat Iskan case, al-Ma'almoun al-Tha'auniya al-Mahduda al-Masuliya, Cooperative Association Legally registered at the Judea and Samaria Area Headquarters v. Commander of IDF Forces in the Area of Judea and Samaria et al.*, at para 13. See unofficial English translation, online: Center for the Defence of the Individual (*Hamoked*) www.hamoked.org/items/160_eng.pdf [*Iskan* Judgment].

24 Peter Maurer, 'Challenges to International Humanitarian Law: Israel's Occupation Policies', (Winter 2012) 94: 888 Int'l Rev Red Cross 1503.

25 Richard Falk and Burns H. Weston, 'The Relevance of International Law to Israeli and Palestinian Rights in the West Bank and Gaza', in Emma Playfair, ed, *International Law and the Administration of Occupied Territories* (Oxford: Clarendon Press, 1992) 125 at 138.

26 The doctrine of military necessity 'has never been internationally recognized as an unqualified licence to disregard the well-being of an occupied people, or as a pretext to undermine their underlying sovereign rights'. Richard Falk and Burns H. Weston, *supra* note 25. One example is article 53 of the Fourth Geneva Convention, which strictly limits the Occupying Power's ability to destroy property in the occupied territory to situations where this is 'rendered absolutely necessary by *military operations* [emphasis added]'. Article 53 of the Fourth Geneva Convention, *supra* note 9. According to the official commentary,

> for unscrupulous recourse to the clause concerning military necessity would allow the Occupying Power to circumvent the prohibition set forth in the Convention. The Occupying Power must therefore try to interpret the clause in a reasonable manner: whenever it is felt essential to resort to destruction, the occupying authorities must try to keep a sense of proportion in comparing the military advantages to be gained with the damage done.
>
> See *Pictet* Commentary, *supra* note 15 at 302

27 Orna Ben-Naftali, 'PathoLAWgical Occupation', *supra* note 18.

28 Ibid. at 23.

29 David Alonzo-Maizlish, 'When does it End? Problems in the Law of Occupation', *supra* note 10.

assumption, at the time of drafting the Convention, was that situations of occupation are of a short duration.[30] This was reflected in the wording of the aforementioned article, that after one year, 'most of the governmental and administrative duties carried out at one time by the Occupying Power had been handed over to the authorities of the occupied territory',[31] and that 'the authorities of the occupied State will almost always have regained their freedom of action to some extent [...]'.[32] However, where the occupation lasts longer than one year, the occupant would be '[...] bound by it, so far as it continued to exercise governmental functions'.[33] It was also stressed that the Convention:

> [...] could only cease to apply as the result of a political act, such as the annexation of the territory or its incorporation in a federation, and then only if the political act in question had been recognized and accepted by the community of States; if it were not so recognized and accepted, the provisions of the Convention must continue to be applied.[34]

Here, it is important to underscore that although under the Oslo Accords of the 1990s, Palestinians were granted a large degree of self-autonomy, the resulting redeployment of Israeli troops and the transfer of powers over certain civil spheres of the government were not tantamount to an Israeli withdrawal from those territories.[35] Nor did it diminish powers of the Israeli military government,[36] which has continued to demonstrate the ability to exercise effective control over that territory after the accords were signed.[37]

30 Article 6(3) of the Fourth Geneva Convention, *supra* note 8. The First Additional Protocol to the Fourth Geneva Convention abrogated article 6(3) by underscoring that the application of the Convention in the case of Occupied Territories shall generally cease only 'on the termination of the occupation'. Article 3(b) of *Protocol Additional to the Geneva Conventions of 12 August 1949, and relating to the Protection of Victims of International Armed Conflicts (1977)* 1125 UNTS 3 (entered into force 7 December 1978) [First Additional Protocol].

31 *Pictet* Commentary, *supra* note 15 at 62.

32 Ibid. at 63.

33 Ibid. at 63.

34 Ibid.

35 UN Economic and Social Council (ECOSOC), *Report of the Special Rapporteur of the Commission on Human Rights, Mr. John Dugard, on the Situation of Human Rights in the Palestinian Territories Occupied by Israel since 1967*, 58th sess, UN Doc E/CN.4/2002/32 (6 March 2002) at para 9(c), online: UN Office of the High Commissioner for Human Rights (OHCHR) https://unispal.un.org/DPA/DPR/unispal.nsf/0/48B2A380133D484085256B87005E1081 [thereafter UN Special Rapporteur Report 2002].

36 The *Declaration of Principles* (DoP) stipulates that Israeli authorities retain, through the military government, responsibility for essential areas of governance not devolved to the PA, such as external security, foreign relations, and jurisdiction over Israelis and Israeli settlements in the territories. Articles I(1), XVII(4) of *Declaration of Principles on Interim Self Government* reprinted in (1993) 4 EJIL 542.

37 UN Commission on Human Rights [UN HR Commission] *Report of the Human Rights Inquiry Commission Established Pursuant to Commission Resolution S-5/1 of 19 October 2000*, 57th Sess, UN Doc E/CN.4/2001/121 (16 March 2001) at para 41, online: UNISPAL https://unispal.un.org/DPA/DPR/unispal.nsf/0/4A5FCB3241D55A7885256A1E006E75AD.

Moreover, since 2002 when the Israeli military forces re-entered Area A of the West Bank as part of military operation 'Defensive Shield', the argument that Israel does not exercise effective control over all of the West Bank (including Area A) is no longer tenable.[38]

'Temporary' security measures? Of Walls, a Seam Zone and special security zones

Three measures stand out as having been contested on the ground that they are not temporary in nature, in violation of the international law of belligerent occupation.

The Wall

In April 2002, the Israeli Cabinet approved a government decision to construct a security 'fence' inside the West Bank.[39] Consisting in some sections of a fence with electronic sensors, 70 km of the structure (both constructed and under construction), is made up of 8–9 m high concrete walls, accompanied by a ditch, an asphalt two-lane patrol road, a trace road running in parallel, groomed sand paths, a buffer zone and depth barriers.[40] Fitted with an electronic monitoring system,[41] its average width is estimated at 50–70 m.[42] Justifying the move by the sharp increase in the frequency of Palestinian suicide attacks against Israelis inside Israel proper, the official Israeli position of the Israeli government has been that the construction of this Wall amounts to a lawful measure of self-defence, in order to 'block [Palestinian] terrorists from entering Israeli population centres'.[43]

Two months after the aforementioned cabinet decision, the government approved the construction of the first phase of the structure.[44] At a length of

38 UN Special Rapporteur Report 2002, *supra* note 35 at para 9.

39 Israeli Ministerial Committee on National Security Affairs (Decision No. 64/B) cited in UN Office for the Coordination of Humanitarian Assistance (OCHA) – Occupied Palestinian Territory (oPt), 'The Humanitarian Impact of the Barrier', Fact Sheet (July 2013), online: OCHA-oPt https://unispal.un.org/DPA/DPR/unispal.nsf/eed216406b50bf6485256ce10072f637/ee597cde07fb400c85257ba30049e6a6?OpenDocument.

40 UN General Assembly (GA), *Report of the Secretary-General Prepared Pursuant to General Assembly Resolution ES-10/13*, UN Doc A/ES-10/248 (24 November 2003), online: UNISPAL https://unispal.un.org/DPA/DPR/unispal.nsf/0/A5A017029C05606B85256DEC00626057 [UN Secretary-General Report 2003].

41 *B'Tselem*, 'Arrested Development: The Long-term Impact of Israel's Separation Barrier in the West Bank', Report (October 2012), at 8, online: *B'Tselem* www.btselem.org/download/201210_arrested_development_eng.pdf.

42 *Beit Sourik* Judgment, *supra* note 1 at para 7.

43 MoFA, 'Saving Lives: Israel's Anti-Terrorist Fence – Answers to Questions', (1 January 2004), online: MoFA www.mfa.gov.il/mfa/foreignpolicy/terrorism/palestinian/pages/saving%20lives-%20israel-s%20anti-terrorist%20fence%20-%20answ.aspx.

44 *Beit Sourik* Judgment, *supra* note 1 at para 4.

712 km (twice the length of the Green Line), 85 per cent of the Wall's route runs inside the occupied West Bank.[45] Per the route of the structure approved, the structure is expected to isolate an estimated 9.2 per cent of the West Bank inside the Wall, including Israeli-annexed EJ and no-man's land.[46] Built in phases,[47] by September 2017, it was estimated that 65 per cent of the Wall's projected route had been completed, while a further 7.5 per cent was under construction.[48]

Initially, government authorities downplayed the relationship between the Wall's route and Israeli settlements.[49] However, an examination of that route reveals that approximately 82 Israeli settlements located in the West Bank (including all the 12 settlements which Israel has built in annexed EJ), and which house 85 per cent of the total settler population in the West Bank, will remain inside the Wall or on what the HCJ refers to as the 'Israeli side' of the 'fence'.[50]

Israeli authorities have claimed that the route has been determined by safety and security considerations of Israeli citizens residing inside Israel proper, and of the Israeli settlements inside the West Bank,[51] including East Jerusalem (EJ).[52] In this regard, government authorities have underscored that it is a temporary

45 UN OCHA-oPt, 'Ten Years since the International Court of Justice (ICJ) Advisory Opinion', Release (9 July 2014), online: OCHA-oPt www.ochaopt.org/sites/default/files/ocha_opt_10_years_barrier_report_english.pdf. See also *B'Tselem*, 'Arrested Development', *supra* note 41 at 13.

46 Dror Etkes, 'A Locked Garden: Declaration of Closed Areas in the West Bank', (*Kerem Navot*, March 2015), online: Kerem Navot http://docs.wixstatic.com/ugd/cdb1a7_5d1ee4627ac84dca83419aebf4fad17d.pdf. Previous estimates put the figure at 9.4 per cent. UN OCHA-oPt, 'Seven Years after the Advisory Opinion of the International Court of Justice', Special Focus (July 2011), online: OCHA-oPt www.ochaopt.org/content/barrier-update-seven-years-after-advisory-opinion-international-court-justice-barrier.

47 *Beit Sourik* Judgment, *supra* note 1 at paras 5–6.

48 *B'Tselem*, 'The Separation Barrier', (11 November 2017), online: *B'Tselem* www.btselem.org/separation_barrier.

49 Consequently, the government's declared objective of providing security to settlements or settlers as one reason for the Wall's construction never featured in the decision of June 2002. It only featured vaguely in a subsequent decision of October 2003, in which the third and fourth stages of the Wall were approved. *B'Tselem* and Planners for Planning Rights (*Bimkom*), 'Under the Guise of Security: Routing the Separation Barrier to enable the Expansion of Israeli Settlements in the West Bank', Report (December 2005), online: *B'Tselem* www.btselem.org/download/200512_under_the_guise_of_security_eng.pdf.

50 UN OCHA-oPt, 'Seven Years after the Advisory Opinion', *supra* note 46.

51 For example (HCJ 426/05) [2006] *Biddu Village et al. v. Government of Israel et al.* [2006] at paras 8–9, unofficial English translation by Avichay Sharon (October 2004) on file with author, [*Biddu Village Council* Judgment]. The petition was dismissed by the HCJ.

52 The Court refers to the West Bank as 'Judea and Samaria', a biblical term also used by Israeli officials. (HCJ 4825/04) [2006], *Muhammad Khaled Alian et al. v. Prime Minister*, unofficial English translation by Avichay Sharon (March 2014), on file with author [*Alian* Judgment]. This petition was dismissed by the HCJ.

defensive measure and not a measure that seeks to consolidate political objectives,[53] such as establishing a new political border.[54]

In addition to its security function,[55] several other features of the Wall allegedly confirm its temporary nature: that wherever possible, the fence is built on state-owned, rather than private lands;[56] that where land that is privately owned by Palestinians has been requisitioned by military authorities[57] it has been done by way of Israeli military orders (MOs), which have specified that the requisition has been conducted for security/military needs;[58] and that these MOs are in themselves valid for a temporary period.[59] Authorities have also expressed readiness to pay compensation to affected landowners for using requisitioned land for the Wall's construction,[60] and that Palestinians are allowed to appeal land confiscation orders.[61] Should the appeal be rejected, the decision can then be appealed to the HCJ.[62]

53 Israel, Ministry of Foreign Affairs (MoFA), 'Saving Lives: Israel's Security Fence', (26 November 2003), online: MoFA http://mfa.gov.il/MFA/ForeignPolicy/Terrorism/Palestinian/Pages/Saving%20Lives-%20Israel-s%20Security%20Fence.aspx.

54 British Broadcasting Corporation (BBC) 'Full Transcript of Sharon Speech to the Harzliyya Institute of Policy and Strategy on 18 December 2003', (19 December 2003), online: BBC News http://news.bbc.co.uk/2/hi/middle_east/3332941.stm.

55 Israel argues that during the first half of 2004 armed attacks inside Israel proper were no less than 83 per cent compared to the same period in 2003. UN HR Commission, *Report of the UN Special Rapporteur of the Commission on Human Rights John Dugard, on the Situation of Human Rights in the Palestinian Territories Occupied by Israel since 1967*, E/CN.4/2005/29 (7 December 2004) at 25, online: UNISPAL https://documents-dds-ny.un.org/doc/UNDOC/GEN/G04/166/92/PDF/G0416692.pdf.

56 *Beit Sourik* Judgment, *supra* note 1 at para 8.

57 Four dunums is equivalent to approximately one acre.

58 Michael Sfard, 'The Fight against the Separation Wall: The Legal Front in Israel', (Paper delivered at the UN International Conference of Civil Society in Support of the Palestinian People (New York, 13–14 September 2004), online: *Hamoked* www.hamoked.org.il/items/7090.pdf. In the Israeli self-declared Jerusalem Municipality; land is requisitioned by the Israeli MoD. UN Secretary-General Report 2003, *supra* note 42.

59 Most of these MOs are valid for three years, after which they are renewable. UN OCHA-oPt, 'Seven Years', *supra* note 46.

60 For example (HCJ 8414/05) [2007] *Ahmed Issa Abdallah Yassin v. Government of Israel* at para 36, online: HCJ http://elyon1.court.gov.il/files_eng/05/140/084/n25/05084140.n25.pdf [*Bil'in* Judgment]. This petition was upheld by the HCJ.

61 The *Ottoman Land Code 1858* had established local land committees for the management of disputes over land ownership. The Jordanian *Initial Registration of Land Law (#6) of 1964*, created two committees for the administration of land registration in the West Bank: the committee for the first registration of land, and the land appeals committee, and which were composed of local judges, lawyers, and government officials. Several Israeli MOs amended the Jordanian law so that both committees were officially run by Israeli institutions. Irus Braverman, '"The Tree is the Enemy Soldier": A Sociological Making of War Landscape in the Occupied West Bank', (September 2008) 42:3 Law and Soc Rev 449.

62 *Beit Sourik* Judgment, *supra* note 1 at para 8.

However, scepticism has been expressed with regards to these assurances. One reason relates to the fact that the Wall's route deviates from the Green Line into the occupied West Bank, in contravention of international law.[63] A second reason is that the Wall seeks to 'effectively incorporate, and make connections with Israeli illegal civilian settlements – whose location it has significantly taken into consideration',[64] in an effort to de facto annex the areas on which these settlements are built in contravention of international law.[65] A third reason is the hefty price of this endeavour, and which underscores that the structure is far from temporary. Representing one of the costliest projects in Israel's history,[66] it is estimated that by 2010, its cost had reached an estimated 1 billion NIS (2.6 billion USD).[67]

To make way for the route, extensive, and in many cases irreversible, destruction and damage of property (for example, olive trees and water wells), took place.[68] Several public statements were made by acting- and ex-Israeli government officials,[69] reiterating that the Wall had been built as a border[70] to unilaterally influence the delimitation of the final frontier between Israel and a future Palestinian state,[71] and that one of the Wall's objectives was to 'include as many Israelis inside [...] and leave as many Palestinians outside'.[72] Last but not least, human rights organizations have criticized on substantive and formal Rule of Law (RoL) grounds, the arbitrary manner in which the land requisitioning act is communicated to the affected Palestinians, as well as the operation of the

63 In 2004, the ICRC reiterated that '[t]he ICRC's opinion is that the West Bank Wall, in as far as its route deviates from the "Green Line" into occupied territory, is contrary to IHL'. See ICRC, 'Israel: "Occupied Autonomous Palestinian Territories": West Bank Barrier Causes Serious Humanitarian and Legal Problems', press release (18 February 2004), online: ICRC www.icrc.org/eng/resources/documents/news-release/2009-and-earlier/5wacnx.htm.

64 Human Rights Watch (HRW), 'Israel's Separation Barrier in the Occupied West Bank: Human Rights and International Humanitarian Law Consequences', Briefing Paper (February 2004), online: HRW http://pantheon.hrw.org/legacy/english/docs/2004/02/20/isrlpa7581_txt.pdf.

65 In 2005, *B'Tselem* had expressed the concern that 'a major aim in planning the route was *de facto* annexation of parts of the West Bank'. *B'Tselem*, 'The Separation Barrier', (updated 11 November 2017), online: *B'Tselem* www.btselem.org/separation_barrier.

66 Shaul Arieli, 'What we have Learned from the Barrier', *Haaretz* (10 July 2012).

67 Haggai Mattar, 'The Wall Ten Years On: The Great Israel Project', (9 April 2012), online: *+972 Magazine* https://972mag.com/the-wall-10-years-on-the-great-israeli-project/40683/.

68 Encyclopedia of the Israeli – Palestinian Conflict vol 2, 'Israeli Supreme Court and the Occupation', by David Kretzmer (Boulder, CO: Lynne Rienner, 2010) 696 at 698.

69 Human Rights Watch (HRW), 'Israel's Separation Barrier', *supra* note 64.

70 *B'Tselem*, 'Arrested Development', *supra* note 41.

71 Yuval Yoaz, 'Justice Minister [Tzipi Livni]: West Bank Fence is Israel's Future Border', *Haaretz* (1 December 2005); Aluf Benn and Yossi Verter, 'Ehud Olmert: Permanent Borders within Four Years', *Haaretz* (9 March 2006).

72 Tirza is a resident of the West Bank Israeli settlement of Kfar Adumim. Scott Wilson, 'Touring Israel's Barrier with its Main Designer', *Washington Post* (7 August 2007).

appeals committees.[73] Many have also criticized the policy of identifying and declaring land as a 'state land', which Israeli authorities allege is the primary type of land that is allocated for the construction of the Wall.

The Seam Zone and its associated permit regime

The second measure addressed here is the Seam Zone, a term which refers to West Bank land that has been trapped between the Wall and the Green Line, or what the HCJ has often referred to as the 'Israeli side' of the Wall. In 2003, upon the completion of phase A of the Wall, the Israeli MC of the Area signed a Territory Closure Declaration, whereby it was announced that large areas between the Green Line and the Wall were to be considered, from now on, a closed military area.[74] By 2011, this area, the Seam Zone, comprised of an estimated 74 per cent of the total area of land inside the Wall, of which an estimated 67.7 per cent consists of land that is privately owned by Palestinians.[75] It also houses some of the most fertile land and water resources of the West Bank.[76] By 2014, approximately 150 Palestinian communities had land located between the Wall and the Green Line.[77] By 2015, the total area of the Seam Zone amounted to 520,000 dunums, of which an estimated 137,219 dunums of land have been declared a closed military area.[78]

Shortly after the creation of the Seam Zone, military authorities decided to institute a regime requiring all Palestinians over the age of 16 to obtain special and provisional permits to enter and remain in the zone. To do so they must prove that they permanently reside in the Zone or that they work and own land

73 Affected Palestinians, have only one week to file an objection with the legal advisory of the Israeli military, to be reviewed by the appeals committee. This committee is also exempt from applying rules of evidence applicable under Israeli law, and the MC has the authority to reverse recommendations by the committee. In most cases, the committee has rejected the appeals. *A Follow-Up Report on the Humanitarian and Emergency Policy Group (HEPG) and the Local Aid Coordination Committee (LACC)* updated (30 November 2003) at para 44, online: UNISPAL https://unispal.un.org/DPA/DPR/unispal.nsf/bc8b0c56b7bf621185256cbf005ac05f/084e7278b1a3491385256d1d0065bc42?OpenDocument. In the past, the HCJ has declared that it will not interfere in the factual findings of the appeals committee, except in extreme cases of serious defects in administrative procedure. (HCJ 277/84) [1984] *Sabri Mahmud Araib v. Custodian of Abandoned and Government Property, Judea and Samaria et al.* at 5, unofficial English translation by Avichay Sharon (March 2014) on file with author.

74 *Territory Closure Declaration No. S/2/03 (Seam Zone) (Judea and Samaria 5764–2003)* cited in (HCJ 9961/03) [2011] *Hamoked et al. v. Government of Israel et al.*, at para 4, unofficial English translation, online: *Hamoked* www.hamoked.org/files/2013/114260_eng.pdf [*Seam Zone* Judgment]. The petition was dismissed.

75 This amounts to an estimated 139,366 dunums. *B'Tselem*, 'Arrested Development', *supra* note 41; *Hamoked* and Association for Civil Rights in Israel (ACRI), 'High Court Approval of West Bank "Permit Regime" – A Green Light to Expulsion of Palestinians from their Lands', update (5 April 2011), online: *Hamoked* www.hamoked.org/Document.aspx?dID=Updates1091.

76 *B'Tselem*, 'The Separation Barrier', *supra* note 65.

77 UN OCHA-oPt, 'Ten Years', *supra* note 45.

78 Dror Etkes, 'A Locked Garden', *supra* note 46.

there.[79] By 2014, it was estimated that approximately 11,000 Palestinians resided in the Seam Zone; and that once the Wall has been completed as planned, this figure will likely increase to 25,000 West Bank Palestinians.[80]

On the one hand, Israeli authorities have claimed that they cannot adopt a generous policy when issuing permits, since the Seam Zone is a buffer zone designed to fend off infiltration into its West Bank settlements (and into Israel proper).[81] Israeli authorities have also published extensive military legislation and processing protocols regulating the permit regime, also known as the Standing Orders for the Seam Zone (thereafter Standing Orders).[82] In addition, they have set up more than 50 gates along the Wall for the alleged objective of enabling Palestinians to cross into and out of the Zone. Palestinians wishing to enter the zone must carry the right kind of permit and must have undergone security checks, as required by the Standing Orders.

On the other hand, Palestinians have argued that the Seam Zone is designed to deprive them of their land, for the sake of 'thickening' Israeli settlements. Together with the permit regime, it has resulted in permanent changes amounting to the de facto annexation of land, in contravention of international law.[83] In fact, it is precisely the manner in which the permit regime is implemented, that underscores that Israel seeks to 'administer this area as if it were part of Israel'.[84]

Similarly, UN agencies and civil society documenting Palestinian access to and from the Seam Zone have criticized the orders on substantive and procedural grounds, particularly highlighting their bureaucratic and arduous nature, and how the process lacks transparency and clarity.[85] Some of the main shortcomings of the Standing Orders includes the lack of their availability to the affected population in Arabic; that they do not allow an applicant to receive a response before the permit in his/her possession expires; that they do not allow for monitoring the application-handling process in real time;[86] and that they are rejected on a routine basis without furnishing the applicant with the precise

79 *Seam Zone* Judgment, *supra* note 74 at para 4.

80 UN OCHA-oPt, 'Ten Years', *supra* note 45. This does not include EJ Palestinians.

81 *Seam Zone* Judgment, Government Response cited in *Hamoked*, 'The Permit Regime: Human Rights Violations in West Bank Areas known as the Seam Zone', Report (31 March 2013), at 5, online: *Hamoked* www.hamoked.org/files/2013/1157660_eng.pdf.

82 *Hamoked*, 'HaMoked to the Military: A Selection of Provisions in the Revised 'Standing Orders for the Seam Zone' Must be Amended', (18 May 2014), online: *Hamoked* www.hamoked.org/Document.aspx?dID=Updates1299.

83 *Seam Zone* Judgment, *supra* note 74.

84 *Hamoked*, 'The Permit Regime', *supra* note 81 at 10; ACRI, 'Demanding Access to Land for Palestinian Villagers in the Seam Zone', Intervention (21 June 2009), online: ACRI www.acri.org.il/en/2009/06/21/demanding-access-to-land-for-palestinian-villagers-in-the-seam-zone/.

85 The applicant is not informed of the procedures and criteria by which the Israeli CA determines the issuance of a permit. *B'Tselem*, 'Ground to a Halt: Denial of Palestinians' Freedom of Movement in the West Bank', Report (August 2007), online: *B'Tselem* www.hamoked.org/files/2012/9260_eng(1).pdf.

86 *Hamoked*, 'HaMoked to the Military: A Selection of Provisions', *supra* note 82.

reasons for the rejection.[87] Because no hearing is held before a decision is made on a permit, Palestinian applicants can only file their appeal after their permit applications have been refused.[88] Moreover, permits are often issued for a less than maximum validity period cited in the order[89] and the processing of permit applications usually fails to respect the time limits as stipulated in the law.[90]

The impact that the permit regime operation has is best illustrated with an examination of challenges facing Palestinians who own agricultural land that remains trapped in that zone and from which they have been separated. Requests for permits by Palestinians seeking to cultivate their land are rejected if they are unable to either provide convincing evidence of ownership of the land or to demonstrate a direct relationship to it. Since much of the West Bank land has not been formally registered during Ottoman, British, or Jordanian rule, 'the demand for the proof of land ownership [...] is often an insurmountable obstacle [for the Palestinian applicant]'.[91] Those who do manage to prove registered ownership of their land were granted a permanent permit (of a maximum two-year validity). When it expired they had to go through the process of renewing it.[92]

Furthermore, the Standing Orders do not regulate the issuing of permits to relatives of Palestinian landowners inside the zone, thereby responding poorly to the needs of people seeking to work their land or harvest their olives.[93] Permit holders must pass through specific agricultural gates located in the Wall,[94] the majority of which are seasonal gates.[95] Those that are open on a daily or weekly basis, operate only for a certain number of hours during the day or limited days during the

87 From 2007–2010, an estimated 746 applications were rejected: 41 per cent of them were turned down for allegedly failing to meet the criteria, 48 per cent for other reasons, and 11 per cent on alleged security grounds. *Hamoked*, 'The Permit Regime', *supra* note 81.

88 *Hamoked*, 'The Permit Regime', *supra* note 81.

89 There are several types of permits for various needs. All permits are 'temporary', with the longest validity period of a permit amounting to two years. *Hamoked*, 'The Permit Regime', *supra* note 81.

90 *Hamoked*, 'Following Hamoked's Petitions, the Military has allowed Three Palestinians to Enter their Lands for the Purpose of Cultivation: in the Hearing, the Justices Criticized the State's Conduct concerning Permits of Entry to the Seam Zone', (15 July 2013), online: *Hamoked* www.hamoked.org/Document.aspx?dID=Updates1232.

91 Economic and Social Council (ECOSOC), *Report of the Special Rapporteur of the Commission on Human Rights, John Dugard, on the Situation of Human Rights in the Palestinian Territories Occupied since 1967*, ECOSOC 62nd Sess, UN Doc E/CN.4/2006/29 (17 January 2006) at para 18, online: UNISPAL https://documents-dds-ny.un.org/doc/UNDOC/GEN/G06/102/18/PDF/G0610218.pdf [UN Special Rapporteur Report January 2006].

92 *Hamoked*, 'The Permit Regime', *supra* note 81.

93 Ibid. *Hamoked*, 'HaMoked to the Military: A Selection of Provisions', *supra* note 82.

94 *Hamoked*, 'HaMoked to the Military: Cancel at Once the Instruction Forbidding Entry of Farmers to their Plots inside the Seam Zone', update (6 August 2014), online: *Hamoked* www.hamoked.org/Document.aspx?dID=Updates1339.

95 They are open only during the olive-harvesting season. UN OCHA-oPt, 'Ten Years', *supra* note 45.

week.[96] The difficulty of reaching the land has created a vicious circle, as it may result in the rejection of applications for farming permits, given that land is then deemed by Israeli authorities to no longer require continuous maintenance.[97]

Once Palestinian landowners are denied regular access to their property in this zone they risk losing that property. According to Israel's interpretation of the law applicable to the oPt, its authorities are entitled to declare unregistered land plots (which make up most of the land) that have not been cultivated for three consecutive years as 'state land'. It becomes land that can be declared as 'state land' as a way of securing land reserves for the construction and expansion of settlements. Arguably, this has also led to a situation of creeping dispossession of Palestinians and their land.[98] One Israeli lawyer, who has dealt with countless cases revolving around the Seam Zone and its permit regime, explains that:

> Many people, including judges we face in court, don't understand the meaning of occupation's bureaucracy. Take farmers who want to reach their lands beyond the fence: they might not get an answer for their request for months, then not get it in writing, and procedures keep changing and growing harder all the time. Even when someone is summoned for a hearing at the DCO [District Coordination Office of the Israeli Civil Administration], they might find themselves waiting for hours only to be informed that the officer in charge just isn't around; so people despair, farmers give up on their trees. People living in the seam zone also lose touch with life in the West Bank and consider leaving home and crossing to the Palestinian side of the wall. The wall is still new, but it's frightening to see the process of annexation happening in front of your eyes.[99]

The special security zones

Established at the height of the *Second Intifada*, the objective is that they serve as buffer zones around Israeli settlements that would remain outside the Wall (on the 'Palestinian side').[100] Each fence marking a particular SSZ runs far from both the immediate fence surrounding a particular settlement and the last line

96 By 2013, there were 81 gates designated for agricultural access. Out of those, only nine were open daily. The majority (63) were open only during the olive-harvesting season. UN OCHA-oPt, 'Ten Years, *supra* note 45.

97 Palestinian farmers have stopped investing in profitable crops that require constant maintenance. *Hamoked*, 'The Permit Regime', *supra* note 81.

98 *Hamoked*, 'The Permit Regime', *supra* note 81.

99 Israeli Attorney Shira Hertzanu, cited in Haggai Mattar, 'The Wall Ten Years On/Part 12: Where Do We Go from Here?', (11 August 2012), online: *+972 Magazine* http://972mag.com/the-wall-10-years-on-part-12-where-do-we-go-from-here/52652/.

100 *B'Tselem*, 'Access Denied: Israeli Measures to Deny Palestinians Access to Land around Settlements', Report (September 2008), online: *B'Tselem*, www.btselem.org/download/200809_access_denied_eng.pdf.

of its houses. Covering a radius of approximately 300–400 m of land, it often includes a significant amount of land that is privately owned by Palestinians. In one report *B'Tselem* examined the impact of SSZs that were established around 12 settlements. Following the creation of these zones, the overall area grew to engulf 3.7 times more land that is privately owned by Palestinians than prior to these zones' demarcation.[101] Sometimes, the SSZ-related fence is an 'engineering fence', which consists of a physical fence and other physical means blocking access. In other instances, it is an 'electronic fence', enabling the supervision of entry by Palestinians into the zone, but which does not physically block it. In other instances, the SSZ has combined both methods.[102] Special rules of engagement apply in these zones, allowing Israeli soldiers to fire at anyone who tries to infiltrate these areas.[103]

Three 'temporary' MOs are issued for the purpose of setting up an SSZ: one to requisition the land on which the SSZ patrol road and fence is constructed; one to declare the area encompassed by the zone a closed military zone; and one which prohibits building on the requisitioned land, even by its owners. These orders, lasting a few months to a few years, are extended time and time again, 'making them permanent for all intents and purposes'.[104] Even where closure orders are not renewed, generally speaking, the prohibition of entry into the SSZ continues to be enforced by the Israeli military on the ground.[105]

In some instances, land had been requisitioned from Palestinians for the construction of a security fence around the SSZs that would eventually be connected to the Wall. This was the situation in the *Ariel Bloc* case.[106] Here, Palestinians from nearby villages challenged the legality of land requisition orders for the construction of a security fence around the SSZ that had been established around the settlements of Immanuel, Karnei Shomron, and Ma'ale Shomron,[107] and whose connection to the actual Wall was pending a full examination and final approval by Israeli government authorities.[108]

101 Ibid. at 35.

102 Ibid.

103 Amos Harel, 'IDF Creating Buffer Zones Around West Bank Settlements', *Haaretz* (26 December 2002).

104 *B'Tselem*, 'Access Denied', *supra* note 100 at 42.

105 In some cases the HCJ noted that closing of land must be preceded by the issuance of a written MO. In other times, it accepted the government's promise to extend them and has not further criticized the lack of renewal. (HCJ 9593/04) [2004] *Rashad Morar et al. v. IDF Commander in Judaea and Samaria et al.* (2006), official English translation, online: HCJ https://supremedecisions.court.gov.il/Home/Download?path=EnglishVerdicts\04\930\095\n21&fileName=04095930_n21.txt&type=4 [*Morar* Judgment]. See also *B'Tselem*, 'Access Denied', *supra* note 100 at 42.

106 (HCJ 2942/05) [2006] *Nafez Mansour et al. v. Government of Israel et al.* at paras 1–10, unofficial English translation by Avichay Sharon (February 2013), on file with author [*Ariel Bloc* Judgment]. The petition was dismissed by the HCJ.

107 Ibid.

108 *Ariel Bloc* Judgment, *supra* note 106 at paras 15–20.

In the past, Israeli military authorities had provided assurances that the creation of these zones would not grant settlements surrounded by them the right to expand the area within their jurisdiction or the right to build houses or other infrastructure in the SSZs. They also noted that they must not infringe on the Palestinians' farmlands. However, developments on the ground contradict these assurances, highlighting that the land that is privately owned by Palestinians, that was encompassed by the SSZs, has traditionally been de facto annexed to the settlements that were surrounded by these zones.

One explanation is that although, in theory, the MOs prohibit the entry of people into what is supposed to be an 'empty buffer zone', in practice, Israeli settlers have often been granted free access to the SSZs. Palestinians, on the other hand, have generally been forbidden from entering the zone to work their land, save for exceptional circumstances: and then only under stringent conditions, and only after fulfilling a number of strict criteria.[109] Even when they are granted entry, Palestinian farmers are unable to dictate the time and length of their stay or to bring in agricultural machines. This has lowered the profit that they can make from agricultural activity on this land, which constitutes their main source of livelihood, and has discouraged many applicants in the long run, from trying to access their land. Farmers have feared that this will lead to their lands' official transfer to Israeli government authorities or that Israeli settlers would consolidate their control over this land by cultivating it.[110]

Once a given SSZ becomes part of the settlement, related structure is often constructed (despite the official building ban).[111] Often, Israeli settlers have then installed fences on their own initiative around adjacent land that belongs to Palestinians, thereby expanding the outer limits of the area included in the jurisdiction of a settlement.[112] By 2008, the overall area of 12 settlements east of the Wall increased by an estimated 2.4 times, from 3,235 dunums (800 acres) to 7,794 dunums (1,825 acres), more than half of which constitute land that is privately owned by Palestinians.[113] In response to petitions by Palestinians challenging these measures, the HCJ's judicial approach has

109 Such as proving ownership of the land they wish to access, obtaining a set date of entry (each time) from the CA and the consent of the Israeli settlement security coordinators. *B'Tselem*, 'Access Denied', *supra* note 100.

110 *B'Tselem*, 'Access Denied', *supra* note 100. They have cultivated an estimated 14,000 dunums of agricultural land in those areas, 60 per cent of which is Palestinian privately owned. Dror Etkes, 'A Locked Garden', *supra* note 46.

111 *B'Tselem*, 'Access Denied', *supra* note 100. Although Israeli settlers are barred from entering closed military areas, statistics indicate that they have cultivated an estimated 14,000 dunums of agricultural land in closed military areas, 60 per cent of which is Palestinian privately owned. Dror Etkes, 'A Locked Garden', *supra* note 46.

112 UN-OCHA-oPt, 'How Dispossession Happens', special focus (March 2012), online: OCHA-oPt www.ochaopt.org/sites/default/files/ocha_opt_springs_report_march_2012_english.pdf.

113 *B'Tselem*, 'Access Denied', *supra* note 100.

followed the approach it had adopted in the *Beit Sourik* judgment,[114] the *Mara'abe* judgment[115] and *Seam Zone* judgment.[116]

Adjudicating the *Beit Sourik* and *Mara'abe* judgments: a judicial blueprint

In 2004, the HCJ rendered its landmark decision in the *Beit Sourik* case, followed by the Mara'abe ruling. These judgments stand out as the two most significant HCJ decisions regarding the legality of the Wall,[117] as it is in these decisions that the Court 'for the first time, found a section of an intended Barrier to be illegal'.[118]

Prior to these judgments, the initial efforts by Palestinians to petition the HCJ, were met by an unreceptive Court, one that had adopted 'the [government's] argument suggesting that the Barrier was needed for security reasons'.[119] Thus, up until mid-2003, the HCJ had refused to interfere, even where the damage caused by the Wall to Palestinian civilians and their property had been significant.[120]

Still, as the route of the Wall made its way, extensive documentation of its human rights and humanitarian impact on nearby Palestinian communities indicated that the harmful consequences arising from this construction were immense.[121] Thus, early petitions that were filed by Palestinians prior to these two judgments focused on bringing:

> [A]bout the cancelation of the government decision concerning the construction of the fence – on the general level as well as with respect to specific aspects concerning different segments of the route of the fence, with respect of which it was argued that they were harmful beyond security needs.[122]

114 *Beit Sourik* Judgment, *supra* note 1.

115 (HCJ 7957/04) [2004] *Mara'abe et al. v. Prime Minister of Israel* (2005), official English translation, online: HCJ https://supremedecisions.court.gov.il/Home/Download?path=EnglishVerdicts\04\570\079\A14&fileName=04079570_A14.txt&type=4 [*Mara'abe* Judgment]. The petition was upheld partially by the HCJ.

116 *Seam Zone* Judgment, *supra* note 74 at para 1.

117 *Beit Sourik* Judgment, *supra* note 1. *Mara'abe* Judgment, *supra* note 128.

118 See Michael Sfard, 'The Fight against the Separation Wall', *supra* note 60 at 4.

119 *Encyclopedia on the Israeli–Palestinian Conflict*, 'Israeli Supreme Court and the Occupation', *supra* note 71 at 702. David Kretzmer 'Introduction to Special Double Issue: Domestic and International Judicial Review of the Construction of the Separation Barrier', (2005) 38:1–2 Isr LR 6.

120 *Encyclopedia on the Israeli–Palestinian Conflict*, 'Israeli Supreme Court and the Occupation', *supra* note 71. Several decisions of the military appeals committees were judicially reviewed at the HCJ by way of an administrative petition. One example is (HCJ 11344/03) [2009] *Faiz Salim et al. v. Military Commander of Judea and Samaria*, unofficial English translation by Avichay Sharon (May 2013), on file with author [*Salim* Judgment]. This petition was dismissed by the HCJ. See also *Beit Sourik* Judgment, *supra* note 1 at para 8.

121 UN OCHA-oPt, 'The Humanitarian Impact of the Barrier', *supra* note 39.

122 *Seam Zone* Judgment, *supra* note 74 at para 1.

However, by the end of 2003, a new wave of petitions reached the HCJ. They questioned the authority of the MC under the law of belligerent occupation to build the Wall or to seize land from Palestinians as protected persons under the Fourth Geneva Convention.[123] By 2012, it was estimated that the HCJ had dealt with at least 150 petitions challenging the legality of the Wall,[124] the majority of which had been filed by Palestinians.[125]

The facts of the cases

Delivered a few days before the ICJ's Wall Advisory Opinion,[126] the *Beit Sourik* case dealt with a petition filed by the Beit Sourik village council and other Palestinian West Bank village councils north-east of Jerusalem. Together with affected landowners, they challenged the decision of the Israeli MC to confiscate plots of village land by way of an Israeli MO, for the purpose of constructing the Wall.[127] This was due to the challenged route having encircled a number of Israeli settlements in the Jerusalem area (to include them on the 'Israeli side' of the Wall), thereby trapping land belonging to them inside the Seam Zone.[128]

Petitioners first underscored that the Wall's route is illegal under international law, because it annexes some of its land to Israel proper. This, they argued, constitutes a political consideration that has been disguised as a pressing security need. The Council for Peace and Security (CPS), an organization of high ranking Israeli reserve officers, joined the petition as amicus curiae to raise strong security-related reservations regarding the usefulness of the route that had been chosen by military authorities.[129] Petitioners also claimed that the Wall's construction does not serve the needs of the occupied population or the military needs of the Occupying Power in the occupied territory,[130] and that

123 Michael Sfard, 'The Fight against the Separation Wall', *supra* note 58 at 7.

124 *B'Tselem*, 'Arrested Development', *supra* note 41.

125 Petitions were also filed by representatives of Israeli settlement councils and towns inside Israel, arguing that the Wall's construction harms their 'fabric of life' or violates their property and other fundamental rights. (HCJ 399/06) [2006] *Susya Agricultural Settlement Association et al. v. Government of Israel et al.*, unofficial English translation by Avichay Sharon (March 2014), on file with author [*Susya* Judgment]. See also (HCJ 10309/06) [2007] *Local Council of Alfei Menashe et al. v. Government of Israel et al.*, unofficial English translation by Avichay Sharon (January 2013), on file with author [*Alfei Menashe Local Council* Judgment]; (HCJ 11651/05) [2006] *Beit Arye Local Council v. Minister of Defense*, unofficial English translation by Avichay Sharon (August 2013), on file with author [*Beit Arye* Judgment]. This petition was dismissed by the HCJ.

126 *Legal Consequences on the Construction of a Wall in the Occupied Territory*, Advisory Opinion [2004] ICJ Rep 136 at para 125 [ICJ *Wall* Advisory Opinion].

127 *Beit Sourik* Judgment, *supra* note 1 at para 9.

128 David Kretzmer, 'The Advisory Opinion: The Light Treatment of International Law', (2005) 99 AJIL 88.

129 *Beit Sourik* Judgment, *supra* note 1 at paras 10 and 16.

130 Ibid. at para 10.

the fence is not of a temporary character.[131] They also highlighted that the injury caused by the Wall to the petitioners and their rights was severe and unbearable:

> Over 42,000 dunums of their lands are affected. The obstacle itself passes over 4,850 dunums, and will separate between petitioners and more than 37,000 dunums, 26,500 of which are agricultural lands that have been cultivated for many generations. Access to these agricultural lands will become difficult and even impossible. *Petitioners' ability to go from place to place will depend on a bureaucratic permit regime which is labyrinthine, complex, and burdensome* [emphasis added]. Use of local water wells will not be possible. As such, access to water for crops will be hindered. Shepherding, which depends on access to these wells, will be made difficult. Tens of thousands of olive and fruit trees will be uprooted. The fence will separate villages from tens of thousands of additional trees. The livelihood of many hundreds of Palestinian families, based on agriculture, will be critically injured. Moreover, the separation fence injures not only landowners to whom the orders of seizure apply; the lives of 35,000 village residents will be disrupted. The separation fence will harm the villages' ability to develop and expand. The access roads to the urban centres of Ramallah and Bir Naballa will be blocked off. Access to medical and other services in East Jerusalem and in other places will become impossible. Ambulances will encounter difficulty in providing emergency services to residents. Children's access to schools in the urban centres, and of students to universities, will be impaired.[132]

As respondents, government authorities reiterated that the Wall is a security (and not a political) border seeking to block the unchecked passage of West Bank Palestinians into Israel proper. Addressing the rationale behind the specific route chosen, they argued that it allows military forces to control their topographic surroundings as a way of preventing direct fire; of protecting the soldiers guarding the 'fence' and of preventing infiltration into Israel proper.[133] While their assessment contradicted that of the CPS's, the respondents underscored that their own assessment as 'the expert who is also responsible for security bears a much greater weight'.[134]

In the *Mara'abe* case, the facts were similar to those of *Beit Sourik.* It involved a petition by Palestinians challenging the legality of the construction of

131 They also highlighted that the land seizure orders were illegal on procedural grounds. *Beit Sourik* Judgment, *supra* note 1 at para 10.

132 *Beit Sourik* Judgment, *supra* note 1 at para 9.

133 Ibid. at para 29.

134 Although government authorities declared that they were ready to modify the Wall's route near the settlement of Har Adar, they reiterated that the remainder of the route proposed by petitioners does not provide an appropriate solution to the security needs that the Wall's construction seeks to address. *Beit Sourik* Judgment, *supra* note 1 at para 20.

the Wall surrounding the Israeli settlement of Alfei Menashe, which had been established 4 km beyond the Green Line, in close proximity to the Palestinian West Bank city of Qalqilya.[135] The structure was to surround the settlement from all sides, leaving a passage containing road 55, which allowed the connection between the settlement and Israel proper.[136] This created an enclave inside the Seam Zone, which included five Palestinian villages of approximately 1,200 residents.[137] Access to these villages was confined to one crossing and three agricultural gates in the Wall.[138] In addition, part of the land requisitioned by Israeli military authorities for the Wall's construction was privately owned by Palestinians.[139]

Delivered after the ICJ Wall Opinion (July 2004), the petitioners reiterated that the Wall's construction in that area serves to de facto annex the enclave's territory to Israel proper and to ensure that the Alfei Menashe settlement and road 55 remain inside the Wall.[140] Addressing the claims of the authorities that the Wall's route is necessary to provide for the security of the settlers, petitioners stressed the illegality of settlements' activity under international law. Consequently, they argued, the protection of Israeli settlers residing in the occupied territory is not a legitimate military necessity. In addition, they reiterated that it is illegal for authorities to restrict their rights as 'protected persons' under the Fourth Geneva Convention for that purpose. Rather than building the Wall inside the occupied territory as a way of guaranteeing the security of those settlers, government authorities should evacuate them back to Israel proper.[141] They also stressed that by enclaving five Palestinian villages inside the Seam Zone, military authorities have created a reality in which hundreds of Palestinians find themselves inside the Wall, without a checkpoint or gate between them and Israel, thereby undermining the security-based rationale for the Wall's route.[142] The impact of the Wall's route on their fundamental rights under both IHL and International Human Rights (IHR) law was also addressed

135 *Mara'abe* Judgment, *supra* note 115 at para 75.
136 Ibid. at paras 9 and 11.
137 Ibid. at para 8.
138 Ibid. at para 9.
139 Ibid. at para 5.
140 Ibid. at para 80.
141 As Attorney Sfard explains further,

> [t]he question of military necessity is deeply connected to legitimate military necessity. It is one thing to say that I have a legitimate military necessity because I need to protect this thing, but this sentence must assume that this thing is a legitimate creature under international law.
>
> Interview with Michael Sfard, by Avichay Sharon on behalf of author (10 July 2014, Tel Aviv) [*Sfard* First Interview]

Mr. Sfard is an Israeli human rights lawyer and legal counsellor who litigates extensively on behalf of Palestinians and of Israeli NGOs challenging measures by the Israeli authorities such as the construction of the Wall. Among other cases, he represented petitioners in the *Mara'abe* case, *supra* note 115.

142 *Mara'abe* Judgment, *supra* note 115 at para 111.

under both IHL and International Human Rights (IHR) law was also addressed by the petitioners' submissions.[143] Lastly, they highlighted that the legal regime in the Seam Zone 'creates legal classes according to ethnicity, and only obfuscates itself with security claims'.[144] Hence, it is discriminatory and illegal in nature.[145]

Respondents on the other hand (including the Alfei Menashe's local settlement council)[146] advocated that the injury caused to the Palestinian petitioners was proportional and that it can be moderated through a series of logistical and structural improvements concerning the Wall and its associated permit regime. They also reiterated that the Wall's construction constitutes a legitimate right to self-defence and 'a security act *par excellence*'.[147] Moreover, it was highlighted that under international law, the Israeli MC is obligated to protect all those present in that territory, including those residents who are not considered 'protected persons' under the Fourth Geneva Convention (in clear reference to Israeli settlers). This duty, would allow him to infringe on other rights for that purpose, provided the infringement was reasonable and was driven by legitimate considerations, such as security needs.[148]

The Court's judgments

In its judgment, several elements of the typology can be discerned. The first is the deference granted by the Court to government/military authorities. On one hand, the Court underscored that where the MC's actions outside Israel proper have military and political implications,[149] his discretion is not absolute.[150] Consequently, the Court is authorized to review whether he had acted reasonably and within the limits and conditions of the law.[151] On the other hand, the

143 These included the right to property, freedom of movement, the right to make a living, the right to education, health, food, dignity and equality. *Mara'abe* Judgment, *supra* note 115 at para 82.

144 *Mara'abe* Judgment, *supra* note 115 at para 82. According to petitioners, improvements which the respondent claims to have made in the structure or permit regime for the Seam Zone were cosmetic. *Mara'abe* Judgment, *supra* note 115 at paras 76 and 92.

145 *Mara'abe* Judgment, *supra* note 115 at para 83.

146 Ibid. at para 93.

147 Emphasis is in the original. *Mara'abe* Judgment, *supra* note 115 at paras 86–87 and 90.

148 Other sources cited by the government for the protection of the settlers are the Oslo Accords as well as the Israeli Basic Laws. *Mara'abe* Judgment, *supra* note 115 at para 91.

149 *Beit Arye* Judgment, *supra* note 125 at paras 8–11. *Alian* Judgment, *supra* note 52 at paras 8–18.

150 It must be one which any reasonable commander in the same situation would make. *Alian* Judgment, *supra* note 52 at paras 8–18 and *Biddu Village Council* Judgment, *supra* note 51 at paras 10–15. See also (HCJ 2577/04) [2007] *Taha El Khawaja et al. v. Prime Minister et al.*, unofficial English translation by Avichay Sharon 2013, on file with author [*Ni'lin* Judgment]. This petition was upheld by the HCJ.

151 *Mara'abe* Judgment, *supra* note 115 at para 16; *Beit Sourik* Judgment, *supra* note 1 at paras 46 and 48; *Susya* Judgment, *supra* note 125 at paras 7–11; *Alian* Judgment, *supra* note 52 at paras 8–18 and (HCJ 3680/05) [2005] *Tene Settlement Committee v. Prime Minister Sharon et al.* at paras 8–14, unofficial English translation by Avichay Sharon (August 2013), on file with author [*Tene* Judgment]. The petition was dismissed by the HCJ.

judges underscored that they are not military experts and that '[a]ll we can determine is whether a reasonable military commander would have set out the route as this military commander did',[152] and doing so is within his legal authority.[153] Moreover, they did not question the authorities' determination that security, and not political considerations, had spearheaded the construction of the Wall in that area.[154] They also accepted the government's assurances that this structure, and its associated regime, are indeed temporary in nature (particularly with land requisition orders being of limited duration) and that the Wall is 'a central security component in Israel's fight against Palestinian terrorism'.[155]

The second element is the extent to which IHL and IHR law applies to the conduct of Israeli authorities in the oPt. According to the Court, Israeli administrative law and public international law form part of the normative framework that influences the scope of the MC's authority to construct the Wall along the chosen route.[156] In other words, the Court underscored the position that Israel's status in the West Bank is that of an occupant,[157] and that henceforth, international law of occupation (consisting of the Hague Regulations[158] and the Fourth Geneva Convention) applies[159] and must therefore guide the MC's actions therein.[160] At the same time, the justices also noted that since the Israeli government has accepted the humanitarian aspects of the Fourth Geneva Convention, there was no need to take a position regarding *de jure* applicability for the Fourth Geneva Convention.[161] The HCJ also noted that '[i]t is not relevant whatsoever [...] to examine whether this settlement activity conforms to international law or defies it, as determined in the Advisory Opinion of the International Court of Justice at The Hague'.[162] In the case of the applicability of

152 *Beit Sourik* Judgment, *supra* note 1 at para 46; *Bil'in* Judgment, *supra* note 60 at para 29.

153 (HCJ 6027/04) [2006] *Taleb Radad Head of a-Zawiya Village Council v. Minister of Defense*, at paras 15–23, unofficial English translation by Avichay Sharon (February 2013), on file with author [*Radad* Judgment]. This petition was dismissed by the HCJ. See also (HCJ 5624/06) [2006] *Beit Ummar Municipality et al. v. Military Commander of the West Bank et al.* at paras 7–11, unofficial English translation by Avichay Sharon (May 2013) on file with author [*Beit Ummar* Judgment]. The petition was dismissed by the HCJ. See also *Beit Arye* Judgment, *supra* note 125 at paras 8–11.

154 *Radad* Judgment, *supra* note 153 at para 10.

155 *Mara'abe* Judgment, *supra* note 115 at para 100. See also *Radad* Judgment, *supra* note 153 at para 2.

156 Ron Dudai, 'The Wall, the Law, and the Court: Reflections on the *Beit Sourik* Case in the Israeli Supreme Court', (2003–2004) 10 Yrbk Islam Mid-East L 477.

157 *Beit Sourik* Judgment, *supra* note 1 at para 1.

158 Hague Regulations, *supra* note 6.

159 *Beit Sourik* Judgment, *supra* note 1 at paras 23, 27 and 33. *Mara'abe* Judgment, *supra* note 115 at para 14.

160 It also concluded that Israeli administrative law applies in the West Bank, since Israel has not annexed the 'area'. *Beit Sourik* Judgment, *supra* note 1 at para 14.

161 *Mara'abe* Judgment, *supra* note 115 at para 14.

162 Ibid. at para 19.

IHR law and whether or not Israel's obligations under the international human rights conventions are legally binding on Israel actions in the oPt, the HCJ decided to leave the question open, even though it did underscore that it 'was willing, without deciding the matter, to rely upon the international conventions'.[163]

A third element, is the meaning afforded to key principles, rules and notions of international law. In this regard, the HCJ justices invoked certain interpretations of a number of legal rules and notions. The first is that situations of occupation are temporary in nature. In this regard, justices underlined that the authority and governance of the MC in the Area (i.e. West Bank) is also of a limited duration,[164] and that the MC '[…] [cannot] take into account considerations beyond the proper administration of the area under belligerent occupation'.[165] The Court then clearly internalized the government's position that the reasons for constructing the Wall along the designated route (such as topography, the need to establish a security zone, etc.) are security considerations par excellence.[166] It also adopted without hesitation the position of the MC:

> [T]hat 'it is not a permanent fence, but rather a *temporary* [emphasis added] fence erected for security needs.' We have no reason not to give this testimony less than full weight, and we have no reason not to believe the sincerity of the military commander.[167]

The second is that of military necessity. Having determined that the Wall constitutes a reasonable means to achieve the intended security objectives,[168] the Court then addressed the legal provisions in the international law of belligerent occupation, which allows an Occupying Power to requisition and destroy private property for the purpose of achieving objectives that are 'rendered absolutely necessary by military operation'.[169] Here, it made extensive reference to articles 23(g), 43 and 52 of the Hague Regulations and to article 53 of the Fourth

163 While the Court made a reference to the International Covenant on Civil and Political Rights (ICCPR), it reiterated its conclusion from a previous judgment (HCJ 1890/03 [2005] *Bethlehem Municipality v. State of Israel*) that:

> [W]e need not, in the framework of the petition before us, take a position regarding the force of the international conventions on human rights in the *area*. Nor shall we examine the interrelationship between international humanitarian law and international law on human rights […].
>
> *Mara'abe* Judgment, *supra* note 115 at paras 25 and 27 (emphasis in original)

164 *Mara'abe* Judgment, *supra* note 115 at para 14.

165 *Beit Sourik* Judgment, *supra* note 1 at para 27; *Mara'abe* Judgment, *supra* note 115 at para 15.

166 *Beit Sourik* Judgment, *supra* note 1 at para 29; *Mara'abe* Judgment *supra* note 115 at para 62.

167 *Beit Sourik* Judgment, *supra* note 1 at para 29.

168 Ibid. at paras 28–31. 'Indeed, our point of departure is that the separation fence is intended to realize a security objective which the military commander is authorized to achieve'. *Beit Sourik* Judgment, *supra* note 1 at paras 44 and 45.

169 *Mara'abe* Judgment, *supra* note 115 at para 16.

Geneva Convention.[170] Listed under Section II of the Regulations (on Hostilities), article 23(g) authorizes the destruction or seizure of enemy property if it is for 'imperative necessities of war'. In stark contrast to the ICJ's conclusion in the Wall Advisory Opinion,[171] the HCJ upheld the relevance of this provision to the action of destroying or requisitioning Palestinian privately owned property for the Wall's construction. In justifying this position, they argued that the situation in the West Bank is one of belligerent occupation in which intermittent periods of combat activity are taking place and that, therefore, the rules and principles of the international law of armed conflict also become applicable in tandem with the law of belligerent occupation.[172]

Subsequently, the Court decided that there was no need to examine whether the Wall's construction is lawful under the international law on the use of force,[173] on the ground that article 52 of the Hague Regulations and article 53 of the Fourth Geneva Convention, provided the legal basis for taking possession of land for military purposes (provided that compensation is paid).[174] In any case, the reasoning suggests that the HCJ did not question the government's position that the Wall is a legitimate act of self-defence, noting that to the extent that '[t]he construction of the fence is part of Israel's combat actions [...] it is a defensive act which serves as an alternative to offensive military activity [...]' and it is permitted by international law.[175]

A fourth element of the typology that features in the Court's adjudication is its attempt to judicially balance between competing interests. Here, the justices highlighted that the principles of Israeli administrative law constrain the actions of the MC, and constitute a legal point of reference for examining whether he had exercised his discretion in a manner that reflected 'substantive and procedural fairness'.[176] They then highlighted that there are three different sets of

170 Article 52 of the Hague Regulations stipulates that possession of property must be for the needs of the army of the occupation). *Hague Regulations supra* note 6; article 53 of the Fourth Geneva Convention, *supra* note 9. See also *Beit Sourik* Judgment, *supra* note 1 at 32.

171 The ICJ had rejected the idea that the occupation is one in which active hostilities and/or armed conflict is taking place. It therefore determined that article 23(g) was not relevant because it is part of Section II of the Hague Regulations applicable during hostilities. ICJ *Wall* Advisory Opinion, *supra* note 126 at para 124.

172 The Court notes, 'there is a view [...] by which the scope of application of regulation 23(g) can be widened, by way of analogy, to cover belligerent occupation as well'. *Mara'abe* Judgment, *supra* note 115 at para 17.

173 *Mara'abe* Judgment, *supra* note 115 at para 17. See also the *Beit Sourik* Judgment, supra note 1 at para 32.

174 Concerning article 46 of the Hague Regulations, the Court stated that the construction of the 'fence' cannot be considered to amount to the confiscation of private property, because it will only amount to a temporary possession, and would be accompanied by payment of compensation of the damage caused. *Mara'abe* Judgment, *supra* note 115 at para 16.

175 *Mara'abe* Judgment, *supra* note 115 at para 17. *Beit Sourik* Judgment, *supra* note 1 at para 32.

176 *Mara'abe* Judgment *supra* note 115 at para 14; *Beit Sourik* Judgment, *supra* note 1 at para 24; *Tene* Judgment, *supra* note 151 at paras 8–14; *Susya* Judgment, *supra* note 125 at paras 7–11; *Ariel Bloc* Judgment, *supra* note 106 at paras 21–33.

considerations and interests, which the MC must take into account when determining the route of the Wall – and that all of these must be balanced against each other. One is the security/military reasons spearheading the implementation of the measure. Here, the HCJ adopted the position that the authority of the MC under article 43 of the Hague Regulations includes the need 'to maintain security in the area and to protect the security of his country and their citizens',[177] as well as the security of the army.[178]

And although the justices emphasized in the *Beit Sourik* judgment that 'the separation fence cannot be motivated by a desire to – annex territories to the state of Israel',[179] and that 'the needs of the army are the army's military needs and not the national security interest in the broad meaning of the term',[180] they did conclude in the *Mara'abe* case, that 'regulation 43 of [t]he Hague Regulations authorizes the military commander to take all necessary action to preserve security. *The acts which self-defence permits are surely included within such action* [emphasis added]'.[181] This, they underscored, includes the duty to protect the safety of Israeli nationals travelling (on road 55) from the settlement to Israel and those wishing to travel from Israel proper to the West Bank settlement of Alfei Menashe.[182]

True, in the *Mara'abe* judgment, the Court ended up requiring government authorities to re-route the Wall sections in this area. However, this was in response to the particularities of this specific case,[183] and not because the justices had decided to question the idea that ensuring the safety of Israelis (including settlers) travelling through the West Bank was not within the scope of the MC's authority. This responsibility can be inferred from the MC's duty to preserve public order and safety, as stipulated in article 43 of the Hague Regulations,[184] and which includes all persons present in the occupied territory even if they are not protected persons as per the meaning of article 4 of the Fourth Geneva Convention.[185] Another cited for the MC's duty to preserve the overall security of Israeli settlements is the Oslo Accords.[186]

177 *Beit Sourik* Judgment, *supra* note 1 at para 34.

178 *Mara'abe* Judgment, *supra* note 115 at para 24.

179 *Beit Sourik* Judgment, *supra* note 1 at para 27. See also (HCJ 10356/02) [2004] *Yoav Haas v. IDF Commander in the West Bank et al.*, unofficial English translation, online: *Hamoked* www.hamoked.org/items/8240_eng.pdf [*Haas* Judgment]. The petition was dismissed by the HCJ. See also (HCJ 2150/07) [2009] *Abu Safiyeh et al. v. Minister of Defense et al.* at para 23, unofficial English translation, online: *Hamoked* www.hamoked.org/files/2011/8865_eng.pdf [*Abu Safiyeh* Judgment]. The petition was upheld by the HCJ.

180 *Beit Sourik* Judgment, *supra* note 1 at para 27.

181 *Mara'abe* Judgment, *supra* note 115 at para 23.

182 Ibid. at para 91.

183 The government had highlighted that road 55 was a temporary road. Hence, the Court was not convinced that from a security perspective, it was necessary to preserve the north-west section of the Wall's route, with its harsh impact on the Palestinians in the area. It ordered government authorities to cancel this road, and to build a new one south-west of the settlement, as originally planned. *Mara'abe* Judgment, *supra* note 115 at para 113.

184 *Mara'abe* Judgment, *supra* note 115 at para 19.

185 This refers to Israeli settlers. *Mara'abe* Judgment, *supra* note 115 at para 18.

186 *Mara'abe* Judgment, *supra* note 115 at para 18.

The Court also discussed a number of non-security-based considerations that can lawfully affect the determination by the MC of the route of the Wall in the area. In the *Mara'abe* proceedings, the respondents had acknowledged that a planning scheme for the expansion of the settlement in the direction of the south-western part of the enclave had been set in motion, thereby implicitly suggesting that it had played a role in determining the Wall's route in the area. Nevertheless, the judges took at face value the assurances by government and military authorities that those development plans were not the primary consideration determining the route of the Wall in the area.[187] This position of the Court is significant, and reappears in subsequent cases in which petitioners challenging the Wall had sought to prove that the objective of providing territorial space for the expansion plans of settlements was one of the main considerations influencing the Wall's route. For, except when there was glaring evidence to the contrary, the Court has accepted the respondents' assurances that security was the determining factor, and that hence, the route was motivated by lawful considerations under international law.

A second consideration is the welfare of the local Palestinian population. According to the Court, the MC must defend '[t]he human dignity of every member of the population, including the local population'.[188] This signifies that his actions 'must refrain from acts which hurt the local residents. That is his "negative" duty; second, he must take the action necessary to ensure that the local residents will not be hurt. That is his "positive" duty.'[189] Hence, he must strive to promote the constitutional human rights of the local population, including 'freedom of movement, religion, and worship, and property rights'.[190] A third consideration for the MC is the protection of the life and safety of Israelis living, in 'Israeli communities in the Judea and Samaria area'.[191] For the justices adjudicating the two cases discussed here, there was little doubt that the MC is obligated to ensure the lives and safety (security) of the Israeli settlers. In the *Mara'abe* judgment for instance, the Court reiterated that the MC:

> [M]ust ensure the wellbeing, safety and welfare of the residents of the *area*. This duty of his applies to all residents, without distinction by identity – Jew, Arab, or foreigner. [...] This sits well with the humanitarian aspect of the military force's responsibility in belligerent occupation.[192]

Again, the relevance of the illegality of settlement activity under international law, as encapsulated by article 49(6) of the Fourth Geneva Convention, was dismissed by the justices. This is because:

187 Ibid. at para 113.
188 Ibid. at para 24.
189 Ibid.
190 Ibid.
191 *Mara'abe* Judgment, *supra* note 115 at paras 18–19 and 101.
192 *Haas* Judgment, *supra* note 179 at para 14, reiterated in *Mara'abe* Judgment, *supra* note 115 at para 19.

> Even if the military commander acted in a manner that conflicted the law of belligerent occupation at the time he agreed to the establishment of this or that settlement and that issue is not before us, and we shall express no opinion on it – that does not release him from his duty according to the law of belligerent occupation itself, to preserve the lives, safety, and dignity of every one of the Israeli settlers.[193]

According to Israeli attorney Michael Sfard, by declining the justiciability of the legality of the settlements under international law and insisting that as long as there are settlements in the occupied territory, the MC is responsible for the security of its settler population, the HCJ came as close as possible to legitimizing the presence of settlements.[194] For even if one were to adopt the point of departure that those Israelis residing illegally in a given territory have legitimate security concerns, under international law the MC is constricted in terms of the measures he can lawfully implement to respond to those needs.[195] Had the HCJ considered the relevance of the question of the illegality of the settlements, it would have found it necessary to examine whether or not, under international law, removing the settlers would have been the more appropriate measure to protect them.[196] In the *Mara'abe* decision, the Court also reiterated another conclusion, namely that:

> In our opinion, the Basic Laws grant rights to every Israeli settler in the area to be evacuated. This jurisdiction is personal. It is derived from the State of Israel's control over the area to be evacuated. It is the fruit of a view by which the state's Basic Laws regarding human rights apply to Israelis found outside the state, who are in an area under its control by way of belligerent occupation […].[197]

Interestingly, the Court noted that scope of human rights that is afforded to Israeli settlers is different from that afforded to Israelis living in Israel proper. Since the West Bank is not part of Israel proper, Israeli settlers live under the regime of belligerent occupation, 'which is inherently temporary'.[198]

193 *Mara'abe* Judgment, *supra* note 115 at para 20.

194 *Sfard* First Interview, *supra* note 141; Interview with Attorney Nasrat Dakwar by Avichay Sharon, translated into English (7 July 2014, Jerusalem) [*Dakwar* Interview]. He is an Arab-Palestinian citizen of Israel (or as commonly referred to, an Arab 48). He is also a staff attorney with the Israeli NGO ACRI.

195 Interview with Israeli Attorney A-04 by Avichay Sharon, in English) (10 July 2014, Jerusalem) [Attorney *A-04* interview].

196 *Encyclopedia of the Israeli–Palestinian Conflict* 'Israeli Supreme Court and the Occupation', *supra* note 71; Daphne Barak-Erez, 'Israel: The Security Barrier between International Law, Constitutional Law and Domestic Judicial Review', (2006) 4:3 Int J Const L 540.

197 (HCJ 1661/05) [2005] *Gaza Coast Regional Council et al. v. Knesset* [*Gaza Regional Council* Judgment] at para 80, cited in *Mara'abe* Judgment, *supra* note 115 at para 21.

198 *Mara'abe* Judgment, *supra* note 115 at para 22.

Consequently, '[t]he rights granted to Israelis living in the area came to them from the military commander. They have no more than what he has.'[199] At the same time, the spectrum of fundamental human rights protected by the Basic Laws was deemed applicable to the Israeli settler population in the West Bank, such as 'the rights to life, dignity and honour, property, privacy, and the rest of the rights which anyone present in Israel enjoys'.[200]

Subsequently, the Court examined whether the MC's decision to construct the Wall had successfully balanced between the various considerations described above. Towards this objective, they invoked the proportionality doctrine and its three sub-tests. According to the justices, both international law and Israeli administrative law recognize the relevance of the proportionality principle[201] 'as a standard for balancing between the authority of the military commander and the needs of the local population'.[202] In international law, this principle seeks to prevent 'incidental consequences *of (lawful) military operations* [emphasis added]'.[203] In Israeli administrative law, the three sub-tests, he argued, give specific content to this doctrine, all of which must be satisfied before determining that 'the means used to realize the governmental objective is of proper proportion'.[204] These are: the 'rational means' test – the means used by the administrative body must rationally lead to the realization of the stated objective; the 'least injurious means' test – that from the spectrum of lawful means which are available to the government authorities to achieve a given objective, they must resort to the means that are the least injurious to the rights of affected individuals; and the 'proportionality in the narrow sense' test – advocating that the 'benefit reaped by the public, against the damage caused to the citizen under the circumstances',[205] must be proportionate. At the same time, the Court stressed that its role is only to determine whether the effect of a given measure falls within a lawful 'zone of proportionality' (similar to the idea of a 'zone of reasonableness').[206]

Thus, applying the first sub-test to the specifics of the *Beit Sourik* case,[207] the Court concluded that it fulfilled the requirement.[208] Similarly in the *Mara'abe*

199 Ibid.
200 *Gaza Coast Regional Council* Judgment, *supra* note 197 at para 127, cited in *Mara'abe* Judgment, *supra* note 115 at para 21.
201 *Beit Sourik* Judgment, *supra* note 1 at para 36.
202 Ibid. at para 39.
203 Ibid. at para 37.
204 Ibid. at paras 40 and 42.
205 Ibid. at para 59. Other Wall-related case law where the sub-tests were applied includes the *Bil'in* Judgment, *supra* note 60 at para 30. See also (HCJ 2645/04) [2007] *Fares Ibrahim Nasser et al. v. Prime Minister et al.* at paras 25–28, unofficial English translation by Avichay Sharon (February 2013), on file with author [*First Dir Qadis Village Council* Judgment]. The petition was dismissed by the HCJ.
206 *Beit Sourik* Judgment, *supra* note 1 at para 42.
207 Ibid. at paras 48–49, 62–63, 73 and 77.
208 Ibid. at paras 57, 66, 70, 75 and 80.

judgment, the Court also concluded that, since the fence separates 'between terrorists and Israelis living in Israel and the area,' the measure fulfilled the rational connection between the objective and the means for its attainment.[209] This conclusion was underlined by the HCJ in a number of other Wall-related cases.[210] For the second sub-test, the Court confirmed in the *Beit Sourik* case that it would not be possible to attain a security objective of the Wall in a way that causes less injury to the local inhabitants.[211] However, it reached a different conclusion in the *Mara'abe* case. On one hand, the justices endorsed the government's reasoning that moving the sections of the 'fence' to run along the Green Line would not achieve the desired security objectives.[212] On the other hand, they disagreed with the authorities' military assessment that leaving the five Palestinian villages (or some of them) inside the fence was absolutely necessary to attain this objective. Instead, they underscored the chokehold effect, which the structure created around its inhabitants and the damage it caused to their 'fabric of life'.[213] This, in the Court's view, was proof that the second sub-test had not been met. Consequently, it ordered authorities to seek an alternative route, one that would possibly remove some or all of the Palestinian villages trapped in the enclave outside of the Wall.[214]

Regarding the third feature of the proportionality test, it was on the basis of this sub-test that the Court concluded in the *Beit Sourik* case that certain Wall segments had failed to fulfil the requirement that the 'injury caused to the local inhabitants by the construction of the separation fence stands in proper proportion to the security benefit from the security fence in its chosen route'.[215] Thus, while the justices took into consideration the allocation by the respondents of gates in the Wall and its associated permit regime as a way of guaranteeing the affected Palestinian villagers access to their land, they nevertheless concluded that:

> This state of affairs injures the farmers severely, as access to their lands (early in the morning, in the afternoon, and in the evening), ***will be subject to restrictions inherent to a system of licensing*** [emphasis added]. Such a system will result in long lines for the passage of the farmers themselves; it will make the passage of vehicles (which themselves require licensing and examination) difficult, and will distance the farmer from his lands (since only two daytime gates are planned for the entire length of this segment of

209 *Mara'abe* Judgment, *supra* note 115 at para 111.

210 For example, see *Alian* Judgment, *supra* note 52 at paras 8–18; *N'ilin* Judgment, *supra* note 150 at paras 30–43; *First Dir Qadis Village Council* Judgment, *supra* note 205 at paras 25–28.

211 *Beit Sourik* Judgment, *supra* note 1 at para 58.

212 *Mara'abe* Judgment, *supra* note 115 at para 112.

213 Ibid. at para 113.

214 The Court ordered that this highway connecting Alfei Menashe to Israel be cancelled and that a new road be built south-west of that settlement. *Mara'abe* Judgment, *supra* note 115 at para 113.

215 *Beit Sourik* Judgment, *supra* note 1 at paras 59 and 60.

> the route). As a result, the life of the farmer will change completely in comparison to his previous life. The route of the separation fence severely violates their right of property and their freedom of movement. Their livelihood is severely impaired.[216]

Subsequently, the Court determined that the Wall in the area disproportionately harms the rights guaranteed to the petitioners under both the Hague Regulations and the Fourth Geneva Convention.[217] Consequently, it ordered military authorities to find a route that was less disruptive to the Palestinian inhabitants.[218] In the *Mara'abe* judgment, however, the justices expressed their relief that there was no need to assess the legality of the Wall in light of the third proportionality sub-test.[219]

Concluding observations

The *Beit Sourik* and *Mara'abe* judgments have been applauded as proof of the Court's ability to rein in Israeli military authorities and their executive powers despite the serious security threats.[220] In light of these judgments, Israeli authorities re-evaluate the disproportionate harm that other segments of the Wall had created for nearby Palestinian communities long before petitions challenging the legality of those segments were to be considered by the Court on merit, and to come up with alternative routes.[221]

However, these two judgments represent the exception and not the norm. For in the majority of cases, the HCJ has granted Israeli authorities a wide discretion in assessing which measures best fulfil the alleged security needs. It has also endorsed the idea that the need to protect its citizens (both inside Israel proper and the occupied territories) and not only its military forces in occupied territory, constitutes a legitimate military purpose under international law. This has allowed it to subsequently conclude that the construction of the Wall is legal under international law. This conclusion comes despite the fact that the majority of the route of this structure runs inside the occupied territory, as opposed to the Green Line.[222] It also explains why, for all practical effects and purposes, it

216 Ibid. at paras 60–71, 73 and 84.
217 Ibid. at paras 67, 70, 76 and 85.
218 Ibid. at para 83. The Court noted that government authorities could opt either for the route presented by the experts of the CPS, or another route to be determined by the MC. *Beit Sourik* Judgment, *supra* note 1 at para 61.
219 *Mara'abe* Judgment, *supra* note 115 at para 116.
220 Michael Lynk (autumn 2005) 'Down by Law: The High Court of Israel, International Law and the Separation Wall', 35:1 JPS, 6 at 7.
221 Michael Sfard, 'The Fight against the Separation Wall', *supra* note 58.
222 In many ways, petitioning the Court on this issue had the opposite effect of what the litigation strategy of petitioning the Court had in mind, namely to receive a ruling that it is unlawful to build a 'fence' on Palestinian land. *Dakwar* Interview, *supra* note 194.

has been difficult for lawyers to challenge the Wall on fundamental principles of international law.[223]

Even in the aftermath of these two rulings, the Court was reluctant to take advantage of any contradictory data and statements that implied that the Wall's construction was driven by considerations other than security,[224] or that the chosen route was not suitable from a topographic, military and humanitarian point of view. As one lawyer explained, this is because:

> It [the Court] believes that it cannot do any better, that this is the maximum ... the Court is not good in declaring a government policy illegal. What it is good with is ordering the State to adhere to its policy.[225]

The Seam Zone and its associated permit regime

The Seam Zone judgment: facts of the case

In 2003, a petition was filed to challenge the MC's legal authority under international law to establish this Seam Zone, which trapped an estimated 7,000 Palestinians.[226] It argued that under article 43 of the Hague Regulations, the MC's authority to administer public life in the occupied territory can only take into account legitimate self-defence purposes, a criteria which the creation of the Seam Zone did not fulfil.[227] To rebut the government's position that the Wall's route deviation from the Green Line was effective from a security point of view, petitioners argued that it created 'a situation in which dozens of Palestinian communities remain west of the barrier'.[228] They also pointed out that the destruction and requisition of Palestinian privately owned property, in order to create the zone, cannot be justified under the exception of military necessity, because the objective was the security of the Israeli settler population and not the defence of the state and its military forces.[229]

223 *Dakwar* Interview, *supra* note 194.

224 *Sfard* First Interview, *supra* note 141.

225 Attorney *A-04* Interview, *supra* note 195.

226 *Seam Zone* Judgment, *supra* note 74.

227 The petition explains that 'the permit regime is [...] directed at the entire Palestinian nation as one'. See '(HCJ 9961/03) *Seam Zone* amended petition for Order Nisi' at para 100, online: *Hamoked* www.hamoked.org/items/6653_eng.pdf [Seam Zone amended petition for Order Nisi].

228 '(HCJ 9961/02) Seam Zone petition for Order Nisi and Interlocutory Order', at para. 31, online: www.hamoked.org/items/3820_eng.pdf [Seam Zone petition for Order Nisi and Interlocutory Order].

229 Article 46 and 52 of the Hague Regulations, *supra* note 6 and article 53 of the Fourth Geneva Convention *supra* note 9, cited in Seam Zone amended petition for Order Nisi, *supra* note 227 at paras 90–92. With respect to Israeli settlers, the Occupying Power has only the authority to administer 'order' and 'public life'. Cited in Seam Zone petition for Order Nisi and Interlocutory Order, *supra* note 228 at para 78.

Petitioners also contended that by seeking to consolidate the political objective of depriving Palestinians as 'protected persons' of their lands, the Seam Zone has 'entailed permanent changes and annexation of territories in a manner which contravened international law'.[230] In addition, military authorities were allegedly violating their duty under IHL to ensure the livelihood and welfare of the residents of the occupied territory.[231] This is because the creation of the Seam Zone and its permit regime has had a 'far-reaching economic, cultural, social and other implications'[232] on entire communities in areas close to the Wall: cutting them off from their farmland,[233] and reducing their access to the rest of the West Bank.[234] The fact that the Seam Zone has been turned into 'a closed military zone for Palestinians who have been living there for hundreds of years, and [into] an open area without any restriction on freedom of movement for any Jew',[235] amounted, in their view, to a discriminatory regime of separation based on group affiliation (akin to apartheid),[236] prohibited under international human rights law, and also to discrimination and collective punishment prohibited under the law of belligerent occupation.[237]

The Court's judgment

The Court decided to uphold the legality of the creation of the Seam Zone and its associated regime on various grounds. First, it reiterated that, 'this Court [had] approved the route of the fence, although a seam zone was created thereby [...]'.[238] Turning to an examination of whether the measures complied with the requirements of international law, the HCJ first held that the MC had the authority to close a certain territory within the West Bank.[239] Addressing the manner in which he had exercised that power, the justices believed that 'the decision to close the seam zone is based on a clear security purpose, ***which complements the original purpose of the security fence*** [emphasis added]'.[240] In other

230 *Seam Zone* Judgment, *supra* note 74 at para 10.

231 Seam Zone amended petition for Order Nisi, *supra* note 227 at paras 68 and 94.

232 Seam Zone petition for Order Nisi and Interlocutory Order, *supra* note 228 at para 97.

233 HRW, 'Israel's Separation Barrier in the Occupied West Bank', *supra* note 64.

234 Daphne Barak-Erez, 'Israel: The Security Barrier', *supra* note 196.

235 Seam Zone amended petition for Order Nisi, *supra* note 227 at para 74.

236 *Seam Zone* Judgment, *supra* note 74 at para 10. According to the petition, '[t]he legal regime that was chosen [...] creates, in fact, a regime of apartheid, unprecedented in Israeli law in all of its manifestations and extent of reach in Israel and in the territories'. Zone case – amended petition for Order Nisi, *supra* note 227 at para 71. See also *Seam Zone* Judgment, *supra* note 74 at para 43.

237 Article 50 of the Hague Regulations, *supra* note 6, Common article 3 of the Four Geneva Conventions and article 27 of the Fourth Geneva Convention, *supra* note 9 and article 75 of the First Additional Protocol, *supra* note 30. Seam Zone case – amended petition, *supra* note 227 at paras 82–85, 98–99. See also *Seam Zone* Judgment, *supra* note 74 at para 45.

238 *Seam Zone* Judgment, *supra* note 74 at para 12.

239 Ibid. at para 15. This was in the *Morar* Judgment, *supra* note 105.

240 *Seam Zone* Judgment, *supra* note 74 at para 16.

words, since the Seam Zone is not separated from Israel proper by any Wall segments, the Court concluded that 'it is difficult not to accept the [government's] argument that there is a security need to establish a mechanism which would enable a close supervision of those who enter through it [...]'.[241] In other words, the Seam Zone and its permit regime contribute to the declared security objective of the Wall.

Although the HCJ acknowledged that the Seam Zone and its permit regime had resulted in severe injury to Palestinians, it quickly pointed out that those harmed rights were relative rights: that is, they can be restricted, for the sake of additional considerations, such as national security, public order and the rights of others.[242] Using the three proportionality sub-tests once again, the Court then proceeded with an examination of whether the MC's Seam Zone declaration and application of the permit regime had achieved a balance between the various considerations. Towards this objective, the Court analysed the legality of three elements, including the mere decision to close the area; the various rules that were established under the permit regime, and various aspects concerning the practical implementation of this process.[243] Since the justices had upheld the government's security assessment, it swiftly concluded that the measures were legal under international law.

It then evaluated whether the harm inflicted by the measure was proportionate. In determining whether the measures fulfilled the first sub-test, (rational link sub-test) and given the justices' earlier conclusions that the closure of the zone and the permit regime complimented the security function of the Wall, they concluded that these measures fulfilled the requirements of that sub-test.[244] Moving on to the second sub-test, the Court believed that, in terms of arrangements for the Seam Zone, petitioners had been unable 'to point at other arrangements which realized the same security objective in a manner that caused less injury to the rights of the Palestinian population'.[245] The justices also accepted the government's position that less harmful measures (such as mere physical individual check-ups as opposed to general closure of the area and the installation of a permit regime) were not sufficient to realize the objective. This led the justices to uphold as reasonable, the arrangements that the government had put in place.[246]

And although justices acknowledged that the practical arrangements put in place by Israeli authorities did not significantly ameliorate the harsh impact of the permit regime for Palestinians, they argued that it was not possible for them

241 Ibid. at para 17.

242 Ibid. at para 22. The Court also reiterated that the legal sources for the rights of Palestinian inhabitants includes the Fourth Hague Convention; the 'humanitarian provisions' of the Fourth Geneva Convention, as well as the various human rights conventions (such as the ICCPR) and Israeli legislation. *Seam Zone* Judgment, *supra* note 74 at para 20.

243 *Seam Zone* Judgment, *supra* note 74 at para 29.

244 Ibid. at para 30.

245 Ibid. at para 32.

246 Ibid. at para 31.

to 'thoroughly examine the condition on the scene and the specific balance system implemented in the case of each resident'.[247] At the same time, they conceded that despite efforts to offer 'reasonable solutions which minimize the violation of the rights of farmers',[248] further improvements in the arrangements and in the processing guidelines, governing the issuance of permit applications could be implemented.[249] Lastly, in terms of the third proportionality sub-test (proportionality in the narrow sense), the justices were satisfied that 'the injury inflicted on the inhabitants – although it should not be taken lightly – is not the kind which may be regarded as over-rides the security benefit which arises from the closing of the zone'.[250] As regards the challenges to the allegations by petitioners that the creation of the Seam Zone is not intended as a temporary measure, the justices only noted that 'we are only hopeful that this need [of restricting Palestinians' access] is temporary in nature [...], as a result of the need to fight terror [...]'.[251]

Subsequent Wall-related case law

No doubt that the HCJ's *Beit Sourik* and the *Mara'abe* decisions have had some significant impacts on several levels. On a positive level, the tests developed by the Court for assessing sections of the Wall and their route, were taken into consideration by government authorities when determining the route of some of its subsequent segments, as a way of fulfilling the requirements set out by the Court under these judgments. One such was the *Salim* case,[252] where the HCJ examined four consolidated petitions challenging the legality of a segment of the Wall's route in the Tulkarem/Qalqilya area and of the Seam Zone permit regime. In this regard, it is known that military authorities had completed the construction of the Wall in the area as early as 2003. However, after the HCJ had rendered the *Beit Sourik* ruling, changes were made to the northern section, thereby leaving one Palestinian village (which by way of the original route had remained in the Seam Zone) on the 'Palestinian side'.[253]

247 Ibid. at para 34.

248 Ibid. The Court noted that the petition had failed to establish whether there is a gap between the government's statements and the situation on the ground. *Seam Zone* Judgment, *supra* note 74 at paras 31–40.

249 *Seam Zone* Judgment, *supra* note 74 at para 49. Measures suggested by the Court include: easing passage for those Palestinians who have managed to receive permits; expanding the criteria based on which persons may be recognized as 'permanent residents'; and establishing a clear time schedule for the handling of the different applications. *Seam Zone* Judgment, *supra* note 74 at para 47.

250 *Seam Zone* Judgment, *supra* note 74 at para 41.

251 Ibid. at para 44.

252 *Salim* Judgment, *supra* note 120.

253 Ibid. at 3. Consequently, government authorities developed several alternative routes before choosing one (route D), and which left an estimated 2,448 dunums of land outside the Wall. *Salim* Judgment, *supra* note 120 at 4.

In the *Tzufin* case, military authorities declared that, considering the HCJ's *Mara'abe* decision, they would re-route the Wall's eastern section. Thus, an estimated 1,000 dunums of land were left on the 'Palestinian side'. Authorities also declared that they would ensure proper access arrangements for the Palestinian farmers to their lands trapped on the 'Israeli side' of the Wall through the agricultural gates.[254] However, despite these statements, Palestinian petitioners decided to challenge the revised route of the Wall in several areas due to the harsh consequences that even this revised route continued to have for them,[255] such as maintaining their disconnection from major urban centres on which they relied for vital social services.[256]

Settlers and Israelis living in Israel proper also challenged the re-routing of the Wall in numerous petitions post-*Beit Sourik*, particularly where the new route chosen by military authorities had left their settlements outside the Wall.[257] In other cases, they argued that the proposed route ran too close to the line of their houses, which reduced the ability of the Israeli military forces to react to any potential attacks.[258] They also claimed that the new route had left land belonging to their settlement's jurisdiction on the 'Palestinian side' and that by failing to include (inside the Wall) an important route allowing Israelis to travel from the West Bank settlements to Israel proper or hilltops that overlook routes inside the Green Line, government and military authorities had failed to adequately provide for their security.[259]

Both Palestinian and Israeli petitioners challenged the new route on the ground that the MC failed to balance between the different considerations that

254 (HCJ 2732/05) [2006] *Abdel Al-Teif Hussein Head of Azzun Municipality Council et al. v. Government of Israel* at para 5, unofficial English translation by Avichay Sharon (January 2013) on file with author [*Tzufin* Judgment]. The petition was upheld by the HCJ.

255 *Biddu Village Council* Judgment, *supra* note 51. In the *First Dir Qadis Village Council* case, petitioners objected to the Wall's construction in the area separating the village from a considerable amount of their land that remained inside Seam Zone. After the petition was filed in 2004 against the original route (thereafter route A), it became clear that government authorities had, when routing the Wall, considered future building plans which had not yet been approved. After studying several alternatives, they adopted route E as the alternative. Still petitioners challenged the alternative route, as it required uprooting 1,000 olive trees, and forced them to succumb to the bureaucratic and arduous requirements of the Seam Zones permit regime. See *First Dir Qadis Village Council* Judgment, *supra* note 205 at paras 1–7.

256 *Biddu Village Council* Judgment, *supra* note 205 at paras 6–7.

257 *Tene* Judgment, *supra* note 151. In another case, Israeli settlers from that settlement challenged the route of the Wall after it had been re-routed by the MC in light of the *Beit Sourik* ruling, thereby leaving them outside the Wall. *Susya* Judgment, *supra* note 125 at paras 1–2.

258 *Alfei Menashe Local Council* Judgment, *supra* note 125. Representatives of settlers and of Israeli towns objected also to the specific route of the certain segments of the Wall. *Beit Arye* Judgment, *supra* note 125 at paras 4–5.

259 This was the case in the *Biddu Village Council* case, where representatives of the Israeli town of Mevaseret Zion argued in petition (HCJ 11409/5) that leaving hilltop 847 on the 'Palestinian side' of the Wall undermined their security. *Biddu Village Council* Judgment, *supra* note 51 at paras 6–7. See also *Tene* Judgment, *supra* note 151.

must guide his actions in an occupied territory. Moreover, they highlighted the detrimental consequences of the Wall on their 'fabric of life'.[260] After alluding to the harmful impact of the permit regime in the Seam Zone,[261] Palestinian petitioners also sought in some cases to convince the justices that government authorities were including some of their land on the 'Israeli side' of the Wall in order to accommodate new Israeli settlement neighbourhoods at various stages of approval or construction. This, they argued, would allow for the future expansion of these settlements, which in turn constituted political considerations. This was the situation in the *Bil'in* case,[262] which involved a petition filed by the Palestinian Bil'in village council against the route of the Wall that separated the village from the Modi'in Illit settlement.[263] Petitioners alleged that the route chosen by military authorities sought to ensure that two of the settlement's new neighbourhoods, at different stages of construction, would be included on the 'Israeli side' of the Wall. In addition, it separated Palestinian villagers from an estimated 50 per cent of their privately held land.[264]

Alternative routes were also suggested by petitioners and their council, including ones that were (closer) to the Green Line, as a way of reducing their separation from less land.[265] This was the argument raised by petitioners in the *Beit Arye Local Council* case,[266] where Palestinians had objected to the route of the Wall, which surrounded the two Israeli settlements of Ofarim and Beit Arye, in addition to an access route connecting them to Israel. Petitioners pointed out that this route separated them from privately owned land,[267] and had caused extensive damage to their property.[268] They also maintained that an alternative

260 Petitioners alleged that this land requisitioning order sought to annex settlements that are part of the Gush Etzion settlement bloc in the Jerusalem area (such as Migdal Oz) to Israel proper. (HCJ 834/07) [2007] *Mahmoud Muhamed Takatka et al. v. Government of Israel et al.*, unofficial English translation by Avichay Sharon (2013), on file with author [*Takatka* Judgment]. See also *Alian* Judgment, *supra* note 52. In the *Radad* case, petitioners highlighted the illegality of the settlements as articulated by the ICJ *Wall* Advisory Opinion. *Radad* Judgment, *supra* note 153.

261 For example, some petitioners argued that despite the changes to the route, 70 per cent of the agricultural land of their villages would remain trapped on the 'Israeli side' of the Wall. In addition, agricultural gates are only open for short periods of time, are not easily accessible and many applicants do not receive permits because of the high standard of proof. *Salim* Judgment, *supra* note 120 at 5 and 6.

262 *Bil'in* Judgment, *supra* note 60.

263 Established 1993, at about 0.6km away from the Green Line, it is part of the Modi'in Settlement Bloc. See 'Modi'in Illit', online: *Peace Now* https://web.archive.org/web/20160323013315/http://peacenow.org.il/eng/content/modiin-illit.

264 *Bil'in* Judgment, *supra* note 60.

265 *Alian* Judgment, *supra* note 52 at para 6. See also *Radad* Judgment, *supra* note 153 at paras 1–8.

266 *Beit Arye* Judgment, *supra* note 125.

267 Petition (HCJ 11651/05) was filed by Israeli settlers, while (HCJ 1998/06) was filed by Palestinians.

268 Of the estimated 2,000 dunums of land required for the Wall's construction, approximately 1,400 dunums are declared 'state land', while 560 dunums are privately owned by Palestinians. The route would also result in uprooting around 1,000 olive trees. *Beit Arye* Judgment, *supra* note 125 at paras 1–3.

Wall route could provide for the same level of security for the settlements/settlers or for Israelis in Israel proper, while resulting in less damage for their fundamental human rights. These allegations were corroborated by the CPS (as amicus curiae).[269] Israeli settlers also requested the re-routing of the Wall, so that their settlement would remain on the 'Israeli side' of the Wall.[270]

Respondents, for their parts, have generally sought to demonstrate that the measures in place reasonably mitigated the Wall's negative impact on the petitioners' lives as a way of balancing Israeli security needs with the human rights of the Palestinian population. They also alleged that, whenever possible, the Wall's route had been moved closer to the line of the houses of the concerned settlements and that the structure had, whenever possible, been built on declared 'state land'. In addition, the access of petitioners to their privately owned lands inside the Seam Zone would be allowed through the construction and operation of agricultural gates,[271] and a number of roads would be built to ensure that Palestinian villages are not cut off from the urban centres in the West Bank (on which they rely for vital social services).[272] In other instances, they argued that the Wall's route is the one that caused the least harm to the Palestinian villagers, even if it was not necessarily the most optimal from a security perspective.[273] Elsewhere, they underscored that they have adopted technology-based security measures in place of a physical barrier as a way of mitigating the harmful impact of the Wall on the petitioners.[274]

In this regard, it is also interesting to note that the government has sometimes alluded to the detrimental impact of the Seam Zone, and its associated permit regime, on the Palestinians to justify arguments that the route of certain Wall sections would be modified. In other instances, it has used the Zone's alleged impact on the Palestinians to cement the opposite argument, namely that the route must be kept as is. For example, in response to objections by Israeli settlers regarding

269 For example, in the *Ni'lin* case, Palestinian petitioners who were separated from over 1,000 dunums of land argued that the declared security objective can also be attained by building the Wall along the line of the settlement's houses. The CPS, joining as an amicus curia, confirmed that both the initial route for the Wall and another route proposed by the government as an alternative were disadvantageous from a military perspective and entailed significant harm for the petitioners. They chose a route that passed closer to the line of the houses of the Hashmoneam settlement. *Ni'lin* Judgment, *supra* note 150 at paras 1–15.

270 *Tene* Judgment, *supra* note 151 at paras 1–3. In the *Susya* case, Israeli petitioners challenged the reasonableness of the route chosen on the ground that by failing to include them on the 'Israeli side' of the Wall. They proposed an alternative route. See *Susya* Judgment, *supra* note 125 at paras 3–4f.

271 *Takatka* Judgment, *supra* note 260 at paras 5–13; *Beit Arye* Judgment, *supra* note 125 at paras 6–7; *Alian* Judgment, *supra* note 52 at paras 1–5 and 7.

272 In one case, such a road was established by the Israeli military authorities between Bir Naballah and Ramallah to allegedly provide the petitioning villagers with access to those urban centres, and minimize the harm to their 'fabric of life'. See *Biddu Village Council* Judgment, *supra* note 51 at paras 8–9.

273 *Ni'lin* Judgment, *supra* note 150 at paras 20–23.

274 *Beit Arye* Judgment, *supra* note 125 at paras 6–7.

the route of the Wall in certain areas, government authorities have argued that from the proportionality point of view, choosing an alternative route for the challenged sections of the structure to accommodate the settlers' request would require more Palestinians to seek a permit to enter the Seam Zone. This would worsen the disruptive effect of the zone and its permit regime on the daily lives of the Palestinians in the area.[275] In other cases, primarily in response to objections by Palestinians, authorities have adopted the opposite position: that the permit regime's operation is reasonable and corresponds adequately to both the needs of the local farmers and to their own professed security needs.[276]

Common denominators

An analysis of these judgments reveals that there are common denominators in the Court's judicial decisions on Wall-related petitions post-*Beit Sourik* and *Mara'abe*. The first one is that in all of these judgments, the Court upheld the idea that the MC enjoys the required expertise, knowledge and responsibility to deal with security considerations and that therefore, he must be afforded a wide discretion in determining which measure best achieves the stated security objective.[277] The justices have generally also upheld the legality under international law of the MC's decision to requisition privately owned property (including land) by the MC for that security-related purpose.[278]

This has been the Court's approach, irrespective of whether petitioners challenging the suitability of the route chosen by the MC were Palestinian or Israeli. For example, in the *Alfei Menashe Local Council* case, representatives of the Alfei Menashe settlement council[279] had filed a petition in 2006 arguing against the route for the Wall that had been amended following the HCJ's judgment in the *Mara'abe* case, on the ground that the proposed route ran too close to their houses. Here, the Court upheld the MC's security-based assessment that this

275 *Tene* Judgment, *supra* note 151 at paras 4–7; *Susya* Judgment, *supra* note 125 at paras 7–11. While emphasizing that the protection of Israelis is the primary consideration for the route of the Wall, it is only one consideration among several which the MC must take into account. *Beit Arye* Judgment, *supra* note 125 at paras 6–7.

276 *Salim* Judgment, *supra* note 120 at 8. In one case, the village of Nabi Samuel was included on the 'Israeli side' of the Wall (with around 200 persons), on the ground that it is located on a strategic hilltop overlooking the settlement of Ramot, in addition to a strategic road inside Israel (road 1). *Biddu Village Council* Judgment, *supra* note 51 at paras 8–9. Although not included in the Seam Zone, residents were subject to similar requirements. *B'Tselem*, 'Arrested Developments', *supra* note 41.

277 *Biddu Village Council* Judgment, *supra* note 51 at paras 10–15. See also *Bil'in* Judgment, *supra* note 60 at para 29.

278 The Court also noted that security-based concerns might also require the violation of the property rights of Israelis. *Alian* Judgment, *supra* note 52 at paras 8–18. See also *Bil'in* Judgment *supra* note 60 at paras 27–28; *First Dir Qadis Village Council* Judgment, *supra* note 205 at paras 20–28.

279 The settlement is located 5 kilometres from the Green Line. *B'Tselem* and *Bimkom*, 'Under the Guise of Security', *supra* note 49 at 33.

route provides the best protection to the settlements, reiterating in the process that petitioners had not succeeded in offering security-based facts that were strong enough to contradict the MC's security assessment.[280]

This was also the situation in the *Beit Arye* case. Here, the Court accepted the government's position that changing the route of the Wall that surrounded the Israeli settlement of Beit Arye to include land that was officially part of the settlement's jurisdiction, and which had been left on the 'Palestinian side' of the structure, would result in disproportionate harm to the Palestinian petitioners (both in terms of land confiscated and in property that would be destroyed).[281] While the justices also agreed with the Israeli settlers challenging the legality of the original route, that maintaining a larger distance between the Wall and their houses and including more land inside the Wall would augment their level of security, they decided that this does not justify the additional harm that would be caused to the Palestinian petitioners.[282]

However, most petitions challenging the route of the Wall have resulted in the requisitioning of predominantly privately owned land belonging to Palestinians, and have separated the former from their source of livelihood. Thus, even where the petitioners and their counsel had proposed several alternatives to the Wall's route as a way of minimizing the harm that it inflicts on them, the Court upheld the validity of the original land requisitioning order. This was especially true in cases where respondents had rejected the proposed routes' suitability from a security point of view. Thus, despite the severe harm incurred by the petitioners, according to the justices, the petitioners failed to demonstrate that their proposed route could achieve the declared security objectives of protecting Israeli lives from terrorist attacks.[283]

According to Israeli lawyer Michael Sfard, since Israeli measures have been implemented in response to alleged security needs, the HCJ has been unwilling and unable to grant more than sporadic acts of protection to the Palestinians in the oPt.[284] True, ascertaining the real motives spearheading the adoption of a given administrative order is often a difficult endeavour.[285] However, in light of the massive documentation by third parties to the contrary, the Court should have scrutinized more carefully, the assurances by government and military authorities that their security-based assessments were conducted in good faith.[286]

280 *Alfei Menashe Local Council* Judgment, *supra* note 125 at 12 and 14.

281 The building plans were in various stages of construction but had not yet been approved. *Beit Arye* Judgment, *supra* note 125 at paras 1–3.

282 *Beit Arye* Judgment, *supra* note 125 at paras 8–11.

283 *Takatka* Judgment, *supra* note 260 at paras 5–13. See also *Biddu Village Council* Judgment, *supra* note 51 at paras 10–15; *Radad* Judgment, *supra* note 153 at paras 15–23.

284 *Sfard* First Interview, *supra* note 141.

285 Marco Pertile, '"Legal Consequences of the Construction of a Wall in the Occupied Palestinian Territory": A Missed Opportunity for International Law?', (2004) 14:1 Italian YB Int'l L 121 at 136.

286 *Dakwar* Interview, *supra* note 194. According to another attorney, the Court 'should have regarded the reality, which was clear to everyone, including some of the judges'. Attorney *A-04* Interview, *supra* note 195.

Embarking on such an exercise would not mean that the Court has substituted its own opinion for that of the military establishment: assessing expert opinions submitted in court is simply part of what justices do when they adjudicate.[287] Furthermore, the law of occupation was designed in the first place to monitor and prevent excess and abuse of power by foreign forces in control of an occupied territory. This state of affairs warrants a narrower interpretation of the exceptions under which the occupant can take measures in the name of security. To assume that good faith underlines the rationale of the occupant's measures, especially security measures, signals that the Court has adopted the view that the Israeli occupation is a benevolent one, and that it only listens to what is being told in the courtroom.[288]

A second denominator common to the HCJ's adjudication of these Wall-related petitions is its determination of the extent to which the rights afforded to the Palestinian population can be lawfully restricted by the MC for the sake of Israeli rights or security. With time, the government's submissions to the Court came to emphasize this as a legitimate reason. As the Attorney General emphasized in one case:

> Indeed, part of the route was planned with the objective of providing protection also for *Israeli residents living in Judea and Samaria* [emphasis added], who also suffer from terror attacks. However, there is nothing wrong in this, for ... in accordance with Supreme Court decisions [...] Israel is of the opinion that the barrier is one of the necessary elements of this protection, so long as the route is proportionate.[289]

Hence, where petitioners contended that the protection of Israeli settlers cannot constitute a valid security consideration under IHL, given that it prioritizes the interests of those settlers at the expense of their interests as 'protected persons' under the Fourth Geneva Convention, the Court has rejected this argument.[290] Instead, the justices have pointed out that an Israeli residing in the West Bank and in the Seam Zone forms part and parcel of the MC's responsibility under

287 Attorney *A-04* Interview, *supra* note 195.

288 *Sfard* First Interview, *supra* note 141. Sfard recalls an incident in which the Deputy Chief Justice at the time (Justice Cheshin) was sitting next to Justice Minister Livni, as part of a conference panel. In it, the latter remarked that the Wall will constitute the political border of Israel. The Justice exclaimed that this is not the position that the government representatives had adopted in court. Still, the Court has never reversed any of its Wall-related decisions in which it had accepted that the structure had indeed been constructed for security reasons. In one of the court proceedings, Attorney Sfard even remarked in court to the justices that 'things are being said outside this court room', underscoring that the motivation guiding the construction of the Wall includes more than just security. However, he was interrupted by one of the justices who assured him that they only 'listen to what they are being told inside this hall'. Ibid.

289 *Alian* Judgment, supra note 52; Statement of Response, Section 469, cited in *B'Tselem* and *Bimkom*, 'Under the Guise of Security', *supra* note 49 at 10.

290 *Takatka* Judgment, *supra* note 260 at para 3.

article 43 of the Hague Regulations to protect all persons who are living under belligerent occupation.[291] For example, in the *Biddu Village Council* case, the Court explained that while granting optimal security to Israeli settlements and residents would entail severe and disproportionate injury to Palestinian rights, avoiding any harm to the latter might put the former at risk. The solution must therefore be sought in 'an appropriate balance' between these two conflicting interests,[292] since the right of both Palestinians and Israelis living in the West Bank are, in the Court's view, relative rights that can be restricted.[293]

This approach was adopted by the Court in several Wall-related decisions. In those judgments, the Court has effectively widened the legitimate military consideration of the MC to include the need to guarantee the security of Israeli travellers to and from Israeli settlements (located partially inside the West Bank), or the security of travellers commuting on roads inside Israel proper. Thus, in the *Alian* case,[294] the Court upheld the government's argument that the Wall's construction in the area was necessary, given that it is close to road 443 connecting Jerusalem and the Tel Aviv region, and therefore represented a convenient entry point into Israel proper (near the Mod'in area).[295] Similar conclusions were reached by the Court in the other petitions such as the *Local Council of Alfei Menashe* case.[296] Following the HCJ's ruling in the *Mara'abe* case, that a section of the Wall's route (which had kept five Palestinian villages trapped in the Seam Zone) was illegal,[297] Israeli military authorities developed three alternative plans for re-routing that section, as a way of reducing the number of Palestinian villages that need to be included on the 'Israeli side' of the Wall. In addition, they were faced with the need to decide whether or not to leave road 55 inside or outside the Wall.[298] After the MC had decided to keep two of the five Palestinian villages inside the Seam Zone, the Court endorsed this decision as proportionate and reasonable, given that it guarantees the security of Israelis, including settlers, travelling on highway 55.[299]

291 *Salim* Judgment, *supra* note 120 at 9. See also *Biddu Village Council* Judgment, *supra* note 51 at paras 10–15.

292 *Biddu Village Council* Judgment, *supra* note 51 at paras 10–15.

293 *Bil'in* Judgment, *supra* note 60 at para 30.

294 *Alian* Judgment, *supra* note 52.

295 Ibid. at paras 1–5, and 7. Similarly in the *Biddu Village Council* Judgment, *supra* note 51 at paras 10–15, the Court upheld the State's argument that there is a need to secure road 436 leading to the settlement of Givat Ze'ev.

296 *Alfei Menashe Local Council* Judgment, *supra* note 125.

297 *Mara'abe* Judgment, *supra* note 115.

298 The three proposed alternatives were: Plan A would re-route the south-western part of the Wall so that three Palestinian villages would remain on the 'Palestinian side' of the Wall, while road 55 (connecting the settlement to Israel proper and used by thousands of Israeli commuters on a daily basis) would remain on the 'Israeli side' of the Wall, with the Palestinian villages of Arab a Ramadin and Abu Fardeh trapped inside the Seam Zone. Route A1, which would keep all the villages and road 55 on the 'Palestinian side' of the Wall; and Plan B, which results in keeping all the villages outside the 'Seam Zone, closing down road 55, and the construction of a new road connecting the southern end of the settlement to Israel proper (through the Israeli towns of Matan and Nirit). Finally, Plan A was adopted. *Alfei Menashe Local Council* Judgment, *supra* note 125 at 5.

299 *Alfei Menashe Local Council* Judgment, *supra* note 125 at 13–14.

This interpretation by the Court took the pressure off the Israeli MC of having to find other means to protect the settlers. This it achieved when it evaded 'the issue of the legality of the settlements altogether and adopt[ed] an individual security premise, which upholds the obligation of the IDF to provide security to all individuals residing in the Occupied Territories – Israelis and non-Israelis alike'.[300] Had the illegality of settlements been taken into account, the Court may have been forced to examine 'the consequent duty of the Occupying Power to return its civilians in those settlements to its own territory'.[301] Had the Court adopted such an approach, it would have restricted the lawful means available for the MC to guarantee the protection of the settler population.[302] And while the Israeli settler population living in the West Bank is under the MC's military jurisdiction, the Court's decision to consider them part of the 'local population' is inaccurate. In fact, its approach is nothing short of misleading because it placed the rights of Israeli settlers to be analysed on the same par with those of the Palestinians, even though it is only the latter population group that qualifies as the 'protected persons' category under the Fourth Geneva Convention.

The third common denominator is the Court's reliance on the proportionality doctrine with its three sub-tests, as a way of assessing the extent to which the MC had succeeded in balancing between the different considerations that can lawfully guide his actions in the occupied West Bank. Here, save for a few cases, the HCJ has been unwilling to strike down segments of the Wall on the basis of the proportionality test.[303] In terms of the first proportionality sub-test (rational link), the justices have usually upheld the existence of a rational link between the measure (the Wall) and the security objective it seeks to achieve, be it the separation between Israelis and 'terror'; between Israelis and the West Bank,[304] or between Israeli settlements and Israel, on the one hand, and Palestinian major cities and areas, on the other.[305]

In the case of the second proportionality sub-test (the least harmful test), they have, for the most part, reaffirmed that the alternative route proposed by the Palestinian petitioners will not achieve the stated security objectives. Even where petitioners had relied on the expert opinion of professionals other than the Israeli military authorities (such as that of ex-Israeli military or of the CPS), the justices have, in the majority of cases, favoured the 'expert opinion' of Israeli

300 An assessment that is questionable, given article 4 of the Fourth Geneva Convention, which excludes the citizens of the Occupying Power from the Convention's scope of protection. Yuval Shany, 'Head against the Wall? Israel's Rejection of the Advisory Opinion on the Legal Consequence of the Construction of a Wall in the Occupied Palestinian Territories', (2004) 7 YB Int'l Human L 352 at 364.

301 David Kretzmer, 'The Advisory Opinion: The Light Treatment', *supra* note 128 at 94.

302 Attorney *A-04* Interview, *supra* note 195.

303 *Alian* Judgment, *supra* note 52 at paras 8–18.

304 Ibid. at paras 8–18.

305 *Salim* case, *supra* note 120 at 9; *Bil'in* Judgment, *supra* note 60 at para 37.

military and/or government authorities.[306] Where and when the Court acknowledged the harmful impact that the Wall had for Palestinian petitioners,[307] it still tended to conclude that the harm was not disproportionate, as 'the purpose of the fence is to save Israeli lives from terrorist'.[308]

In this regard, the determination of the topographic conditions, etc., is not the only thing the Court considered when assessing the proportional impact of the measure (or the lack of it). In analysing whether the Wall meets the requirements of the second sub-test, for example, it was crucial for the judges to evaluate the impact of the Seam Zone and its permit regime. In some cases, the route of the Wall had succeeded in including fewer Palestinians in this zone, which implied that less people would have to submit themselves to the permit regime. In other cases, the route of the Wall had not separated Palestinians from essential services. The Court alluded to this as proof that military authorities were taking all reasonable measures to alleviate the harmful impact of the Wall's construction on the petitioners.[309]

Other factors which the Court has traditionally considered were: the MC's assessment that the amended route of the Wall had reduced the amount of land inside the Wall;[310] the assurances by government authorities that it would grant petitioners regular access to their privately owned land in the Seam Zone by establishing a gate or granting them more access permits; that they would put in place or improve the quality of measures that seek to ameliorate the 'fabric of life' of Palestinian communities remaining in that zone and their connectivity to other West Bank villages outside the Wall;[311] that Palestinians would be offered compensation for land that had been requisitioned and for property that had been damaged (such as trees) as a result of the Wall's construction;[312] and that affected *individuals* would have the opportunity to petition the Court if the specific arrangements at the gate proved unsatisfactory.[313]

306 *Alfei Menashe Local Council* Judgment, *supra* note 125. See also *Salim* Judgment, *supra* note 134; (HCJ 1882/08) [2010] *Abdel Rahman Shaib Naser et al. v. Government of Israel et al.* at 4, unofficial English translation by Avichay Sharon (January 2013), on file with author [*Umm Saffa* Judgment]. The petition was dismissed by the HCJ. See also *Bil'in* Judgment, *supra* note 60 at para 37.

307 In the *Alfei Menashe Local Council* case, the HCJ acknowledged the remaining harmful effect of the Wall on the villagers. An estimated 2,500 dunums of land that is privately owned by Palestinians remained inside that zone. *Alfei Menashe Local Council* Judgment, *supra* note 125 at 14.

308 *Alian* Judgment, *supra* note 52 at paras 8–18; *Beit Arye* Judgment, *supra* note 125 at paras 8–11, *Biddu Village Council* Judgment, *supra* note 53 at paras 10–15; *Radad* Judgment, *supra* note 169 at paras 15–23.

309 *Alian* Judgment, *supra* note 52 at paras 8–18. *Salim* Judgment, *supra* note 120 at 9.

310 *Salim* Judgment, *supra* note 120 at 9.

311 Ibid. at 10. *Beit Arye* Judgment, *supra* note 125 at paras 1–3.

312 *Alfei Menashe Local Council* Judgment, supra note 125 at 15; *Takatka* Judgment, *supra* note 260 at paras 5–13.

313 *Biddu Village Council* Judgment, *supra* note 51 at paras 10–15.

Concluding observations

One main consequence of the *Beit Sourik* and *Mara'abe* rulings is that lawyers litigating on behalf of Palestinians have realized that they have little chance of convincing the Court that any considerations other than security have influenced the route chosen by authorities for the Wall's construction. Nevertheless, they continue to gather as many facts and indicators as possible to substantiate their claims that political considerations are the driving force behind the respondents' decision to route the Wall along a certain way, hoping it would then be 'easier [for the Court] to decide on the proportionality which it so loves', to strike down the route as illegal.[314]

The very fact that the Court has traditionally assessed the proportionality of the harm of each segment of the Wall, rather than the proportionality of the harm of the structure as a whole, has profoundly influenced the outcome of its Wall-related adjudication.[315] To begin with, adopting a segment-by-segment approach has allowed the HCJ to regulate the impact of security-based measures[316] on the rights of the petitioners more specifically and the impact on the Palestinian local population more generally. This also explains why the proportionality sub-tests ended up representing the most likely ground that the Court invokes to strike down the legality of the Wall. This has provided an avenue for remedy for petitioners on a case-by-case basis.[317]

Still, in assessing whether a given route fulfils the proportionality sub-test, it is very indicative that the route of that structure has hardly ever been considered by the Court as failing to fulfil the requirements of the first test (rational link) or the third proportionality sub-test (proportionality in the narrow sense). In the former, it is again the result of the Court's acceptance of the alleged security-based rationale of the Wall. In the case of the latter sub-test, whenever the question did arise as to whether the added benefit of increased security for the settlers or for Israelis travelling on the route justifies the extra harm inflicted on the Palestinians' right to property, the answer of the justices had usually been in the affirmative. Consequently, while it is true that Palestinian petitioners are left with an opportunity to challenge the legality of the Wall based on the second sub-test (least harmful measure), these opportunities are narrow and only have the potential to be exhausted in cases where a specific local remedy is being sought by the petitioners, as opposed to a change in the general policy of government and military authorities.[318]

Moreover, it remains an extremely challenging endeavour for petitioners to provide evidence that the Court would consider strong enough to refute the

314 Attorney *A-04* Interview, *supra* note 195.

315 *Sfard* First Interview, *supra* note 141.

316 Guy Harpaz and Yuval Shany, 'The Israeli Supreme Court and the Incremental Expansion of the Scope of Discretion under Belligerent Occupation', (2010) 43 Isr LR 514 at 515.

317 Yishai Blank, 'Legalizing the Barrier: The Legality and Materiality of the Israel/Palestine Separation Barrier', (2011) 46 Tex Int'l L 309 at 341.

318 *Dakwar* Interview, *supra* note 194.

security-based assessment of military authorities who, in the words of the HCJ, remain the security experts. As the case law suggests, in most situations, the Court has also accepted that measures taken by the government reflect a reasonable attempt to reduce the harm on the Palestinians (thereby rendering the harm proportional to the objective sought). Examples include: the promises of the military authorities to grant permits to farmers to access their land or to grant them physical access through gates, even though the functioning of the permit regime or opening of those gates has not ensured Palestinians with the regular access that they were promised.[319] This was particularly evident in the *Seam Zone* case, in which as part of the defence, the counsel for the petitioners had highlighted the inconsistencies between the promises made by authorities and what actually took place on the ground. Yet:

> The HCJ did not follow up and really check how these permit procedures work and what this *whole* complex bureaucracy means for the residents. Even more so in some cases the state outright lied and misled the court. For example in some cases the state issued permits for deceased people in order to spike up the numbers of permits it presented to the court. We asked the court to actually go into the small details and see that in fact on the ground for example many people are not allowed to cross the fence and reach their lands. But the court failed here and took the bait of the state and believed that living under such a complex regime of permits is in fact possible and therefore it allowed it.[320]

In other cases, the severe impact of the Wall's route and the creation of the Seam Zone were not considered of sufficient gravity by the Court to merit changing the route of the Wall in a manner that would exclude more land or more Palestinians from remaining in that zone. This, in the Court's view, is the case as long as the effect of the measure falls within a zone of proportionality:

> So even when for instance you show the court that a farmer will have to walk now 4 km to reach his land instead of 500 meters the court says – yes this is inconvenient but still proportional especially when balanced against security. In what sense is this proportional? In one of these cases I tried to explain to [Justice] Beinisch, using a power point presentation and maps and everything, that when you see it so close on the map in reality it is 2 km each direction. For a farmer to carry his goods and tools by foot, because he can't cross with a vehicle, means a detour of 4 km. But this is extremely

319 A third example is where state authorities decided to route the Wall so it runs on 'state land'; the Court commended the authorities' effort to reduce its disproportionate impact, even though the 'state land' declaration process has been severely criticized on substantive and formal RoL grounds.

320 *Dakwar* Interview, *supra* note 194.

difficult to explain in theory. Therefore, the language of 'proportionality' can easily cover for all these different situations.[321]

There have been instances in which the Court's willingness to go to great lengths to question the security-based justifications of the government representatives for the route of a specific segment of the Wall did arise. This was particularly the case where information coming to light during court proceedings had revealed that the decision by the respondents to establish the Wall along a certain route was influenced by their desire to encompass unauthorized building plans inside settlements so they remain on the 'Israeli side' of the Wall. However, the Court's tougher stance was only possible because domestic Israeli law requirements stipulate the fulfilment of certain criteria before the construction in new neighbourhoods can proceed.

Future plans to construct new neighbourhoods in existing settlements: are they a legitimate consideration?

Once the construction of the Wall had begun, senior government officials began to allude more directly to the fact that the consolidation of settlement blocs on the 'Israeli side' of the Wall constitutes a major objective guiding its route.[322] In a 2005 study, conducted by the two Israeli NGOs *B'Tselem* and *Bimkom*, highlighted that at least in 12 cases, the main consideration in determining the route of the Wall was the government authorities' desire to accommodate future expansion plans of Israeli settlements.[323] Thus even where evidence had come to the forefront suggesting that future expansion plans had indeed been taken into account in determining the Wall's route in the area, authorities continued to underline that ensuring the safety of those future neighbourhoods constituted legitimate considerations of military security.[324] In this regard, the Court has for the most part accepted at face value the assurances by the respondents that despite the existence of these future expansion plans, the only element that was instrumental in determining the route of the Wall in the area is security.[325]

321 Ibid.

322 *B'Tselem* and *Bimkom*, 'Under the Guise of Security', *supra* note 49.

323 Including plans for which the process of obtaining approval from the CA's Supreme Planning Council had not even commenced. *B'Tselem* and *Bimkom*, 'Under the Guise of Security', *supra* note 49.

324 *Bil'in* Judgment, *supra* note 60 cited in Aeyal Gross, 'The *Construction of a Wall* between The Hague and Jerusalem: The Enforcement and Limits of Humanitarian Law and the Structure of Occupation', (2006) 19 Leiden J Int'l L 393. Emphasis in the title is in the original.

325 In one case, the respondents had stated in court that a planning scheme for the development of the Israeli settlement of *Alfei Menashe* in the direction of the south-western part of the enclave had been filed. Nevertheless, the Court took at face value the assurances of the government that the Wall's route was chosen based on security considerations. *Mara'abe* Judgment, *supra* note 115 at para 113.

Nevertheless in a few judgments, the HCJ did conclude that illegal political considerations had filtered into the determination by military authorities of the route of the Wall. This was the case, for example, where it became clear that plans for the expansion of existing settlements have been taken into account by the MC when determining the route of the Wall, even though these plans had not yet gained the necessary political approval from relevant government authorities. However, this only took place if and when strong unequivocal evidence had emerged during the case proceedings that government authorities had indeed misled the Court regarding the main considerations motivating their determination of the Wall's route.

One example is the *Bil'in* case, where Palestinian petitioners had submitted several petitions to challenge the decision of the MC to requisition land for the construction of the Wall in the area. In them, they alleged that the Wall's route, which kept land belonging to the village, together with the Israeli settlement of Modi'in Illit, on the 'Israeli side' of the Wall was chosen to secure land for the settlement's eventual expansion. They also pointed out that the objective was to make way for the two new neighbourhoods of Naot HaPisga and East Mattityahu. Petitioners also claimed that, in the case of the latter neighbourhood, construction had been carried out without conforming to Israeli domestic regulations governing the expansion and building inside settlements.[326]

The petitioners' counsel also underscored that the Wall's route followed the line of a planning scheme (plan 210/8), which had allowed for the development of the East Mattityahu neighbourhood after it had been revised (plan 210/8/1).[327] This took place even though the revised plan had not yet received the final approval by the Ministry of Defence.[328] Once the scheme had been re-deposited it also became evident that the Wall's route had deviated from the area of the settlement's municipal jurisdiction, to include enclaves of privately owned land by Palestinians from Bil'in, and that several hundreds of dunums of land, which lay outside the jurisdictional limit of the settlement, had been

326 Either without a permit (in some part of the neighbourhood) or according to illegal permits (in other parts. *Bil'in* Judgment, *supra* note 60 at para 12.

327 The revised scheme, which lies within the jurisdictional area limit of the settlement, was designated among other things, for the construction of approximately 3,000 housing units, as opposed to only 1,500 housing units under the original plan. *B'Tselem* and *Bimkom*, 'Under the Guise of Security', *supra* note 49 at 56.

328 As the decision explains, '[i]t turns out that the developers took the law into their own hands and began to build the neighbourhood according to the future plan 210/8/1 before it had come into force'. *Bil'in* Judgment, *supra* note 60 at paras 5 and 13. Upon inquiring with the CA about the illegal construction taking place, Israeli human rights organizations were assured that 'stop work' orders had already been issued. However, site visits confirmed that the construction works were still moving ahead quickly. *Bil'in* Judgment, *supra* note 60. Moreover, while various faults in the process to approve the new planning scheme had been established by the Attorney General (including the fact that there were no building permits), construction had already begun in the area by an Israeli Real Estate Company. Agencies of the government had also ordered the annulment of the planning proceedings of the scheme and for the plan to be resubmitted. *Bil'in* Judgment, *supra* note 60 at paras 6 and 7.

attached to the revised plan of the neighbourhood. Moreover, information had emerged that this land had been allocated for the construction of more than 1,000 additional settlement housing units.[329]

The petitioners' counsel explained that instead of following the topographic line, or the line of settlement houses (traditionally considered by the military authorities when determining the route for a given section of the Wall), the route set by the MC followed the line of the revised planning scheme (plan 210/8/1).[330] This, they argued, cast doubt on whether the Wall's route had indeed been chosen for security reasons (as alleged by the government) or whether its main purpose was to secure more territory for the future development of the settlement of Modi'in Illit.[331] Government authorities, however, maintained that the route of the Wall in that area was chosen based on security considerations for the aforementioned settlement, including the need to provide for the safety of any future residents, and that doing so is a legitimate military consideration.[332]

During the proceedings, severe faults in the original planning scheme 210/8 and the revised planning scheme (210/8/1) came to light.[333] After affirming that the MC had the authority to build the Wall[334] and examining whether lawful considerations had indeed been considered, the justices concluded that:

> Due to the planning situation of the 'East Mattityahu' neighbourhood and the decisive weight which the military commander granted to the defence of this future neighbourhood, difficulty arises regarding the legality of the route that takes that construction into account. As is known, the planning of the route of the security fence ***should not be based on the desire to include on the 'Israeli' side of the fence territory intended for the expansion of settlements*** [emphasis added], specifically when the planning schemes ***are not about to be implemented in the near future*** [...] [emphasis added].[335]

329 *B'Tselem* and *Bimkom*, 'Under the Guise of Security', *supra* note 49 at 28.

330 *Bil'in* Judgment, *supra* note 60 at paras 6, 7 and 16.

331 And to annex it to Israel proper, in contravention of the ICJ's *Wall* Advisory Opinion. *Bil'in* Judgment, *supra* note 60 at paras 13 and 19.

332 They also argued that the MC was authorized to take new neighbourhoods into account and 'to consider valid planning schemes that have real chances of being implemented within a reasonable period, as there is no logic in building the fence and leaving new neighbourhoods beyond it'. *Bil'in* Judgment, *supra* note 60. Furthermore, the fact that the developers of the East Mattityahu

> took the law into their own hands and chose to commence illegal construction in the area of the neighborhood, should not prevent the assigning of appropriate weight, in determination of the route, to the fact that a new neighborhood will be built on site.

The respondents, therefore, required that the petition be rejected *in limine*. *Bil'in* Judgment, *supra* note 60 at para 22.

333 This includes the deviation of the former from the Modi'in Illit's area of municipal jurisdiction and the fact that construction was taking place in the enclave of land that is privately owned by Palestinians. *Bil'in* Judgment, *supra* note 60 at para 33.

334 *Bil'in* Judgment, *supra* note 60 at para 34.

335 Ibid. at para 35.

Consequently, when information came to light that the particular building plan had not yet received the final approval from the relevant government authorities, the justices opted for an assessment of the legality of the measure using the proportionality doctrine. Once the justices had underscored that the route chosen for the construction of the Wall's segment had fulfilled the requirements of the first proportionality sub-test (rational link),[336] they moved on to the second sub-test (least harmful measure). Here they determined that phase B (east) was conditional upon approval by the Ministry of Defence, an approval which, at the time, had not been granted. Given that no construction or development work had already been conducted there, the justices then concluded: 'we cannot accept the argument that defending the eastern part of the "East Mattityahu" neighborhood is a necessary security objective'.[337] Addressing more forcefully and directly, the government's argument that it had been a security need to construct the Wall on topographically controlling territory, the Court then explained:[338]

> [I]t seems that due to the desire to ensure the future construction of the eastern neighborhood in the future, the fence route was determined in a place which lacks security advantages. [...] The current route of the fence also *raises questions pertaining to the security advantage it offers* [emphasis added]. It is uncontroversial that the route mainly passes mostly through territory which is topographically inferior, both to Modi'in Illit and Bil'in. It leaves a number of hills on the Palestinian side and two hills on the Israeli side. It endangers the forces patrolling the route: In general, the military commander presents the possession of controlling hills as a significant security advantage in many cases regarding fence route planning, but in this case a route has been determined that is partially on territory which is inferior vis-à-vis the hills.[339]

The justices also indicated that the route of the Wall does not fulfil the third proportionality test (proportionality in the narrow sense). In their analysis, they held that the government's intention of developing the eastern part of the aforesaid settlement neighbourhood does not justify leaving the hundreds of dunums of land that is privately owned by Palestinians on the 'Israeli side' of the Wall. Nor did it justify the severe harm and hardship caused by the Wall's route to the petitioners' 'fabric of life', which had resulted from

336 '[W]hich is the separation between the Israeli settlements and the Palestinian settlements in the Judea and Samaria area, and protection of Israelis from terrorist attacks'. *Bil'in* Judgment, *supra* note 60 at para 37.

337 *Bil'in* Judgment, *supra* note 60 para 37.

338 The contested route had passed mostly through territory which is topographically inferior to the settlements it purports to protect *Bil'in* Judgment, *supra* note 60 at para 38.

339 *Bil'in* Judgment, *supra* note 60 at paras 37–38.

restricted access to their land due to checkpoints and agricultural gates.[340] Consequently, the Court ordered Israeli military authorities to devise an alternative route for the Wall.[341]

The Court's assessment in this case is commendable and demonstrates that, where petitioners have been able to provide strong evidence to counter the arguments of the government – indicating that political considerations were at play – it was emboldened to strike down the legality of the Wall's route in certain areas. However, and despite the strong evidence indicating that government authorities had taken political considerations into account,[342] the justices stated:

> [D]ue to the conclusion we have reached on the question of proportionality, *we refrain from deciding* [emphasis added] the question whether the fact that the 'East Mattityahu neighborhood' was a decisive consideration in the planning of the route leads to the conclusion *that a fault occurred regarding the military commander's very authority* [emphasis added] to order the erection of the fence on Bil'in land, or whether it should be determined that it is a fault in discretion, as opposed to lack of authority. We thus assume for the sake of the discussion that the construction of the fence was within the authority granted to the military commander.[343]

A second example is the *Tzufin* case,[344] and which involved a petition by Palestinians from the villages of Azzoun and Nabi Elias (in the Qalqilya area of the West Bank), who had challenged the legality of the Wall's route in that area. To surround the Israeli settlement of Tzufin, the route chosen by military authorities had kept 1,000 dunums of agricultural land belonging to the petitioners inside the Wall.[345] Here, petitioners who in the past had twice petitioned the Court in

340 *Bil'in* Judgment, *supra* note 60 at para 41.

341 It also demanded that land that was planned to allow for the future construction of phase B of the *East Mattityahu* neighbourhood remain on the 'Israeli side' of the Wall. *Bil'in* Judgment, *supra* note 60 at paras 36–42.

342 As the HCJ explained,

> it turned out that scheme 210/8/1 replaced, *de facto*, scheme 210/8 which had been in effect since 1999 but had not been implemented. The route of the fence thus took into account a planning scheme which had been abandoned, prior to the approval of the new planning scheme.
>
> *Bil'in* Judgment, *supra* note 60 at para 35

In this regard, the Court underlined that even though it was aware that the new scheme had passed the new approval proceedings, the implementation of 'phase B' in the eastern part was still conditional upon approval to be granted by the Minister of Defense. *Bil'in* Judgment, *supra* note 60 at para 35.

343 *Bil'in* Judgment, *supra* note 60 at para 35.

344 *Tzufin* Judgment, *supra* note 254.

345 Some 650 dunums of which were privately owned by Palestinians on the west side of the Wall. *Tzufin* Judgment, *supra* note 254 at paras 1–4.

relation to the route, argued that new information had come to light confirming that plan 194/5 allowing for the future expansion of the settlement (and which had not yet been approved),[346] had been taken into consideration by government authorities when determining that route. This contradicted assurances by these authorities, which they had made in previous cases, that only security considerations had influenced their decision regarding the Wall's route in the area.[347]

After the Court issued an order nisi, government authorities filed a new response in which they admitted to the fact that 'in planning the route in the area, consideration was given to the existence of a plan that is under preparation, but has not yet gained official approval'.[348] This new admission was received rather sternly by the justices, who added that:

> In the petition before us, a grave phenomenon has occurred: In the first petition, the Supreme Court was not presented with the full picture. The court dismissed the first petition on the basis of information only partially correct [...]. [T]he petition before us alludes to an event with which we cannot be reconciled in terms of which information that was provided to the court did not reflect the overall considerations with which the decision makers were faced. [...] We hope this will not be repeated.[349]

The Court subsequently decided to make the order nisi permanent and upheld the petition. According to one Israeli lawyer, familiar with the case:

> The HCJ [here] determined that it was not lawful on the grounds that the source of the authority to erect the fence stems from the necessity to protect people that at the relevant period of time are already present in the

346 The land under this plan was allocated for the establishment of an industrial zone. *B'Tselem* and *Bimkom*, 'Under the Guise of Security', *supra* note 49 at 6.

347 *Tzufin* Judgment, *supra* note 254 at para 4. Petitioners had petitioned the Court back in 2002. (HCJ 8172/02) [2002] *Ibrahim v. Military Commander*.

348 State response, section 17 cited in *B'Tselem* and *Bimkom* 'Under the Guise of Security', *supra* note 49 at 4.

349 *Tzufin* Judgment, *supra* note 254 at para. 7, cited in *Hamoked*, '(HCJ 2732/05) *Abdel Al-Teif Hussein Head of Azzun Municipality Council et al. v. Government of Israel et al*: Application for an Order of Contempt of Court', at para 6, online: *Hamoked* www.hamoked.org.il/items/6656_eng.pdf. It also reiterated that the respondent must ensure free passage by the petitioners to their land until the section of this Wall is constructed on a new route. *Tzufin* Judgment, *supra* note 254 at paras 6–7. Two years after the ruling was issued, the government had not implemented that ruling. In September 2008, *Hamoked* filed an application under the Contempt of Court Ordinance. Only then did the State begin to dismantle the route. *Hamoked*, 'In a decision on an application under the Contempt of Court Ordinance filed by *HaMoked* regarding the state's delay in implementing the judgment establishing that the route of the separation wall in the area of the villages of 'Azzun and An Nabi Elyas is unlawful and therefore null and void, the court harshly criticized the state's conduct in the case highlighting that its judgments are not merely recommendations and ordered the state to pay expenses to the sum of NIS 20,000'. (October 2009), online: *Hamoked* www.hamoked.org/Document.aspx?dID=847_update.

area and not potential future residents. In this case we can see a narrow interpretative approach of the court. The court restricted and minimized the lands that can be taken by the commander under the claim of 'security' and that under this objective, lands cannot be taken in order to expand settlements.[350]

A third example is the *Nilin* case, where the contradictory actions of Israeli military authorities furnished proof that security considerations were not the primary consideration for the route of the Wall, despite assurances to the contrary. In this case, Palestinian residents of the West Bank village of N'ilin had challenged the military's decision to requisition land (including land that is privately owned by Palestinians) for the construction of a section of the Wall. The construction had also effectively kept other parts of their land inside the Seam Zone. The MC had alleged that the route of the Wall in the area was influenced by the desire to include an area of land where several future building plans for the expansion of the Modi'in Illit bloc had been initiated (but which had not been approved at the time), so that they remain on the 'Israeli side' of the Wall.[351] The Wall's route, first decided upon in 2003 had, in light of the *Beit Sourik* ruling, been re-routed. From among the three alternatives which the MC considered at the time, it was determined that the southern route option, which left the lands for a future building plan (plan 208/03) on the 'Israeli side', would strike the necessary balance between the security considerations on the one hand, and the rights of the Palestinians on the other.[352]

However, soon thereafter, this route was challenged by the Hashmoneam Local Settlement Council because moving the Wall's route closer to the line of their houses would undermine the ability of the military forces to protect them.[353] In response, government authorities decided to drop that option in favour of another alternative route (thereafter the intermediate route). While this route expanded the distance between the Wall and the line of the settlement's houses, it also separated Palestinians from more of their lands than what had been envisaged, had the initial southern route of the Wall been followed.[354]

In their petitions, the affected Palestinian residents argued that the intermediate route chosen for the Wall confirmed that the main objective was to

350 Written response by an Israeli attorney, who wishes to remain anonymous, to Questionnaire (English) (10 July 2014) at 4, [*Attorney A 03-B* Written Submission].

351 The main plan (208/3) was intended for the construction of the future neighbourhood of Ganei Modi'in Illit over a surface of more than 147 dunums. *Ni'lin* Judgment, *supra* note 150 at paras 1–15.

352 Even though the State claimed that it was not the optimal route from a security perspective. *Ni'lin* Judgment, *supra* note 150 at paras 1–15.

353 *Ni'lin* Judgment, *supra* note 150 at paras 20–23.

354 This would take up 326 dunums for the construction of the Wall and would leave 3,490 dunums in the Seam Zone. Among these lands are 1,355 dunums of privately owned lands while the rest are 'state' lands. *Ni'lin* Judgment, *supra* note 150 at paras 1–15.

accommodate the future building plans of Hashmoneam and to trap land on the 'Israeli side' of the Wall for the proposed expansion of the settlement.[355] Joining as amicus curiae, the CPS underscored that both the initial route and the intermediate route for the Wall were disadvantageous from a military/ security perspective and resulted insignificant harm to the Palestinians and their rights.[356]

In employing the proportionality sub-tests, the Court ruled that the intermediate route did not meet the second proportionality sub-test (the least harmful sub-test).[357] Pointing out that the respondents had already commenced issuing requisitioning orders for land based on the 'southern route' option, it noted that it was only after the plea had been made by the settlement council that government authorities had decided to adopt the 'intermediate route'. Given the previous assurances by authorities that the optimal distance between the Wall and the line of settlement houses was necessary from a security point of view (as laid out in the initial 'southern route'),[358] the justices were concerned that the respondents had failed to explain why the necessary distance between the Wall and the settlement's line of houses had to be increased.

Finally, the Court concluded that government authorities had also failed to fulfil the third proportionality sub-test (proportionality in the narrow sense) because the proposed security-added value of the northern route did not justify the great harm inflicted on the petitioners from N'ilin.[359] In their conclusion, the justices reiterated that the route of the fence cannot take into consideration future building plans, particularly if those plans had not been approved.[360] The petition was consequently accepted and the land requisition orders for the intermediate route cancelled.

Neighbourhoods at an advanced stage of construction

In petitions where the expansion plans for an Israeli settlement neighbourhood to be included on the 'Israeli side' of the Wall were taken into consideration by government authorities, the Court remained open to the possibility of considering the route to be lawful. This was the case where government authorities were able to convince the Court that security remains either the only or the primary factor that has influenced the determination of the route. Thus, in the *Bil'in Village Council* case, the justices noted that, since the Israeli settlement

355 *Ni'lin* Judgment, *supra* note 150 at paras 20–23.

356 Here they chose a route which passed closer to the line of the houses of the Hashmoneam settlement and, hence, closer to the southern route which had initially been chosen by the respondents *Ni'lin* Judgment, *supra* note 150 at paras 1–15.

357 *Ni'lin* Judgment, *supra* note 150 at paras 30–43.

358 At the same time, the Court did not see any reason to prefer the alternative route suggested by the CPS. *Ni'lin* Judgment, *supra* note 150 at paras 30–43.

359 *Ni'lin* Judgment, *supra* note 150 at paras 30–43.

360 Ibid. at paras 30–43.

neighbourhood of Naot HaPisga had been built according to valid domestic planning schemes and regulations and was at an advanced stage of construction, a 'legitimate' need for defending it has arisen.[361]

Concluding observations

According to lawyer Nasrat Dakwar who was involved in litigating the *Tzufin* case, the Court only decided to uphold the petition in this case because petitioners had succeeded in refuting the security-based argument of government authorities:

> We were able to put our hands on the future plans themselves and could show the correlation between the plans and the route of the fence [...] we could show that the fence was distanced way beyond what is necessary from the existing houses in the settlement.[362]

According to another lawyer, who has litigated extensively in front of the HCJ on behalf of Palestinians, this represents one of the rare instances in which the Court chose to apply a more rigorous test and 'might have to do with the fact that the government was caught presenting false and partial information before the court'.[363] Another reason is 'the fact that we were able to present the expansion plans [which] made a difference in this regard'.[364]

The special security zones: overview of the case law

With the creation of these zones, the Court has followed the blueprint it developed in the Wall-related decisions to adjudicate the petitions challenging the legality of establishing these zones around settlements.

The position of the parties

Palestinians challenging the legality of confiscated land (including privately owned land) for the purpose of establishing those zones[365] highlighted that the primary objective is to annex occupied West Bank land or, at the very least, to secure indefinite control by Israeli authorities of this land for the benefit of Israeli settlements. To do so, they have articulated several arguments. One is the

361 *Bil'in* Judgment, *supra* note 60 at para 35.
362 *Dakwar* Interview *supra* note 194.
363 Attorney *A03-B* Written Response, *supra* note 350 at 4.
364 Ibid.
365 (HCJ 11395/05) [2006] *Mayor of Sebastia et al. v. Government of Israel et al.* at para 3, unofficial English translation by Avichay Sharon (August 2013) on file with author [*Sebastia* Judgment]. The petition was dismissed by the HCJ. In another case, an SSZ was established around the settlement of Carmei Tzur. See *Beit Ummar Municipality* Judgment, *supra* note 153.

illegality of settlement activity under international law and that, consequently, Israeli military authorities do not have the legal authority to provide for the settlement's security.[366] A second argument is the disproportionate impact of their establishment in terms of the appropriation of land, the uprooting of trees and the restrictions on access.[367] A third is that Israeli authorities could establish the fence surrounding the SSZ closer to the settlement's line of houses and/or adopt a technological system for surveillance (instead of a physical fence), as a way of reducing the amount of their privately owned land to be included in the SSZ and its disproportionate harm.[368]

Meanwhile, the respondents first contended that the location of land owned by Palestinians close to the settlements has been a source of ongoing security risks for the settlements' inhabitants.[369] Thus, the creation of a buffer zone of 200–400 m from the first settlement houses was necessary to fend off any attempts to infiltrate or target these settlements. Second, they also claimed that the distance between the SSZ fence and the line of houses of the settlements constitutes the minimum distance that is needed to provide the military forces with the necessary time to respond to any security breaches.[370] Third, the measure was allegedly both reasonable and proportionate for the following reasons: it required the confiscation of only a limited amount of land (for the purpose of constructing the SSZ fence); compensation will be offered to the affected Palestinian landowners/farmers and the affected individuals would have access to their lands, which would remain inside the SSZ, through gates set up for this purpose.[371]

The Court's assessment

The justices first reiterated that the relevant legal framework is the same as the one it had followed in the *Beit Sourik* and *Mara'abe* judgments. Subsequently, they underlined that the MC was authorized under international law to construct a 'fence' in 'Judea and Samaria' and to confiscate private property (including land) if this was necessary to meet genuine security-based objectives. Here, as well, the Court has generally upheld the government's position that the SSZ's establishment was necessary from a security/military point of view. It also reiterated that, as a matter of principle, the MC was authorized to implement

366 *Ariel Bloc* Judgment, *supra* note 106 at paras 11–14. See also *Beit Ummar Municipality* Judgment, *supra* note 153 at paras 1–5.
367 *Sebastia* Judgment, *supra* note 365 at para 3.
368 *Beit Ummar* Judgment, *supra* note 153 at paras 1–5.
369 (HCJ 5139/05) [2007] *Falah Mitzah Ahmed Shaib, Head of Beit Lid Village Council et al. v. Government of Israel et al.* at 1 and 3, unofficial English translation by Avichay Sharon (March 2013), on file with author [*Shaib* Judgment]. The petition was dismissed by the HCJ.
370 *Sebastia* Judgment, *supra* note 365 at paras 1–2, and at 4; *Ariel Bloc* Judgment, *supra* note 106 at paras 15–20 and *Beit Ummar* Judgment, *supra* note 153 at paras 1–4.
371 *Sebastia* Judgment, *supra* note 365 at paras 1–2.

measures that are allegedly geared towards enhancing the security of the Israeli settlers in 'the Area', even if the former are not 'protected persons' under the Fourth Geneva Convention.[372] It also stressed that the issue of the legality/illegality of the settlements under international law did not impact the obligation of the MC to secure the lives, dignity and freedom of all persons living under the law of belligerent occupation.[373]

Subsequently, the justices assessed whether or not the MC had balanced between the three main considerations which can lawfully guide his actions, and which are: the security of the State and its military forces; the human rights of the Palestinians as 'protected persons'; and the human rights and/or security of the Israeli settlers. In the first place, the justices assessed whether the MC's decision to establish the SSZ was reasonable. Again here, the justices underscored that they do not replace the MC as the security/military expert and that it is the latter who is entitled to establish which measure best addresses the declared security objective.[374] They then accepted the assessment of the military authorities that establishing an electronically based surveillance system (as opposed to a physical fence) around the SSZs would not suffice to respond to the security needs of the settlers.[375]

Invoking the proportionality doctrine, the Court then moved on to the first proportionality sub-test (rational link test). Here, it reaffirmed that, since the primary aim of the SSZs was to separate between the Israeli settlement and the neighbouring Palestinian villages, this measure (the fence and its route) was rationally linked to the objective it aims to achieve (security).[376] The Court has also generally upheld that the measure satisfied the second sub-test (least harmful measure). In this regard, the justices pointed out that petitioners had not succeeded in proving that their alternative routes would achieve the security objective that was laid out by the MC.[377] At the same time, when concluding that the route identified by the MC was the most optimal from a security perspective, the justices reiterated that they have taken into account promises made by government authorities that they would implement measures which would reduce the harm resulting from these zones on the petitioners. They also accepted the idea that these measures demonstrated that authorities have made a reasonable effort to strike an appropriate balance between the different considerations. These measures include: ensuring that the SSZs would not block the access of petitioners to any nearby Palestinian cities or villages and their essential services;[378] that only a limited amount of land that is privately owned by Palestinians would be appropriated

372 Ibid. at paras 5–6.
373 *Beit Ummar* Judgment, *supra* note 153 at paras 7–11.
374 *Sebastia* Judgment, *supra* note 365 at paras 5–6.
375 *Beit Ummar* Judgment, *supra* note 153 at paras 7–11.
376 *Ariel Bloc* Judgment, *supra* note 106 at paras 25–32.
377 Ibid. at paras 25–32.
378 *Sebastia* Judgment, *supra* note 365 at paras 5–6.

for the purpose (with the majority of land requisitioned to constitute 'state land');[379] that compensation will be offered to the affected landowners; and that the access of the landowners to their land in the SSZs for farming purposes will be guaranteed.[380]

In this regard, there is no doubt that petitioning the Court in and of itself could result, and has indeed resulted, in authorities deciding to modify the scope of their MOs. It also reduced some of the harm that would have been incurred by the petitioner. This was the situation in the *Beit Lid* case, where the respondents assured the Court that they have decided to modify the MOs requisitioning the land to stipulate that certain parts of the SSZ-related fence would run closer to the settlement line of houses. This effectively reduced the amount of land belonging to Palestinians that would have otherwise been included in those zones. Authorities also declared that they would replace some physical sections of it by an electronic surveillance system-based fence and that they would ensure access of farmers to the land that lay in the SSZ through agricultural gates and to offer compensation.[381]

Similarly, in the *Beit Ummar* case, after objections had been filed by the affected Palestinians against the MOs requisitioning their land, government authorities claimed that despite a certain compromise to their declared security objectives, they would modify these orders to move the outer fence of the SSZ closer to the line of settlement houses. They also expressed readiness to rely on technological surveillance in some parts surrounding the zone. Moreover, they committed themselves to granting access permits to all Palestinian landowners, to construct agricultural gates through the fence for this purpose and to offer compensation and rental fees.[382]

Closing remarks

On a positive note, the Court provided isolated and individual windows of legal remedy to affected Palestinian petitioners by reducing some of the harmful impacts of those security-based measures. Moreover, it consistently underscored that the occupation must remain temporary in nature to be lawful, and that an Occupying Power cannot be guided by political considerations, such as annexation, or the desire to establish a political boundary when implementing measures in the occupied territory. It has also made extensive reference to the principles of IHL when examining the legality of these measures.

Nevertheless, the HCJ has first generally upheld the legality of the measures that have been proposed by the government and has confined its efforts to

379 *Ariel Bloc* Judgment, *supra* note 106 at paras 15–20.
380 *Beit Ummar* Judgment, *supra* note 153 at paras 7–11.
381 *Shaib* Judgment, *supra* note 369 at 3.
382 Ibid. at paras 1–4 and 6.

regulating their impact. This is because, in the majority of cases, the Court has refused to accept that any considerations, other than security, have spearheaded the actions of government and military activities in the West Bank. It has also widened the military necessity exceptions under the international law of belligerent occupation, authorizing an Occupying Power to implement measures such as requisitioning land or destroying private property, to include the need to preserve the security and well-being of Israeli settlers living there and Israelis travelling in and out of the West Bank.

Second, through its combined approach to international law and Israeli administrative law, the Court has bolstered the rights and protection afforded to the Israeli settler population living in the occupied territory, while undermining the substantive protection afforded to the Palestinian occupied population by international law. This is achieved through the way in which the Court has sought to balance between different considerations affecting the decision of the MC. In fact, the way the Court has understood these considerations and what they can lawfully entail, has undermined the justice's willingness to entertain the idea that certain political considerations were at play (as opposed to strictly security-based considerations), or that these measures have resulted in a long-term and more permanent form of changes in the West Bank, not justified by legitimate considerations of security, thereby rendering them unlawful under international law.

This has undermined for all practical intents and purposes the human rights guarantees afforded to the Palestinian local population under the Fourth Geneva Convention. Moreover, the Court's refusal to rule on the legality of settlement activity reflects a pick-and-choose attitude towards upholding fundamental principles of international law. This cannot be seen in isolation from the Court's silence on the issue of whether the rights of the Palestinian population are also anchored in international human rights conventions that have been deemed applicable to the oPt.[383]

The Court's internalization of the security rationale furnished by government authorities is clearly reflected in the language it uses in its judgments. For example, the West Bank is referred to in its biblical term 'Judea and Samaria' or simply as 'the Area', a term that does not include EJ. Settlements are referred to as 'Jewish communities in Judea and Samaria' or more generally as 'Yishuv', while Israeli settlers are considered 'residents'. West Bank areas remaining outside the Wall are described by the Court as lying on the 'Palestinian side' of the 'fence', while the term 'Israeli side' is used interchangeably by the Court to refer to those areas of the West Bank that have been included inside the Wall (including the Seam Zone).[384]

383 *Mara'abe* case, *supra* note 115 at para 27.

384 The Court also uses the Hebrew words *tfisah lohmatit* (belligerent possession). Nimer Sultany, 'The Legacy of Justice Aharon Barak: A Critical Review', (2007), Harv ILJ 48.

This has provided a stepping stone for upholding the legality of the land requisition orders for the sake of the construction of the Wall as a temporary possession of the land.[385] As long as the requisition orders meet formal RoL requirements,[386] the Court has upheld them, irrespective of other indications that are underscoring the physical long-term permanence of the Wall or of other security-related measures and the legal consequences arising from them.[387] This has been facilitated by the fact that many of the measures discussed here have been cloaked in formal legality. As Blank explains:

> [T]he barrier is erected on the basis of authorized government decisions, administrative regulations, and military orders. Every piece of land confiscated, each section of erected wall, and every area declared a 'special security zone' – these were all done in a highly legalized fashion according to legal chains of authorizations. I am not arguing, of course, that some of the actions were not in violation of international law or contradictory to Israeli constitutional or administrative law [...]. Yet, the state of Israel behaved as if it were bound by law.[388]

Even where the ability of some of the security-based measures to fulfil procedural criteria or formal aspects of the RoL has been seriously questioned, the Court refrained from examining their legality. This remained the case unless the Court determined that there was strong evidence indicating that a government-implemented measure had been arbitrary in nature.

Third, the HCJ's adjudication has not ensured that the actions of government authorities do not undermine the first normative principle underlying the law of belligerent occupation. Agencies and organizations documenting the Wall's impact and that of its associated regime have maintained that Israel is seeking to consolidate its control of large swaths of the West Bank, in an effort to de facto annex significant portions of this territory.[389] Yet, the Court has consistently refused to seriously examine the wider and long-term consequences

385 According to the Court, '[c]onstruction of the fence does not involve transfer of ownership of the land upon which it is built. [...]. Taking of possession is temporary. The seizure order orders its date of termination.' *Mara'abe* Judgment, *supra* note 115 at para 16.

386 *B'Tselem* and *Bimkom*, 'Under the Guise of Security', *supra* note 49. Hence, even where land requisition orders for the Wall's construction are renewed on a constant basis, the Court preferred to consider this requisitioning to amount to a temporary takeover of land for a limited period of time. David Kretzmer, 'The Advisory Opinion: The Light Treatment', *supra* note 128.

387 Seam Zone petition for Order Nisi and Interlocutary Order, *supra* note 228 at para 3.

388 Yishai Blank, 'Legalizing the Barrier', *supra* note 317 at 317.

389 By contrast, the ICJ concluded that 'the construction of the wall and its associated regime, create a "fait accompli" on the ground that it "*could well become permanent* [emphasis added], in which case [...] it would be tantamount to *de facto* annexation" [emphasis in the original]'. ICJ *Wall* Advisory Opinion, *supra* note 126 at para 121.

arising from the implementation of these measures, and how they compare to government assurances that these policies respect the temporary nature requirement.[390]

It has also allowed the Court to brush aside the question of why: (a) military authorities have confiscated thousands of dunums of land (including land that is privately owned by Palestinians) for the construction of the Wall under temporary but renewable requisition orders; (b) significant and often irreversible damage to much property and land has resulted from this construction; (c) massive financial investment by the government into the Wall's construction has taken place; (d) a majority of Israeli settlements and its population have been deliberately included on the 'Israeli side' of the Wall;[391] (e) building plans for Israeli settlements are developed for implementation in areas that the military has declared a buffer zone; (f) the permit regime has contributed to the 'de-Palestinianization' of the Seam Zone;[392] and (g) severe and long-term harm has been caused by the creation of this Zone and its permit regime to the collective and individual rights of Palestinian communities.[393] Although, at the time of the *Beit Sourik* and *Mara'abe* judgments, the Court was not in a position to declare that the Wall was anything other than a temporary measure, it is hard to justify those conclusions 'after so many cases are still being litigated against the wall'.[394]

In the case of the SSZs, the Court's adjudication of petitions has done little to preclude the inclusion of vast areas of land inside these zones. Here too, the justices have accepted that these zones are temporary and necessary security-based measures. However, if seen in tandem with other elements that have effectively limited the Palestinians' use of land, and the weak enforcement on Israeli settler-building or cultivation activities in those zones, the emerging picture is of a consolidated Israeli control over these areas, for the long-term benefit of its settler population.[395] According to Attorney Sfard, several steps have narrowed the gap between being an occupant and a sovereign, such as 'having your own national community, imposing your own laws, creating settlements that by definition are not temporary … and the refusal to advance to an end of occupation'.[396]

390 The *Seam Zone* and *Mara'abe* judgments are good examples.

391 'The separation wall is designed to separate between the territory subject to Israeli law, governance and administration and the occupied territories, ***which are an entirely different political and legal being*** [emphasis added]'. Seam Zone petition for Order Nisi and Interlocutary Order, *supra* note 228 at para 4.

392 UN Special Rapporteur Report January 2006, *supra* note 91 at para 26.

393 *B'Tselem*, 'Arrested Development', *supra* note 41.

394 Attorney N. Amar-Shiff, Interview with Avichay Sharon on behalf of author (24 August 2014, Jerusalem) [*Amar-Shiff* Interview]. Mrs. Amar-Shiff is a lawyer and legal advisor for the Israeli NGO Rabbis for Human Rights (RHR).

395 The creation of these SSZs has added approximately 18,000 more dunums to the total closed areas in the West Bank. Dror Etkes, 'A Locked Garden', *supra* note 46.

396 *Sfard* First Interview, *supra* note 141.

One cannot dismiss the fact that the Court remains a government branch pursuing state interests. Moreover, public polls conducted among the Israeli Jewish public confirm that the majority have supported the Wall's construction when it began,[397] a feature of which the judiciary is mindful.[398] It also explains why the chances of Palestinians receiving effective legal remedy on security-related petitions have remained very slim,[399] and why the Court in almost all cases has upheld the policy of the government.[400] Moreover, the claim by military authorities that there have been fewer infiltrations by West Bank Palestinians into Israel proper as a result of the Wall's construction clarifies why the Court has been unwilling to question the temporary nature of these measures.[401] Therefore, petitioning the Court cannot effectively hinder the Occupying Power from channelling political considerations through the back door of alleged security-based measures. As early as 2004, Former UN Special Rapporteur for Human Rights in the oPt warned that:

> Like the settlements it seeks to protect, the Wall is manifestly intended to create facts on the ground. It may lack an act of annexation, as occurred in the case of East Jerusalem and the Golan Heights. But its effect is the same: annexation. Annexation of this kind goes by another name in international law – conquest.[402]

In terms of the provisions of the international law of belligerent occupation, applying this body of law to a determination of whether Israeli measures described here have resulted in the de facto annexation of parts of the West Bank has its own sets of challenges. First, although the law of occupation provides useful indications as to when a situation of occupation has started, it offers no concrete answers as to when it has ended.[403] Second, while the label 'de facto annexation' has frequently been invoked to describe the legal effect of Israeli

397 Ephraim Yaar and Others, 'Peace Index: Most Israelis Support the Fence despite Palestinian Suffering', *Haaretz* (10 March 2004).

398 *Beit Sourik* Judgment, *supra* note 1 at para 86.

399 *Sfard* First Interview, *supra* note 141.

400 Attorney *A-04* Interview, *supra* note 195. According to Sfard, many liberal Israelis sleep well at night because they know the Court is 'on it' and that 'we are not going completely crazy in terms of breaches of human rights'. Furthermore, the Court is perceived as a domestic court that is 'making sure Israeli policies are not arbitrary or violating international law'. *Sfard* First Interview, *supra* note 141.

401 This is because '[i]n terms of results, there are results, so why give in to the [un]temporary argument. [the judge] must be a very courageous judge to negate the temporary aspect … you go against a whole facade of temporariness'. *Amar-Shiff* Interview, *supra* note 393.

402 UN Special Rapporteur Report 2004, *supra* note 55 at para 14.

403 Tristan Ferraro, ed, 'Expert Meeting: Occupation and Other Forms of Administration of Foreign Territory', Report (March 2012), online: ICRC www.icrc.org/eng/assets/files/publications/icrc-002-4094.pdf.

policies,[404] the words do not feature in any of the relevant treaties and conventions. Third, there is a big disconnect between what Israeli authorities underscore, namely that their security-based measures are temporary in nature, and the documented impact of the policies in practice. Fourth, due to the prolonged nature of Israel's occupation of the West Bank, authorities have claimed that they are lawfully entitled to implement measures that might have far-reaching consequences for the legal and political landscape of that territory.

404 Interview with Charles Shamas, Partner in the Mattin Group, with author via Skype (21 November 2014, Ramallah) [*Shamas* Interview]; Aeyal Gross, 'The *Construction of a Wall*', *supra* note 324.

3 Security and welfare of the 'local population'

Implications of the HCJ's adjudication for the normative principle that occupation is a form of 'trust'

> It is sufficient for us to say that within the framework of the duty of the military commander to exercise his discretion reasonably, he must also take into account, among his considerations, the interests and rights of the local population [...].[1]
>
> – Dorit Beinisch, Chief Justice at the HCJ

Introduction

The adjudication by the Israeli High Court of Justice (HCJ) of petitions by Palestinians which has challenged Israeli security-based measures, has had implications for the second normative principle underlying the law of belligerent occupation, namely that occupation is a form of 'trust'.[2] Initially developed to cover situations of colonial trusteeship as well as government-conducted foreign territorial forms of administration under international mandate and trusteeship systems,[3] the concept of 'trusteeship' has also been invoked by the ICJ[4] and by legal scholars[5] as a way of understanding not only

1 (HCJ 1890/03) [2003] *Bethlehem Municipality et al. v. Government of Israel et al.* at para 15, online: HCJ http://elyon1.court.gov.il/files_eng/03/900/018/n24/03018900.n24.pdf, [*Bethlehem Municipality* Judgment]. The petition was dismissed by the HCJ. All links in this chapter last accessed on 1 June 2018.

2 Adam Roberts, 'What is Military Occupation', (1984) 55 Brit YB Int'l L 249.

3 Ralph Wilde 'From Trusteeship to Self-Determination and Back Again: The Role of the Hague Regulations in the Evolution of International Trusteeship and the Framework of Rights and Duties of Occupying Powers', (2009) 31 Loy LA Int'l and Comp LJ 85.

4 The mandate system was established on 'the principle that the well-being and development of such people form a sacred trust of civilization' and 'that the 'trust' had to be exercised for the benefit of the peoples concerned [...]'. *Legal Consequences of the Continued Presence of South Africa in Namibia (South West Africa) notwithstanding Security Council Resolution 276* (1970), Advisory Opinion, [1971] ICJ Rep 16 at paras 45 and 46. It also applies to the occupied Palestinian territory, 'as a former mandated territory, on whose behalf the international community holds a sacred trust'. *Legal Consequences on the Construction of a Wall in the Occupied Territory, Advisory Opinion*, Advisory Opinion (2004) ICJ Rep 136 at para 89 [ICJ *Wall* Advisory Opinion], *Opinion of Judge Koroma* at para 7.

5 Sir Arnold Wilson, 'The Laws of War in Occupied Territory', (1932) 18 Transactions of the Grotius Society 17 at 38.

those aforementioned systems, but also situations of occupation. Similarly to a trustee, the Occupying Power is perceived to be under the obligation to administer the occupied territory as a sacred 'trust', in the interests of both the local inhabitants and the sovereign government.[6] The analogy is derived from the manner in which legal and beneficial ownership is split in a 'trust' between the trustees on the one hand, who exercise legal discretion regarding the disposition of the assets of this 'trust', and the beneficiaries on the other hand, who receive the benefits flowing from it.[7]

Those who advocate understanding occupation as a form of trusteeship explain that this is guided by the two other main normative principles underlying the law of belligerent occupation, namely that occupation is supposed to be temporary in nature and that the Occupying Power does not enjoy sovereignty over the occupied territory.[8] This implies that the occupant is left with de facto administrative powers,[9] until a peace treaty is concluded.[10] The notion that acting on behalf of the beneficiary obliges it to refrain from enacting changes that may alter the status of the occupied territory, finds ground in article 43 of the Hague Regulations[11] which, in the authoritative French version, notes that:

> L'autorité du pouvoir légal ayant passé de fait entre les mains de l'occupant, celui-ci prendra toutes les mesures qui dépendent de lui en vue de rétablir

6 Ralph Wilde 'From Trusteeship to Self-Determination and Back Again', *supra* note 3. This characterization is used to describe in broad terms the kind of obligations on the Occupying Power, and is not intended to describe the juridical nature of the occupation in a strict sense. It also should not be confused with 'trusteeship occupation', a concept that has been used to describe control over territory that had not been under full sovereignty prior to occupation and where allegedly the occupation seeks to develop the territory economically and socially. Allan Gerson, 'Trustee Occupant: The Legal Status of Israel's Presence in the West Bank', (1978) 14 Harv Int'l LJ 1.

7 The obligation of usufruct and administration of public assets in article 55 of the Hague Regulations is practically similar to the way in which legal and beneficial ownership is split in a trust. McCarthy, 'The Paradox of the International Law of Military Occupation: Sovereignty and the Reformation of Iraq', (2005) 10:1 J Confl and Sec L.

8 Ralph Wilde 'From Trusteeship to Self-Determination and Back Again', *supra* note 3.

9 Jean Pictet, ed, *Commentary: IV Geneva Convention Relative to the Protection of Civilian Persons in Time of War*, reprinted (Geneva: ICRC, 1994) at 273 [*Pictet* Commentary]. Lassa Oppenheim, 'The Legal Relations between an Occupying Power and the Inhabitants', (1917) 33 L Q Rev 363.

10 Robert Kolb 'Etude sur l'occupation et sur l'article 47 de la quatrième convention de genève du 12 aout 1949 relative à la protection des personnes civiles en temps de guerre: le degrée d'intangibilité des droit en territoire occupé', (2002) 10 Afr YB Int'l L 267.

11 *Convention (IV) respecting the Laws and Customs of War on Land and its Annex: Regulation concerning the Laws and Customs of War on Land*, 18 October 1907, Cons TS No 25, 277 (entered into force 26 January 1910) [Hague Regulations].

> et d'assurer, autant qu'il est possible, l'ordre et la vie publics en respectant, sauf empêchement absolu, les lois en vigueur dans le pays.[12]

Often viewed as 'the gist of the law of occupation'[13] or the 'mini constitution' of an occupation regime,[14] this article provides a 'general framework for the manner by which the military commander exercises its duties and powers in the occupied territory'.[15] It also sets out the considerations that may influence the decision of the occupant to embark on changing the status quo (i.e. the state of affairs existing on the eve of the occupation).[16] The first consideration is the security needs of the Occupying Power.[17] At the time that the Hague Regulations were developed, 'military necessity' or the 'exigencies of war' were deemed to be the only concern that may prevent an occupying power from maintaining the old order in the occupied territory. In light of the minimal interaction between the occupier and the occupied population, article 43 of the Hague Regulations envisaged that the former would not be interested in the laws of the area under its control except for the security of its military forces and the maintenance of public order.[18]

12 French version of the Hague Regulations, *Convention (IV) concernant les lois et coutumes de la guerre sur terre et son Annexe: Règlement concernant les lois et coutumes de la guerre sur terre. La Haye, 18 octobre 1907*, online: International Committee of the Red Cross (ICRC) www.icrc.org/applic/ihl/dih.nsf/Article.xsp?action=openDocumentanddocumentId=48B0C736A648E654C12563BD002BA3EF. The term 'l'ordre et la vie publics', (public order and life) is rendered in the English translation as 'public order and safety'. Hence, the English version reads as follows:

> The authority of the legitimate power having in fact passed into the hands of the occupant, the latter shall take all the measures in his power to restore, and ensure, as far as possible, public order and safety, while respecting, unless absolutely prevented, the laws in force in the country.

Only the French version is the authentic one. Yoram Dinstein, 'Legislation under Article 43 of the Hague Regulations: Belligerent Occupation and Peacebuilding', (Fall 2004), online: Program on Humanitarian Policy and Conflict Research Harvard University https://web.archive.org/web/20170123155734/www.hpcrresearch.org/sites/default/files/publications/OccasionalPaper1.pdf.

13 Eyal Benvenisti, *The International Law of Occupation* (Princeton, NJ: Princeton University Press, 2004) at 7.

14 David Kretzmer, 'The Law of Belligerent Occupation in the Supreme Court of Israel', (Spring 2012) 94: 885 Int'l Rev Red Cross 207 at 213 and 218.

15 (HCJ 2164/09) [2011] *Yesh Din – Volunteers for Human Rights v. the Commander of IDF Forces in the Judea and Samaria Area et al.*, at para 8, unofficial English translation, online: *Yesh Din* https://s3-eu-west-1.amazonaws.com/files.yesh-din.org/עתירות/מחצבות/HCJ+2164-09+Judgement+%5BYD+Quarries+case%5D.pdf [*Quarry* Judgment]. The petition was dismissed by the HCJ.

16 Iain Scobbie and Alon Margalit, 'The Israeli Military Commander's Powers under the Law of Occupation in Relation to Quarrying Activity in Area C', (July 2012), online: *DIAKONIA* – International Humanitarian Law Resource Center www.DIAKONIA.se/globalassets/documents/ihl/ihl-resources-center/expert-opinions/quarrying-in-area-c---final---july-2012.pdf [*Scobbie* and *Margalit* Expert Opinion].

17 Lassa Oppenheim, 'The Legal Relations', *supra* note 9.

18 Eyal Benvenisti, 'The Security Council and the Law on Occupation: Resolution 1483 on Iraq: Historical Perspective', (2003) 1 IDF LR 19.

The second consideration consists in preserving the interests of the ousted sovereign or the duly constituted successor in title. In the case of conflict between the interests of the ousted government and the interests of the 'local population' (the third consideration), the Occupying Power was supposed to grant more consideration to the interests of the former.[19] The third consideration is the interests of the 'local population' in the territory under the effective control of the occupant. The advent of the Fourth Geneva Convention accorded great weight to the need to safeguard the interests and rights of individuals under foreign rule by granting them the status of 'protected persons'.[20] A common assumption is that the term 'local population' in the Hague Regulations refers to the 'protected persons' and the original inhabitants of the occupied territory.[21] The developments in international human rights (IHR) law, particularly the principle of the self-determination of people, led to greater recognition of the proposition that sovereignty is vested in the population under occupation.[22] This factor gained prominence in determining what is to be done during a trusteeship.[23] Palestinian petitioners addressing the HCJ have also made this argument.[24]

As a way of preserving the interests of the occupied population and the ousted government, the law of belligerent occupation imposes limitations on the ability of the Occupying Power to change the status quo in the occupied territory. Two limitations that are particularly relevant are the limitation that it imposes on the ability of the occupant to change the laws that exist in the territory on the eve of its occupation, and the restrictions imposed on the occupant's use of that territory's local resources.[25]

The restrictions on the occupant's ability to change the laws that exist in the territory on the eve of its occupation

For the purpose of local government, the Occupying Power has been described as the entity that 'stands in the shoes of the legitimate sovereign'.[26] However,

19 Ibid.

20 Eyal Benvenisti, *The International Law of Occupation*, *supra* note 13 at 110. See article 4 of the Fourth Geneva Convention *(IV) Relative to the Protection of Civilian Persons in Time of War* (12 August 1949)', 75:973 UNTS, 287 (entered into force 21 October 1950) [Fourth Geneva Convention]. It explicitly excludes nationals of that power. Yuval Shany and Guy Harpaz, 'The Israeli Supreme Court and the Incremental Expansion of the Scope of Discretion under the Law of Belligerent Occupation', (2010) 43 Isr LR 514.

21 Noam Lubell, 'Human Rights Obligations in Military Occupation', (Spring 2012) 94: 885 Int'l Rev Red Cross 317 at 333.

22 Orna Ben-Naftali, Aeyal Gross and Keren Michaeli, 'Illegal Occupation: Framing the Occupied Palestinian Territory', (2005) 23 Berkeley J Int'l L 551, at 579–592.

23 Ralphe Wilde 'From Trusteeship to Self Determination and Back Again', *supra* note 3.

24 '(HCJ 2164/09) *Yesh Din – Volunteers for Human Rights v. the Commander of IDF Forces in the Judea and Samaria Area et al.* – Petition', at para 39, unofficial English translation, online: *Yesh Din* https://s3-eu-west-1.amazonaws.com/files.yesh-din.org/תוריתע/תובצחמ/Quarries+Petition+English.pdf [*Quarry* Case – petition].

25 Eyal Benvenisti, 'Water Conflicts during the Occupation of Iraq', 97:4 AJIL (October 2003) 860.

26 Philip C. Jessup, 'A Belligerent Occupant's Power over Property', 38:3 AJIL (July 1944) 457 at 460.

an occupation is supposed to be a temporary state of affairs and does not bestow sovereignty on the Occupying Power in the occupied territory. Consequently, the law of belligerent occupation imposes certain restrictions on that power's ability to revise criminal and penal laws[27] as a way of maintaining the status quo.[28] These duties are set out in broad terms in article 43 of the Hague Regulations. The basic principle underscored by this article is that the Occupying Power is prohibited from extending its own legislation over the occupied territory.[29]

Two diverse obligations are imposed on the Occupying Power by article 43: (a) to restore and ensure, as far as possible, 'public order and life' in the occupied territory. This has been interpreted as an obligation that extends beyond the guaranteeing of security to relate to 'the whole social and economic and commercial life of the community'.[30] Changes to existing legislation or institutions are only lawful if they enhance 'civil life', compared with the situation under previous legislation.[31] (b) The second point refers to respecting the local laws in force in the occupied territory 'unless absolutely prevented'. This requirement underscores that the Occupying Power is prohibited from repealing or suspending existing laws,[32] as a way of preserving the status quo that was in effect at the beginning of the occupation.[33]

At the same time, the law of belligerent occupation entitles the occupant to make changes to the civil laws and penal laws in effect in the occupied territory if they meet a number of considerations. The first is that it meets the security needs of the Occupying Power's armed forces, administrative staff

27 Although article 43 refers to 'laws', it is widely recognized that the term must be understood to broadly include decrees, ordinances, court precedents (especially in territories of common-law tradition), as well as administrative regulations and executive orders. Dr. Theó Boutrouche and Marco Sassòli, 'On International Humanitarian Law Requiring the Occupying Power to transfer back Planning Authority to Protected Persons regarding Area C of the West Bank', (February 2012), online: *DIAKONIA* – International Humanitarian Law Resource Center www.DIAKONIA.se/globalassets/documents/ihl/ihl-resources-center/expert-opinions/ihl_expert_opinion_transfer_planning_authorities_feb2011.pdf [*Boutrouche* and *Sassòli* Expert Opinion].

28 Eyal Benvenisti, *The International Law of Occupation*, *supra* note 13.

29 *Boutrouche* and *Sassòli* Expert Opinion, *supra* note 27.

30 Ibid.

31 Ibid.

32 Yoram Dinstein, *The International Law of Belligerent Occupation* (Cambridge: Cambridge University Press, 2009).

33 Yuteka Arai-Takahashi, 'Preoccupied with Occupation: Critical Examinations of the Historical Development of the Law of Occupation', (Spring 2012) 94:885 Int'l Rev Red Cross 51. See also 'Occupation', online: *DIAKONIA* – International Humanitarian Law Resource Center www.diakonia.se/en/IHL/The-Law/International-Humanitarian-Law-1/issues-addressed-by-ihl-2/Occupation/?_t_id=1B2M2Y8AsgTpgAmY7PhCfg%3d%3d&_t_q=Occupation&_t_tags=language%3aen%2csiteid%3adfed4c1a-bbd8-450f-954a-02cff1abcc09&_t_ip=24.201.7.109&_t_hit.id=Diakonia_Web_Models_Pages_ArticlePage/_f5911847-6f4f-4f5c-91f4-35ab4c4eebe2_en&_t_hit.pos=1.

and those employed in its service.[34] The second is that it is needed for the preservation of 'public order and civil life'. The third consideration is whether it proves necessary for the occupant in order to 'abrogate any discriminatory measures incompatible with humane requirements',[35] and to discharge its obligations under the Fourth Geneva Convention.[36] This has been stipulated by article 64(2) of the Fourth Geneva Convention, a provision that has been interpreted as amplifying rather than replacing article 43 of the Hague Regulations.[37] Together, these two articles (43 and 64(2)) emphasize the idea that the occupant can make legislative changes to implement measures that fulfil its obligations towards the 'local population'.[38]

Restrictions on the occupant's use of the local resources of the occupied territories

Under the law of belligerent occupation, privately owned property in the occupied territory is generally immune from being taken by the occupant, save for a few exceptions. For example it cannot be destroyed unless this is deemed 'absolutely necessary by military operations'.[39] In the case of public property, movable public property and most immovable public property can be used, subject to certain restrictions. Where movable public property is concerned, the army of occupation can take possession of property 'of the State which may be used for military operations'.[40] In the case of immovable public property, article 55 of the Hague Regulations entitles the Occupying Power to use all property of such

34 This also includes the purpose of maintaining safe lines of communication. Yoram Dinstein, 'Legislation under Article 43', *supra* note 12. 'The provision is sufficiently comprehensive to cover all civilian and military organizations which an Occupying Power normally maintains in occupied territory'. When referencing the Occupant, the Convention is 'referring to the members and property of the occupying forces or administration' so that general activities such as activities on behalf of enemy armed forces are covered'. *Pictet* Commentary *supra* note 9 at 337.

35 *Pictet* Commentary, *supra* note 9 at 335.

36 This requirement is stipulated more specifically in article 64(2) of the Fourth Geneva Convention, which provides that existing penal laws in the occupied territory must be suspended by the Occupying Power where they constitute a threat to the application of the Fourth Geneva Convention. Marco Sassòli, 'Legislation and Maintenance of Public Order and Civil Life by Occupying Powers', (2005) 16:4 EJIL 661.

37 Conor McCarthy, 'The Paradox of the International Law of Military Occupation', *supra* note 7.

38 Eyal Benvenisti, 'Water Conflicts during the Occupation of Iraq', *supra* note 25. When reading article 43 of the Hague Regulations is supplemented by the Fourth Geneva Convention (most notably article 64), it becomes clear that 'this concept has been adjusted in the direction of promoting the rights and wellbeing of civilian populations under occupation'. Yuteka Arai-Takahashi, 'Preoccupied with Occupation', *supra* note 33 at 68.

39 Article 53 of the Fourth Geneva Convention, *supra* note 20. Requisition may not be deemed necessary 'except for the needs of the army of the occupation'. Article 52 of the Hague Regulations, *supra* note 11.

40 Article 53(1) of the Hague Regulations, *supra* note 11. Brice M. Clagett and O. Thomas Johnson, 'May Israel as a Belligerent Occupant Lawfully Exploit Previously Unexploited Resources?', (1978) 72 AJIL 558.

nature,[41] provided it safeguards the capital of that property and administers it in accordance with the principle of *usufructs.*[42]

In accordance with this principle, the occupant must ensure that the resources of the occupied territory are protected against potential damage, destruction, theft, overuse or the diminution of its quality and quantity.[43] This is because under the rules of the law of belligerent occupation, the economy of the occupied territory can only be required to bear the 'expenses of the occupation'[44] and cannot be made to cater to general 'military needs' or the needs of the occupant's civilian population.[45] The Occupying Power may also use these resources to meet its own security needs to defray the occupation-related administration costs and to promote the needs of the 'local population'.[46]

For an occupant's actions to enjoy a solid basis under international law, the use of the resources must be carried out in good faith, for the management of the 'local population' and not for its own enrichment.[47] The occupant's duty to respect article 55 of the Hague Regulations does not allow for a change in its scope depending on the duration of the occupation.[48] Violations by the occupant of this prohibition amount to pillage, which constitutes a war crime under the Rome Statute of the International Criminal Court (ICC).[49]

41 Hague Regulations, *supra* note 11.

42 Usufruct is a distinctively civil law concept; the obligations of a common-law life tenant are practically identical with those of civil law usufructuary. Brice M. Clagett and O. Thomas Johnson, 'May Israel as a Belligerent Occupant Lawfully Exploit Previously Unexploited Resources?', (1978) 72 AJIL 558, *supra* note 40. It has been defined as the right:

> [T]o draw from them profit, interest or advantage, without reducing or wasting them [...]. It may be established in any property which is capable of being used as far as is compatible with the substance not being destroyed or injured.

US States Military Tribunal at Nuremberg, 'The Flick Trial: Trial of Friedrich Flick and Five Others', Law Reports of Trials of War Criminals Vol IX (1945), at 42, online: www.loc.gov/rr/frd/Military_Law/pdf/Law-Reports_Vol-9.pdf [*Flick* Judgment]. While the Hague Regulations did not offer a specific definition of the term 'usufruct', the drafters chose a well-defined legal term of the art that included within its meaning the widely shared practices of applying the rules of usufruct at the time, and which included within its meaning the prohibition on usufructuaries from opening new mines. Brice M. Clagett and O. Thomas Johnson, 'May Israel as a Belligerent Occupant Lawfully Exploit Previously Unexploited Resources?', (1978) 72 AJIL 558, *supra* note 40. The HCJ has defined 'usufruct' as the 'right to use and enjoy the fruits of another's property for a period without damaging or diminishing it, although the property might naturally deteriorate over time'. See *Quarry* Judgment, *supra* note 15 at para 7.

43 Eyal Benvenisti, 'Water Conflicts during the Occupation of Iraq', *supra* note 25.

44 *Flick* Judgment, *supra* note 42 at 22.

45 Dobie R. Langenkamp and Rese Zedalis, 'What Happens to Iraqi Oil? Thoughts on some Significant Unexamined International Legal Questions', (2003) 14:3 EJIL 417.

46 Eyal Benvenisti, 'Water Conflicts during the Occupation of Iraq', *supra* note 25.

47 Philip C. Jessup, 'A Belligerent Occupant's Power over Property', *supra* note 26.

48 Vaois Koutroulis, 'The Application of International Humanitarian Law and International Human Rights Law in Situations of Prolonged Occupation: Only a Matter of Time?', (Spring 2012) 94:885 Int'l Rev Red Cross 165.

49 *Quarry* Case – petition, *supra* note 24 at paras 113 and 114.

The Israeli occupation of the West Bank is of a prolonged nature. While this does not render the law of belligerent occupation inapplicable, it introduces an important time-related factor.[50] It also 'places the law under considerable strain'.[51] Moreover, it begets the question of whether the Occupying Power is entitled to affect a wider spectrum of changes in the occupied territory.

How much change is lawful? The challenges of a prolonged occupation

The ever-increasing regulation of markets and other social activities by central governments in the twentieth century, has granted an occupant the authority to prescribe and create changes in a wide spectrum of affairs.[52] It has also been suggested that the factual situation arising from the prolonged nature of an occupation, coupled with the changing needs of the 'local population' during that time, create the need for increased governmental activity and regulation in different spheres of life, including social and economic.[53] These elements must be taken into account when analysing the duties of the Occupying Power,[54] particularly regarding its obligation to restore and ensure public order, civil life and safety.[55] Over-emphasizing the need to maintain the status quo would be counter-productive since it would lead to the territory's economic and political stagnation[56] and prevent the occupant from effectively responding to the evolving needs of local inhabitants.[57]

On the other hand, while International Humanitarian Law (IHL) treaties provide only general guidelines regarding the extent to which the occupant is obliged to preserve the status quo ante,[58] they are flexible enough to accommodate some of the needs arising in a situation of prolonged occupation[59] or other more recent forms of occupation/control.[60] Nevertheless, the criteria which they spell out for assessing the legitimacy of the changes that an Occupying Power can make remain relevant. This is because the long-term nature of the occupation does not entitle the occupant to import special rules that deviate from its IHL

50 Yuval Shany, 'Forty Years after 1967: Reappraising the Role and Limits of the Legal Discourse on Occupation in the Israeli–Palestinian Context', (2008) 21 Isr LR 6.

51 Christopher Greenwood, 'The Administration of Occupied Territory in International Law', in Emma Playfair, ed, *International Law and the Administration of Occupied Territories* (Oxford: Clarendon Press, 1992) 241 at 263.

52 Eyal Benvenisti, 'Water Conflicts during the Occupation of Iraq', *supra* note 25.

53 Grant T. Harris, 'Human Rights, Israel, and the Political Realities of Occupation', (2008) 41 (1–2) Isr LR 87.

54 Vaois Koutroulis, 'The Application of International Humanitarian Law', *supra* note 48.

55 *Boutrouche and Sassòli* Expert Opinion, *supra* note 27.

56 Eyal Benvenisti, *The Law of Belligerent Occupation*, *supra* note 13.

57 Robert Kolb and Gloria Gaggioli, eds, *Research Handbook on Human Rights and Humanitarian Law* (Cheltenham: Edward Elgar, 2013).

58 Eyal Benvenisti, *The International Law of Occupation*, *supra* note 13.

59 Christopher Greenwood, 'The Administration of Occupied Territory', *supra* note 51.

60 Eyal Benvenisti, 'The Security Council and the Law of Occupation', *supra* note 18.

obligations.[61] They also underscore that the Occupying Power must not abuse the powers granted for the purpose of implementing far-reaching changes that are intended to further its own political and economic objectives in the occupied territory,[62] or that 'serve as a means of oppressing the population'.[63]

Thus, while the prolonged nature of the occupation should in principle allow the occupant to deviate from the general rule of preserving the status quo by granting it a wider latitude to enact new legislation,[64] this is only permitted insofar as it benefits the 'local population'.[65] Since a situation of occupation bears an inherent conflict of interest between the occupant and the occupied,[66] in a situation of long-term occupation it becomes all the more pertinent to take the welfare and benefit of the population into consideration.[67] Hence, any effort to recognize wider powers for the occupant, risks granting it 'all the powers a modern sovereign would yield'.[68]

Even where the Military Commander (MC) is allegedly acting for the benefit of the 'local population', he must also ensure that the measures he implements in the occupied territory do not have a long-term effect that is designed to 'outlive' the occupation itself or to bring about changes in the fundamental institutions of the occupied territory.[69] A more conservative interpretation of the right of the occupant to change or amend existing legislation or institutions would ensure that the law is not abused to render the interests of the 'local population' secondary to the security concerns of the occupant.[70]

Israeli government authorities have argued that a narrow interpretation of the duties of the MC under article 43 of the Hague Regulations would not allow the occupant to carry out its duty vis-à-vis this population and, therefore, run contrary to the rationale guiding the duties imposed under the international law on them as the authorities of the Occupying Power.[71] They have also argued

61 David Alonzo-Maizlish, 'When does it End? Problems in the Law of Occupation', in Roberta Arnold and Pierre-Antoine Hildebrand, eds, *International Humanitarian Law and the 21st Century Conflicts: Changes and Challenges* (Lausanne: Editions Interuniversitaires Suisses, 2005) 97.

62 David Kretzmer, *The Occupation of Justice: The Supreme Court of Israel and the Occupied Territories* (Albany, NY: SUNY Press, 2002).

63 *Pictet* Commentary, *supra* note 9 at 337.

64 Yoram Dinstein, 'Legislation under Article 43 of the Hague Regulations', *supra* note 12.

65 *Scobbie* and *Margalit* Expert Opinion, *supra* note 16 at para 18.

66 Eyal Benvenisti, *The International Law of Occupation*, *supra* note 13 at 4.

67 Adam Roberts, 'Prolonged Military Occupation: The Israeli-Occupied Territories since 1967', (January 1990) 84:1 AJIL 44.

68 Eyal Benvenisti, *The International Law of Occupation*, *supra* note 13 at 147.

69 Yoram Dinstein, 'Legislation under Article 43 of the Hague Regulations', *supra* note 12.

70 Eyal Benvenisti, *The International Law of Occupation*, *supra* note 13 at 143.

71 See '(HCJ 2164/09) *Yesh Din – Volunteers for Human Rights v. the Commander of IDF Forces in the Judea and Samaria Area et al.* – State Response', (May 2010) at paras 46–47, unofficial English translation, online: *Yesh Din* https://web.archive.org/web/20160405015816/www.yesh-din.org/userfiles/file/Petitions/Quarries/Quarries%20State%20Response%20May%202010%20ENG.pdf [*Quarry* Case – Government Response 2010].

that the settlers constitute part and parcel of the 'local population' whose interests, security and well-being the MC is entitled to uphold as part of his duties under the aforementioned article. Moreover, they have underscored that many policies, have been implemented with the benefit of the local Palestinian population in mind.

This position stands in stark contrast with criticism by the international and local human rights community, and legal scholars. The first is that government and military authorities have implemented far-reaching changes in the occupied territory to guarantee the security and interests of the Israeli settlers in the West Bank, which are not legitimate considerations of the MC under the law of belligerent occupation. Second, measures implemented have allegedly allowed the Occupying Power to channel some of its vested general political and economic interests into the occupied territory in a manner that facilitates its indefinite control of that territory. This has promoted considerations that exceed what can legitimately influence the decision of the MC under article 43 of the Hague Regulation.[72] This is particularly the case of Israeli measures in Area C of the West Bank, where most of the Israeli settlements are located.[73] Towards this objective, criticism has underscored that government authorities have amended local laws and institutions in the occupied territory, and implemented strategies and policies, in order to promote a privileged access by Israeli citizens, including settlers, to the natural resources of the West Bank, particularly in regard to water use[74] and the use of the physical infrastructure (including road networks).[75]

72 Yuval Shany and Guy Harpaz, 'The Israeli Supreme Court and the Incremental Expansion', *supra* note 20.

73 More than 60 per cent of the West Bank is considered Area C and houses 150,000 Palestinians living in 542 communities. UN Office for the Coordination of Humanitarian Assistance (OCHA)-oPt, 'Area C of the West Bank: Key Humanitarian Concerns', (January 2013), online: OCHA-oPt. www.ochaopt.org/content/area-c-west-bank-key-humanitarian-concerns-january-2013 [OCHA-oPt Area C Report]. Forty-two per cent of the West Bank, mostly in Area C, is included within the jurisdiction of settlements. *B'Tselem*, 'Acting the Landlord: Israel's Policy in Area C, the West Bank', Report (June 2013), online: *B'Tselem* www.btselem.org/download/201306_area_c_report_eng.pdf.

74 UN Human Rights Council (HR Council), *Report of the Independent International Fact-finding Mission to Investigate the Implications of the Israeli Settlements on the Civil, Political, Economic, Social and Cultural Rights of the Palestinian People throughout the Occupied Palestinian Territory, including East Jerusalem*, HRC 22nd Sess, UN Doc A/HRC/22/63 (7 February 2013) at paras 80–88, online: OHCHR www.ohchr.org/Documents/HRBodies/HRCouncil/RegularSession/Session22/A-HRC-22-63_en.pdf [UN Fact-finding Mission on Settlements Report 2013]. Water consumption dips to 20 litres/capita/day in most Palestinian herding communities in the Jordan Valley. This stands in stark contrast to the average settlement consumption of 300 litres/capita/day. See UN OCHA-oPt, 'Humanitarian Fact Sheet on the Jordan Valley and the Dead Sea', (February 2012), online: OCHA-oPt. www.ochaopt.org/sites/default/files/ocha_opt_jordan_valley_factSheet_february_2012_english.pdf.

75 David Kretzmer, *The Occupation of Justice*, *supra* note 62. See also *B'Tselem*, 'Access Denied: Israeli Measures to Deny Palestinian Access to Land around Settlements', Report (2008), online: *B'Tselem* www.btselem.org/download/200809_access_denied_eng.pdf.

It also guaranteed a privileged allocation of land in the West Bank that has been declared 'state land'.[76] While an Occupying Power has the duty to proclaim and make known what land amounts to 'state land',[77] the policy of a 'state land' declaration as implemented by Israeli authorities in the West Bank has also been criticized on numerous grounds.[78] One major criticism is that state lands have been allocated to the exclusive use of Israeli settlers,[79] thereby undermining the requirement that they must be allocated to serve the needs of the local occupied population.[80] By 2006, an estimated 54 per cent of the land in the West Bank on which settlements have been built constitutes land that has been declared as

76 According to the *Ottoman Land Code*, most land in the West Bank constitutes *miri* land. Unless a private claim to the land arose, it hence belonged to the ruling power. If a farmer proves uninterrupted cultivation of a parcel of *miri* land for 10 consecutive years, without objection from any parties, he can claim this land. Otherwise, the possession reverts back to the government. After 1967, Palestinian farmers who could not prove registered ownership had the parcel of land confiscated by Israel and subsequently declared as 'state land'. It was then placed under the control of the Custodian of Government and Absentee Property. Quamar Mishriqi-Assad, 'Legal Recourse Based in Local Law for Palestinians in the West Bank against Settler Takeover of Private Palestinian Land', (Appendix II) in Dror Etkes 'Israeli Settler Agriculture as a Means of Land Takeover in the West Bank', Report (August 2013) at 106, online: *Rabbis for Human Rights* (RHR) https://web.archive.org/web/20171109112728/http://rhr.org.il/heb/wp-content/uploads/Kerem-Navot.pdf. Israeli military authorities ended the process of land registration by promulgating the MO, *Order Regarding the Regulation of Land and Water (Judea and Samaria) (No. 291), 5729–1968. Peace Now*, 'Breaking the Law in the West Bank – One Violation Leads to Another: Israeli Settlement Building on Private Palestinian Property', Report (October 2006), online: *Peace Now* https://web.archive.org/web/20160315082904/http://peacenow.org.il/eng/sites/default/files/Breaking_The_Law_in_WB_nov06Eng.pdf. This made it extremely difficult at the time, for Palestinian landowners to register their landownership, in spite of documents or other proof of ownership they might have had. While military appeals committees were established to hear appeals against the 'state land' declaration order, in the majority of cases, these committees displayed a built-in bias towards the aforementioned Custodian. *B'Tselem*, 'Under the Guise of Legality: Israel's Declaration of State Land in the West Bank', Report (February 2012), online: *B'Tselem* www.btselem.org/download/201203_under_the_guise_of_legality_eng.pdf.

77 As one lawyer explains, this is because 'under the Hague Regulations, the occupant has a duty to protect public property. Therefore, if the protection of public property is the purpose, then the declaration can serve a needed tool, and is a legal one.' Interview with Attorney Michael Sfard by author (21 October 2014, Tel Aviv) via Skype [*Sfard* Second Interview].

78 One primary criticism is that the policy's implementation has promoted an interpretation of the *Ottoman Land Code* in a manner that is detrimental to the Palestinians' right to private property. A second one is that through the promulgation of MOs to amend existing local laws, Israeli authorities have violated the obligation to maintain local laws that were, in effect, intact in the occupied territory (unless the proposed amendments fulfilled the considerations provided for by article 43 of the Hague Regulations). Third, this policy has shifted the burden of proof from the government to the individuals objecting to the 'state land' declaration. Interview with Raja Shehadeh (2 October 2014, Ramallah), by author via Skype [*Shehadeh* Interview].

79 In the majority of cases, the land is leased by the *Custodian for Absentee and Government Property* for 49 years to the Settlement Division of the WZO which sub-leases it to specific settlement associations and occasionally also to private persons. Written response by Former Head of Settlement Watch at *Peace Now* (Dror Etkes), via email (1 February 2015) at 1 [*Etkes* Written Submission].

80 *Sfard* Second Interview, *supra* note 77. See also *B'Tselem*, 'Acting the Landlord', *supra* note 73. Written response by Israeli Attorney A03-B to Questionnaire by author via Avichay Sharon (10 July 2014) [Attorney *A 03-B* Written Submission].

'state land'.[81] Often, once the land was seized; settlers would embark on cultivating the land and physically preventing Palestinians from reaching it,[82] before applying to the CA to have it declared as 'state land'.[83] In this regard, it must be noted that Israeli military rule has been applied to the entire territory of the West Bank and its residents, so that Israeli settlers residing in the occupied territory are also subject to the military legislation of the MC.[84]

However, both Israeli lawmakers and the MC have, over the years, gradually applied Israeli law to the Israeli settlements and its population. This has had the effect of removing, in practice, those settlements and their residents from the jurisdiction of the military law. It has also allowed the settler population to enjoy a legal environment and rule of law (RoL) resources, similar to the ones that prevail in Israel proper.[85]

This has been possible through two legal processes: The first is through the application of Israeli domestic law to the Israeli settler population by way of MOs.[86] The second one is the application of Israeli domestic law to the settlers through Israeli legislation. Not only has this allowed Israeli civilians who have committed offences in the occupied territories to be tried in Israeli civil courts,[87] but has also ensured that a number of laws become applicable *in persona* to Israeli citizens living in the West Bank.[88]

81 *Peace Now*, 'Breaking the Law', *supra* note 76 at 15–17.

82 (HCJ 9593/04) [2004] *Rashad Morar et al. v. IDF Commander in Judaea and Samaria et al.* (2006) at paras 1, 2, 4 and 6, official English translation, online: HCJ https://supremedecisions.court.gov.il/Home/Download?path=EnglishVerdicts\04\930\095\n21&fileName=04095930_n21.txt&type=4 [*Morar* Judgment]. The petition was upheld by the HCJ.

83 Because of their uninterrupted cultivation of the land, they could declare ownership of it, based on the *Ottoman Land Code 1858*. Meron Rapoport, 'Court Case Reveals How Settlers Illegally Grab West Bank Lands', *Haaretz* (17 March 2008).

84 (HCJ 1661/05) [2005] *Gaza Coast Regional Council v. Knesset*, unofficial English translation of extracts by Avichay Sharon (December 2013), on file with author, at para 13 [*Gaza Coast Regional Council* Judgment]. Where military orders (MOs) applied differently to Palestinians than to Israelis in the West Bank, the Court attributed it to the existence of valid distinctions between the two populations that were not discriminatory in nature. (HCJ 4400/92) [1992] *Kiryat Arba Local Council v. Yitzhack Rabin*, at 2, 3 and 5 unofficial English translation by Avichay Sharon (September 2013) on file with author [*Kiryat Arba Local Council* Judgment].

85 Raja Shehadeh, 'Negotiating Self-Government Arrangements', (Summer 1992) 21:4 J Palest Stud 22.

86 Association for Civil Rights in Israel (ACRI), 'One Rule, Two Legal Systems: Israel's Regime of Law in the West Bank', Report (October 2014), online: ACRI www.acri.org.il/en/wp-content/uploads/2015/02/Two-Systems-of-Law-English-FINAL.pdf. Examples of such orders are those concerning the administration of local and regional settlement councils that have bestowed upon settlement councils a set of powers and responsibilities that are identical to those enjoyed by Israeli municipalities in Israel proper. Eyal Benvenisti, *The International Law of Belligerent Occupation*, *supra* note 8.

87 Shortly after the 1967 war, the *Knesset* enacted the *Emergency Regulations Law Offenses in the Occupied Territories – Jurisdiction and Legal Assistance 5727–1967*. *B'Tselem*, 'Dual System of Law', (1 January 2011), online: *B'Tselem*. www.btselem.org/settler_violence/dual_legal_system.

88 This includes laws regarding taxation, product supervision, national insurance and the right to participate in Israeli elections. Khaled Diab, 'Why Palestinians should Demand to be Ruled by Israeli Law', *Haaretz* (20 November 2014). ACRI, 'One Rule, Two Legal Systems', *supra* note 86.

These strategies have been criticized as creating and maintaining an official institutionalized legal regime consisting of two separate legal systems and sets of institutions for the two population groups living in the same territory. It has also resulted in systematic discrimination that affects every aspect of the lives of the Palestinians.[89] Moreover, they have been responsible for bringing about long-term and profound changes in the occupied territory that are likely to last beyond the end of the occupation.[90]

In terms of specific measures challenged by Palestinians with alleged consequences for the second normative framework, the first is the requisition of land (including land that is privately owned by Palestinians) by way of an MO, for the construction and/or expansion of roads which primarily service Israelis.[91] The second are measures that have restricted or completely denied them access on certain roads throughout the occupied West Bank, on the ground that they constitute a legitimate response to ongoing security threats against Israeli nationals residing or commuting through the West Bank.[92] In addition, reference will be made to a petition that was filed by Palestinians in order to challenge the decision of the Israeli military to restrict farmers from accessing their lands, on the ground that it was necessary for the protection of those farmers against 'settler violence'.[93] Since the security of Israelis was not at stake, this helps to demonstrate that the Court can adopt a more robust stance vis-à-vis Israeli military authorities, both in terms of the language it employs and the judicial conclusions it reaches. This takes place when two conditions are fulfilled: (a) that the security of Israelis or their rights are not the main focus of a given petition, and (b) that the challenged measure raises domestic RoL issues as opposed to international law-related arguments.

The movement restrictions and land requisition for building roads

Movement restrictions in the West Bank in the name of security

A few months into the *Second Intifada* (2000), Israel stepped up its policy of closure and movement restrictions on Palestinians, thereby constricting their ability to enter, leave or remain along large areas throughout the West Bank.[94]

89 ACRI, 'One Rule, Two Legal Systems', *supra* note 86.

90 Ian Lustick, 'Israeli State-Building in the West Bank and the Gaza Strip: Theory and Practice', (Winter 1987) 41:1 Intl Org 15 at 152.

91 Piet Van Nuffel, 'The Story of the Israeli Settlements in the West Bank as it is told in International Law', (1994) 33 Mil L and L War Rev 354.

92 OCHA-oPt, 'Area C: Vulnerability Profile', (March 2014), Fact Sheet, online: OCHA-oPt: www.ochaopt.org/documents/ocha_opt_fact_sheet_5_3_2014_en_.pdf [OCHA-oPt, Area C: Vulnerability Profile].

93 *Morar* Judgment, *supra* note 82 at paras 1, 2, 4 and 6.

94 *B'Tselem*, 'Ground to a Halt: Denial of Palestinians' Freedom of Movement in the West Bank', Report (August 2007), at 7–9, online: *B'Tselem* www.btselem.org/sites/default/files2/publication/200708_ground_to_a_halt_eng.pdf.

Although these restrictions were officially in response to the outbreak of that second uprising, they are also a by-product of the construction and expansion of Israeli settlements.[95] According to Israeli authorities, many of these measures were put in place for the protection of not only Israelis in Israel proper, but also to provide security for the Israeli settler population, citing an increased frequency of attack against them since 2000.[96] They have also been employed to surround settlements with areas that are 'off-limits' to the Palestinians, all the while connecting those settlements with Israel proper and with each other and facilitating the unhindered commute of settlers to and from Israel.[97]

Requisitioning land for the construction of 'by-pass' roads

The idea of 'by-pass' roads was first raised by government and military authorities in the 1970s on the ground that '[t]he road is the factor that motivates settlement in areas where settlement is important, and [where] its advancement will lead to development and demand'.[98] This encouraged the development of a new transportation grid and road system in the West Bank, the objective of which was to 'by-pass' Palestinian towns and villages, connecting Israeli settlements to each other, and linking them to the Israeli transportation grid inside Israel proper. Located for the large part throughout Area C of the West Bank,[99] 'by-pass' roads formed 'a grid that crisscrossed the entire West Bank [...]'.[100] Often, Palestinians are restricted (completely or partially) from accessing these roads.[101]

At the time that these roads were constructed, government authorities had argued that this comes as a way of fulfilling the duty of the MC under article 43 of the Hague Regulations to promote the welfare of the Palestinian local population. Land that is privately owned by Palestinians has also been requisitioned for the sake of widening roads used by Israelis in the West Bank. The fact that these roads have been dedicated for the needs of the Israeli settler population has contributed to 'a situation where for the average Israeli, the distinction

95 UN OCHA-oPt, 'West Bank Movement and Access', Special Focus (June 2010), at 3, online: OCHA-oPt www.ochaopt.org/content/west-bank-movement-and-access-update-june-2010.

96 *B'Tselem*, 'Ground to a Halt', *supra* note 94.

97 UN OCHA-oPt, 'Movement and Access in the West Bank', (September 2012), online: United Nations Information System on the Question of Palestine (UNISPAL) https://unispal.un.org/DPA/DPR/unispal.nsf/0/BB7BD3D5A0DCB21785257A77004D5730.

98 *Peace Now*, 'Bypass Roads in the West Bank', (August 2005), online: *Peace Now* https://web.archive.org/web/20160306060603/www.peacenow.org.il/eng/content/bypass-roads-west-bank. This was articulated in the *Master Plan for Settlement of Judea and Samaria [West Bank] Plan for Development of the Area (1983–1986)*, cited in *B'Tselem*, 'Forbidden Roads: The Discriminatory West Bank Road Regime', Report (August 2004), online: *B'Tselem* www.btselem.org/download/200408_forbidden_roads_eng.pdf.

99 *B'Tselem*, 'Ground to a Halt', *supra* note 84.

100 *Peace Now*, 'Bypass Roads', *supra* note 88.

101 While sometimes restrictions have been imposed by way of a written military order (MO), in other instances, no written order was issued. *B'Tselem*, 'Ground to a Halt', *supra* note 94 at 98.

between Israel and the West Bank is increasingly blurred'.[102] Moreover, the large scale of the Israeli financial investment in this road network 'raises troubling questions about Israel's long-term intentions for the West Bank'.[103] It is also propagating a system of separation between Israelis and Palestinians residing in the West Bank based on national origin.[104]

In terms of restricting Palestinian access and movement, three different types of roads exist: (1) completely prohibited roads, designated for the exclusive use and mobility of Israelis (including settlers) and foreign nationals;[105] (2) partially prohibited roads, on which Palestinians are only allowed to travel, if they have successfully obtained special permits issued by the Israeli Civil Administration (CA);[106] and (3) roads on which Palestinian access is not prohibited.[107]

Up and until 1979, the promulgation of Israeli MOs has been one of the most common ways by which Israeli authorities have taken over land that is privately owned by Palestinians for the construction of settlements on the ground that this constitutes a military necessity. In the 1980s and 1990s, they also began taking over such land for the construction of 'by-pass' roads.[108] Theoretically speaking, requisitioning land under this pretext leaves the land's official ownership in the name of its original owners and only results in the transfer of control of the land for a designated and temporary period of time to the military authorities. This authority is also obliged to pay compensation for the land's use, after which the military must either renew the seizure MO or relinquish control of the land back to the owners.[109] Practically speaking, however, relinquishing control over requisitioned land is something that rarely happens.[110] From 1968 to 1979, an estimated 47,000 dunums of private-owned Palestinian land was confiscated,[111] (allegedly for military purposes, on which many Israeli settlements were established).[112] Moreover, while several petitions were

102 *Peace Now* 'West Bank Settlement Blocs', (May 2008), online: *Peace Now* http://archive.li/5u9EM.

103 *Report of the UN Human Rights Inquiry Commission Established Pursuant to Commission resolution S-5/1 of 19 October 2000*, UN CHR, 57th Sess, UN Doc E/CN.4/2001/121 (16 March 2001) at para 70, online: OHCHR https://documents-dds-ny.un.org/doc/UNDOC/GEN/G01/118/72/PDF/G0111872.pdf?OpenElement.

104 This road network bears alleged similarities to the one that existed in South Africa during the Apartheid era. *B'Tselem*, 'Forbidden Roads', *supra* note 98 at 3.

105 *B'Tselem*, 'Ground to a Halt', *supra* note 84.

106 *B'Tselem*, 'Forbidden Roads', *supra* note 98.

107 Also known as the 'fabric of life' roads, they intersect with the roads that are designated for the use of Israeli travellers. *B'Tselem*, 'Alternative Roads for Palestinians', (1 January 2013), online: *B'Tselem* www.btselem.org/freedom_of_movement/alternative_roads_for_palestinians.

108 Piet Van Nuffel, 'The Story of the Israeli Settlements in the West Bank', *supra* note 91.

109 *Peace Now*, 'Methods of Confiscation: How does Israel Justify and Legalize Confiscation of Land', online: *Peace Now* https://web.archive.org/web/20160306031030/http://peacenow.org.il/eng/content/methods-confiscation-how-does-israel-justify-and-legalize-confiscation-lands.

110 Ibid.

111 Ibid.

112 *Peace Now*, 'Breaking the Law in the West Bank', *supra* note 76.

submitted to HCJ in the 1970s to challenge Israel's land requisitioning policy, on the ground that using this land for the purpose of establishing settlements violates provisions of IHL, the HCJ has habitually dismissed those petitions.[113]

The situation changed significantly in October 1979 when the HCJ rendered its *Elon Moreh* judgment.[114] In this judgment, the Court ruled that such land requisitioning could be considered lawful under Israeli domestic law, only if and when the establishment of that settlement serves a clear and predominant security interest.[115] Subsequently, Israeli government authorities committed themselves to implementing the Court's decision,[116] and did not resort to MOs in order to seize land for the explicit purpose of settlement construction.[117]

However, the policy was reintroduced after the signing of the Oslo Accords in the 1990s for the construction of 'by-pass' roads,[118] alleging that this was necessary to facilitate the travel of Israelis (civilians and military) to and from oPt.[119] The Court has upheld the government's position that the construction of these 'by-pass' roads was carried out for absolute security needs.[120] After 2000, Israeli authorities once again argued that there is a need for such roads in light of the increased attacks by Palestinians against Israeli settlements and settlers in the West Bank.[121] Consequently, MOs to requisition land were issued.[122]

113 For example (HCJ 302/72) [1972] *Abu Hilu v. Government of Israel*, English summary in (1975) 5 Isr YB Hum Rts 384, [*Hilu* Judgment – Summary]; (HCJ 606/78) [1979] *Ayub et al. v. Minister of Defense et al.* English summary in (1979) 9 Isr YB Hum Rts 338, [*Ayub* Judgment – Summary]; (HCJ 834/78) [1978] *Al-Salam Salameh et al. v. Minister of Defense et al.*, English summary in (1980), 10 Isr YB Hum Rts 330 [*Salameh* Judgment – Summary], and (HCJ 258/79) [1979] *Amira et al. v. Minister of Defense et al.*, English summary in (1980) 10 Isr YB Hum Rts 331 [*Amira* Judgment – Summary].

114 (HCJ 390/79) [1979] *Azat Muhammad Mostafa Dweikat et al. v. Government of Israel et al.* unofficial English translation, online: *Hamoked*: www.hamoked.org/Document.aspx?dID=1670 [*Elon Moreh* Judgment].

115 The Court ordered the settlement to be dismantled, and the land to be returned to its Palestinian owners. *Elon Moreh* Judgment, *supra* note 114 at 15 and 20.

116 Israel Prime Minister's Office, Israel State Archives, 'Prime Minister Menachem Begin on Justice and the Rule of Law': Selected Documents on the 20th Anniversary of his Death', online: Government of Israel https://web.archive.org/web/20160304081008/www.archives.gov.il/ArchiveGov_Eng/Publications/ElectronicPirsum/MenachemBegin. The government also decided that from then onward, settlements would only be established on state-owned land. *B'Tselem*, 'The Ofra Settlement: An Unauthorized Outpost', Report (October 2008), online: *B'Tselem* www.btselem.org/download/200812_ofra_eng.pdf.

117 *B'Tselem*, 'Seizure for Military Needs and the Elon Moreh Ruling', (13 March 2013), online: *B'Tselem* www.btselem.org/settlements/seizure_of_land_for_military_purposes.

118 Ibid.

119 Ibid.

120 (HCJ 2717/96) [1996] *Wafa v. Minister of Defense et al.*, unofficial English translation by Avichay Sharon, September 2013 (on file with author) [*Wafa* Judgment].

121 UN OCHA-oPt, 'Fragmented Lives: Humanitarian Overview 2013', Report (March 2014), online: OCHA-oPt www.ochaopt.org/sites/default/files/ocha_opt_annual_review_2014.pdf.

122 *B'Tselem*, 'Land Grab: Israel's Settlement Policy in the West Bank', Report (May 2002), online: *B'Tselem* www.btselem.org/download/200205_land_grab_eng.pdf.

Sometimes, Israeli authorities also expropriated privately owned land for 'public' use by relying on the provisions of a local Jordanian law (amended by way of Israeli MOs).[123] While this method of land control had not been extensively used for the purpose of building settlements, it has been applied towards the construction of 'by-pass' roads on the ground that they help meet the transportation needs of the Palestinian local population.[124] This argument has been upheld by the Court.[125]

Palestinian petitioners have challenged the requisition order for the purpose of constructing roads of this nature or contested the movement restrictions that have been imposed on them. In response, and as part of an effort to demonstrate that they seek to reduce the harm incurred by the Palestinian civilian population, Israeli authorities have pointed out their efforts to construct what has become known as 'fabric of life' roads.

Running north–south (parallel to the roads on which Palestinian vehicles are forbidden to travel),[126] these roads were allegedly constructed to meet the Palestinians' transportation needs.[127] Although these roads do improve the flow of their traffic in certain areas, they have also effectively diverted it further away from the main roads, thereby allowing the latter to become 'Israeli roads' de facto.[128] Hence, petitioners have argued that constructing those roads has paved the way for the creation of a dual road system in the West Bank: one for settlers and one for Palestinians.[129]

123 *Jordanian Law No 2, Expropriation of Land for Public Purposes (1953)* in Raja Shehadeh, *Occupier's Law: Israel and the West Bank* (Beirut: Institute for Palestine Studies, 1988). This law was amended by way of Israeli MO No. 131, 321 and 949. Meron Benvenisti, *West Bank Data Project: A Survey of Israel's Policies* (Washington, DC: American Enterprise Institute for Public Policy Research, 1984). This allowed authorities to abolish the requirements to publish the decision in the official gazette and to deliver them to the landowner. It also moved the legal authority entitled to examine appeals against the expropriation order to a military appeals committee. In the 1980s, an amendment forced the 'empowered authority' to publish its decisions in the compilation of proclamations and to inform the landowner personally or through the *mukhtar* (mayor) of the village in which he resides. *B'Tselem*, 'Land Grab', *supra* note 122.

124 The law specifically states that the expropriated land must be used for a public purpose. *B'Tselem*, 'Land Grab', *supra* note 122.

125 (HCJ 202/81) [1981] *Tabib et al. v. Minister of Defense*, English summary in (1983) 13 Isr YB Hum Rts 364 [*Tabib* Judgment – Summary]. See also (HCJ 2056/04) [2004] *Beit Sourik Village Council v. Government of Israel* (2005), official English translation, online: HCJ https://supremedecisions.court.gov.il/Home/Download?path=EnglishVerdicts\04\560\020\A28&fileName=04020560_a28.txt&type=4 [*Beit Sourik* Judgment]. The petition was upheld partially by the HCJ.

126 *B'Tselem*, 'Ground to a Halt', *supra* note 94.

127 *B'Tselem*, 'Alternative Roads for Palestinians', *supra* note 107.

128 *B'Tselem*, 'Ground to a Halt', *supra* note 94 at 27.

129 'The interaction between the two networks is intentionally kept to a minimum'. Meron Benvenisti, *The West Bank Data Project*, *supra* note 123 at 23.

Overview of petitions

Palestinians have primarily focused their efforts on challenging three kinds of measures. The first ones are the land requisition orders allegedly issued by the Israeli MC to enhance the security of settlers and other Israelis in the West Bank, including those who commute on the road to and from Israel. For example, in the *Haas* case, they objected to the MC's decision to issue MOs to requisition privately owned land and to demolish two buildings belonging to the petitioners, for the purpose of building a concrete wall and for widening a road accessed by Israeli worshippers.[130] In the *Ad-Dhahiriya* case,[131] Palestinians together with Israeli human rights NGOs – the *Association for Civil Rights in Israel* (ACRI) and *Rabbis for Human Rights* – asked the Court to rule against the requisitioning of land for the purpose of building a concrete barricade along roads between the Israeli settlements of Tene and Carmel (South Hebron Hills).[132]

In a third one, the *Bethlehem Municipality* case,[133] two Palestinian municipalities filed a petition challenging a 2003 Israeli MO requisitioning large amounts of land for the purpose of building a 'by-pass' road for Jewish worshippers travelling from Jerusalem to Rachel's Tomb. The road, which is protected by walls that formed part of the sections of the Wall in the Jerusalem area, was declared by Israeli authorities to constitute an essential security measure in light of an alleged increase in attacks against Jewish worshippers in the area since 2000.[134] In other instances, petitioners challenged a land requisition order for the purpose of constructing a road to service a particular settlement[135] (and which was allegedly being built on privately owned land)[136] or in relation to a train line which the Israeli authorities sought to establish as a way of connecting Tel Aviv and Jerusalem.[137]

130 (HCJ 10356/02) [2004] *Yoav Haas v. IDF Commander in the West Bank et al.* at paras 1 and 2, unofficial English translation, online: *Hamoked* www.hamoked.org/items/8240_eng.pdf [*Haas* Judgment]. The petition was dismissed by the HCJ.

131 (HCJ 1748/06) [2006] *Mayor of Ad-Dhahiriya v. IDF Commander in West Bank.* (2006) 2 Isr LR 603 [*Mayor of Ad-Dhahiriya* Judgment]. The petition was upheld by the HCJ.

132 The requisition order covered approximately 320 dunums of land (4 dunums = 1 acre). *Mayor of Ad-Dhahiriya* Judgment, *supra* note 131 at paras 2–3. Located in Area C of the West Bank the south Hebron hills are home to approximately 30 Palestinian villages with an estimated 4,000 Palestinians. *B'Tselem* 'South Hebron Hills', (1 January 2013), online: *B'Tselem* www.btselem.org/south_hebron_hills.

133 *Bethlehem Municipality* Judgment, *supra* note 1.

134 Ibid. at para 7.

135 This was the settlement of Nili located on the 'Palestinian side' of the Wall in the Ramallah district, at 3.8 km from the Green Line. See *Peace Now*, 'Nili', online: *Peace Now* https://web.archive.org/web/20160423234132/http://peacenow.org.il/eng/content/nili.

136 (HCJ 5098/11) [2011] *Head of Dir Qadis Village Council et al. v. Minister of Defense et al.*, unofficial English translation by Avichay Sharon (2013), on file with author, [*Second Dir Qadis Village Council* Judgment]. The petition was dismissed by the HCJ.

137 (HCJ 281/11) [2011] *Head of Beit Iksa Council et al. v. Minister of Defense*, unofficial English translation, online: *Hamoke*d www.hamoked.org/files/2012/115140_eng.pdf, [*Beit Iksa* Judgment]. The petition was dismissed by the HCJ on grounds of latency.

The second type of the MC authorized measures challenged by petitioners involve those which have effectively restricted the movement of Palestinians and their vehicles alongside parts of roads in the West Bank, while these roads continue to be made available to Israelis including settlers and other Israeli citizens living in Israel proper. This was the situation in the *Dir Samit Village Council* case,[138] where several Palestinian village councils had petitioned the Court to revoke an Israeli MO that led to the closing off of sections of roads 3265 and 345 to Palestinian vehicles and pedestrians, and which were located at a distance of a few kilometres from an Israeli settlement and an 'unauthorized outpost'.[139]

Similarly, in the *Abu Safiyeh* case,[140] ACRI, together with residents of Palestinian villages, objected to the imposition of a complete travel ban on Palestinians' vehicles and pedestrians on a major road throughout the West Bank (also known as road 443), which represented the sole route connecting the Palestinian city of Ramallah and the Palestinian villages lying to the west.[141] At the same time, the route was being used daily by thousands of Israelis commuting between towns inside Israel proper[142] and which is known to connect the coast of Israel proper to Jerusalem (including annexed EJ) and to the Modi'in Illit settlement bloc.[143]

Here it should be noted that, in the 1980s, the requisitioning of land for the construction of this very road had been the subject of an earlier petition by Palestinians in the *Iskan* case. At the time, petitioners had challenged the assertions by government authorities that the road's construction was driven by a desire to benefit the Palestinian local population. The petition was dismissed by the HCJ. Following the outbreak of the *Second Intifada*, Palestinians were increasingly banned from using this vital road, after several attacks by Palestinians against Israeli vehicles using the road were alleged.[144] In 2002, the

138 (HCJ 3969/06) [2009] *Dir Samit Village Council et al. v. Military Commander*, unofficial English translation, online: *Hamoked* www.hamoked.org/files/2011/1294_eng.pdf, [*Dir Samit Village* Judgment]. The petition was upheld partially by the HCJ.

139 The Israeli settlement in question is Negohot, established on the 'Palestinian side' of the Wall at 2.6km from the Green Line and the unauthorized outpost of Mitzpeh Lachish. *Peace Now*, 'Negohot', online: *Peace Now* https://web.archive.org/web/20160804013303/http://peacenow.org.il/eng/content/negohot and https://web.archive.org/web/20140911234255/http://peacenow.org.il/eng/content/mitzpe-lachish. Road 3265 was completely closed off to Palestinian movement between the Green Line and the Palestinian village of F'qaiqis. In addition, Palestinian movement was prohibited on the south–north road (road 345). *Dir Samit Village* Judgment, *supra* note 138 at paras 1–4 and 7–9.

140 (HCJ 2150/07) [2009] *Abu Safiyeh et al. v. Minister of Defense et al.*, unofficial English translation, online: *Hamoked* www.hamoked.org/files/2011/8865_eng.pdf [*Abu Safiyeh* Judgment]. The HCJ upheld the petition.

141 ACRI, 'Route 443: Fact Sheet and Timeline', (25 May 2010), online: ACRI www.acri.org.il/en/2010/05/25/route-443-fact-sheet-and-timeline/.

142 *B'Tselem*, 'Route 443 – West Bank Road for Israelis Only', (1 January 2011), online: *B'Tselem* www.btselem.org/freedom_of_movement/road_443.

143 *Abu Safiyeh* Judgment, *supra* note 140 at para 1.

144 *B'Tselem*, 'Road 443', *supra* note 142.

ban against was made absolute on the ground that their continued use of the road facilitated terrorist attacks against Israeli travellers and their vehicles.[145]

The third type of measures challenged by Palestinians is the decision of the MC to prohibit Palestinians from entering areas adjacent to, or in the vicinity of, Israeli settlements. This was deemed necessary both for the purpose of protecting both the Israeli settler population in those 'Israeli towns' and the Palestinian farmers accessing these lands from settler violence.[146]

The petitioners' arguments

Petitioners have mainly challenged the MC's authority to implement a certain security-related measure on the ground that this exceeds the scope of this authority under international law. One argument advanced by several petitioners is that the decision of the Commander has been motivated by (irrelevant) political considerations, as opposed to genuine security or military needs.

This was the situation in the *Haas* case, in which petitioners alleged that the decision of military authorities to confiscate land for the widening of a road used by Israeli worshippers under the guise of security, served political considerations of creating 'territorial continuity between [the settlement of] Kiryat Arba and the Machpela Cave [Tomb of the Patriarchs] by means of establishing a promenade that will, in the future, allow the expansion of Jewish settlement in the area'.[147] In the *Dir Samit* case, petitioners also argued that the MC's closure decision was to allow the Israeli residents of the outpost to expand their community and to take over more land.[148] In the *Mayor of Ad-Dhahiriya* case, petitioners highlighted that the route of the barricade is very close to the original route that had initially been chosen by military authorities for the route of the Wall (before they decided to re-route the Wall in light of the HCJ's *Beit Sourik* ruling) and that the decision to put in place a barricade in that area constituted a 'way of circumventing the requirement of determining a proportionate route for the separation fence'.[149]

In other instances, petitioners backed their petitions with security expert opinions by the *Council for Peace and Security* (CPS) as a way of challenging the reasonableness of the respondent's assertion that the measures they wanted to

145 *Abu Safiyeh* Judgment, *supra* note 140 at paras 3–4. After the petition was filed, Israeli military authorities signed a written MO officially banning the Palestinians from using the road. ACRI, 'Road 443', ibid.

146 *Morar* Judgment, *supra* note 82 at paras 1, 2, 4 and 6.

147 *Haas* Judgment, *supra* note 130 at para 3. In the Hebron district, the settlement is located outside the Wall. See *Peace Now* 'Kiryat Arba', online: *Peace Now* http://peacenow.org.il/eng/content/kiryat-arba. In the *Bethlehem Municipality* case, petitioners argued that the contested measure was motivated by irrelevant political considerations of seeking to annex Rachel's Tomb to Israel proper. See *Bethlehem Municipality* Judgment, *supra* note 1 at para 7.

148 *Dir Samit Village* Judgment, *supra* note 138 at para 20.

149 *Mayor of Ad-Dhahiriya* Judgment, *supra* note 131 at para 10.

implement would indeed reduce the alleged security risks.[150] This was the situation in the *Dir Samit* case where the counsel for the petitioners contended that by turning the road into one that caters exclusively for the travel of Israelis, the security risks posed to those travellers would increase.[151] Expert opinions also sought to demonstrate that less harmful alternatives were available to enhance the protection of Israeli settlers. For example, in the *Bethlehem Municipality* case, petitioners put forward the argument that safeguarding the Jewish worshippers visiting Rachel's Tomb can be addressed through other less invasive means, such as the construction of a tunnel under the tomb to be used by those worshippers.[152]

A second line of arguments advanced by petitioners is that the challenged measure was not implemented for the benefit of the occupied territory or its 'protected persons', thus violating the MC's obligations under article 43 of the Hague Regulations. This was the situation in the *Abu Safiyeh* case.[153] There, petitioners claimed that, by closing off road 443 to Palestinian traffic, the road was effectively reduced to an internal Israeli traffic route. Hence, it no longer addressed the transportation needs of the occupied population. By closing off this road, the government had, they argued, contradicted its position in the *Iskan* case. At the time, government authorities had argued that building that very same road was necessary to respond to the needs of the Palestinian local population.[154] Petitioners also cast doubt on the idea that the Israeli settler population was entitled to use the public resources of the occupied territory, underscoring that a better way of ensuring the settlers' safety would be to prevent them from entering the occupied territory.[155]

Another case in point is the *Beit Iksa Council* case, where the petition challenged the requisition of land for the construction of a railway line that would connect Tel Aviv and Jerusalem. Since the planned railway intends to only serve Israeli commuters, petitioners argued that this declared purpose did not serve one of the two legitimate considerations of the MC under international law: imperative security needs or the interests of the Palestinian local population.[156]

150 In *Ad-Dhahiriya* case the CPS asserted that the barricade's construction fails to provide the alleged protection needed for persons travelling on the roads. *Mayor of Ad-Dhahiriya* Judgment, *supra* note 131 at para 11.

151 *Dir Samit Village* Judgment, *supra* note 138 at para 6.

152 *Bethlehem Municipality* Judgment, *supra* note 1 at para 7.

153 *Abu Safiyeh* Judgment, *supra* note 140 at para 8.

154 Ibid. at para 8. See also (HCJ 393/82) [1983] *Jam'iat Iskan case, al-Ma'almoun al-Tha'auniya al-Mahduda al-Masuliya, Cooperative Association Legally registered at the Judea and Samaria Area Headquarters v. Commander of IDF Forces in the Area of Judea and Samaria et al.*, unofficial English translation, online: *Hamoked* www.hamoked.org/items/160_eng.pdf [*Iskan* Judgment].

155 *Abu Safiyeh* Judgment, *supra* note 140 at para 31. *Dir Samit Village* Judgment, *supra* note 138 at para 5.

156 The railway connects Tel Aviv–Jerusalem without any stations inside the West Bank. *Beit Iksa* Judgment, *supra* note 137 at paras 1 and 27.

Moreover, they cast doubt on the government's assurances that the railway might in future serve Palestinians living in the West Bank, noting that this constitutes nothing short of a pretext for legitimizing the illegal route and for effectively annexing the expropriated land to Israel proper.[157]

Third, petitioners have highlighted the disproportionate harm inflicted on their ability to move within the West Bank and to access agricultural and grazing land,[158] and which disrupted all aspects of their 'fabric of life'.[159] Even where certain changes had been introduced by the MC,[160] petitioners insisted that the measures imposed a heavy burden.[161] In other instances, they alleged that the practice amounted to collective punishment, prohibited under IHL,[162] and that it constitutes discrimination on the basis of nationality.[163]

On the procedural levels, petitioners challenged the imposition of restrictions without written authorization[164] and that land has been requisitioned from them without their being afforded a fair and effective hearing.[165] This was the situation in the *Morar* case, where petitioners alleged that their access to the land for farming and harvesting purposes was done without a formal closure order being promulgated by way of an Israeli MO.[166]

157 *Beit Iksa* Judgment, *supra* note 137 at paras 5 and 25.

158 *Mayor of Ad-Dhahiriya* Judgment, *supra* note 131 at paras 6 and 7; *Beit Iksa* Judgment, *supra* note 137 at paras 5 and 25 and *Morar* Judgment, *supra* note 82 at para 10.

159 It allegedly infringed on their right to earn a living, their right to education, family life, and their right to life in dignity. *Abu Safiyeh* Judgment, *supra* note 140 at paras 8 and 30.

160 Following the *Beit Sourik* ruling, government authorities in the *Bethlehem Municipality* case introduced changes to the proposed route of the 'bypass' road. While this reduced the number of Palestinian residents who were to be in an area completely surrounded by walls, it did not alleviate the severe limitation on the freedom of movement of those living in the tomb's vicinity. *Bethlehem Municipality* Judgment, *supra* note 1 at paras 3, 5, 6 and 18.

161 (HCJ 11235/04) [2011] *Hebron Municipality and Others v. Government of Israel et al.* at 1, unofficial English translation by Avichay Sharon (2013), on file with author, [*Hebron Municipality* Judgment]. The petition was dismissed by the HCJ. During the *Second Intifada*, military authorities had created a contagious strip of land in the Old City of Hebron, along which the movement of Palestinian vehicles was forbidden. In 2009 Palestinian vehicle owners who hold individual permits were allowed to use one of these roads (Othman Bin Affan/Zion road). *B'Tselem*, 'Hebron City Center', (updated January 2011), online: *B'Tselem* www.btselem.org/hebron.

162 *Abu Safiyeh* Judgment, *supra* note 140 at para 8.

163 *Dir Samit Village* Judgment, *supra* note 138 at paras 5 and 6.

164 In the *Dir Samit Village* case, one of the claims by petitioners was that the movement restrictions were not anchored in a written MO, *Dir Samit Village* Judgment, *supra* note 138 at para 7. In the *Abu Safiyeh* case, petitioners showed that restrictions had been in place for seven years and that there was no intention to lift them in the near future. Petitioners had also requested that the Betouniya road (connecting road 443 to the Palestinian city of Ramallah), be made accessible to Palestinian private cars. However, the Court rejected the argument, noting that expanding the crossing would leave it prone to attacks. See *Abu Safiyeh* Judgment, *supra* note 140 at paras 8, 9, 13 and 38.

165 *Beit Iksa* Judgment, *supra* note 137 at paras 4–5.

166 Section 90 of the *Security Measures (Judaea and Samaria) (no. 378) Order, 5730–1970*, cited in the *Morar* Judgment, *supra* note 82 at para 11.

The position of respondents

According to respondents, the MC has a duty and authority 'to ensure [that] security in the territory appl[ies] with regard to all the persons who are present in the territory that is subject to belligerent occupation', including Israeli nationals travelling or residing therein.[167] Where the challenged measure involved the requisition of land that is privately owned by Palestinians for the benefit of security-related measures, they claimed that these requisition orders were temporary in nature and driven by two genuine security needs: (a) the need to protect Israelis inside the West Bank from attacks by Palestinians;[168] and (b) the need to protect Israelis travelling to and from settlements in the West Bank, to Israel proper.[169] Hence they were lawful under international law.[170]

In addition, they have denied that the harm incurred by the Palestinian local population was disproportionate to the security advantage gained, on the ground that it would allow Israeli citizens to exercise some of their essential human rights (such as the right to worship).[171] Moreover, they allege to have often modified the implementation of a given security-based measure to significantly reduce the injury to the petitioners' daily lives. For example, in the *Abu Safiyeh* case, they constructed 'fabric of life' roads for the Palestinian local population.[172] In the *Bethlehem Municipality* case, instead of requisitioning land for the purpose of constructing a ring road that would guarantee the safe passage of the Jewish worshippers travelling to Rachel's Tomb, a 'by-pass' road secured by walls was built instead.[173]

In other instances, government authorities contended that resort to the implementation of a specific security measure was necessary to protect Palestinians. They also underscored even though the impact of this measure was harsh, there was no better alternative capable of resulting in less harm for them or their property.[174]

In response to claims of a more procedural nature, the government also argued that Israeli MOs in force in the occupied territory authorized the MC to restrict movement within the occupied territory in the absence of a written

167 *Morar* Judgment, *supra* note 82 at para 13. See also *Abu Safiyeh* Judgment, *supra* note 140 at para 9; *Mayor of Ad-Dhahiriya* Judgment, *supra* note 131 at paras 10 and 15.

168 *Dir Samit Village* Judgement, *supra* note 138 at para 8. See also *Abu Safiyeh* Judgment, *supra* note 140 at para 35; *Haas* Judgment, *supra* note 130 at para 1; *Bethlehem Municipality* Judgment, *supra* note 1 at para 7.

169 *Mayor of Ad-Dhahiriya* Judgment, *supra* note 131 at paras 10 and 11; *Dir Samit Village* Judgement, *supra* note 138 at paras 8–9.

170 *Haas* Judgment, *supra* note 130 at para 4.

171 *Abu Safiyeh* Judgment, *supra* note 140 at para 9. *Dir Samit Village* Judgment, *supra* note 138 at paras 8–9. *Haas* Judgment, *supra* note 130 at para 5.

172 *Abu Safiyeh* Judgment, *supra* note 140 at paras 8, 9, 13 and 34.

173 *Bethlehem Municipality* Judgment, *supra* note 1 at paras 2, 3, 7 and 18.

174 In the *Morar* case, government authorities argued that, since the Palestinian farmers often suffered from harassment by Israeli settlers, particularly during the olive-harvesting seasons, closing off the area to those farmers is the only viable means for ensuring their safety. *Morar* Judgment, *supra* note 82 at para 23.

order.[175] They also underscored that the challenged roads were built (for the most part) on 'state land', or that they would only be used by the security personnel of the settlement.[176]

In other cases, most notably *Head of Beit Iksa Council*, the respondents provided a variety of arguments to justify the requisitioning of land for the building of an alternative road to service emergency rescue operations that may be necessary during the construction of the railway.[177] First, they argued that the Occupying Power can implement measures to ensure the safety of its citizens in the West Bank. Second, they alleged that under international law, the MC was authorized to use property of the occupied territory and to reap its benefits, as long as the residents of the occupied territory also benefit.[178] Hence, the utility of the measure should be:

> [...] examined from a broad perspective in which the railroad is seen as a single component of an overall plan for a regional steel railway, including such that would allow connecting the Judea and Samaria Area to the railway infrastructure inside Israel [...].[179]

The HCJ's interpretation of key aspects of article 43 of the Hague Regulations

The Court has gradually expanded the authority of the MC to implement a wide spectrum of measures for the declared purpose of promoting the welfare of the 'local population'. This it has done by relaxing the definition of 'local population' to include, other than the 'protected persons' (i.e. the Palestinians), the Israeli settler population. Moreover, it has maintained that, in light of the prolonged nature of Israel's occupation, the MC can introduce institutional and legislative changes of a more profound nature in the occupied territory. This is despite the fact that there is no distinct category of 'prolonged occupation' in the law of belligerent occupation.[180]

175 Section 88 of the MO *regarding Defense Regulations (Judea and Samaria) (No. 378) 5730–1970. Dir Samit Village* Judgment, *supra* note 138 at paras 5 and 7. In other instances they highlighted that a retroactive written authorization had been issued, thereby rendering the petitioners' argument regarding the procedural flaws redundant. *Abu Safiyeh* Judgment, *supra* note 140 at para 8; *Morar* Judgment, *supra* note 82 at para 11.

176 In the *Dir Qadis* case, they maintained that the road built to service the settlement of *Nili* was on 'state land'. They also pointed out that, even though the roadwork had not fulfilled planning and construction requirements, it would only be used by the security personnel of that settlement. *Second Dir Qadis Village Council* Judgment, *supra* note 136 at paras 2–3.

177 *Beit Iksa* Judgment, *supra* note 137 at paras 2–3 and 7.

178 Ibid. at para 10.

179 Ibid. at para 7.

180 The HCJ began referring to 'prolonged occupation' just over four years after the Israeli occupation of the West Bank had begun. See (HCJ 337/71) [1972] *Christian Society for the Holy Places v. Minister of Defense* (1972) 2 Isr YB Hum Rts 354 [*Christian Society* Judgment – Summary].

On the interests guiding the lawful actions of the military commander

In 1972, the *Christian Society Place* judgment was the first landmark decision requiring the Court to interpret article 43 of the Hague Regulations.[181] In this case, a Palestinian charitable society with headquarters in the United States of America had challenged the decision of the Israeli MC for the West Bank to amend Jordanian labour laws in effect in the West Bank, to facilitate the settlement of a labour dispute through the use of compulsory arbitration.[182] Petitioners argued that the MC had exceeded the scope of his legislative powers under article 43 of the Hague Regulations, obligating him to respect the local laws in force in the occupied territory, 'unless absolutely prevented'.[183]

In its judgment, the HCJ reiterated that under article 43, the MC's duty revolved around two axes: the need to ensure the legitimate security interests of the Occupying Power and its forces in the territory under belligerent occupation; and the obligation to respond to the needs and interests of the 'local population' 'and to ensure its "civil life"'.[184] It also reiterated that the French version of article 43 was the authoritative one.[185]

In another case, *Abu Aita*, the Court was tasked with ruling on the legality of the MC's decision to impose the value added tax (VAT) in the oPt, in conjunction with a decision to impose it in Israel proper.[186] After 1967, government authorities had devised and implemented 'numerous policy measures aimed at increasing the level of physical integration between Israel and the occupied territory primarily through the creation of a common market'.[187] This allowed the occupied territories to continue to exist in principle as a separate economic entity, 'while practically speaking, ensuring that it becomes fully integrated within that of Israel'.[188]

181 *Christian Society* Judgment – Summary, *supra* note 180. See also Sharon Weill, *The Role of National Courts in Applying International Humanitarian Law* (Oxford: Oxford University Press, 2014.

182 *Christian Society* Judgment – Summary, *supra* note 180 at 344–345.

183 Ibid. at 354–355.

184 Ibid. at 355. See also the (HCJ 256/72) [1972] Electric *Corporation for Jerusalem District LTD v. Minister of Defense* 5 Isr YB Hum Rts 381 at 383 [*Electric Corporation* Judgment – Summary]; *Iskan* Judgment, *supra* note 154 at para 16.

185 Therefore, the term 'safety' in this article is more precisely translated as 'civil life', which refers to the 'whole commercial, economic and social life'. Sharon Weill, *The Role of National Courts*, *supra* note 181.

186 The decision was imposed by way of an MO. See (HCJ 69/81) [1981] *Bassel Abu Aita v. the Regional Commander of Judea and Samaria*, unofficial English translation, online: *Hamoked* www.hamoked.org/files/2011/290_eng.pdf [*Abu Aita* Judgment].

187 Eyal Benvenisti, *The International Law of Occupation*, *supra* note 13 at 123–134.

188 The dependency was enhanced by interconnecting all roads, electricity, water and communication grids. Meron Benvenisti, *The West Bank Data Project*, *supra* note 123 at 9. This continued until the 1980s, when Israel adopted a policy of separating from the Palestinians. Neve Gordon, 'From Colonization to Separation: Exploring the Structure of Israel's Occupation', in Adi Ophir, Michal Givoni and Sari Hanafi, eds, *The Power of Inclusive Exclusion: Anatomy of Israeli Rule in the Occupied Palestinian Territories* (New York: Zone Books, 2009) 239.

In its judgment, the justices explained that they will not consider legislative changes implemented in response to legitimate security needs or to further the welfare of the 'local population' to be a violation of the law of belligerent occupation, just because the MC had not been 'absolutely prevented' from making those changes.[189] In addressing the criteria which 'absolutely prevent' an MC from introducing amendments, Justice Shamgar noted that they:

> [...] arise from the legitimate interests of the military government and the maintenance of public order, or from *interests of concern for the local population* [emphasis added] and the assurance of its public life, all, of course, whilst maintaining a reasonable balance between the considerations [...].[190]

The Court then ruled that imposing an additional tax in the occupied territory conforms with article 43 of the Hague Regulations if they proved necessary.[191]

In a subsequent case, *Iskan*, the Court interpreted the MC's duty to restore and ensure 'public order and safety' as stipulated by article 43 to amount to a twofold duty on the MC: first, to restore 'public order and safety' in places where it had been interrupted and, second, to ensure the continued existence of 'public order and safety' in situations in which 'these had not been disrupted, or where 'public order and safety' had already been restored'.[192] According to the Court, this can encompass all aspects of public order and safety and can apply to a variety of civilian issues, such as economy, society, education, welfare[193] and transportation.[194] Otherwise, the MC will not be able to respond to the constant changing needs of the inhabitants of the occupied territory,[195] and to address the needs arising in a situation of prolonged occupation.[196] At the same time, and given that occupation is inherently a temporary situation, the justices underscored that:[197]

189 David Kretzmer, 'The Law of Belligerent Occupation and the Supreme Court', *supra* note 14.

190 *Abu Aita* Judgment, *supra* note 186 at 129 and 130.

191 Ibid. See also an English summary in (HCJ 69/81) [1981] *Bassel Abu Aita v. the Regional Commander of Judea and Samaria*, English summary in 13 Isr YB Hum Rts 348 [*Abu Aita* Judgment – Summary].

192 *Iskan* Judgment, *supra* note 154 at paras 18 and 25.

193 Ibid. at para 18. This is because the original French version of this provision refers to: 'l'ordre et la vie publics', which has a wider meaning than the equivalent English term 'public order'. It includes all social, commercial and economic life of the community. *Abu Aita* Judgment, *supra* note 186 at para 35. In another case, the Court reiterated that the term 'public order and safety' encompasses 'all its agencies' practices in a civilized country'. *Iskan* Judgment, *supra* note 154 at para 18. This idea was first spelled out by the Court in the *Tabib* Judgment, *supra* note 125.

194 In the *Tabib* Judgment, the HCJ concluded that the term 'public life' includes proper administration of all its branches in a well-functioning country, such as health, welfare and quality of life and transportation. *Tabib* Judgment – Summary, *supra* note 125.

195 *Iskan* Judgment, *supra* note 154 at paras 21–22.

196 Ibid. at para 26. The idea was initially elaborated in the *Christian Society* Judgment – Summary, *supra* note 180.

197 *Iskan* Judgment, *supra* note 154 at paras 20 and 23–24.

> The military commander *may not weigh the national, economic and social interests of his own country* [emphasis added], insofar as they do not affect his security interest in the Area or the interest of the local population [...]. Military necessities *are his military needs and not the needs of national security in the broader sense* [emphasis added].[198]

Years later, the Court relied on this concept to rule that the MC's decision to purchase the undertaking of Jerusalem District Electricity Company relative to the West Bank was null and void. This was the case because the modifications which he introduced by purchasing the company were too far-reaching to amount to a legitimate action under international law. The government argued that the reason they had submitted a notice of purchase of the company's undertaking in the West Bank was to ensure the proper administration of vital services to the 'local population'. The Court rejected this argument, explaining that:

> [G]enerally, in the absence of special circumstances, the Commander of the region should not introduce in an occupied area modifications which, even if they do not alter the existing law, would have far-reaching and prolonged impact on it, far beyond the period when the military administration will be terminated one way or another, save for actions undertaken for the benefit of the inhabitants of the area.[199]

However, this 'decision was a voice in the wilderness'.[200] Over the years, the important principle that had been developed by the Court in the *Iskan* judgment lost much of its significance because of two elements: (a) the willingness of the Court to grant a wider interpretation to the authority of the MC to enact changes under article 43 of the Hague Regulations due to the long-term nature of the occupation; and (b) the Court's decision to uphold the government's interpretation of the term 'local population' to include the Israeli settler population.

The authority of the military commander to effect changes in a situation of 'prolonged occupation'

The *Christian Society Place* judgment, rendered less than a decade after Israel's occupation of the West Bank began, highlights the evolution in the Court's approach regarding the lawful considerations that can guide the MC's decision under international customary law. Addressing the legality of the MC's decision

198 Ibid. at para 13.

199 (HCJ 351/80) [1980] *Jerusalem District Electricity Company Ltd. v. Minister of Energy and Infrastructure et al.* (1981) 11 Isr YB Hum Rts 354 at 357 [*Jerusalem District Electricity Company* Judgment – Summary].

200 David Kretzmer, 'The Law of Belligerent Occupation and the Supreme Court', *supra* note 14 at 219.

to amend the Jordanian labour law by way of an MO, the justices noted that the prohibition on his ability to do so unless 'absolutely prevented' must be interpreted in a manner that allows him to respond to the changing economic, commercial and social needs of the 'local population'. Since, in a prolonged occupation, those needs are constantly evolving, he may adapt local laws to those evolving needs. Consequently the justices ruled that by promulgating an MO that led to the appointment of a person in the arbitration council, the MC had acted within the scope of his authority under international law.[201] Noteworthy is that a minority opinion disagreed, noting that the authority of the occupant must remain focused on restoring public order and civil life to the status quo ante (i.e. to restore it to the level that had existed before the beginning of Israel's occupation of the West Bank), and not on bringing about a novel situation that had not existed in the occupied territory prior to the MC's decision.[202]

Similarly, in the *Electric Corporation* judgment, the justices reiterated that military authorities must respect the laws in force in the occupied territory, unless 'absolutely prevented'.[203] In this specific case, the petitioners had challenged the MC's decision to have electricity needs in the city of Hebron be supplied through the Israeli Electric Corporation on the ground that this runs counter to an existing Jordanian law. Since the Court had concluded that the MC's duties under international law include the need to respond to the needs of the 'local population', it upheld the MC's decision to amend the law.[204] As the Court elaborated elsewhere, the longer the duration of the military occupation, the more extensive are the obligations that arise for the MC,[205] on the ground that the 'time element is a factor affecting the scope of the powers, whether we regard military needs, or whether we regard the needs of the territory, or maintain equilibrium between them'.[206]

The aforementioned *Iskan* case provided the Court with another opportunity to develop its interpretation of the scope of the MC's duty under article 43 of the Hague Regulations. In this case, the requisitioning of land for the construction of road 443 was presented as a necessary step in response to an out-of-date road system. Military authorities argued that the main objective of the plan was to serve the Palestinian local population.[207] This was challenged by the

201 The petition was dismissed. *Christian Society* Judgment – Summary, *supra* note 180 at 355.

202 *Christian Society* Judgment – Summary, *supra* note 180 at 355–356.

203 *Electric Corporation* Judgment – Summary, *supra* note 184 at 381. As the Court explains, under article 43 of the Hague Regulations the 'existing laws in the occupied territory may not be altered unless a legislative change is required in order to realize the powers of the military government (whether on the civilian or military level'. *Iskan* Judgment, *supra* note 154 at para 17.

204 *Electric Corporation* Judgment – Summary, *supra* note 184 at 383.

205 *Abu Aita* Judgment, *supra* note 186 at 134.

206 Ibid. at 134.

207 *Iskan* Judgment, *supra* note 154 at para 5. The Interchange would connect between two highways to be built in the West Bank. The same road became the subject of the petition in the *Abu Safiyeh* Judgment, *supra* note 140.

Palestinian petitioners, who argued that, under the temporary nature requirement underlying the normative framework of the law of occupation, an Occupying Power 'is not permitted to plan, and implement an action, which creates permanent facts, that are designed to continue to exist following the termination of military rule in the Area'.[208]

In its judgment, the Court first determined whether the MC had the authority to plan and implement a civilian project in the West Bank, if it was not driven by military considerations. This was necessary, given that the road creation would result in 'long-term permanent ramifications, [which continue] sometimes beyond the limits of the term of the military government itself'.[209] Then it pointed out that although the Hague Regulations were formulated 'against the backdrop of a short-term occupation',[210] 'in a "long-term" military occupation, the needs of the "local population" receive extra validity',[211] and required investments in all domains of life.[212]

Addressing the legality of constructing the road, the Court accepted at face value that the development of the road had been carried out for the benefit of the Palestinians. Hence, even though the infrastructural changes would result in permanent changes that are likely to outlast the end of the occupation itself, they were not illegal. In justifying his decision, Justice Barak argued that the changes fulfilled two criteria: (i) 'they are reasonably required for the needs of the local population'[213] and (ii) they do not 'bring about a substantive change in the fundamental institutions of the Area'.[214] The Court subsequently upheld the requisition order and dismissed the petition.[215]

In the more recent *Naale Association* judgment,[216] the Court examined a petition filed by Israelis from the settlements of Naale and Nili, which challenged the legality of the CA's decision to allow an Israeli company to build and operate a nearby quarry.[217] Petitioners maintained that, under article 55 of

208 *Iskan* Judgment, *supra* note 154 at para 8.
209 Ibid. at para 16.
210 Ibid. at para 22.
211 Ibid. at para 22.
212 Ibid. at para 26.
213 Ibid. at para 27.
214 Ibid. at para 27.
215 However, compensation must be paid and the right to a fair hearing must be granted (prior to expropriation), in line with the requirements of Israeli administrative law. *Iskan* Judgment, *supra* note 154 at paras 31 and 37.
216 (HCJ 9717/03) [2004] *Naale – Association for Settlement in Samaria of Employees of the Israel Aerospace Industries et al. v. the Civil Administration for Judea and Samaria et al.*, unofficial English translation, online: *Hamoked* www.hamoked.org/items/112080_eng.pdf [*Naale Association* Judgment]. The petition was dismissed by the Court.
217 The settlers contended that the decision to establish a quarry would undermine the quality of their life, because of the noise and pollution that would result from its operation. The Mining and Excavation Committee decided to approve the plan while imposing various limitations and determining specific conditions regarding the operation of the quarry. *Naale Association* Judgment, *supra* note 216 at paras 1–3 and 7.

the Hague Regulations, the Occupying Power was prohibited from utilizing local resources of the occupied territory for its own benefit. Hence, the decision to build a quarry was also not consistent with the limited authorization of the MC under the international customary law (to administer and generate fruit).[218] The justices disagreed. In addressing the legality of the action under the Hague Regulations, the justices explained that although they were:

> [...] [d]eveloped against the background of various wars which led to the belligerent occupation lasting a relatively short period of time [...] there appears to be a justification to acknowledging that the occupying state [during a long-term occupation] is entitled to make moves which can have a long-term effect on the area which is under belligerent occupation.[219]

The petition was dismissed.[220]

The notion of 'local population'

In examining this element, the *Electric Corporation* judgment sheds light on the HCJ's interpretation of the notion of 'local population'. To determine the scope of the MC's duty to provide for the welfare of that population, it concluded that the Israeli residents of the settlement of Kiryat Arba are also part of the 'local population' in the occupied territory and that therefore, the MC was obliged to provide them with a regular supply of electricity.[221]

In the aforementioned *Na'ale Association* judgment, the Court initially admitted that excavation acts cannot be included within the scope of the MC's prerogatives, because of their tendency to deplete natural resources of the occupied territory. However, it subsequently concluded that, given that the material extracted from the quarries would go towards construction works in the West Bank settlements and since Israeli settlers are part of the 'local population', the MC's decision meets the test of benefiting the 'local population' and does not violate article 55 of the Hague Regulations.[222]

The welfare and interests of the 'local population': must they be a primary consideration?

An analysis of earlier landmark judgments indicates that the Court has generally upheld the decision of the MC to implement measures that might be driven by

218 *Naale Association* Judgment, *supra* note 216 at para 6.
219 Ibid. at para 6.
220 Ibid. at para 8.
221 David Kretzmer, 'The Law of Belligerent Occupation and the Supreme Court', *supra* note 14.
222 *Naale Association* Judgment, *supra* note 216 at para 6.

non-security objectives (such as servicing its own nationals) provided that the dominant factor guiding the measure was the security or welfare of the 'local population'.[223]

Again in the *Abu Aita* judgment, the Court appears to sanction the efforts of government authorities to create (at the time) a common market consisting of the economies of both Israel and the oPt, noting in this regard that 'to separate them [...] would impede the possibility of return to orderly life and prevent the effective observance of the duty regarding the assurance of "la vie publique"'.[224] The justices also accepted the claim advanced by government authorities that uncoupling those two economies would be detrimental first and foremost to the Palestinian local population.[225] Once again, the justices suggested that one relevant criterion which would guide their determination of whether genuine considerations for the welfare of the civilian population had spearheaded the proposed amendments to local laws is whether or not authorities would have implemented the measure in Israel proper out of a similar concern for the welfare of its own population.[226] However, the Court's approach was criticized for sidelining how beneficial the integration was primarily to the Israeli economy and Israeli citizens, but not necessarily as beneficial for the occupied Palestinian population.[227]

In a second case, the petitioners argued that the road which Israeli authorities had sought to build, mainly served the transportation needs of the Israelis going to and from Israeli cities to the West Bank and that, therefore, it had 'nothing to do with the benefit of the Area'.[228] Government authorities, for their part, remained adamant that 'the benefit of the [Palestinian local] population stands at the center of this plan',[229] thereby rendering the relevant land requisition order lawful.[230] At the same time, the respondents did not refute the fact that:

> [...] this plan is connected to planning inside Israel, it takes it into consideration and forms a joint project for Israel and the Area. It [the plan]

223 *Christian Society* Judgment – Summary, *supra* note 180 at 355. This test was recognized explicitly in the *Elon Moreh* Judgment, where the HCJ used the test to determine that the claimed interest of government authorities (security) had been secondary to the main and illegal interest (of a political nature). 'Expert Legal Opinion (HCJ 2164/09) [2011] Yesh Din *Volunteers for Human Rights v. Commander of IDF Forces in Judea and Samaria* (December 26 2011)', at para 43, online: *Yesh Din* https://s3-eu-west-1.amazonaws.com/files.yesh-din.org/עתירות/מחצבות/Quarries+Expert+Opinion+English.pdf [*Quarry* Case – Expert Legal Opinion].

224 *Abu Aita* Judgment, *supra* note 186 at 143.

225 Ibid. at 143.

226 In other words, the litmus test would be to establish 'whether the military government is filled with the same concern in regard to its *own people* and applies the same measures taken in the area of military government in its own area'. *Abu Aita* Judgment, *supra* note 186 at 136.

227 Eyal Benvenisti, *The International Law of Occupation*, *supra* note 13 at 142–144.

228 *Iskan* Judgment, *supra* note 154 at para 7.

229 Ibid. at para 5.

230 Ibid. at para 6.

> ***will serve not only the residents of the Area but also residents of Israel and the traffic between Judea and Samaria and Israel*** [emphasis added].[231]

Therefore, despite strong indications by the respondents regarding some of the considerations driving the construction of the road,[232] Justice Barak (writing the opinion) accepted the assertion that the civilian needs of the Palestinian local population did indeed constitute the dominant consideration guiding the decision of the authorities to build the road.[233] This is true even though the action being challenged admittedly also served Israeli nationals.[234]

The same approach was adopted by the HCJ in a third case, that of *Beit Iksa Council*. Having initially decided to reject the petition,[235] the Court subsequently decided to determine whether or not the petition 'should be heard despite its late submission'.[236] Addressing in the first place the petitioners' argument that by connecting Tel Aviv and Jerusalem, the construction of the railway had amounted to an illegal action under international law,[237] the justices reiterated that 'the military government may not implement a road system in an area held under belligerent occupation, if the purpose had been to provide a 'service road' *for its own state* [emphasis added]'.[238] This, it argued, was not lawful since:

> There is also no dispute that expropriating lands for the purpose of a project that would serve only residents of a country who do not live in the territory under belligerent occupation contravenes international law and as such exceeds the competency of the military commander.[239]

The Court then addressed the requisition and whether or not the fact that, in addition to the Palestinian local population, Israeli travellers were also benefiting from this measure could render it lawful under international law. Here, the justices did not to elaborate on whether or not the interests of the former (i.e. the Palestinians) must constitute the primary consideration, noting that it was not entirely clear whether:

231 Ibid. at para 8.

232 In this regard, the Court explained that '[a]lthough the development of the Area for the benefit of the population therein stands at the centre of his plan [...] [*i*]*t will serve not only the residents of the Area, but also residents of Israel and the traffic between Judea and Samaria and Israel* [emphasis added]'. *Iskan* Judgment, *supra* note 154 at para 5.

233 *Iskan* Judgment, *supra* note 154 at paras 9 and 14–16.

234 David Kretzmer, 'The Law of Belligerent Occupation and the Supreme Court', *supra* note 14.

235 This was because of the petitioners' delay in submitting the petition in a timely fashion amounted to a subjective and objective delay. *Beit Iksa* Judgment, *supra* note 137 at paras 12–22.

236 *Beit Iksa* Judgment, *supra* note 137 at para 24.

237 Petitioners pointed to the lack of any railway stations in the West Bank as proof that it was not meant to serve their needs as was claimed. *Beit Iksa* Judgment, *supra* note 137 at para 27.

238 *Iskan* Judgment, *supra* note 154 at para 13 cited by the HCJ in *Beit Iksa* Judgment, *supra* note 137 at para 26.

239 *Beit Iksa* Judgment, *supra* note 137 at para 27.

> [...] land expropriation in the Judea and Samaria Area for a purpose that serves *both protected persons and Israelis living inside the Green Line* [emphasis added] [can] be considered as ensuring the needs of the population in the territory held under belligerent occupation[.][240]

To bolster their conclusion, they highlighted that government authorities had declared that they would ensure that the Palestinian population would benefit from the overall project, and that future plans would link the West Bank to the railway infrastructure inside Israel.[241] Finally, they declined to rule on the merits of the petition,[242] thereby forfeiting an important opportunity to provide legal accuracy on this matter.

The fourth case relevant to our discussion is the *Quarries* judgment.[243] This concerned a petition filed by the Israeli human rights NGO *Yesh Din* against the government and 10 Israeli quarries operating in the West Bank.[244] Most of the quarried material had been transported into Israel proper. Moreover, the CA had been collecting significant payments (which included leasing fees and royalties) from these quarries.[245] Petitioners argued that article 55 of the Hague Regulations allows the occupant to manage and yield fruit from the quarries for the benefit of the 'protected persons',[246] except when their exhaustion or use is required for security reasons.[247] Therefore, even if during a prolonged occupation the occupying power was entitled to mine resources in a way that causes damage to the capital,[248] this still could not take place 'to benefit the occupying

240 Ibid. at para 27.

241 *Beit Iksa* Judgment, *supra* note 137 at paras 29–32.

242 This is because 'the extent of this harm does not exceed the harm that would be caused to the interests of the railway, third parties and the public interest in a manner that would justify hearing the petition despite its late submission' *Beit Iksa* Judgment, *supra* note 137 at paras 27, 28 and 32.

243 *Quarry* Judgment, *supra* note 15.

244 An estimated 94 per cent of the production of the active private Israeli quarries operating in that area had been transported within the border of Israel proper. *Quarry* Case – Government Response 2010, *supra* note 71.

245 The total amount of royalties paid in 2009 for the exploitation of the quarries stood at approximately 25 million NIS [New Israeli Shekels]. See *Quarry* Judgment, *supra* note 15 at para 1.

246 Article 55 of the Hague Regulations *supra* note 11 cited in the *Quarry* Judgment, *supra* note 15 at para 3.

247 *Quarry* Case – Petition, *supra* note 24 at paras 46, 48, 53, 54, 56.

248 Petitioners acknowledged that there exist more lenient interpretations, certainly in the context of long-term occupation, which allows for a limited use of natural resources in the occupied territory as a way of addressing the gap between the permission to use the fruit of public property on the one hand, and the ban on the exploitation of non-renewable material, on the other. They cited the writings of some scholars who have called for the adherence to a principle *of continuity*, whereby the occupier can exploit the mineral resources at the same pace that had existed prior to the beginning of the occupation. However, that use must still respect the rules of occupation: observing the administrative trust and adhering to the usufructuary rules. *Quarry* Case – Petition, *supra* note 24 at para 70. The production of new minerals is prohibited. *Quarry* Judgment, *supra* note 15 at para 8.

power or any other body that is not the occupied people'.[249] Since the mining is yielding products that almost exclusively serve the population of the occupying power and its economic needs, the measures, they argued, were illegal under international law.[250]

The respondents acknowledged that most of the quarried material from the Israeli-operated quarries in the West Bank was being transferred into Israel proper and announced that they would freeze the establishment of any new quarries that would produce quarrying material for the sale thereof inside or to the country.[251] In addition, they noted that some of the quarried material had in any case been allocated for use inside the occupied territory (including for the use by Israeli settlements). On the merits, the respondent also argued that, given the prolonged nature of the Israeli occupation, the interpretation of article 43 of the Hague Regulations must consider the unique circumstances of that situation.[252] Hence, a broader interpretation of this article, they argued, is warranted: one that would allow the Occupying Power to exploit new minerals in an occupied territory as long as this did not exhaust the capital in question.[253] Moreover, the respondents sought to demonstrate that the activities were contributing to the economic development and modernization of the West Bank and that they served as a source of livelihood for the Palestinians employed therein.[254]

After contemplating the possibility of rejecting the petition on preliminary grounds,[255] the Court nevertheless decided to address it on its merits.[256] Addressing the relevance of article 55 of the Hague Regulations, it reiterated that the occupant's administration of public property might not result in the depletion or the exhaustion of the exploited natural resource. However, as long as quarrying was not exhausting the resource, its use by the Occupying Power remained lawful, even if that usage took place outside the boundaries of the occupied territory.[257] And while the Court did acknowledge that it was debatable whether the occupant could undertake quarrying activities of new resources, it noted that the resource exploitation did not amount to a depletion of the mine. Taking into consideration that the government had committed itself to refraining from establishing new quarries, the Court then concluded that the respondent's interpretation of article 55 of the Hague Regulations was reasonable.[258]

249 *Quarry* Case – Petition *supra* note 24 at para 92.
250 Ibid. at paras 44, 65 and 75. See also *Quarry* Judgment, *supra* note 15 at paras 1–3.
251 *Quarry* Judgment – Government Response 2010, *supra* note 71 at para 77.
252 *Quarry* Judgment, *supra* note 15 at paras 4, 8 and 9.
253 *Quarry* Case – Government Response 2010, *supra* note 71 at paras 41–43, 52–54.
254 Ibid. at paras 5, 54 and 55.
255 *Quarry* Judgment, *supra* note 15 at para 6.
256 'So finally the case was not exactly deemed to be not justiciable due to the political nature'. Written response by Israeli Attorney A03-B to Questionnaire by author via Avichay Sharon (10 July 2014) at 2, [Attorney *A 03-B* Written Submission].
257 *Quarry* Judgment, *supra* note 15 at paras 7 and 8.
258 Ibid. at paras 11 and 12.

More significantly, the Court consolidated its earlier interpretation that the MC enjoys a considerably wider scope of authority to enact measures for the alleged benefit of the 'local population' during a situation of prolonged occupation. Thus, even if the benefit accruing to the 'protected persons' is a side result of a given measure implemented by the MC rather than the direct objective, this did not render the measure unlawful.[259] To support this conclusion, three elements were highlighted: that some of the quarried stone was used by the 'local population', a notion, which legitimately also included the Israeli settlers; that the quarries provided employment opportunities to a significant number of Palestinians; and that royalties paid to the CA by the operators of the quarry were being used to finance the administration and projects of the Israeli military authorities in the West Bank for the benefit of the Palestinians. The justices concluded that the measure was indeed in 'the best interests of the Area [...]'[260] and dismissed the petition.[261]

Concluding observations

The Court can be commended for spelling out in theory, that the MC cannot be guided by national, economic or social interests of his own country when introducing changes that are lawful under article 43 of the Hague Regulations. However, the Court's approach must be criticized for relaxing the limitations placed on the MC's authority under customary international law.[262] This is because the Court adopted an approach of not questioning more rigorously whether the interests of the Palestinian population constituted the dominant factor spearheading the measure's implementation. This allowed illegal considerations (most notably in the form of the economic interests of the Occupying Power) to filter into the MC's decision to implement this activity, without much judicial scrutiny.[263] It also permitted the MC to take into account the interests of third parties (such as the quarrying companies in

259 David Kretzmer, 'The Law of Belligerent Occupation and the Supreme Court', *supra* note 14.

260 *Quarry* Judgment, *supra* note 15 at para 13.

261 On 10 January 2012, *Yesh Din* submitted a request to the Court to hold a further hearing, arguing that the judgment was both erroneous and dangerous and likely to implicate Israel in the commission of grave violations of the provisions of IHL applicable to the Occupied Territories. *Yesh Din*, 'Legality of Quarry Activity in the West Bank', (9 March 2009), online: *Yesh Din* https://web.archive.org/web/20120317160014/http://yesh-din.org/infoitem.asp?infocatid=15. The HCJ dismissed the request of the NGO to reopen the case on procedural ground. Since the petition had been rejected outright, there was no need to re-examine the ruling. However, it also noted that 'nothing prevents future petitioners from raising these arguments again in the future, especially in the case of a petition against opening a new quarry'. Written response by Attorney *A 03-B*-Written Submission, *supra* note 256.

262 Eyal Benvenisti, 'Water Conflicts during the Occupation of Iraq', *supra* note 25.

263 Even though several factors had indicated that at best, the interests of the Palestinian local population are subordinate to the interests of Israel.

the *Quarry* case), even though their interests do not constitute a legitimate consideration for the MC under the law of occupation.[264]

A second element characterizing the Court's approach is that Israeli settlers were deemed part and parcel of the 'local population', whose interests (in addition to their security) the MC is entitled to take into consideration under article 43. This took place even though 'the Israeli settlers are not mentioned directly or indirectly as beneficiaries of the occupation by article 43 of the Hague Regulations'.[265] Such an interpretation, 'smacks of a colonial approach, under which the activities of the colonial power are claimed to bring benefit to the colonized peoples'.[266] Furthermore, it has watered down the consideration that the MC must grant to the rights of the 'protected persons' (the Palestinians).[267] It has also undermined the very rationale guiding this provision and 'which was meant to protect the interests of the community of occupied civilians'.[268]

Third, this approach has considerably widened the scope of the MC's authority under article 43 of the Hague Regulations to implement significant changes in the occupied West Bank, all in the name of promoting the welfare, rights and security of the Israeli settler as part of the 'local population'. In addition to amending existing local laws for purposes beyond what is permissible under the law of belligerent occupation (for immediate security needs and/or the welfare of the 'protected persons'), the Court's approach has left the door wide open for national laws of the Occupying Power to be duplicated in the occupied territory in a manner that is resulting in the 'assimilation of the legal landscape of the two regions'.[269]

Whose 'rights', and which 'local population'? Adjudicating security-related petitions in light of article 43 of the Hague Regulations

The source of the military commander's authority: the normative framework

The HCJ has emphasized that the West Bank is under a regime of belligerent occupation, and that as the 'long arm of the State', the MC derives his powers from:

264 The NIS 25 million/year which government authorities declared that they would transfer to the CA are only part of an estimated benefit of USD90 million/year. This underscores that the larger part of the royalties has still been allocated towards the interests of the Occupying Power outside the occupied territory. There was also no guarantee that they would be used only to fund projects for the benefit of the Palestinian population, as opposed to the mere operation of the CA. *Quarry* – Expert Legal Opinion, *supra* note 223 at paras 5, 59 and 61.

265 *Quarry* – Expert Legal Opinion, *supra* note 223 at para 33.

266 David Kretzmer, 'The Law of Belligerent Occupation and the Supreme Court', *supra* note 14 at 222.

267 Ibid.

268 *Quarry* Case – petition, *supra* note 24 at para 99.

269 Eyal Benvenisti, *The International Law of Occupation*, *supra* note 13 at 16.

> [T]he rules of public international law relating to belligerent occupation; from local laws in effect in the Area which comprise of the law prior to the military occupation; from new local statutes enacted by the military administration; and from the principles of Israeli law.[270]

It has also reiterated that the main norms applicable are the Hague Regulations, which reflect customary international law and the customary provisions of both the Fourth Geneva Convention and of the First Additional Protocol to the Geneva Conventions, which have become part of Israeli law.[271] At the same time, it has maintained its refusal to rule on the *de jure* applicability of the Fourth Geneva Convention, emphasizing instead the government's willingness to uphold the humanitarian provisions of this Convention.[272]

In the case of international human rights law (IHR law), although the Court has, to date, not ruled on its applicability to the occupied territory, in some of the decisions it has explained that 'where there is a gap in the aforesaid laws of armed conflict, it may be completed from within international human rights law'.[273] It has also alluded to specific IHR treaties and conventions.[274] Still, in other decisions, the Court has underscored IHR law as the normative source for these rights (in tandem) with Israeli law.[275] The Court has also maintained that, in addition to international law and local law, the applicable legal framework consists of 'fundamental principles of Israeli administrative law, [...] including the norms of fairness, reasonableness and proportionality that are to be exercised when using power',[276] and that accordingly, the MC must strike a balance 'between individual liberty and the public interest, all whilst taking security needs into account'.[277]

It is interesting to note that in petitions where the interests/rights of Israelis were at stake and where they had to be balanced against the rights of the Palestinians, the justices stressed that the rights enjoyed by both populations were fundamental rights, which are protected by Israeli constitutional law.[278] Moreover, they have often embarked on a constitutional balancing between

270 *Abu Safiyeh* Judgment, *supra* note 140 at para 14; *Morar* Judgment, *supra* note 82 at para 12.

271 *Abu Safiyeh* Judgment *supra* note 140 at para 16. See also *Dir Samit Village* Judgment, *supra* note 138 at para 10.

272 *Haas* Judgment, *supra* note 130 at para 8 and *Dir Samit Village* Judgment, *supra* note 138 at para 10.

273 *Abu Safiyeh* Judgment, *supra* note 140 at para 16. See also *Dir Samit Village* Judgment, *supra* note 138 at para 10.

274 Such as the ICCPR. See *Dir Samit Village* Judgment, *supra* note 138 at paras 10 and 17.

275 In one case, the Palestinians' right to freedom of movement was referred to as a fundamental right enshrined in both Israeli law and IHR law. *Dir Samit Village* Judgment, *supra* note 138 at para 17.

276 *Beit Iksa* Judgment, *supra* note 137 at para 25. *Abu Safiyeh* Judgment, *supra* note 140 at para 14; *Haas* Judgment, *supra* note 130 at para 8; *Morar* Judgment, *supra* note 82 at para 10.

277 *Dir Samit Village* Judgment, *supra* note 138 at para 11. See also *Bethlehem Municipality* Judgment, *supra* note 1 at paras 8 and 9.

278 Yaël Ronen, 'Applicability of Basic Law: Human Dignity and Freedom in the West Bank', (2013) 46 Isr LR 135.

these rights as a way of determining whether the restrictions on the rights of the Palestinian petitioners for the sake of the realization of the rights of the Israelis had been warranted.

However, the Court's invocation of Israeli constitutional law, as well as its interchangeable reference to this body of law and to other normative frameworks (Israeli administrative law, IHL, IHR law) has not been consistent.[279] In some cases the Court has stressed that the rights enjoyed by Palestinians and Israelis were constitutional rights and expressly referred to Israeli constitutional law.[280] In other instances, the Court explained that there was no need to address the applicability of basic constitutional rights since the restricted rights of the Palestinians were also entrenched in international law.[281] Still elsewhere (such as in the *Morar* judgment), the Court held that the rights enjoyed by the Palestinian petitioners were not only basic rights at the heart of the international law of belligerent occupation, but were also rights that were enshrined in, and protected by, Israeli constitutional law.[282] The lack of clarity is compounded by the fact that the Court has upheld the applicability of the Basic Law: *Human Dignity and Liberty in personae* to Israeli settlers in the West Bank.[283] In this regard, the justices reiterated that 'Israelis present in *the area* have the rights to life, dignity and honour, property, privacy, and the rest of the rights which anyone present in Israel proper enjoys'.[284]

At the same time, it did not stipulate whether the Basic Law applies to the Palestinians living in the same territory.[285] The Court's decision to restrict the extra-territorial applicability of this and other Basic Laws to Israeli nationals has first been criticized for distinguishing between nationals and non-nationals when it comes to the protection of rights that are in essence universal rights.[286]

279 One author described the Court's approach as 'chaotic', and one that ignores 'the differences in the substantive and normative distinctions between these bodies of law'. Yaël Ronen, *supra* note 278 at 164.

280 *Hass* Judgment, *supra* note 130 at paras 14, 15 and 17.

281 The right to property being one example. *Beit Iksa* Judgment, *supra* note 137 at para 26.

282 *Morar* Judgment, *supra* note 82 at para 14.

283 Basic Law: *Human Dignity and Liberty* (Isr), online: *Knesset* website as amended by Basic Law: *Human Dignity and Liberty – Amendment*, 1994, online: *Knesset* http://knesset.gov.il/laws/special/eng/BasicLawLiberty.pdf [Basic Law: *Human Dignity and Liberty*].

284 (HCJ 7957/04) [2004] *Mara'abe and Others v. Prime Minister of Israel and Others* at para 21, official English translation, online: HCJ https://supremedecisions.court.gov.il/Home/Download?path=EnglishVerdicts\04\570\079\A14&fileName=04079570_A14.txt&type=4 [*Mara'abe* Judgment]. The petition was upheld partially by the HCJ.

285 Orna Ben-Naftali, 'PathoLAWgical Occupation: Normalizing the Exceptional Case of the Occupied Palestinian Territory and Other Legal Pathologies', in Orna Ben-Naftali, ed, *International Humanitarian Law and International Human Rights Law* (Oxford: Oxford University Press, 2011) 129 at 141.

286 While there may be a legitimate distinction under constitutional law between nationals and non-nationals, this is less justifiable with regards to the kind of rights protected by the Basic Law: *Human Dignity and Liberty*. Furthermore, section 11 of this Basic Law suggests that the obligations on government authorities to respect certain rights must take place regardless of where they act and who the beneficiary is. Yaël Ronen, 'Applicability of Basic Law', *supra* note 278.

Second, it has constitutionalized existing legal discriminations between Israeli settlers and Palestinian residents in the occupied territory.[287] Third, applying a human rights discourse (grounded in domestic law) to a conflict of interest between an Occupying Power and the occupied population (especially when the civilian population of the occupant is also involved), risks rendering the law of belligerent occupation meaningless.[288] Fourth, it creates 'a semblance of uniformity of law between Israel and the West Bank, at least in so far as Israelis are concerned'.[289] Lastly, the applicability of the Basic Law to Israeli settlers in the West Bank suggests that for all practical purposes, Israeli settlements have been de facto annexed to Israel.[290]

The military commander's scope of discretion

On one hand, the Court has stressed the idea that Palestinians of the West Bank constitute 'protected persons' under the Fourth Geneva Convention,[291] while Israeli settlers do not.[292] On the other hand, the Court has also cemented the idea that the Israeli settler population constitutes part of the 'local population' whose rights and needs the MC can lawfully take into consideration as part of his duties under article 43 of the Hague Regulations.

Thus, in the *Haas* judgment, the Court established that the duty of the MC under international law, 'to ensure proper living conditions, applies to all spheres of life, extending beyond security and essential needs to include economic and social needs that arise in a modern society'.[293] The aforementioned duty concerns 'both the Arab and Israeli inhabitants' of the occupied territory.[294] This, they opined allows the MC to lawfully restrict rights that are enjoyed by the 'protected persons', including their property rights.

In that case, petitions had challenged the decision of the MC to requisition land belonging to Palestinians for the purpose of widening the path used by Israeli worshippers to access the Tomb of the Patriarchs. In its decision, the Court upheld the legality of the land requisition on the ground that 'where it

287 Since the rights enshrined in the Fourth Geneva Convention allow for restricting those rights to respond to legitimate needs of the Occupying Power, the scope of these rights is narrower than for those protected under constitutional law in ordinary circumstances. Daphne Barak-Erez, 'Israel: The Security Barrier – Between International Law, Constitutional Law and Domestic Judicial Review', (July 2006) 4:3 Int J Const L 540 at 551.

288 Yaël Ronen, 'Applicability of Basic Law', *supra* note 278.

289 Ibid. at 162.

290 Ibid.

291 *Morar* Judgment, *supra* note 82, *Dir Samit Village* Judgment, *supra* note 138 at para 32; *Abu Safiyeh* Judgment, *supra* note 140 at paras 20 and 28.

292 *Morar* Judgment, *supra* note 82 at para 20; *Mayor of Ad-Dhahiriya* Judgment, *supra* note 131 at para 12; *Abu Safiyeh* Judgment, *supra* note 140 at para 21. It was also underlined in the *Gaza Beach Regional Council* Judgment, *supra* note 84 at para 12.

293 *Haas* Judgment, *supra* note 130 at para 14. See also *Morar* Judgment, *supra* note 82 at para 13.

294 *Haas* Judgment, *supra* note 130 at para 8.

shall be required *in order to satisfy essential living needs of the population residing in the* area [emphasis added], [...] the need for the requisition of private land for the purpose of paving roads and access routes to various locations in the area has been recognized'.[295]

The HCJ reiterated that the normative point of departure is 'identical to the normative position that was determined for considering the petitions concerning the separation fence'.[296] Its judges have underscored that they are not experts on security and military issues, that 'determining the security limits in the specific case is of course within the jurisdiction of the military commander',[297] and that their judicial role is confined to the examination of the legality of this Commander's discretion, not to replacing this discretion with that of the Court.[298] Moreover, they underscored that special weight would be granted to the MC's expertise and that his decision enjoys 'the presumption of administrative propriety as long as no factual basis has been established to the contrary'.[299]

As a logical conclusion, the Court has refrained from entertaining the possibility that irrelevant political considerations or hidden objectives may have enticed the MC to implement the contested measure. It has also concluded that, by contrast to the factual analysis provided by the government which alleges the existence of real security risks for the Israeli settlers and other nationals, the petitioners had failed to prove that considerations other than security had influenced the decision of the MC.[300] For example, this was the Court's assessment in the *Hebron Municipality* judgment. Hence, despite taking note of the improvements in the overall security situation in the West Bank city of Hebron (which had resulted in lifting several movement restrictions imposed in some parts of the city)[301] the Court did not question the assessment of military authorities that it was necessary to maintain other measures restricting the movement of Palestinians elsewhere.[302]

295 Ibid. at para 9.

296 *Mayor of Ad-Dhahiriya* Judgment, *supra* note 131 at para 12.

297 *Morar* Judgment, *supra* note 82 at para 21.

298 *Haas* Judgment, *supra* note 130 at para 10; *Abu Safiyeh* Judgment, *supra* note 140 at para 27.

299 *Haas* Judgment *supra* note 130 at para 12; *Abu Safiyeh* Judgment, *supra* note 140 at para 27.

300 *Bethlehem Municipality* Judgment, *supra* note 1 at paras 9 and 19. See also *Haas* Judgment, *supra* note 130 at para 12; *Abu Safiyeh*, *supra* note 140 at para 12.

301 Hebron has more than 600 Israeli settlers living in four settlements with approximately 1,500 Israeli soldiers to protect them. The part of the Wall constructed in this area is approximately 125.5 km long, 109 km of which has been semi-finished. The 'H2 area' of the city of Hebron, which includes four downtown Israeli settlements that house 500 settlers and is inhabited by an estimated 30,000 Palestinians, is surrounded with checkpoints, roadblocks and military barriers. Temporary International Presence in Hebron (TIPH), 'Hebron', online: TIPH www.tiph.org/hebron/.

302 Israeli military authorities had decided to allow some Palestinians living on one main road to access it with their vehicles by granting several permits. The HCJ expressed its confidence that the MC will lift the remaining restrictions and would allow for the reopening of shops when the 'security situation' permits. *Hebron Municipality* Judgment, *supra* note 161 at 2. See also *Bethlehem Municipality* Judgment, *supra* note 1 at para 18.

This was also the case in the *Dir Samit Village Council* case, in which petitioners alleged that closing off the road had forced residents of 12 Palestinian villages along that road to make a long detour to reach essential social service centres.[303] The Court was reluctant to question the government's security-based assessment and also dismissed alternative military opinions presented by the petitioners on the ground that:

> [...] the question of the proportionality of the chosen security measure cannot be decided by presenting an alternative security position or security approach which differs from that of the military commander, who has the power and duty with regards to the security of the residents of the Area. The military commander is the professional body with expertise in the area of security and those wishing to refute the security position of the military commander bear a great burden.[304]

In this regard, the Court emphasized that it would not intervene in the discretion of the MC as to which methods best respond to an alleged security risk, particularly since he had not departed from the margin of proportionality and reasonableness.[305] Similarly, in the *Second Dir Qadis* case, the Court accepted the government's assurances that the road would only be used by the security personnel of the settlement, thereby avoiding having to rule on whether government authorities had failed to fulfil all of the planning procedures related to the road.[306]

Managing conflicting human rights values and interests through the balancing act

A review of the HCJ decisions indicates that the manner in which the Court balanced the various rights and interests can be divided into three main categories. The first category is one where the Court balanced the security of Israelis with the human rights of the Palestinian local population. The second category is where it sought to balance between the need to protect the rights of the Palestinians to physical security and safety against the restriction of other fundamental rights that they enjoy, such as freedom of movement and the right to property. And the last category is one in which a balance was required between the various rights of the Israelis (mainly, but not exclusively Israeli settlers) and the fundamental rights of the Palestinians.

303 *Dir Samit Village* Judgement, *supra* note 138 at para 1. As a result, residents of 12 Palestinian villages along the road have been forced to make a long detour to reach service centres – OCHA-oPt, 'West Bank Movement and Access Update', (November 2009), online: UNISPAL https://unispal.un.org/DPA/DPR/unispal.nsf/0/EAD44F7163AF410F8525767700593335.

304 Petitioners furnished an expert opinion that creating roads that are exclusively dedicated to the movement of Israelis would increase rather than decrease the overall security risks. See *Dir Samit Village Council* Judgment, *supra* note 138 at para 23.

305 *Bethlehem Municipality* Judgment, *supra* note 1 at para 19.

306 *Second Dir Qadis Village Council* Judgment, *supra* note 136 at paras 2–4.

To assess whether the MC had adequately balanced the security of the Israeli settler population against the rights of the Palestinians, the Court followed two steps: establishing whether the security of those Israelis lies within the scope of the authority of the MC; and conducting the three-pronged proportionality test. Having determined that the MC is responsible for the security of all persons under his effective authority, the Court has traditionally treated the security of Israeli settlers, and/or other Israeli citizens (including travellers) as a derivative of the security military consideration which the MC can lawfully take into consideration, and which then must be balanced against the rights of the Palestinian civilian population.[307] Clarifying the duty of the MC further in the *Haas* case, the justices explained the decision that the MC must:

> [...] *ensure the safety, security and welfare of the area inhabitants. The said duty applies to him in respect of all the inhabitants, regardless of their identity – Jews, Arabs or foreigners* [emphasis added] [...]. The duty of the Area Commander to guard the safety of their lives and their human rights is derived from *their mere residence in the area* [emphasis added].[308]

As in previous cases, the Court did not consider the illegality of an occupant's transfer of its own civilians into occupied territory under international law to be an element that casts doubt on the MC's authority to guarantee the settlers' security. This was the situation in the *Morar* judgment where, upon considering whether the decision of the MC to close off areas adjacent to Israeli settlements was lawful, the justices stressed that 'the protection of the security of the Israeli inhabitants in the territories is the responsibility of the military commander, even though these inhabitants do not fall within the scope of protected persons'.[309]

In several judgments, the Court upheld the idea that the MC is also responsible for providing for the security of Israeli nationals who usually reside in Israel proper and who were travelling inside the West Bank. Consequently, the justices determined that the rights and security of these Israeli citizens need to be balanced against the rights of the Palestinian population.[310] This was the

307 In a judgment dating from the 1980s, the Court underlined that '[t]his power is quite broad, and applies to any person who is present in the Area, whether a permanent resident of the Area or a new resident thereof'. (HCJ 72/86) [1987] *Zalum et al. v. the Military Commander of the Judea and Samaria Area,*) at para 8, unofficial English translation, online: *Hamoked* www.hamoked.org/files/2013/1158750_eng.pdf [*Zalum* Judgment].

308 *Haas* Judgment, *supra* note 130 at para 14. See also *Abu Safiyeh* Judgment, *supra* note 140 at para 20; *Dir Samit Village Council* Judgment, *supra* note 138 at para 16.

309 *Morar* Judgment, *supra* note 82 at para 20.

310 *Abu Safiyeh* Judgment, *supra* note 140 at para 28. The worshippers in another case included Israelis living in West Jerusalem (Israel proper). *Bethlehem Municipality* Judgment, *supra* note 1 at para 7. In the *Beit Iksa* case, the railway benefited Israeli travellers between Tel Aviv and Jerusalem and therefore includes, among those who benefited, Israeli nationals not living in annexed EJ. *Beit Iksa* Judgment, *supra* note 137 at para 5.

situation in the *Abu Safiyeh* case, where the Court concluded that in addition to Palestinians and Israeli settlers, the MC has a duty to ensure the 'public order and safety' vis-à-vis the 'residents and citizens of Israel who do not reside in the Area, mainly for the purpose of travel between the coast and Jerusalem'.[311]

Similarly, in the *Dir Samit* case, the Court noted that the 'security considerations indeed justify measures to protect the Israelis using the road', in clear reference to the fact that Israelis – who are not necessarily settlers – also travel between Israel proper and Israeli settlements in the West Bank. Again, in this case, the Court upheld that, as a matter of principle, the MC was entitled to restrict the Palestinians' freedom of movement. Only when the subsequent examination of whether 'there is justification to take such an extreme measure as *completely closing* [emphasis added] the breadth road to a large population that depends on freedom of movement in the area in order to maintain the basic necessities of life',[312] did the Court strike down the legality of his measure.

The same stance was adopted by the Court to uphold the legality of an MO that had led to the requisitioning of land belonging to Palestinians for the alleged protection of settlers and other Israeli citizens who are present in the West Bank (for travel, worship, etc.). For example, in the *Haas* case, the Court was faced, on the one hand, with the fact that the laws of belligerent occupation strictly do not authorize the destruction of buildings in the occupied territory except for imperative operational military needs. However, the Court effectively widened the existing exceptions under that body of law by ruling that the objective of 'paving roads in order to protect Israeli inhabitants residing in the area' can be considered part of the MC's legitimate military/security considerations and that, therefore, the land requisition order by the MC fulfilled the requirements of article 52 of the Hague Regulations.[313]

Implicitly, the manner in which the Court has approached the security considerations of article 43 has allowed the security of not only the settlers, but also of Israelis in Israel proper to constitute part of the balancing equation. Thus although the Court had underscored that the Palestinians' rights to freedom of movement are protected in Israeli constitutional law,[314] it decided that '[w]hen there is a direct confrontation and there is a concrete risk to security and life, the public interest indeed overrides protected human rights, and the same is the case where there is a concrete *likelihood* of a risk to life'.[315]

The Court also stressed that, in order to prevent an absolute negation of one's ability to exercise a protected right, the MC must maintain a balance between the conflicting values. To assess whether the Commander had indeed struck the appropriate balance, the justices applied the proportionality doctrine and its three

311 *Abu Safiyeh* Judgment, *supra* note 140 at para 20.
312 *Dir Samit Village* Judgment, *supra* note 138 at para 19.
313 *Haas* Judgment, *supra* 130 at para 9.
314 This is in addition to freedom of worship and property rights, which the HCJ underscored, are constitutional law, to be enjoyed by both Israelis and Palestinians in the West Bank.
315 *Morar* Judgment, *supra* note 82 at para 16. Emphasis is in the original.

sub-tests.[316] A review of the petitions discussed here underscores the central role that the HCJ has afforded to the proportionality doctrine as a way of determining the legality of the actions of the MC in the occupied territories under IHL.[317] When balancing the security of Israelis against the rights of the Palestinian inhabitants, the Court has generally upheld the idea that the security measure implemented by the MC fulfilled the requirement of the first proportionality sub-test (i.e. the rational connection test) in all cases discussed here.[318] Similarly, to other cases, the Court continued to prioritize the assessment of the military authorities, even where alternative military sources had questioned the soundness of the former's decision from a security perspective.[319]

It is when the Court embarked on examining whether the challenged security-based measure fulfilled the second proportionality sub-test (the least harmful sub-test) that the justices demonstrated in some cases, a certain readiness to strike down its legality. Thus, in several judgments, they held that less harmful alternative measures were available to government authorities and that, if implemented, they could achieve the same security benefits. This was the case in the *Mayor of Ad-Dhahiriya* judgment.[320] Although the justices ordered government authorities to dismantle the concrete barricade that had impeded the access of the Palestinians in the area, they did not rule out that 'the respondents may construct an alternative barrier that is consistent with this judgment'.[321]

Adopting a similar stance in the *Dir Samit* judgment, the Court decided to strike down the MC's decision to close off road 443 almost entirely to Palestinian movement. The justices explained that 'even if we were to accept the position that the existing threats justify the measure of separation and prevention of friction between the Israeli population and the Palestinian population', the respondent had not examined all possible alternative measures for protecting the Israeli settlers and other Israelis travelling on the road. They also noted that the existing threat did not justify such sweeping measures, which completely barred Palestinians from using the road, while allowing Israelis to access it.[322] Similarly in the *Abu Safiyeh* case, the Court noted that less invasive security measures had been at the disposal of Israeli authorities, which could secure the

316 *Abu Safiyeh* Judgment, *supra* note 140 at para 29.

317 Sharon Weill, *The Role of National Courts*, *supra* note 181. See *Morar* Judgment, *supra* note 82 at para 18; *Mara'abe* Judgment, *supra* note 284 at para 30.

318 *Morar* Judgment, *supra* note 82 at para 20; *Abu Safiyeh* Judgment, *supra* note 140 at para 30; *Dir Samit Village* Judgment, *supra* note 138 at para 23.

319 Petitioners highlighted the security assessment of a reserve Brigadier General in the Israeli army in another petition, in which he had underscored that allowing only Israeli vehicles to travel along a given road, addresses in a satisfactory manner the threat of drive-by shooting attacks, but may facilitate attack by other methods. *Abu Safiyeh* Judgment, *supra* note 140 at para 30 and *Dir Samit Village* Judgment, *supra* note 138 at para 6.

320 *Mayor of Ad-Dhahiriya* Judgment, *supra* note 131 at paras 21–22.

321 Ibid. at para 22. A lower barricade would allow Palestinian pedestrians and their livestock to pass through. *Mayor of Ad-Dhahiriya* Judgment, *supra* note 131 at paras 19–20.

322 *Dir Samit Village* Judgment, *supra* note 138 at para 26.

safety of Israeli passengers on the road, and be less injurious to the Palestinian inhabitants of the area.[323]

As for the third proportionality sub-test (proportionality in the narrow sense), the justices concluded in some cases that the benefit of protecting Israelis and their security justified the level of harm that the Palestinian petitioners would have to incur. At the same time, they called upon government authorities to put in place measures that would be more proportionate. For example, in the *Morar* judgment, while noting that the MC had the authority to determine the range of the area to be closed off to the access of Palestinian farmers, and its distance from the boundaries of the Israeli settlements, it remains necessary to grant Palestinians the opportunity to access the land to complete their agricultural work 'to the last olive'. Moreover, while preserving in principle the right of the MC to give oral instructions for closing off an area, it held that, as a general policy, closing off an area should be preceded by a written order.[324]

In some judgments where the Court had already struck down the legality of a given measure under the second sub-test, it decided that there was no need to examine whether the contested measure had also fulfilled the requirements of the third sub-test.[325] In other judgments, it did embark on this analysis, most notably in cases where petitioners had argued that the security-based measure that they were challenging was sweeping in nature. This was the case in the *Dir Samit* judgment. Here, the government had argued that the injury caused to the petitioners centred on a longer commuting time. The Court disagreed, underscoring that the injury undermined the 'fabric of life' of thousands of Palestinians. Furthermore, it was so disproportionate, in their view, that it made it impossible for them to conduct 'a reasonable daily life'.[326]

Equally, in the *Abu Safiyeh* case, the Court concluded that the complete travel ban on Palestinians had not satisfied the criteria of the third proportionality sub-test. The justices explained that:

> The additional security achieved by the *flat ban* [emphasis added] does not equal a complete denial of the right of protected persons to travel on a road which was designed for their needs and built on lands some of which were expropriated from them.[327]

It does not justify that the road is exclusively used for the needs of the Occupying Power, while the 'protected persons' are barred from using the very same road.[328] According to the Court, the resulting situation was unacceptable because:

323 *Abu Safiyeh* Judgment, *supra* note 140 at paras 32 and 35.

324 *Morar* Judgment, *supra* note 82 at para 21.

325 *Mayor of Ad-Dhahiriya* Judgment, *supra* note 131 at para 21.

326 *Dir Samit Village* Judgment, *supra* note 138 at paras 28–32. However, while it rendered the *order nisi* absolute, it suspended the judgment for three months to allow the Commander to formulate a more reasonable security solution. *Dir Samit Village* Judgment, *supra* note 138 at paras 34–35.

327 *Abu Safiyeh* Judgment, *supra* note 140 at para 35.

328 Ibid. at para 35.

> [...] it is possible to say that, as a rule, a *sweeping measure is constitutionally 'suspect'* [emphasis added]. Absolute measures require, even more so than usual, substantiated reasoning powerful enough to persuade that they are justified. This is due to the inherent contradiction between blanket measures and the protection of human rights.[329]

However, the Court refused to hold that the segregation/separation between the Palestinian and the Israeli population in terms of their access to the road was illegal as a matter of principle,[330] or that it amounted to an institutionalized form of discrimination as petitioners had alleged.[331] Instead, it recalled that in the past it had upheld the right of the MC to requisition land for the purpose of constructing 'by-pass' roads for the use of Israelis (primarily settlers) in the West Bank, in order to reduce friction between the two populations.[332]

Concluding observations

In analysing the Court's interpretation of the MC's scope of authority under article 43 of the Hague Regulations, a number of elements stand out. First, the Courts position vis-à-vis the government and military authorities' assessment of existing security threats and their gravity underscores that it does not question, as a matter of principle, that the measures they have chosen to implement best respond to these threats. Only when there was a clear misfit – that is, when the Court had a *prima facie* factual basis brought to its attention, indicating that the action of the MC was arbitrary or not performed in good faith – did it deem the security-based measure unlawful.[333] Even when the Court did so, it left it to the authorities to come up with alternative measures, and did not provide any concrete suggestions.[334]

329 Ibid. at para 5.

330 Ibid., *Separate opinion by Chief Justice Beinisch* at para 2.

331 'Not every instance of distinguishing between people under any circumstances necessarily constitutes wrongful discrimination, and not every instance of wrongful discrimination constitutes Apartheid'. *Abu Safiyeh* Judgment, *supra* note 140, *Separate opinion by Chief Justice Beinisch* at para 6.

332 In this specific case, it was to allow the settlers in the settlement of Kiryat Arba and other settlements to reach their destinations without having to pass through Palestinian population centres. *Wafa* Judgment, *supra* note 120 at 5.

333 'The Court does not dispute that the Palestinians may have suffered serious injury to their rights, but confines itself to applying Israeli administrative law in such cases. It is just concerned with whether or not the MC acted arbitrarily – disproportionately or unnecessarily'. Interview with Charles Shamas, Partner in the Mattin Group, with author via Skype (21 November 2014, Ramallah) [*Shamas* Interview].

334 For example, although it declared the absolute travel ban imposed by Israeli authorities against the Palestinians unlawful, it granted the MC five months, 'to formulate a different security solution which would provide protection for the Israeli residents who use the Road'. *Abu Safiyeh* Judgment, *supra* note 140 at para 39. However, it did not call for the opening of the Beituniya crossing, which connects the Palestinian villages to the metropolitan centre of Ramallah. ACRI, 'Route 443: Fact Sheet and Timeline', (25 May 2010), online: ACRI www.acri.org.il/en/2010/05/25/route-443-fact-sheet-and-timeline/. Time to formulate another plan was also granted to authorities in the *Dir Samit Village* Judgment, *supra* note 138 at para 35.

Second, the Court again relied on the proportionality doctrine to regulate some of the harsher impacts of a given measure on the rights of the Palestinians. This approach is effective insofar as it has allowed the Court to strike down measures that are sweeping in nature or arbitrary. In addition, it has proven to be a less effective tool for challenging the very authority of the MC to implement a given action as a matter of principle. A very clear demonstration can be found in the *Abu Safiyeh* judgment: rather than conclude that the MC did not have the authority to exclude Palestinian vehicles from using a highway (ostensibly built for the benefit of the Palestinian local population), the justices maintained that he had the authority to impose travel restrictions (as a rational response to security concerns) and preferred to focus their criticism on the fact that the ban was absolute and, therefore, disproportionate in nature.[335] This highlights the detrimental impact of invoking the proportionality doctrine in the context of a military occupation: it shifts the judicial discourse to an analysis of the extent to which the human rights violations are still proportional, and not on whether the contested measure is lawful or unlawful to begin with. It also:

> [A]ssumes an accountable democratic government committed to the collective good of its citizens, but occasionally forced to violate the rights of whole or part of the population in order to attain legitimate ends. The benefits to the population are then weighed against the infringement of their rights, the point being that the benefits accrue to the *same* population whose rights were violated. But it is questionable whether this logic can apply when the government is a military occupier promoting the collective security interests of its *own* citizens while violating the rights of the people it occupies.[336]

The end result is that the security of the Israelis almost always trumps the rights of the Palestinians, thereby relegating the rights of the latter to second place.

Third, the Court's decision to consider Israeli settlers as part of the 'local population' whose safety and security the MC must protect under article 43 of the Hague Regulations has also granted a stamp of approval to both the presence of Israeli nationals in the occupied territory and their right to use the territory's resources and infrastructure.[337] It has also added one extra layer to the many layers of 'military need' exception under the international law of belligerent occupation, which allows the MC to lawfully restrict the rights of

335 Had the Court done so, this would have been a much more powerful statement regarding the rights of the 'protected persons'. David Kretzmer, 'The Law of Belligerent Occupation and the Supreme Court', *supra* note 14.

336 Aeyal Gross, 'The *Construction of a Wall* between The Hague and Jerusalem: The Enforcement and Limits of Humanitarian Law and the Structure of Occupation', (2006) 19 Leiden J Int'l L 393. Emphasis in the quote is in the original.

337 Yuval Shany and Guy Harpaz, 'The Israeli Supreme Court and the Incremental', *supra* note 20.

Palestinians as 'protected persons'. No doubt, this latter element cannot be viewed in isolation from the fourth element, namely that the Court has consistently refused to rule on the illegality of settlement activity under article 49(6) of the Fourth Geneva Convention.[338] It has also refused to entertain the possibility that the illegal presence of those settlers in the occupied territory[339] has implications for the scope of the MC's authority under article 43 of the Hague Regulations.[340]

Even if one assumes that every natural person under the MC's effective control deserves protection (i.e. including Israeli settlers), the justices should have demanded that these security-related measures take note of the question of the illegality of the transfer by the Occupying Power of its civilian population into the occupied territory.[341] Had this been the case, the Court could (and should) have instructed the MC to restrict the presence of settlers in the occupied territory, as a less invasive way to ensure their personal safety:[342]

> [...] the commander's responsibility and obligation to guarantee that person's security and the security of others meant not allowing that person to settle there. Not the opposite and creating a new friction zone. The commander has the authority and obligation to prevent people from entering certain areas in order to prevent precisely these security risks. The court should have started from the basic principle in IL [international law] which forbids the transfer of population into that area. This is what should have guided the court and based on that the obligation of the commander is clearly to prevent that presence [...].[343]

The Court's position was only possible because it decided to treat the presence of the Israeli settlers in the West Bank as the only significant factor irrespective of its illegality under international law.[344]

338 This goes back to the Court's position that the issue of the settlement is unjustifiable because it is a political question. *Shehadeh* Interview, *supra* note 78.

339 *Sfard* Second Interview, *supra* note 77. Interview with Attorney Nasrat Dakwar by Avichay Sharon on behalf of author and translated into English (7 July 2014, Jerusalem) at 2 and 7 [*Dakwar* Interview].

340 'There is a fundamental principle and rule in law that an unlawful act cannot give rise to legal claim'. *Dakwar* Interview, *supra* note 339.

341 Daphne Barak-Erez, 'Israel: The Security Barrier', *supra* note 287 at 549. This is because from a legal perspective, 'your citizens are not allowed to be there'. Interview with Israeli Attorney by Avichay Sharon on behalf of author (23 July 2014, Jerusalem) [Attorney *A-04* Interview].

342 David Kretzmer, 'The Law of Belligerent Occupation and the Supreme Court', *supra* note 14. Interview with Attorney Michael Sfard by Avichay Sharon on behalf of author (10 July 2014, Tel Aviv) [*Sfard* First Interview].

343 Attorney *Dakwar* Interview, *supra* note 339 at 6.

344 That is, it was not interested in 'why they are there', but only in the fact that 'they are there'. *Shamas* Interview, *supra* note 333.

Balancing the security needs of the Palestinians vis-à-vis their rights

In one case, the *Morar* case, Palestinians challenged the MC's decision to close off an area of land that is privately owned, thereby preventing their landowners from accessing it. What distinguishes this case from others is that military authorities argued that this was necessary for ensuring the Palestinians' own physical security from possible acts of violence by Israeli settlers against them and their property.[345] Petitioners representing five Palestinian villagers challenged the decision of the MC to prevent them from accessing their lands nearby an Israeli settlement, a measure which was declared necessary both for the protection of Israelis and of the Palestinian farmers.[346] They also highlighted that Israeli military forces had consistently failed to take effective measures against settlers, in violation of the MC's obligations under international law and of Israeli administrative law.[347]

In its judgment, the Court endorsed again the idea that it was within the MC's authority under international law to decide whether or not movement restrictions were necessary.[348] It also underscored that the purpose for which the closure was exercised was a proper one, namely to protect public order and security under article 43 of the Hague Regulations. This, as a duty of the MC, applies 'with regard to all persons who are present in the territory that is subject to belligerent occupation'.[349] It also included the Israeli settlers, 'even though these inhabitants do not fall within the scope of the category of protected persons'.[350]

For the Court, the heart of the issue was to determine the extent to which the MC had successfully balanced between the two opposing poles: the security of the inhabitants of the territories and the rights of the Palestinian inhabitants.[351] After stressing that the 'right to life and to physical integrity' was protected under both the international law of belligerent occupation and Israeli constitutional law,[352] it emphasized that: 'the existence of risks to public safety does not justify in every case an absolute denial of human rights'.[353] Thus, after

345 Dror Etkes, 'Israeli Settler Agriculture as a Means of Land Takeover in the West Bank', *supra* note 76.

346 *Morar* Judgment, *supra* note 82 at paras 1–2, 7 and 19.

347 Ibid. at paras 5, 11 and 13.

348 In the *Morar* case the Court underscored that the MC is authorized to:

> [M]ake an order to close the whole of the territories or any part thereof, and thereby to prevent anyone from entering or leaving the closed area [...] [and that] this power of the military commander is derived from the rules of belligerent occupation under public international law [...].
>
> *Morar* Judgment, *supra* note 82 at para 12

349 Ibid. at paras 13 and 14.

350 Ibid. at para 20.

351 Ibid. at para 15.

352 Thereby amounting to a right 'that is on the highest normative echelons'. Here the Court cited section 2 and 4 of the *Basic Law on Human Dignity and Liberty*, *supra* note 387. *Morar* Judgment, *supra* note 82 at para 14.

353 Ibid. at para 16.

acknowledging that the Palestinians' right to freedom of movement is a basic right entrenched in Israeli constitutional law and in international law, the Court stressed that the restrictions imposed by government authorities to this right must be reduced to a minimum.[354] In the particular situation of the *Morar* case, this was all the more necessary since the petitioners were trying to access land '*that belongs to them*'.[355]

Moving on to an assessment of the legality of the measure based on the three-pronged proportionality test, the Court first explained that the measure did not meet the requirements of the first sub-test. This was because the closure, while likely to achieve its declared objective of protecting the Palestinian farmers, 'results in serious harm to basic rights while giving into violence and criminal acts'.[356] Addressing the second and the third proportionality sub-test requirements, the justices were not convinced that there were not less harmful measures capable of achieving the objective of protecting the Palestinian petitioners without disproportionately violating their rights to access their land.[357] At the same time, they did not rule out that the MC retained, as a matter of principle, the authority to close off any given area to the party that is facing threats to its safety and security. In this particular case, the decision to restrict the access of Palestinian farmers to their privately owned land was deemed illegal because of the sweeping nature of the closure, and the fact that it had been put in place over a protracted period of time.[358]

The subsequent discussion by the Court of the problem of law enforcement against settler violence is very insightful for a number of reasons. It offers a glimpse into the forceful language that the Court can adopt, and has adopted, vis-à-vis government authorities in situations in which the Court concluded that they have not done enough to address the inadequate standards of law enforcement. This is because ensuring proper law enforcement is 'a fundamental element of the rule of law [...] [and] one of the main functions of any government'.[359] In addition, the judgment demonstrates a clear departure from the Court's traditional approach of not challenging the respondent's version of the facts on the ground and of accepting – at face value – that the measures adopted by the government were implemented in 'good faith':

> It would appear that the facts on the ground speak for themselves and that too little has been done in order to protect the rights of the petitioners

354 According to the Court, the restrictions on the freedom of movement in public areas should be examined differently than restrictions imposed on a person's freedom of movement within an area, to which he is connected to 'his home'. *Morar* Judgment, *supra* note 82 at para 14.

355 Emphasis in the original by the Court. The Court cited the *Bethlehem Municipality* Judgment, *supra* note 1. *Morar* Judgment, *supra* note 82 at para 14.

356 In the Court's words, 'it is like a policy that orders a person not to enter his home in order to protect him from a robber who is waiting for him in order to attack him'. *Morar* Judgment, *supra* note 82 at para 25.

357 *Morar* Judgment, *supra* note 82 at para 26.

358 Ibid. at para 27.

359 Ibid. at para 33.

> [...]. We are aware that the declaration of intentions made by the counsel for the respondents in this matter is not mere words. We are persuaded that the establishment of the inter-ministerial committee and the experience in dealing with law enforcement in the territories are steps that were chosen in good faith and in recognition of the duty imposed on the army and the police operating in the territories. *But plans and intentions are one thing and results another, and the results do not indicate success in the field of law enforcement* [emphasis added].[360]

The justices then conclude by giving a number of clear directives on how the law enforcement by Israeli military authorities can be significantly improved.[361]

Analysis

The *Morar* judgment provides an interesting illustration of how the Court can adopt a more reprimanding attitude towards Israeli authorities. This was possible for two reasons: (a) that the aspect of the petition addressing allegations of settler violence against Palestinians touched on a domestic RoL enforcement issue (and not so much on issues of international law); and (b) that the security of Israelis was not really the main focus of this part of the petition, so the rights of the Palestinians did not need to be balanced against concern for the former. This has allowed the Court to adopt a much stronger stance with government authorities, regarding the discrepancy between intentions and the hard facts on the ground, and to question the extent to which they have respected domestic RoL requirements. The manner in which the Court addressed the issues also reinforces the Court's distaste for the implementation of sweeping measures.[362]

Balancing the rights of Israelis versus the rights of Palestinians

In some of the judgments, the Court determined that the MC's duty to ensure the needs of the civilian population includes not only the preservation of public order and the safety of these residents, but also the safeguarding of their human rights enshrined in constitutional status.[363] Consequently, when assessing conflicting rights of Israelis and Palestinians, the HCJ justices have, in some cases, embarked on a horizontal balancing, a method 'which is practiced in Israel in the context of conflicting rights between two equal rights-holding communities'.[364]

360 Ibid. at paras 32–33.

361 Such as giving precise instructions to the military forces on how to protect Palestinians accessing their land and ensuring that they are not prevented from doing so. *Morar* Judgment, *supra* note 82 at para 33.

362 *Separate Opinion of Justice Jubran* in *Morar* Judgment, *supra* note 82 at para 6 at 85.

363 *Mara'abe* Judgment, *supra* note 284 at para 28. *Haas* Judgment, *supra* note 130.

364 Sharon Weill, *The Role of National Courts*, *supra* note 181 at 32.

In conducting this assessment, after first establishing that the measure/limitation has fulfilled the constitutional requirements of being prescribed by law and of satisfying an appropriate goal, the justices examined whether the challenged security-based measure was proportional. Here, the Court invoked the proportionality doctrine and its three sub-tests, as established in Israeli constitutional law, to determine the extent to which constitutional rights can be limited.[365] This test establishes that for a measure to be deemed constitutional three requirements must be fulfilled: (1) that there must be a rational connection between the appropriate goal and the means utilized by the law; (2) that the objective cannot be achieved by means that are less restrictive of the constitutional rights; and (3) that there must be a proportionate balance between the social benefit of realizing the appropriate goal and the harm caused to the right.[366]

Of constitutional balancing

The Court's adjudication of the *Haas* case illustrates how the justices have sought to balance conflicting constitutional rights. In this case, the justices sought to establish whether the MC's administrative decision to requisition land and to demolish the two buildings belonging to Palestinians for the purpose of widening the road used by Jewish worshippers visiting the Machpela Cave is consistent with constitutional standards. In terms of the first constitutional requirement (that there must be a rational connection between the goals and the means) the Court endorsed the respondent's position that the MOs allowing for the requisition of the lands and buildings were issued in response to genuine security considerations.[367] In relation to the second constitutional requirement (that the objective cannot be achieved by less restrictive measures), the Court did not question the authorities' position that 'any other alternative involves much greater costs in terms of security risks for the worshippers and anticipated harm and damage to the area's inhabitants'.[368]

The Court then analysed whether the third constitutional requirement (that a proportionate balance between the benefit and the harm) has been attained, by conducting the analysis in two stages. The first stage was to determine whether the MC has properly balanced between the Jewish worshippers' constitutional right of praying at the holy site and their constitutional right to safety of life.[369] According to the justices:

365 Basic Law: *Human Dignity and Liberty*, *supra* note 383. See also Mordechai Kremnitzer, 'Constitutional Proportionality: (Appropriate Guidelines', in Gideon Sapir, Daphne Barak-Erez and Aharon Barak, eds, *Israeli Constitutional Law in the Making* (Portland, OR: Hart, 2013) 225.

366 Aharon Barak, 'Proportionality and Principled Balancing', (April 2010) 4:1 L & Ethics Hum Rts 1.

367 *Haas* Judgment, *supra* note 130 at paras 11 and 12.

368 Ibid. at para 21.

369 Ibid. at paras 17 and 18.

> Where the exercise of the right of worship creates near certainty of the occurrence of severe and heavy damage to the public's safety [...], then the value of the public's safety shall prevail and the constitutional right shall give way to it [...].[370]

The measure, they argued, did not justify an absolute negation of the worshippers' right of worship particularly if military authorities can take certain measures to bolster order and public safety in the area. Hence, with regards to the first stage, they concluded that, since the constitutional right to prayer at a holy site is of great value, the MC must seek to facilitate the passage (of the Jewish worshippers) to these sites 'while taking enhanced security measures'.[371]

The second stage consisted of examining whether the MC balanced between the freedom of worship of the Israelis and the value of protecting the Palestinians' right to property, the latter also qualifying as 'a protected constitutional right'.[372] This required an assessment of whether the security of the Israeli worshippers justified the requisitioning of land and the demolition of the houses of the Palestinian petitioners.[373] Here, the justices first stressed that the Palestinians' constitutionally protected right to property was not an absolute right, but one that can be restricted for the purpose of guaranteeing the Israelis' constitutional right of worship.[374] They concluded that the MC's decision satisfied the test because of the following: it befitted an acceptable social value; it was designated for a proper purpose and was not excessive in the harm it renders to Palestinian right to property.[375] The petition was dismissed.[376]

A similar approach was in the *Bethlehem Municipality* judgment. The justices first reiterated that when determining the extent to which the MC can restrict the Israelis' right to worship at certain places, he must first examine whether or not the adoption of certain security-based measures could help realize this right.[377] Subsequently, they effected a balancing between constitutional rights in two stages. In the first stage, they examined whether the MC's measure had struck a balance between the Israelis' right to worship and the Palestinians' freedom of movement.[378] While the Court acknowledged on one hand, that the right to freedom of

370 Ibid. at para 19.
371 Ibid. at para 19.
372 Ibid. at para 17.
373 Ibid. at para 16.
374 Ibid. at paras 17 and 20.
375 Therefore fulfilling the requirements set out by the limitation clause in section 8 of the Basic Law: *Human Dignity and Liberty*, *supra* note 387; *Haas* Judgment, *supra* note 130 at paras 20 and 21. The Court noted the assurances by Israeli military authorities that the road was widened only a few metres on each side, that all the buildings that are being contemplated for requisition were abandoned and that affected individuals had a right to receive compensation. *Haas* Judgment, *supra* note 130 at para 21.
376 Ibid. at para 20.
377 *Bethlehem Municipality* Judgment, *supra* note 1 at para 14.
378 According to the HRC, the two constitutional rights are of equal weight, and hence require horizontal balancing. *Bethlehem Municipality* Judgment, *supra* note 1 at paras 1 and 16.

movement of Palestinians is protected under international HR law (ICCPR and UDHR) and is enshrined in the Hague Regulations and the Fourth Geneva Conventions, its emphasis was that these rights were protected by Israeli constitutional law.[379] In analysing the extent of harm inflicted on the Palestinian petitioners, it then highlighted that Israeli authorities had implemented measures to reduce the geographic scope of the restrictions of movement imposed on the petitioners and maintain the interests of the persons seeking to realize this right. Furthermore, it highlighted the government's assurances that these restrictions were temporary and that they would be lifted once the security situation improves.[380] Thus it concluded that the harm incurred by the petitioners was not sufficiently grave to render the security measure disproportionate or unreasonable and, therefore, illegal.[381]

The second stage consisted of the need to determine whether the MC had struck a balance between the Israelis' right to worship on one hand, and the Palestinians' right to property on the other. In this regard, the justices took note of the claims by military authorities that the petitioners' parcels of land had suffered only marginal damage (as a result of the requisition orders) and that compensation had been offered. The Court concluded that the balance between the competing rights has been achieved and dismissed the petition.[382]

Concluding observations

The Court underlined the idea that different legal regimes apply to different populations: Palestinians as 'protected persons' and Israelis who are not. However, practically speaking, it has refrained from 'following the consequences of those statements to their logical end'.[383] The Court's adjudication demonstrates the shortcoming of assessing the conflicting rights of Palestinians and Israelis through the prism of Israeli constitutional law and the balancing of constitutional rights. It explains why it does not constitute an adequate formula for evaluating the conflict of rights in the situation of occupation, particularly if the balancing involves the interests of the nationals of the Occupying Power.

379 Although it recognized that the Palestinians' right to freedom of movement is a fundamental right under international human rights law, and that the right to property is enshrined in the Hague Regulations and the Fourth Geneva Conventions, it framed the value of these rights in Israeli constitutional law. *Bethlehem Municipality* Judgment, *supra* note 1 at paras 17 and 20.

380 *Bethlehem Municipality* Judgment, *supra* note 1 at para 17. According to the Court, MOs remain in place as long as the security situation required, '*which may continue for a long time* [emphasis added]'. *Bethlehem Municipality* Judgment, *supra* note 1 at para 18.

381 Although the Court conceded that the time of travel will increase for Palestinians travelling east of Bethlehem, because of the need to circumvent the Rachel's Tomb area, this required less time than the level of harm that they would have incurred had authorities decided to keep the roadblocks in place. *Bethlehem Municipality* Judgment, *supra* note 1 at para 18.

382 The Court also took into consideration the promise by the respondents that they 'will be prepared to examine any application for an amendment of the route at a specific point, in order to reduce the harm to the owners of the land'. *Bethlehem Municipality* Judgment, *supra* note 1 at para 18.

383 Yaël Ronen, 'Applicability of Basic Laws', *supra* note 378 at 149.

The first reason for this conclusion is that adopting such a judicial approach has diluted the special weight accorded to the rights of the occupied population as 'protected persons' under the law of belligerent occupation. One good example is the right to property, which, under the law of belligerent occupation, is considered a fundamental right of those persons, and must be protected by the occupant, save for very stringent exceptional situations. By turning this right into a constitutionally protected one that can be balanced against other constitutionally protected rights of Israelis (who are not 'protected persons'), the exceptions to the prohibition on the Occupying Power to refrain from violating this right are further relaxed.

Second, by grounding the analysis of the rights in a domestic human rights framework, the Court has transformed the relationship between the occupier and the occupied into a relationship requiring constitutional protection, as if the clash of interests is taking place between equal parties.[384] This may have worked if the Palestinians of the West Bank were a minority that is part of a democratic polity in which they have a say.[385] However, given that they are not citizens of the State, their rights will, in the majority of cases, be relegated to second place whenever they are balanced against those of the Israelis. In this regard, one has only to recall the statement by former HCJ justice Barak highlighting the weight that should be accorded to each side of the scale of the balancing act:

> I contend that the criterion is that of the relative social importance attached to each of the conflicting principles or interest at the point of conflict, which assesses the *importance to society of the benefit gained* [emphasis added] by realization of the law's goal as opposed to the importance to society of preventing the limitation of human rights. Even rights of the same normative level are not necessarily of the same social importance. The social importance of a right – and by extension its weight in relation to conflicting principles – is derived from its underlying rationale and its importance within the framework of *society's fundamental conceptions* [emphasis added].[386]

384 Aeyal Gross 'Human Proportions: Are Human Rights the Emperor's New Clothes of the International Law of Occupation?', (2007) 18:1 EJIL 1. As one lawyer explains:

> I see no problem in incorporating basic human rights of settlers, [but] Palestinians have more rights as 'protected persons'. But the judiciary gives them less rights always (not on a formal level though). They usually say they have equal rights. This is incorrect. They have more rights.
>
> Interview with Attorney *Netta Amar-Shiff* by Avichay Sharon (24 August 2014, Jerusalem) on file with author [*Amar-Shiff* Interview]

385 'If norms demand obedience by virtue of one's association to a particular political community, how can binding "outsiders" who can neither identify nor shape an alien society's institutions ever be justified?' Karen Eltis, 'The Democratic Legitimacy of the "International Criminal Justice Model": The Unilateral Reach of Foreign Domestic Law and the Promise of Transnational Constitutional Conversation', in Christopher P.M. Waters, ed, *British and Canadian Perspectives on International Law* (Netherlands: Martinus Nijhoff, 2006) 349 at 360.

386 Aharon Barak, 'Proportionality and Principled Balancing', *supra* note 366 at 7 and 9.

Hence, there is little doubt that, whenever the interests of the Palestinians (who are not citizens) do conflict with those of Israeli citizens, the social importance granted by Israeli society to the former would be second best.

Third, even if one presumes that the HCJ's constitutional balancing is an appropriate tool for determining the value that should be granted to the conflicting rights of both Israelis and Palestinians, the fact that the Basic Law: *Human Dignity and Liberty* applies only to the Israeli settler population in the West Bank but not *de jure* to Palestinians living therein has exacerbated the gap in terms of formal legal protection afforded to both. This is not to suggest that the solution lies in extending the applicability of the Basic Law to Palestinians, given that this would amount to a recognition of a *de jure* annexation of the West Bank. However, extending the Basic Law to Israelis living therein but not to the Palestinians is not a tenable situation either: it has created an impossible situation in which annexation is taking place de facto while a dual legal system of law is allowed to prevail. By refusing to rule on the applicability of IHR law to the actions of Israeli authorities in the occupied territory and to their relationship with its Palestinian population,[387] the Court has diluted the relevance of this body of law as a point of reference for the protection of the rights of the Palestinians.[388] The result is a significant protection gap.

Closing remarks

On the one hand, the Court should be commended for stressing the centrality of article 43 of the Hague Regulations and for reiterating that Palestinians are 'protected persons' under the Fourth Geneva Convention, and that the MC is obligated under international law to balance between military/security needs and the welfare of the 'local population'. On the other hand, it has upheld the government's position that the security of Israeli settlers and commuters is part of the legitimate security interests that can guide the MC's actions under international law. This has significantly widened the security considerations beyond the strict military needs of the armed forces in the occupied territory. Along with the tendency to uphold the MC's security assessments[389] and the limited usefulness of the proportionality doctrine in challenging the very authority of

387 Federica d'Alessandra 'Israel's Associated Regime, Exceptionalism, Human Rights and Alternative Legality', (2014) 30 Utrecht J. Int'l and Euro L 30.

388 This is because many of the guarantees provided to Israelis through the Basic Laws are provided to Palestinians under IHR law. *Sfard* Second Interview, *supra* note 77. In this regard it is important to note that some basic rights expressly mentioned in IHR conventions and treaties were not included in the Basic Law: *Human Dignity and Liberty*, such as the right to equality. David Kretzmer, 'New Basic Laws on Human Rights: A Mini-Revolution in Israeli Constitutional Law', (1992) 26 Isr LR 238.

389 'I can understand any act from the court can jeopardize its place as a domestic court. I don't have a solution of what is the wise thing to do, but it is unacceptable to do this'. *Attorney A-04* Interview, *supra* note 341.

the MC to implement the security-based measure as a matter of principle, it is hardly surprising that the security and interests of the settlers will almost always trump those of the Palestinians.[390]

The Court's approach has slowly but surely expanded the considerations which the MC can take into account under article 43 of the Hague Regulations in a manner that has relaxed the limitations imposed on that Commander's authority.[391] By upholding the idea that Israeli settlers are part of the former for whose rights the MC is also responsible under international law, the Court has rendered the notion of 'local population' and its composition as a 'factual question devoid of any normative meaning'.[392] This interpretation stands at odds with the manner in which article 43 of the Hague Regulations has been understood to limit the powers of an occupant.

Several factors have further limited the ability of the Court to scrutinize whether the measures and changes implemented in the occupied territory were carried out in response to lawful considerations under international law. The first factor is that the Court has rarely questioned the government's assurances that the welfare of the Palestinians constitutes the dominant factor spearheading a policy's implementation.[393] Moreover, it has, in the majority of cases, accepted the government's argument that the contested policy was implemented in good faith to serve the Palestinian local population (even when other considerations involving the interests of Israeli nationals cast significant doubt on these contentions). This has provided the Occupying Power with a backdoor through which professed humanitarian concerns may camouflage the hidden agenda of the occupant.[394]

Given the prolonged nature of the occupation and that there is no foreseeable end in sight for Israeli control, the Court's approach has allowed for the creation of a legal environment and the allocation of natural resources and physical infrastructure therein in a manner that favours the rights and interests of the nationals of the Occupying Power. This has allowed the occupant to consolidate its long-term non-security-related interests in the territory (both economic and political),[395] and to distort the delicate balance reflected in the law of belligerent occupation, between the needs of the occupier and the occupied population.[396]

Second, the Court has focused on the micro-level or details of the specific case at hand, devoid of any considerations for the larger (macro-level) political context of occupation. As in the Wall-related decisions,[397] it chose to

390 Orna Ben-Naftali, Aeyal Gross and Keren Michaeli, 'Illegal Occupation', *supra* note 22.

391 Sharon Weill, 'The Legitimating Role of the Israeli High Court of Justice: From Occupation to Segregation', (2015) 15:2 Global Jurist 139.

392 Yuval Shany and Guy Harpaz, 'The Supreme Court and the Incremental', *supra* note 20 at 531.

393 David Kretzmer, 'The Law of Belligerent Occupation and the Supreme Court', *supra* note 14.

394 Yoram Dinstein, *The International Law of Belligerent Occupation*, *supra* note 32 at 122.

395 Sharon Weill, *The Role of National Courts*, *supra* note 181.

396 Noam Lubell, 'Human Rights Obligations', *supra* note 21.

397 In those decisions, the Court chose to rule on the Wall segment by segment, thereby evading the need to look at its impact as a whole on the spectrum of rights of the Palestinians.

present Israeli settlers and the Palestinian occupied population as equals who are entitled to the same treatment.[398] Reaching this conclusion was possible, because the justices did not examine the bigger picture of the context in which the alleged security-based measures are being implemented: one in which government and military authorities have systematically dedicated much of the resources, infrastructure and RoL features of the occupied territory to the well-being of the Israeli settlers. They have also discarded the illegality of the presence of those settlers under international law. The end result is that:

> A complex reality that involves a matrix of political actors and interests is reduced into the distant courtroom to a calculated selection and evaluation of evidence and facts, which are taken out of any broader context of power relationships and transformed into an anonymous dispute on which so-called *neutral* legal codes are applied.[399]

This stands in stark contrast to the Court's approach in other decisions involving the rights of Israeli settlers, in which it has proven that it would take the general political context into consideration. Again the *Kiryat Arba Local Council* judgment offers a good demonstration. Here, Israeli petitioners had argued that the freezing of settlement construction by Israeli authorities constituted unlawful discrimination because it is applied only to Israelis and their settlement. However, the Court remained unconvinced, noting that even if the court was willing to entertain this argument, it must first examine the full context. It then noted that for many years the state has provided generous advantages and aid to the Israeli settlements. Hence, it would be difficult to conclude that there has been discrimination, particularly since for many years these settlements have enjoyed a wide range of benefits. It then concluded that the policy does not amount to unlawful discrimination but a valid and relevant distinction between the two communities.[400]

Third, the Court's decision to apply standards of Israeli constitutional law on an 'equal' basis to both Palestinians and Israelis is ill-suited to the context of occupation, as it dilutes the special protection afforded to Palestinians under international law.[401] Thus, even if one were to assume that the Court's resort to constitutional balancing was driven by a sincere desire to augment the protection afforded to Palestinians, given the Court's refusal to rule on the *de jure* applicability of IHR law to the oPt, this approach has allowed the Israeli

398 Sharon Weill, 'The Legitimating Role of the Israeli High Court of Justice', *supra* note 391.

399 Ibid. at 165–166.

400 *Kiryat Arba Local Council* Judgment, *supra* note 84 at 5 and 6.

401 Aeyal Gross, 'Human Proportions', *supra* note 384.

authorities to maintain two separate legal regimes in the occupied territory.[402] Recent legislative initiatives are pushing for the wholesale applicability of Israeli laws to Israeli settlers and/or settlements,[403] and for the *de jure* annexation of the jurisdictional areas of Israeli West Bank settlements (primarily Area C[404] and the Jordan Valley).[405] This indicates a shift in the Israeli political discourse towards a more readily accepted idea of the *de jure* annexation of large parts of the West Bank.[406]

In the meantime the situation has been described as one of de facto annexation that is taking place in the context of a military regime,[407] and as having 'the effect of leaving a whole population in legal and political limbo: neither entitled to the citizenship of the occupying state, nor able to exercise any other political

402 Sharon Weill, 'The Legitimating Role of the Israeli High Court of Justice', *supra* note 391. Dror Etkes explains that:

> What can't be disputed is the fact that in the West Bank there are two separate legal and political regimes. Now, how do you want to call this type of reality? It has certainly some similar aspect to the South African reality and some distinct one as well. I think that it is not irresponsible to use the term apartheid in this case, though one has to be aware of the fact that this is not exactly as the South African model of apartheid.
>
> *Etkes* Written Response, *supra* note 79

403 In November 2014, the Ministerial Committee for Legislation approved a draft bill entitled the 'Norm Law', which would have made it mandatory for the West Bank Israeli Regional MC, within 45 days of a law's passage in the *Knesset*, to promulgate an identically phrased MO that effectively ensures that all ratified legislation also applies to Israeli settlers living in the West Bank. If passed, this bill would effectively limit the authority of the MC who, temporarily speaking, occupies the position of the legal and legitimate 'sovereign' under international law (for as long as he has effective control over the occupied territory), and subordinates it to the will of the *Knesset*. This would change 'the status of the region from territories subject to 'belligerent occupation' to territories that have undergone de facto unilateral annexation to the State of Israel'. See Gilead Sher and Keren Aviram, Insight No. 638, 'The Application of Israeli Law to the West Bank: De Facto Annexation?', (4 December 2014), online: Institute for National Security Studies www.inss.org.il/index.aspx?id=4538andarticleid=8272. See also Reuters, 'Israeli Ministers Approve Applying Israeli Law to West Bank Settlers', (9 November 2014).

404 In June 2011, a draft bill was introduced to *de jure* annex Area C endorsed by the parliamentary caucus that was established earlier for that purpose. And while deliberations on the draft bill were ultimately postponed, they could resume any time. *DIAKONIA*, 'Rule of Law: A Veil of Compliance in Israel and the oPt 2010–2013', Report (March 2014) at 11, online: *DIAKONIA* www.DIAKONIA.se/globalassets/documents/ihl/ihl-resources-center/rule-of-law_final_mar5.pdf.

405 The second bill is one in which the parliamentary caucus tabled, in July 2012, a bill calling for the annexation of the Jordan Valley and the application of Israeli sovereignty to all Israeli settlements. While the draft bill was approved in December 2013 by the Ministerial Committee for Legislative Affairs, it was later appealed by then Justice Minister Livni and is opposed by Prime Minister Netanyahu. *DIAKONIA*, 'Rule of Law', *supra* note 404.

406 *DIAKONIA*, 'Rule of Law', *supra* note 404.

407 *Amar-Shiff* Interview, *supra* note 384.

rights, except of the most rudimentary character [...]'.[408] While Israeli settlers participate in electing representatives for the government institutions of the Occupying Power that controls the West Bank, Palestinians, although subjected to the actions and decisions of that power, cannot do the same.[409] This has granted Israel the benefits of annexation without requiring it to extend formal citizenship or its associated rights and privileges to the Palestinians, while shielding its military and government authorities from state responsibility arising from the de facto annexation of that area in violation of international law.

408 Adam Roberts, 'Prolonged Occupation', *supra* note 10.

> [T]he real inequality on the West Bank is that the Israeli settlers have political rights in the state that controls their lives and the Palestinians do not. That is one of the grounds for the claim that the system there has elements of apartheid.
>
> David Kretzmer, 'Bombshell for the Settlement Enterprise in Levy Report', *Haaretz* (10 July 2012)

409 ACRI, 'One Rule, Two Legal Systems', *supra* note 86.

4 The HCJ's examination of security-related measures in light of the requirement that occupation does not bestow sovereignty

> Even if I were to accept the supposition that domestic Israeli legislation is inconsistent with customary international law – and I do not accept this supposition as it is baseless – Israeli law trumps international law.[1]
>
> – Justice *Aharon Barak*, Chief Justice at the HCJ

Introduction

Occupation is considered a temporary situation resulting from the occupant's ability to impose its de facto authority on the occupied territory through the projection of its military might.[2] However, the use of this force 'cannot imply any right whatsoever to dispose of the territory',[3] and does not entitle the occupant to annex the occupied territory or change its political status.[4] This is the case irrespective of whether or not the belligerent power's use of that force qualifies as a war of aggression or had been carried out in self-defence.[5]

True, major treaties and conventions do not specifically state that occupation does not bestow sovereignty over the occupied territory.[6] However, '[t]he foundation upon which the entire law of occupation is based, is the principle of inalienability of sovereignty through the actual or threat of the use of force'.[7] In

1 (HCJ 256/01) [2002] *Ibrahim Rabah et al. v. Jerusalem Municipal Court and Government of Israel* at para 6, unofficial English translation, online: *Hamoked* www.hamoked.org/files/2012/115170_eng.pdf [*Rabah* Judgment]. All links in this chapter last accessed 1 June 2018.

2 Christopher Greenwood, 'The Administration of Occupied Territory in International Law', in Emma Playfair, ed, *International Law and the Administration of Occupied Territories* (Oxford: Clarendon Press, 1992) 241.

3 Jean Pictet, ed, *Commentary: IV Geneva Convention Relative to the Protection of Civilian Persons in Time of War* reprinted (Geneva: ICRC, 1994) at 275 [*Pictet* Commentary].

4 Eyal Benvenisti, *The International Law of Occupation* (Princeton, NJ: Princeton University Press, 2004).

5 John Quigley, 'Sovereignty in Jerusalem', (1995) 45 Cath U L Rev 765.

6 '[A]s long as hostilities continue, the Occupying Power cannot therefore annex the occupied territory, even if it occupies the whole of the territory concerned. A decision on that point can only be reached in the peace treaty'. *Pictet* Commentary, *supra* note 3 at 275.

7 Eyal Benvenisti, *The International Law of Occupation*, *supra* note 4.

the case of the Hague Regulations, this is reflected in article 43's emphasis on the duty of the occupant to respect the laws that are in force in the occupied territory at the time of occupation. By virtue of the same provision, the occupant is prohibited from implementing legislative changes or structural reforms therein,[8] as a way of 'protecting the separate existence of the State, its institutions, and its laws'.[9]

This normative principle is also reflected in the restrictions that the article places on the ability of this power to legislate, save for limited exceptions, as a way of guaranteeing the rights of the ousted government.[10] However, with the ushering of the era of decolonization and self-determination of people, the focus on 'sovereignty' has shifted from a state-centred approach to one of 'popular sovereignty', expressed as the will of the people in the quest for their right to self-determination.[11] This shift also found expression in the Fourth Geneva Convention, where many provisions guarantee a spectrum of fundamental rights and welfare to populations who 'find themselves, in case of a conflict or occupation, in the hands of a Party to the conflict or Occupying Power of which they are not nationals'.[12] As 'protected persons', they remain entitled in all circumstances to respect for certain fundamental rights including the right to move freely, respect for their religious convictions and practices, humane treatment and family rights.[13] And although an occupant may implement security-related measures 'in regard to protected persons as may be necessary as a result of war',[14] including practices that restrict their freedom of movement:

> [T]he regulations concerning occupation [...] are based on the idea of the personal freedom of civilians remaining in general impaired. [...] What is essential is that the measures of constraint they adopt should not affect the

8 Convention (IV) respecting the Laws and Customs of War on Land and its Annex: Regulation concerning the Laws and Customs of War on Land, 18 October 1907, Cons TS No 25, 277 (entered into force 26 January 1910) [Hague Regulations]. Christopher Greenwood, 'The Administration of Occupied Territory in International Law', *supra* note 2.

9 *Pictet* Commentary, *supra* note 3 at 273.

10 Other articles include article 45, which prohibits the Occupying Power from forcing the occupied population to swear allegiance to it; article 55, which states that the occupant is only an administrator or usufructuary of public buildings and resources; and articles 48 and 49, concerning the collection of taxes. Hague Regulations, *supra* note 8.

11 The principle of self-determination underscores that sovereignty over people and territory must be derived from a source other than the State, namely from the people it claims to represent. Nathaniel Berman, 'Self-Determination in Abeyance: Self-Determination and International Law', (1986–1989) 7 Wis Int'l L J 51.

12 Article 4 of the *Geneva Convention (IV) Relative to the Protection of Civilian Persons in Time of War* (12 August 1949), 75:973 UNTS, 287 (entered into force 21 October 1950) [Fourth Geneva Convention]. See also Martti Koskenniemi, 'Occupied Zone – "A Zone of Reasonableness?"', (January 2008) 41: 1–2 Isr LR 13.

13 Article 27(1) of the Fourth Geneva Convention, *supra* note 11. See also *Pictet* Commentary, *supra* note 3 at 202–207.

14 Article 27(4) of the Fourth Geneva Convention, supra note 11.

> fundamental rights of the persons concerned. […] [T]hose rights must be respected even when measures of constraint are justified.[15]

In addition, the Fourth Geneva Convention underscores that these persons may not be:

> [D]eprived in any case or in any manner whatsoever of the benefits of the present Convention by any changes introduced, as a result of the occupation […] *nor by annexation by the latter of the whole or part of the occupied territory* [emphasis added].[16]

The Wall in and around Jerusalem

In 1967, Israel occupied the West Bank including EJ.[17] Shortly thereafter, the Israeli government applied Israeli law, jurisdiction and administration over it. At the time, these measures were understood by the international community to effect an annexation,[18] 'in all but name'.[19] It also provoked strong criticism by the United Nations (UN), the Security Council (SC) and the General Assembly (GA).[20]

Israel's subsequent adoption of the 1980 Basic Law: *Jerusalem*, declaring 'unified Jerusalem' to be the capital of Israel, forced about a similar wave of strongly worded resolutions in response. Indeed, the UN SC adopted Resolution 478, in which it affirmed 'that the enactment of the basic law by Israel constitutes a violation of international law and does not affect the continued application of the [Fourth] Geneva Convention in the […] territories occupied since 1967, including East Jerusalem'.[21] It also decided 'not to recognize the "basic law" and such other actions by Israel that, as a result of this law, seek to alter the character and status of Jerusalem'.[22] The language employed in the resolution can be explained by the prohibition on the acquisition of territory by force under customary international

15 *Pictet* Commentary, *supra* note 3 at 202 and at 207.

16 Article 47 of the Fourth Geneva Convention, *supra* note 12. '[A]n Occupying Power continues to be bound to apply the Convention as a whole, even when, in disregard of the rules of international law, it claims during a conflict to have annexed all or part of an occupied territory'. *Pictet* Commentary, *supra* note 3 at 276.

17 *Encyclopedia of the Israeli–Palestinian Conflict*, vol 2, 'Jerusalem' by Michael Dumper (Boulder, CO: Lynne Rienner, 2010) 731.

18 Eyal Benvenisti, *The International Law of Occupation*, *supra* note 4.

19 John Quigley, 'Sovereignty in Jerusalem', *supra* note 5 at 775.

20 *Measures Taken by Israel to Change the Status of the City of Jerusalem*, GA Res 2253 (ES-V), 5th Emergency Session, UN Doc A/RES/2253 (ES-V) (4 July 1967) at para 2, online: UN www.un.org/en/ga/search/view_doc.asp?symbol=A/RES/2253(ES-V); UN SC, Resolution 252 UN Doc S/RES/252 (1968) (2 May 1968), online: UN www.un.org/en/ga/search/view_doc.asp?symbol=S/RES/252(1968).

21 UN SC Resolution 478, UN Doc S/RES/478 (1980) (20 August 1980), para 2, online: UN www.un.org/en/ga/search/view_doc.asp?symbol=S/RES/478(1980).

22 Ibid. at para 5.

law.[23] This prohibition and the obligation of third States not to recognize as lawful any territorial changes brought about by this serious violation also form part of customary international law that is of a peremptory character.[24]

Following EJ's annexation, the Palestinians of the city, who at the time of the occupation were physically present therein, were also granted 'Israeli residency' status.[25] This amounted to a status that was distinct from that of 'West Bank' Palestinians, who were subjected to the rules and regulations of a military regime. According to human rights non-governmental organizations (NGOs), a series of Israeli measures were designed to consolidate this status of EJ as part of 'Jewish Jerusalem: Capital of Israel'.[26] One of these latest measures is the construction of the Wall, including in and around EJ. Officially referred to as *Otef Yerushalaym*, government representatives have argued that the Wall's route in the area was guided by two main sets of legitimate considerations: the first is the desire to provide security for residents of Israel proper, including 'all of Jerusalem'.[27] The second is the need to protect the residents of the major Israeli settlement blocs in the 'West Bank' that have been built around the Israeli self-declared Jerusalem Municipality (JM).[28] At the same time, there is a proclaimed need to allow '[m]inimum disruptions to the daily life of the [Palestinian] population residing on both sides of the Security Fence [...] along its course'.[29]

23 Rainer Hofmann (February 2013), 'Annexation', in Rüdiger Wolfrum, ed, *Max Planck Encyclopedia of Public International Law* (Oxford University Press, 2008), online edition: http://opil.ouplaw.com/home/epil. The majority of States have not moved their embassies from Tel Aviv to Jerusalem. Monique Chemillier-Gendrau, 'Jérusalem, le droit international comme source de solution', (2013) 3:86 Confluences Méditerranée 57.

24 Art. 41 (2), 'Responsibility of States for International Wrongful Acts', article 41(2), Annex to UN GA Resolution 56/83, 56th Sess, Agenda Item 162, UN Doc A/RES/56/83 (28 January 2002), online: UN www.un.org/en/ga/search/view_doc.asp?symbol=A/RES/56/83. That States may not encourage violations of IHL by parties to an armed conflict has been established by state practice and *opinio juris* as a norm of customary international law applicable in both international and non-international armed conflicts. 'Rule 144: Ensuring Respect for International Humanitarian Law *Erga Omnes*', in J.M. Henckaerts and L. Doswald-Beck, eds, *Customary International Humanitarian Law* (Cambridge: Cambridge University Press, 2005) at 462–463, online: ICRC www.icrc.org/customary-ihl/eng/docs/v1_rul_rule144#Fn_11_6 [ICRC Customary Law Study].

25 Ruth Lapidoth, 'Jerusalem: Some Legal Issues', (2011) at 162, online: Jerusalem Institute for Israel Studies www.jiis.org/.upload/lapidoth-jerusalem.pdf.

26 'Response of *Ir Amim* to the Fourth Periodic Report of Israel (CCPR/C/ISR/4) in accordance with the List of Issues adopted by the Human Rights Committee at its 105th Session 9–27 July 2012', (September 2014), online: UN Office of the High Commissioner for Human Rights (OHCHR) http://tbinternet.ohchr.org/Treaties/CCPR/Shared%20Documents/ISR/INT_CCPR_CSS_ISR_18193_E.pdf [*Ir Amim* Response 2014].

27 (HCJ 5488/04) [2006] *Al-Ram Local Council et al. v. Government of Israel et al.*, unofficial English translation by Avichay Sharon (January 2014), on file with author at 2–3 [*Al-Ram Local Council* Judgment]. The petition was dismissed by the HCJ. The term 'West Bank' will be used in this chapter to refer to all of the West Bank excluding those parts of Jerusalem that were annexed by Israel in 1967.

28 For example (HCJ 11205/05) [2006] *Al-Ezariyah Village Council et al. v. Government of Israel et al.*, unofficial English translation by Avichay Sharon (February 2014), on file with author, at para 7 [*Al-Ezariyah Village Council* Judgment]. The petition was dismissed by the HCJ.

29 Israeli Ministry of Defense (MoD), 'Israel's Security Fence: Route', online: Israeli MoD https://web.archive.org/web/20120325000339/www.securityfence.mod.gov.il/Pages/ENG/route.htm.

Israeli authorities have made it clear that they do not consider EJ to be occupied territory. Thus, government authorities have admitted in court that the route of the sections of the Wall in and around Jerusalem, challenged by Palestinians, is not only driven by security considerations, but also by considerations that support 'diplomatic political state interests'.[30] Hence, they do not consider the requirement that an Occupying Power's measures in an occupied territory be guided only by security or by the interest of the 'local population' to apply.

However, the Wall's construction cannot be viewed in isolation from other policies and considerations that have been spearheaded by the objective of consolidating the annexation of EJ.[31] The first set of political considerations and their associated policies relate to the consolidation of physical control over EJ, and the 'West Bank' land outside the Jerusalem Municipal Border (JMB), on which some of the largest 'West Bank' Israeli settlement blocs are located. Here, the Wall's route contributes towards this objective by following the JMB in some parts, while veering sharply away from that border in other areas, deep into the West Bank, to include major Israeli settlements inside the Wall, as a prelude to their de facto annexation to Israel proper.[32]

The second set of political considerations is demographic in nature and seeks to ensure the prevalence of a demographic majority in favour of the Israeli Jewish inhabitants. This comes at the expense of its Palestinian population, who carry 'Israeli residency' Identification Documents (IDs) [thereafter Palestinians with Jerusalem IDs].[33] A population of approximately 300,000 to 370,000, they constitute an estimated 31 to 39 per cent of the overall population of the JM,[34] and 8–10 per cent of all Palestinians living in the West Bank.[35]

In relation to this latter consideration, the Wall cordons off densely populated EJ Palestinian neighbourhoods, which to date, are part of the jurisdiction

30 *Al-Ram Local Village Council* Judgment, *supra* note 27 at paras 31–39.

31 Francesco Chiodelli, 'Reshaping Jerusalem: The Transformation of Jerusalem's Metropolitan Area by the Israeli Barrier', (2013) 31 Cities 417.

32 *Peace Now*, 'The Etzion Bloc and the Security Barrier', (November 2006), online: *Peace Now* https://web.archive.org/web/20140821131830/http://peacenow.org.il/eng/content/etzion-bloc-and-security-barrier.

33 *B'Tselem*, 'Revocation of Israeli Residency', (January 2011), online: *B'Tselem* https://web.archive.org/web/20140328034228/www.btselem.org/jerusalem/revocation_of_residency.

34 This amounts to an estimated 371,000 persons. Association for Civil Rights in Israel (ACRI), 'East Jerusalem – By the Numbers', (updated 7 May 2013), online: ACRI www.acri.org.il/en/2013/05/07/ej-figures/. Another figure puts the total number of Palestinians in EJ at 300,000. Office for the Coordination of Humanitarian Assistance OCHA, oPt, 'Key Humanitarian Concerns: East Jerusalem', (August 2014), online: OCHA-oPt https://web.archive.org/web/20150421094637/www.ochaopt.org/documents/ocha_opt_jerusalem_factsheet_august 2014_english.pdf.

35 Figure for 2011. United Nations Conference on Trade and Development (UNCTAD), *The Palestinian Economy in East Jerusalem: Enduring Annexation, Isolation and Disintegration*, UN Doc UNCTAD/GDS/APP/2012/1, online: UNCTAD http://unctad.org/en/PublicationsLibrary/gdsapp2012d1_en.pdf.

of the JM.[36] At the same time, it consolidates the physical integration of the nearby Israeli settlements and its population within the bigger Jerusalem metropolis. Although the Wall leaves a little over 200,000 Palestinians with Jerusalem IDs on the 'Israeli side' of the Wall, in other areas it deviates away from the JMB. This excludes an estimated eight Palestinian neighbourhoods, together with a population of 55,000–80,000 Palestinians (with Jerusalem IDs) to remain outside the Wall (on the 'Palestinian side' of the Wall). Hence, by cutting into the JMB at select locations, 'the barrier achieves a substantial reduction, de facto, in the number of Palestinian residents in the city'.[37]

Nevertheless, the Wall includes, on the 'Israeli side' a significant number of settlements. Although physically located outside the JMB, today they constitute some of the most densely populated settlements that Israel has created in the West Bank.[38] However, and despite Israeli unilateral measures and efforts to step up construction of settlements and housing units in EJ 'neighbourhoods' beyond the Green Line,[39] the accepted international legal position, the official one, has been that EJ's legal status is the same as that of the entire West Bank (as an occupied territory), to which the Fourth Geneva Convention applies.[40] A third political consideration is the desire by government authorities to fracture EJ's position as the cornerstone of the occupied West Bank in functional, economic, social, religious and symbolic terms.[41]

Israeli practices in EJ

Consolidating physical control over annexed EJ

When Israel secured control of West Jerusalem (1948), it extended its domestic law to that part of the city by way of a proclamation issued by the Ministry of Defence and by means of the *Areas of Jurisdiction and Powers Ordinance 5708–1948*.[42] Shortly thereafter, this part was declared an inseparable part of the State of Israel and as its eternal capital.[43] Following its occupation of the West Bank and EJ in 1967, authorities extended the municipal boundaries of 'Unified

36 *Ir Amim* and *Yachad:* Together for Israel, 'Frequently Asked Questions about Jerusalem', reference document (2013), online: *Yachad* http://yachad.org.uk/wp-content/uploads/2013/07/FAQ-about-Jersualem.pdf.

37 *Ir Amim*, 'Beyond the Wall', Report (January 2007) at 3, online: *Ir Amim* www.ir-amim.org.il/en/reports_1/641.

38 Menachem Klein, 'Jerusalem as an Israeli Problem – A Review of Forty Years of Israeli Rule over Arab Jerusalem', (Summer 2008) 13:2 Israel Stud 54 at 5.

39 Jack Khoury, 'Israel Issues 558 Permits for East Jerusalem Housing', *Haaretz* (5 February 2012).

40 *Legal Consequences of the Construction of a Wall in the Occupied Palestinian Territory* [2004] ICI Rep 136 at paras 78 and 97 [ICJ *Wall* Advisory Opinion].

41 Francesco Chiodelli, 'Re-shaping Jerusalem', *supra* note 31.

42 Ruth Lapidoth, 'Jerusalem: Some Legal Issues', *supra* note 25.

43 Ruth Lapidoth (May 2013) 'Jerusalem' in *Max Planck Encyclopedia of International Law* (Oxford University Press, 2008), online edition: http://opil.ouplaw.com/home/epil.

Jerusalem', to include two additional areas: the 6 km² comprising the newly occupied EJ, and an estimated 64 km² of additional West Bank territory.[44] On 28 June 1967, they applied the *Law and Administrative Ordinance (Amendment No. 11) Law, 5727–1967*, declaring that 'the state's law, jurisdiction, and administration will apply to any area of the Land of Israel that the government decides by decree'.[45] The area, to which those elements would be applied, was delineated by the Ministry of Interior under another law, the *Municipalities Ordinance (Amendment No. 6) Law, 5727–1967*. This law authorized the extension of the JMB where Israel's jurisdiction had been applied in accordance with the above amendment.[46] This left heavily populated Palestinian villages and/or neighbourhoods of EJ outside the JMB, while some of their lands were included.[47] Today, the Israeli-defined JM spans an estimated 108 km².[48]

Government authorities also conducted a census in the annexed areas and granted permanent residency status to those Palestinians who were resident and present at the time in those areas (an estimated 66,000 Palestinians). This granted them the right to buy property, to work and move freely in Jerusalem and in Israel, and to receive social benefits (in return for the payment of taxes).[49] Palestinians, who traditionally resided in EJ but who, for whatever reason, were not present in the city at the time of the census, forever lost their right to reside in the city.[50] Instead, they were granted, together with the rest of the 'West Bank' residents, 'West Bank' IDs.[51] Moreover, an estimated 30,000 Palestinian residents of Jerusalem, who lived nearby the Israeli declared JMB, were also excluded.[52]

In June 1980, the Israeli *Knesset* adopted the Basic Law: *Jerusalem: Capital of Israel* [Basic Law: *Jerusalem*], which expressed 'unequivocally Israel's claim to the right to exercise its sovereignty over the area',[53] and that 'Jerusalem

44 *B'Tselem*, 'Legal Status of Jerusalem and its Residents', (1 January 2013), online: *B'Tselem* www.btselem.org/jerusalem/legal_status.

45 Israeli MoFA, 'Law and Administration Ordinance – Amendment No. 11-Law', online: MoFA http://mfa.gov.il/MFA/ForeignPolicy/MFADocuments/Yearbook1/Pages/13%20Law%20and%20Administration%20Ordinance%20-Amendment%20No.aspx.

46 Ruth Lapidoth, 'Jerusalem: Some Legal Issues', *supra* note 25.

47 *B'Tselem*, 'Legal Status of Jerusalem and its Residents', *supra* note 44.

48 *Ir Amim* and *Yachad:* Together for Israel, 'Frequently Asked Questions about Jerusalem' *supra* note 36.

49 This includes health insurance, social security and public schooling. Danielle C Jefferis, 'Institutionalizing Statelessness: The Revocation of Residency Rights of Palestinians in East Jerusalem', (2012) Int'l J Refugee L 1.

50 International Crisis Group (ICG), 'Extreme Makeover? (I): Israel's Politics of Land and Faith in East Jerusalem', Middle East Report No.134 Report (20 December 2012), online: ICG www.crisisgroup.org/middle-east-north-africa/eastern-mediterranean/israelpalestine/extreme-makeover-i-israel-s-politics-land-and-faith-east-jerusalem.

51 OCHA-oPt, 'The Humanitarian Impact of the Barrier on Palestinian Communities: East Jerusalem', (June 2007), online: OCHA-oPt https://web.archive.org/web/20160305132859/www.ochaopt.org/documents/jerusalem-30july2007.pdf.

52 Ibid.

53 Eyal Benvenisti, *The International Law of Occupation*, *supra* note 4 at 113.

complete and united is the capital of Israel',[54] The Law also explained that '[t]he jurisdiction of Jerusalem includes, [...] all of the area that is described in the appendix of the proclamation expanding the borders of municipal Jerusalem beginning [...] (June 28, 1967)'.[55]

Israeli authorities also constructed and expanded settlements in and around EJ. By the end of 2015, Israel had built 15 settlements in EJ (as part of the JMB).[56] An estimated 210,000 Israeli settlers live in large settlement blocs, while another estimated 2,000–3,000 live in small enclaves in the heart of Palestinian EJ neighbourhoods.[57] Attempts to consolidate control over EJ have also resulted in the creation of 'concentric belts of Jewish presence' [58] around Jerusalem. This term refers to large settlement blocs that extend approximately 10 km from the JMB into the 'West Bank'.[59] The Israeli residents of these blocs are also integrated in their daily life with the JM and with Israel proper, commuting to and from them for work, school and social activities.

One of these blocs east of Jerusalem is the Adumim Bloc, which includes the Ma'ale Adumim settlement.[60] A second bloc is that of Giv'at Zeev (also called the Givon bloc), located north-west of Jerusalem.[61] The third bloc, also known as the Gush Etzion bloc, is situated south-west of Jerusalem. All of these blocs remain within the Israeli political and public consensus as settlements that should be incorporated into Israel,[62] irrespective of the outcome of Palestinian–Israeli peace negotiations.[63] By including all of them on the 'Israeli side' of the

54 Basic Law *Jerusalem: Capital of Israel* (unofficial translation) at section 1, online: *Knesset* www.knesset.gov.il/laws/special/eng/basic10_eng.htm [Basic Law: *Jerusalem*].

55 Ibid. at section 5.

56 These have been commonly referred to by the HCJ as 'Jewish neighbourhoods', *B'Tselem*, 'Statistics on Settlements and Settler Population', (updated 11 May 2017), online: *B'Tselem* www.btselem.org/settlements/statistics.

57 *Israeli settlements in the Occupied Palestinian Territory, including East Jerusalem, and the occupied Syrian Golan: Report of the United Nations High Commissioner for Human Rights*, Human Rights Council (HRC) 37th Sess, UN Doc A/HRC/37/47 (6 March 2018) at para 26, online: OHCHR www.ohchr.org/EN/HRBodies/HRC/RegularSessions/Session37/_layouts/15/WopiFrame.aspx?sourcedoc=/EN/HRBodies/HRC/RegularSessions/Session37/Documents/A_HRC_37_43.docx&action=default&DefaultItemOpen=1.

58 ICG 'Extreme Makeover?' *supra* note 50 at 7.

59 Ibid.

60 Encompassing approximately 4,800 hectares, it is the largest Israeli settlement in its jurisdictional area and the third largest in population size (after Beitar Illit and Modi'in Illit). *B'Tselem* and *Bimkom*: Planners for Planning Rights, 'The Hidden Agenda: The Establishment and Expansion Plans of Ma'ale Adummim and their Human Rights Ramifications', Report (2009), online: *B'Tselem* www.btselem.org/download/200912_maale_adummim_eng.pdf.

61 Edward Cody, 'Israeli Settlements: A Link to Jerusalem', *Washington Post* (14 August 1979).

62 Ibid.

63 Aluf Benn, 'Olmert: Israel will Separate from most Palestinians', *Haaretz* (8 February 2006). The permanent status of EJ is to be determined and shall be addressed in final status negotiations between the two sides to begin no later than 1996. 'Declaration of Principles on Interim Self-Government Arrangements 13 September, 1993' 32 ILM (1993) 1535.

Wall, it has been argued that 'the barrier mothers a "Greater Jewish Jerusalem" a 10/15 km radius predominantly Jewish metropolitan area'.[64]

In the case of Israeli settlements that were built in the Jerusalem area but outside the JMB, Israeli authorities have requisitioned the land for this purpose, using the same land confiscation procedures that they have used for this purpose elsewhere in the 'West Bank'.[65] Authorities have also confiscated land on the ground that it would be necessary for public use. In many cases, once this land has been confiscated, it has been allocated for the construction of settlements.[66]

Maintaining a Jewish majority in the city

The second category of measures through which Israeli authorities have sought to control the number of EJ Palestinians, includes the requirement that those Palestinians demonstrate that EJ continues to be their 'centre of life'. As 'Israeli residents', they are entitled to live and work in Israel and to receive Israeli social benefits.[67] However, if an individual has lived outside of those areas for seven years or more, he/she risks the revocation of his/her permanent residency.[68] The onus lies on Palestinian East Jerusalemites to prove (through the submission of extensive documentation) that Jerusalem remains their 'centre of life'.[69] This equally applies if the individual has physically moved to other parts of the 'West Bank' even if he/she resides in close proximity to the JMB. It also applies if the person obtained citizenship or residency in another country.[70] This policy

64 Francesco Chiodelli, 'Reshaping Jerusalem', *supra* note 31 at 418.

65 This includes declaring the land as 'state land'. In the case of settlements built inside EJ, other methods for confiscating land include declaring the land as absentee property and confiscating land for 'public use'. *Absentees' Property Law (5710–1950)*, unofficial English translation, online: Israel Law Resource Center https://web.archive.org/web/20160326012134/www.israellaw resourcecenter.org/israellaws/fulltext/absenteepropertylaw.htm [*Absentees' Property* Law 1950].

66 This was under the *1943 Land (Acquisition for Public Purposes) Ordinance*. Usama Halabi, 'Legal Status of the Population of East Jerusalem since 1967 and the Implications of Israeli Annexation on their Civil and Social Right', Report, online: Civic Coalition for Defending the Palestinian Rights in Jerusalem https://web.archive.org/web/20140204035434/http://civiccoalition-jerusalem.org/system/files/documents/chap._1-legal_status_of_the_population_of_ej.pdf.

67 *B'Tselem*, 'Legal Status of Jerusalem and its Residents', *supra* note 44. Jews from anywhere in the world, are entitled to automatically receive Israeli citizenship by virtue of Israel's *Law of Return (1950)*. For an English translation of the law, online: *Hamoked* www.hamoked.org/Document.aspx?dID=2240.

68 UN OCHA-oPt, 'East Jerusalem: Key Humanitarian Concerns' Special Focus (March 2011), online: OCHA-oPt www.ochaopt.org/documents/ocha_opt_jerusalem_report_2011_03_23_web_english.pdf.

69 UN OCHA-oPt, 'The Humanitarian Impact of the West Bank Barrier', (June 2007), *supra* note 51. Jewish settlers are exempt from having to prove that Jerusalem is their 'centre of life'. Human Rights Watch (HRW), 'Separate and Unequal: Israel's Discriminatory Treatment of Palestinians in the Occupied Palestinian Territories', Report (19 December 2010), online: HRW www.hrw.org/reports/2010/12/19/separate-and-unequal.

70 UN OCHA-oPt, 'Fragmented Lives: Humanitarian Overview 2011', Report (May 2012), online: UNISPAL https://unispal.un.org/DPA/DPR/unispal.nsf/0/65EF204C475CFFC685257A0D00494E3F.

has been criticized for allowing government authorities to treat EJ Palestinians 'as immigrants without the basic right to live in their homes'.[71] During the period 1967 to 2013, the Ministry of Interior has revoked an estimated 14,309 residency statuses of Palestinian East Jerusalemites.[72] This includes residency permits of those who have relocated to the 'West Bank'.[73]

Another policy is to ensure unequal access of Palestinians with Jerusalem IDs to planning and building in EJ.[74] Following EJ's annexation, Israeli law, such as the *Planning and Building Law (1965)*, was applied to that part of the city. With that, Jordanian outline plans that had been valid for the area were largely annulled.[75] In the 1980s, the JM began preparing outline plans for all of the EJ Palestinian neighbourhoods. Of the 70.5 km^2 of land in EJ, 35 per cent was expropriated for the construction of Israeli settlements.[76] This resulted in a corresponding reduction in land and resources available for construction and development in the Palestinian EJ neighbourhoods.[77] Outline plans, meanwhile, covered only a small part of the total area of land in those neighbourhoods.[78]

This resulted in a severe shortage in housing units available in the EJ Palestinian neighbourhoods, including in the number of buildings performing public needs.[79] Other contributing elements include the difficulty and high costs of obtaining building permits;[80] the allocation of substantial areas in that part of the city to the establishment of national parks;[81] and difficulties encountered by Palestinians (who were seeking to build) in the licensing stage.[82] In addition,

71 *B'Tselem*, 'Revocation of Israeli Residency in East Jerusalem', *supra* note 33.

72 *Ir Amim* Response 2014, *supra* note 26.

73 *B'Tselem*, 'Revocation of Residency in East Jerusalem', *supra* note 33.

74 *B'Tselem*, 'Discrimination in Planning, Building and Land Expropriation', (1 January 2011), online: *B'Tselem* www.btselem.org/jerusalem/discriminating_policy.

75 Ibid.

76 By 2001, 461,978 housing units for Israeli Jews were established, but not one unit for Palestinians ibid.

77 OCHA-oPt, 'East Jerusalem: Key Humanitarian Concerns', *supra* note 68.

78 From the entire area of the JM (around 126,000 dunums), only 17 per cent was included in outline plans for the Palestinian neighbourhoods of EJ. Of the aforementioned 17 per cent, a mere 46 per cent has been designated for housing purposes, in accordance with detailed outline plans that are still valid. *Bimkom and ACRI v. Chair of the Jerusalem District Planning and Building Committee* (extracts from petition in English) (April 2013) at para 42, online: ACRI www.acri.org.il/en/wp-content/uploads/2013/04/Planning-Petition-ENG.pdf [*ACRI* and *Bimkom* Petition].

79 This has led to a severe shortage in social welfare offices, health centres, kindergartens and other service providers. [*ACRI* and *Bimkom* Petition, *supra* note 79 at para 86 and paras 89–90.

80 From 2005–2009, an estimated 3,215 residential building permits were granted in the JM, 20.6 per cent in the EJ Palestinian neighbourhoods, while 19.3 per cent were granted for construction in Israeli settlements therein, and 60.1 per cent to construction in West Jerusalem. *Bimkom*, 'Violation of Civil and Political Rights in the Realm of Planning and Building in Israel and the Occupied Territories: Shadow Report – Response to the State of Israel's Report to the UN regarding the Implementation of the International Covenant on Civil and Political Rights', (September 2014), at 14, online: OHCHR http://tbinternet.ohchr.org/Treaties/CCPR/Shared%20 Documents/ISR/INT_CCPR_CSS_ISR_18128_E.pdf [*Bimkom* Shadow Report 2014].

81 *B'Tselem*, 'National Parks as a Tool for Constraining Palestinian Neighbourhoods in East Jerusalem', (16 September 2014), online: *B'Tselem* www.btselem.org/jerusalem/national_parks.

82 *Ir Amim and Yachad*, 'Frequently Asked Questions about Jerusalem', *supra* note 36.

while the *Jerusalem 2000 Local Outline* plan[83] allowed for the improvement in the planning situation of EJ Palestinian neighbourhoods,[84] in practice it stipulated conditions that were exceedingly difficult to meet.[85] Concern was also expressed about the extent to which the plan bases efforts of zoning and planning in the JM on an officially adopted government policy of maintaining a ratio of 70 per cent Jewish Israelis and 30 per cent Arab Palestinians.[86]

Prior to the construction of the Wall in the Jerusalem area, the resulting severe housing crisis led thousands of Palestinians with Jerusalem IDs over the years to move into the 'West Bank' villages and suburbs of Jerusalem (outside the JMB).[87] Others have resorted to illegal construction inside the city, to which the JM has responded by issuing administrative demolition orders.[88] Estimates for the year 2013 projected that 33 per cent of all Palestinian homes in EJ lacked an Israeli-issued building permit, thereby placing approximately 93,000 Palestinians at risk of displacement.[89]

Severing East Jerusalem from the rest of the 'West Bank'

The third category of measures sought to isolate EJ from the rest of the West Bank. Up until the 1990s, however, the Israeli unilateral act of annexing the territory had little implications for the ability of Palestinians with 'West Bank' IDs to continue to physically access the eastern part of the city for work, education, health care or the maintenance of family and cultural ties.[90]

Following the outbreak of the *First Intifada* (1987–1993), Israel began to 'sever East Jerusalem from its social, political, and economic hinterland in the West Bank'.[91] In 1993, they began demanding that those Palestinians wishing to access EJ obtain special permits from the Israeli Civil Administration (CA), a process that was time-consuming and bureaucratic.[92] Many permits were denied for security reasons, the most specific reasons for the denial of permits being rarely given to the applicant.[93] Many Palestinians with 'West Bank' IDs continued to make their way

83 *Bimkom*, 'From Public to National: National Parks in East Jerusalem', Report (2012), online: *Bimkom* http://bimkom.org/eng/from-public-to-national-national-parks-in-east-jerusalem/.

84 *Bimkom* Shadow Report 2014, *supra* note 80.

85 Ibid. at 4 and 13.

86 The plan offers suggestions on how to achieve a 60/40 ratio instead, because of high birth rates among the Palestinian population. OCHA-oPt, 'East Jerusalem: Key Humanitarian Concerns', *supra* note 68.

87 Usama Halabi, 'Legal Status of', *supra* note 66.

88 UN OCHA-oPt, 'Report 4–17 June 2013', online: OCHA-oPt www.ochaopt.org/sites/default/files/ocha_opt_protection_of_civilians_weekly_report_2013_06_21_english.pdf.

89 UN OCHA-oPt, 'Humanitarian Monthly Report: November 2013', online: OCHA-oPt www.ochaopt.org/sites/default/files/ocha_opt_the_humanitarian_monitor_2013_12_16_english.pdf.

90 UNCTAD, 'The Palestinian Economy in East Jerusalem', *supra* note 35.

91 Menachem Klein, 'Jerusalem as an Israeli Problem – A Review of Forty Years of Israeli Rule over Arab Jerusalem', (Summer 2008) 13:2 Israel Studies 54 at 65.

92 OCHA-oPt, 'The Humanitarian Impact of the Barrier', *supra* note 51.

93 Ibid.

into the city, often illegally, in order to access social services and employment opportunities or places of worship.[94] With the beginning of the *Second Intifada* (2000), access was further restricted, through additional military checkpoints on the major access routes from the 'West Bank' to Jerusalem and into Israel proper.[95]

The route of the Wall in and around Jerusalem: security or political considerations?

Overview

In June 2002, the Israeli government approved the first stage of the Wall, which included the first two sections of this structure north and south of Jerusalem. This was followed by a decision in 2003, to approve the Wall's route along the eastern JMB.[96] However, in 2005, and in light of numerous HCJ landmark Wall-related rulings, the government approved an entirely new route for the structure. However, while it made significant changes to this route in various areas, it remained largely the same in the Jerusalem area.[97]

Much of the route of the Wall runs along the JMB, as opposed to the Green Line. However, in some segments in and around the Jerusalem area, the route makes an important deviation in two ways: the first one is by deviating from the JMB in some areas, thereby leaving EJ Palestinian neighbourhoods which are officially part of the JM, outside the Wall. Where the route runs inside the JM or along the JMB, authorities have considered the Wall to be physically located on Israeli sovereign territory. Therefore, to requisition land for the Wall's construction, government authorities have invoked the *Emergency Land Regulation Law (5710–1949)*.[98] This law enables relevant authorities to make land

94 *Al-Haq*, 'Building Walls, Breaking Communities: The Impact of the Annexation on East Jerusalem Palestinians', Report (October 2005), online: *Al-Haq* www.alhaq.org/publications/publications-index/item/building-walls-breaking-communities-the-impact-of-the-annexation-wall-on-east-jerusalem-palestinians.

95 OCHA: oPt, 'The Humanitarian Impact of the West Bank Barrier', *supra* note 51.

96 *B'Tselem* and *Bimkom*, 'Under the Guise of Security: Routing the Separation Barrier to enable the Expansion of Israeli Settlements in the West Bank', Report (December 2005), online: *B'Tselem* www.btselem.org/download/200512_under_the_guise_of_security_eng.pdf.

97 Ibid. With the exception of adding an additional 40 km to surround the settlement of Ma'aleh Adumim.

98 For an English version of the law, see *Emergency Land Requisition (Regulation) Law (5710–1949)*, online: Israel Law Resource Center https://web.archive.org/web/20110928035857/www.israellawresourcecenter.org/emergencyregs/fulltext/emergencylandreglaw.htm. [*Emergency Land Regulation Law*]. See also (HCJ 1300/06) [2006] *Rabbi Abu Ziad et al. v. Government of Israel et al.*, unofficial English translation by Avichay Sharon (April 2014), on file with author, at 2 [*Abu Ziad* Judgment]. The petition was dismissed by the HCJ. See also (HCJ 7136/09) [2011] *Qawasmeh Iado et al. v. Ministry of Defense et al.*, unofficial English translation by Avichay Sharon (May 2013), on file with author [*Iado* Judgment]. The petition was dismissed by the HCJ. See also (HCJ 1073/04) [2006] *Omar Salameh et al. v. IDF Commander of Central Command*, unofficial English translation by Avichay Sharon (May 2014), on file with author, at paras 1–4 [*Salameh* Judgment]. The petition was dismissed by the HCJ.

requisitions if it 'is necessary for the Defence of the state, public security [...] or essential public services'.[99] Individuals affected by the requisition have the opportunity to challenge the order by appearing in front of specific appeals committees, established and provided for by the *Emergency Land Regulation Law*.[100]

The second way is that elsewhere; the Wall's route makes incursions inside the 'West Bank', beyond the JMB, in order to include Israeli settlements inside the Wall (on the 'Israeli side'). The land is requisitioned by the Israeli Military Commander (MC), by way of an Israeli Military Order (MO). As already discussed, affected individuals have the opportunity to appeal the land requisition order before specific appeals committees established as part of the Israeli CA.[101]

Cementing physical control of a 'Greater Jerusalem'

Not too long after the Wall's route was determined, the Israeli and international human rights community expressed concerns that it suggests that government authorities are seeking to redraw the size of the JM that it considers part and parcel of sovereign Israeli territory and thus ensure that within this municipality, a Jewish majority prevails. In some areas it runs along the JMB to consolidate control over the parts of EJ that had been formally declared part of the municipality. In other areas, it runs inside the JMB, thereby excluding neighbourhoods of EJ with predominantly large EJ Palestinian populations so that they remain outside the Wall. Elsewhere, it makes incursions inside the 'West Bank' beyond the JMB, to include a large number of 'West Bank' Israeli settlements inside the Wall.

Running the route along the JMB: consolidating EJ's de jure *annexation*

Where the Wall's route runs along the JMB, it has been argued that this has been driven by a desire to consolidate control over the parts of EJ that have already been *de jure* annexed by Israel. By 2005, it was projected to include 12 Israeli settlements built in EJ on the 'Israeli side' of the Wall, together with their estimated 192,918 settlers.[102] One consequence has been that thousands of Palestinians with 'West Bank' IDs (residing in communities that are part of the JM but without Jerusalem IDs), have also been included on the 'Israeli side' of the Wall. The village of Walajeh is a case in point. Located beyond the Green Line, a third of its area had been annexed by Israel to form part of the JM, with the majority of its Palestinian residents (an estimated 2,500 persons) not granted Jerusalem IDs.[103] With the construction of the Wall along the JMB, these residents were cut off from the rest of the 'West Bank' and have since

99 *Emergency Land Requisition Regulation Law*, *supra* note 98 at article 3(b).

100 Ibid. at articles 16 and 17.

101 See Chapter 2.

102 *B'Tselem*, 'The Separation Barrier – Statistics', (updated 16 July 2012), online: *B'Tselem* www.btselem.org/separation_barrier/statistics.

103 *Ir Amim*, 'Walajeh – A Village under Siege', (November 2010), online: *Ir Amim* www.ir-amim.org.il/sites/default/files/Walajeh.pdf.

faced daily challenges in accessing social services, employment, etc., therein. At the same time, by virtue of holding 'West Bank' ID, they are denied the right to move freely in the JM unless they carry Israeli-issued valid permits to do so.

Another example is the community of Al Nu'man in the Bethlehem Governorate ('West Bank').[104] Surrounded by the Wall on three sides, an Israeli military checkpoint was set up in 2006 at the entrance of the village. Residents were required to register their names whenever they entered and left the village, and have since experienced regular delays at the checkpoint.[105] Moreover, Palestinians with 'West Bank' IDs are only allowed to cross the checkpoints on foot; are restricted from bringing in basic products, farming equipment and livestock, and can only access social services (such as schools and clinics) available on the 'Palestinian side' of the Wall.[106]

Running the Wall inside the 'West Bank' beyond the JMB

In some areas, the Wall's route makes incursions inside the 'West Bank', primarily to include, on the 'Israeli side', some of the largest Israeli 'West Bank' settlement blocs that surround annexed EJ, yet are located outside the JMB. By making these incursions, the Wall allegedly seeks to undermine any possibility of seceding control over EJ to the Palestinians as part of a future peace settlement.[107] It also threatens the territorial contiguity of any future state that the Palestinians seek to establish in the West Bank.[108] To the east, where the route of the Wall deviates 14 km from the Green Line, this will comprise the Adumim settlement bloc, where an estimated 53 km^2 of 'West Bank' territory surrounding the settlement of Ma'aleh Adumim will be enclosed by the Wall. The structure will also enclose on the 'Israeli side' of the structure, the controversial E-1 plan,[109] whose northern and southern edges of the plan largely correspond to the route planned for the Wall. If construction plans go ahead as planned, it would complete the isolation of EJ from the rest of the 'West Bank'. It would

104 OCHA-oPt, 'Shrinking Space: Urban Contraction, Rural Fragmentation in the Bethlehem Governorate' Special Focus (May 2009), online: OCHA-oPt www.ochaopt.org/content/shrinking-space-urban-contraction-and-rural-fragmentation-bethlehem-governorate-may-2009.

105 Ibid.

106 This is despite the fact that the community has no shops, schools, mosques or health facilities. *B'Tselem*, 'Nu'man, East Jerusalem – Life under Threat and Expulsion', Status Report (September 2003), online: *B'Tselem* www.btselem.org/download/200309_numan_east_jerusalem_eng.pdf.

107 *Ir Amim*, 'Beyond the Wall', *supra* note 37 at 2.

108 ICG, 'The Jerusalem Powder Keg', (2 August 2005), Middle East Report No. 44, online: ICG www.crisisgroup.org/middle-east-north-africa/eastern-mediterranean/israelpalestine/jerusalem-powder-keg.

109 It covers 12,000 dunums of land inside the 'West Bank', the majority of which has been declared as 'state land' and has been made part of the jurisdiction of the Ma'ale Adumim settlement. *B'Tselem*, 'The E1 Plan and its Implications for Human Rights in the West Bank', (updated 27 November 2013), online: *B'Tselem* www.btselem.org/settlements/20121202_e1_human_rights_ramifications.

also undermine the territorial contiguity between the north and south of the 'West Bank'.[110]

In the north-east, the Wall's route – which intrudes 10 km from the Green Line into the 'West Bank' – it encircles the Giv'at Ze'ev settlement bloc, cutting off approximately 34 km^2 of land from the Jerusalem and the Ramallah governorates to isolate it on the 'Israeli side' of the Wall. Finally, in the south-west, the route will enclose approximately 64 km^2 of some of the most fertile 'West Bank' land and deviates about 10 km from the Green Line, to include the Gush Etzion settlement bloc.[111] In addition on the 'Israeli side', the Wall's route includes some of the major roads, highways, and even railroads which settlers and other Israeli travellers use daily to commute to and from the JM and Israel proper to their settlements.[112]

As with segments of the Wall elsewhere in the 'West Bank', its route around Jerusalem leaves 'West Bank' land – including land that is privately owned by Palestinians – on the 'Israeli side' of the Wall. Here again, it has been alleged that the objective is to provide Israeli settlements in the area with open space that would accommodate their future expansion eastward.[113] One of these settlements is Neve Ya'akov, located in the north-east corner of Jerusalem, where the desire to expand the settlement to the east (beyond the JMB) was a decisive factor in determining the route of the Wall in the area.

One of the consequences has been the inclusion of medium- and small-sized Palestinian communities into enclaves between the Wall and the JMB, often surrounded by the Wall from more than one side. This has prevented residents (the majority of whom are Palestinians with 'West Bank' IDs) from accessing Jerusalem. It has also made it difficult for them to move freely from those enclaves towards other areas of the 'West Bank'. Those wishing to do so must travel long distances and are required to access specifically designated gates in the Wall, where they undergo protracted security checks. Others must cross through physical checkpoints at the entrance of their communities every time they wish to exit or enter them, thereby disrupting every aspect of their daily lives.[114]

One example is the 'West Bank' village of Al-Ram, whose residents have been completely cut off from Jerusalem, and whose village has been deprived of

110 Yet the Court has dismissed previous petitions that have challenged earlier versions of the E1 plan on the ground that it raises issues of a political nature and, therefore, are non-justiciable. Ibid. See also *Iado* Judgment, *supra* note 98 at 3.

111 OCHA-oPt, 'Seven Years after the Advisory Opinion of the International Court of Justice', July 2011), online: OCHA-oPt www.ochaopt.org/content/seven-years-after-advisory-opinion-international-court-justice-barrier.

112 Many of these roads are 'bypass' roads. UN OCHA-oPt, 'The Humanitarian Impact of the West Bank Barrier', *supra* note 51.

113 *B'Tselem* and *Bimkom*, 'Under the Guise of Security', *supra* note 96.

114 *Bimkom*, 'Between Fences: The Enclaves Created by the Separation Barrier' Abstract in English (October 2006), online: *Bimkom* http://bimkom.org/eng/wp-content/uploads/Between-Fences.pdf.

space for urban development on the south-east.[115] Another example is Bir Nabala. Situated north-west of Jerusalem, the Wall's route has trapped an estimated 15,000 Palestinians in five villages, encompassing an area of 270 acres, completely surrounded by that structure from all sides. Residents wishing to leave and enter the enclave towards other parts of the 'West Bank' can only do so by travelling in designated tunnels. The enforced disconnection of these villages from Jerusalem has led 'to the atrophy of the villages in the enclaves possibly resulting in their disintegration'.[116]

Other internal enclaves include Al-Ezariyah and Sawahreh Al Sharqiyeh.[117] Prior to the Wall's construction, these and other localities represented flourishing commercial centres in the area, and depended on the influx of Palestinians with Jerusalem IDs who were able to move freely across the JMB into the 'West Bank'. However, after its construction and the difficulties that many Palestinians with Jerusalem IDs faced in commuting to and from the JM to the 'West Bank', many shops have closed and unemployment has soared, thus marking a clear impoverishment of the area.[118] For example, in the case of the village of Abu Dis (at a distance of only 5 km from the old city of Jerusalem) what once took a 10 minute journey to reach the hospitals in EJ, 'now takes at least one hour and often longer when there are queues and delays at the checkpoints'.[119]

Similarly (north-west of Jerusalem), the Wall's construction has included the entire village of Al-Nabi Sammuel inside the structure.[120] To the east and west, the Wall surrounds the village, while in the north it is blocked by a highway, which is a major 'by-pass' road connecting the nearby Israeli settlement of Pisgat Ze'ev and other settlements with Jerusalem and with the coastal cities of Israel proper.[121] Since the Wall's construction began, its Palestinian residents have faced severe limitations on their ability to build on and farm their land;[122] they have been prohibited from accessing Jerusalem 'a distance of only a few hundred meters from their home'.[123] Those wishing to access major 'West Bank'

115 Case Study: 'Ne'eve Ya'akov' in *B'Tselem* and *Bimkom*, 'Under the Guise of Security', *supra* note 151 at 45. The route of the Wall in the area and its implications was the subject of the petition *Al-Ram Local Village Council* Judgment, *supra* note 27.

116 *Bimkom*, 'Between Fences', *supra* note 114 at VIII. The 5 villages are Bir Nabala, Al Judeira, Beit Hanina, al Balad and Qalandia.

117 *Bimkom*, 'Between Fences', *supra* note 114.

118 UN OCHA-oPt, 'The Humanitarian Impact of the West Bank Barrier', *supra* note 51.

119 Ibid. at 25.

120 This village is home to approximately 200 Palestinians (the majority of whom carry 'West Bank' IDs). Moriel Rothman, 'Living inside an Invisible Cage: Welcome to Nabi Samuel', (18 May 2014), online: *+972 Magazine* http://972mag.com/living-inside-an-invisible-cage-welcome-to-nabi-samuel/91020.

121 (HCJ 426/2005) [2006] *Biddu Village et al. v. Government of Israel et al.*, unofficial English translation by Avichay Sharon (October 2014), on file with author [*Biddu Village Council* Judgment].

122 HRW, 'Israel: Military Chocking Palestinian Village, Planning Tourist Site', (4 February 2014), online: HRW www.hrw.org/news/2014/02/04/israel-military-choking-palestinian-village-planning-tourist-site.

123 Amira Hass, 'Holiday Marred for Hundreds of Palestinians outside Jerusalem as Israeli Army Limits Entry into Villages', *Haaretz* (15 October 2013).

population centres (such as Bir Naballa and Ramallah), have to go through the Al-Jib Wall checkpoint, where they have to endure long waiting hours, thereby prolonging their daily commute to jobs, schools and medical centres in nearby villages.[124] The checkpoint is one example of a 'list checkpoint': a terminology which refers to checkpoints where only those people and vehicles of residents 'registered' as living in the village are permitted to pass through it:

> The lists are updated infrequently, which causes great difficulties in the case of changes of residency. For instance, new brides from other villages who marry men from Nabi Samwil may be unregistered for months (at least) which makes it impossible for them to pass through the checkpoint, and there is no other way for them to access the village. On the other hand, relatives who have moved to the villages on the West Bank side of the wall cannot visit the village.[125]

In 2006, Israeli authorities declared that they will be building 'fabric of life' roads for the purpose of minimizing the harm on residents, primarily by connecting the villages trapped in those enclaves with the rest of the 'West Bank'. However, no such roads connecting Nabi Samwil have been constructed.[126]

The Wall: a demographically driven measure?

Palestinian petitioners have been concerned that the Wall's demographic objectives in the Jerusalem area are twofold. The first one is to exclude a number of Palestinian neighbourhoods and their residents who remain part and parcel of the JM to remain outside the Wall (on the 'Palestinian side'). The second one is to include a significant number of the Israeli settlement population residing in major Israeli settlements in the 'West Bank' to remain inside the Wall (on the 'Israeli side').

Where the Wall runs inside the JM short of the JMB: excluding EJ Palestinian neighbourhoods and their residents, both of which are officially part of the JM

Where the Wall's route runs inside the JM, it has resulted in the exclusion of an estimated eight EJ Palestinian neighbourhoods, on the 'Palestinian side'. Unofficial estimates point to around 60,000 Palestinians (the majority of who hold Jerusalem IDs) residing in those densely populated neighbourhoods which, to

124 Amira Hass, 'The Civil Administration is Preventing the Transfer of Water Tanks to Two Isolated Palestinian Communities in the West Bank', *Haaretz* (14 October 2013).

125 Email response to questions from Michaela Rahat, volunteer activist with *Machsom Watch:* Women against the Occupation and for Human Rights (22 March 2015), on file with author, [*Rahat* Written Response]. The organization is a volunteer activist of Israeli female peace activists who since 2001 monitor and report on the operation of the checkpoints, the Wall and its agricultural gates. See online: *Machsom Watch* www.machsomwatch.org/.

126 Amira Hass, 'Holiday Marred for Hundreds of Palestinians', *supra* note 124.

date, remain part of the jurisdiction of the JM.[127] According to Israeli authorities, the primary reason for the diversion from the JMB is the illegal presence of many Palestinians with 'West Bank' IDs in those neighbourhoods.[128] However, criticism paints a very different picture: one where the objective for cutting into the JMB seeks to achieve 'a substantial reduction, de facto, in the number of Palestinian residents in the city',[129] thereby betraying political considerations of a demographic nature.[130]

The impact of the Wall's route has particularly affected the daily lives of the Palestinians with Jerusalem IDs and their ability to maintain the JM as their 'centre of life'. Because of the route of the structure, thousands have found themselves living on the 'Palestinian side' of the Wall.[131] This has required them to go through checkpoints and gates in the Wall on a daily basis to access employment on the 'Israeli side' of the Wall and obtain other social benefits that they are entitled to as 'Israeli residents'.[132]

One Palestinian EJ neighbourhood facing such reality is Kufr 'Aqab, located in the most northern part of Jerusalem (at the point closest to Ramallah). Cut off from the rest of the JM by the Wall, its residents, the majority of whom are Palestinians with Jerusalem IDs, must go through the traffic heavy Qalandiya/Atarot checkpoint[133] every time they want to enter the rest of the municipality on the 'Israeli side' of the Wall. Despite Israeli government assurances that it would facilitate the access of petitioners, to prevent their quality of life from being undermined,[134] they have, since the Wall's construction, regularly experienced delays at Wall gates and checkpoints which suffer from the lack of clear and consistent crossing times and opening hours:[135]

127 Official government figures regarding the total number of Palestinian Jerusalemites living within the JMB yet on the 'Palestinian side' of the Wall are lacking. A figure given by *Hagihon*, the Jerusalem water company, cites an estimated 60,000 to 80,000 people living by 2014 in the Shuafat Refugee Camp area. ACRI, 'Shadow Report: ICCPR Implementation in East Jerusalem', (August 2014) at 8–9, online: OHCHR http://tbinternet.ohchr.org/_layouts/treatybodyexternal/Download.aspx?symbolno=INT%2fCCPR%2fCSS%2fISR%2f18195andLang=en [ACRI Shadow Report 2014].

128 (AC 405/04, 72/04, 73/04) Residents *of Shuafat Village and Others v. Certified Authority – Ministry of Security*, cited in *Ir Amim*, 'Beyond the Wall', *supra* note 37.

129 Ibid.

130 *Ir Amim*, 'Jerusalem Neighborhood Profile: Shuafat Refugee Camp', Report (September 2006), online: *Ir Amim* www.ir-amim.org.il/en/report/jerusalem-neighborhood-profile-shuafat-refugee-camp.

131 *Ir Amim*, 'Beyond the Wall', *supra* note 37.

132 UN OCHA-oPt, 'Preliminary Analysis: The Humanitarian Implications of the February 2005 West Bank Barrier Route', (February 2005) at 2, online: Relief Web https://reliefweb.int/sites/reliefweb.int/files/resources/68CEAD5936442010C1256FD5002B5E4B-ocha-opt-analysis-22mar.pdf.

133 ACRI Shadow Report 2014, *supra* note 127.

134 These assurances were made, for example, in *Al-Ram Local Village Council* Judgment, *supra* note 27 at paras 31–39.

135 *Ir Amim* Response 2014, *supra* note 26 at 18.

> ACRI's researcher was at Qalandiya Checkpoint on 24 August 2014 and reported that it took car drivers more than an hour to pass through the checkpoint, including the traffic jams to and from. This figure is consistent with about a dozen visits by our field researcher to Qalandiya throughout 2014, and consistent with accounts of the residents of Kufr 'Aqab who pass through the checkpoint daily on their way to work, studies, family visits, etc. During a High Court hearing, the State had assured the judges that passing with a vehicle through Qalandiya would take no longer than 15 minutes at most.[136]

Frequently, only two of the five pedestrian lanes are made operational, including during the busiest hours of the day.[137] This has detrimentally affected all areas of life, particularly health[138] and education.[139]

A second example is the densely populated Shu'afat ridge, situated between Jerusalem and the 'West Bank' city of Ramallah, and which is home to tens of thousands of Palestinians.[140] Many of those Palestinians are either Israeli citizens or carry Jerusalem IDs.[141] Palestinians with Jerusalem IDs must pass daily through the Shu'afat camp/Anata checkpoint:[142]

> Throughout the day and night, including rush hour, only 2 of the vehicular lanes are open; As such, every morning, between 8:00 and 8:45 AM, traffic jams from the exit of the neighbourhoods toward Jerusalem cause delays of up to half an hour. In the direction toward the neighbourhoods, only one of the lanes is open, and it is often blocked by traffic police who stop and check vehicles from within the lane itself [...].[143]

At other smaller checkpoints, such as the Sawahreh Al Sharqiyeh (highlighted in some petitions), its residents must be registered with the military authorities if they want to cross that checkpoint:

> Anyone not registered, including visiting family members, cannot pass through ... [G]aining new permits to pass through a checkpoint can take months if not longer [...]. The result is that in these instances and others,

136 ACRI Shadow Report 2014, *supra* note 127 at 11.
137 *Ir Amim* Response 2014, *supra* note 26.
138 *ACRI* Shadow Report 2014, *supra* note 127.
139 UN OCHA-oPt, 'The Humanitarian Impact of the West Bank Barrier', *supra* note 51.
140 This ridge is comprised of the Shuafat Refugee Camp as well as the three Palestinian EJ neighbourhoods of Ras Khamis, Ras Shehada, and Dahiyat al-Salaam. *Ir Amim*, 'Jerusalem Neighbourhood Profile: Shuafat Refugee Camp', *supra* note 130.
141 They add up to a few more thousand Palestinians with 'West Bank' IDs. *B'Tselem*, 'A Wall in Jerusalem: Obstacles to Human Rights in the Holy City', Report (2006), online: *B'Tselem* www.btselem.org/download/200607_a_wall_in_jerusalem.pdf.
142 ACRI, Shadow Report 2014, *supra* note 127.
143 *Ir Amim* Response 2014, *supra* note 26 at 18–19.

long detours and winding roads that can take an hour or longer are used instead of the checkpoint situated only minutes away from one's home.[144]

Yet, despite these difficulties, Israeli authorities have sought to reassure Palestinians with Jerusalem IDs that the Wall's construction 'does not change their status as 'Israeli permanent residents'.[145] In a government decision (2005), they also promised to invest in heavy financial and other resources at the municipal level to ensure that the ordinary life of the residents of these communities continues. This included setting up offices of service provision at the checkpoints themselves and building more schools. However, '[t]he majority of sections included in the decision had not been implemented to this day, more than 9 years after the decision was passed'.[146]

One of the primary concerns of EJ Palestinians is that the Wall's route would, in the long run, result in the loss of their 'Israeli residency' status. These fears have been compounded by recent developments, such as the marked neglect and/or halt of basic services provided by the JM to the Palestinian EJ neighbourhoods remaining on the 'Palestinian side' of the Wall.[147] The absence of Israeli police presence in many of these neighbourhoods has led to thriving crime, as well as drugs and arms trade in some of these communities.[148] It has also augmented the worries of those Palestinians that their continued residence in those neighbourhoods will jeopardize their ability to continue receiving social benefits.[149] Many are also apprehensive that their physical separation from the rest of the JM and the abdication of the JM from providing social services in the area signals Israel's intention to redraw in the future the JMB, so that it matches the route of the Wall, and that soon their 'Israeli residence' status will also be revoked.[150]

Where the Wall runs along the JMB: excluding Palestinians with Jerusalem IDs living in 'West Bank' neighbourhoods of the city

Where Israeli government authorities decided to place the route of the Wall along the JMB (as opposed to the Green Line), this resulted in the physical

144 ACRI Shadow Report 2014, *supra* note 127 at 11–12.

145 Israeli Ministry of Justice (MoJ), The Department for International Agreements and International Litigation, 'Reference to the B'Tselem Draft Report Regarding Restrictions on Movement', Ref. 287 (5 August 2007) in *B'Tselem*, 'Ground to a Halt: Denial of Palestinians' Freedom of Movement in the West Bank', Report (August 2007) at 7–9, online: *B'Tselem* www.btselem.org/sites/default/files2/publication/200708_ground_to_a_halt_eng.pdf.

146 Government of Israel decision no. 3873 concerning the 'Jerusalem Envelope' and the impact of the Wall on residents in Jerusalem passed on 10 July 2005: cited in ACRI Shadow Report 2014, *supra* note 127 at 10.

147 Such as sewage and drainage services, classrooms in official schools, and provision of health care sanitation, and access to water. Ibid.

148 *Ir Amim* Response 2014, *supra* note 26 at 20.

149 This was reported by residents of the Shu'afat ridge. Ibid.

150 *Iado* Judgment, *supra* note 98 at para 4. Barak Ravid, 'Netanyahu Mulls Revoking Residency of Palestinians beyond E. Jerusalem Separation Barrier', *Haaretz* (25 October 2015).

separation of many Palestinian neighbourhoods from each other, depending on whether their neighbourhood is officially part of the jurisdiction of the JM or not.[151] The impact has been particularly severe for Palestinians with Jerusalem IDs residing in the 'West Bank' neighbourhoods/suburbs of EJ.[152]

Despite Israel's unilateral annexation of this city, the built-up areas of the Palestinian neighbourhoods of the JM have, since 1967, spread geographically beyond the JMB into the 'West Bank', thereby forming an urban continuum with the former.[153] One example of such a 'West Bank' village is Al-Ram, north-east of Jerusalem (just outside the JMB), which has been surrounded by the Wall from three sides, cutting it off from the JM. Stretching between the residential houses, the Wall has included portions of the neighbourhood of Dahiyet Al-Bareed, south of Al-Ram, as part of the JM on the 'Israeli side', while the rest of the neighbourhood has, as a result of the route of the Wall, remained on the 'Palestinian side' of the structure.[154]

A second example is the village of Anata. Located in the 'West Bank', it forms one urban continuum with the Palestinian EJ neighbourhood of Dahiyat Al-Salam (which is part of the JM). A third example is the town of Abu Dis. Considered before 1967 to be part of the Jerusalem district, only a segment of it was included by Israeli authorities within the JMB, while the remaining parts were labelled as constituting part of the 'West Bank'.[155] However, with one continuous urban fabric of Palestinian neighbourhoods connecting the walls of the Old City of Jerusalem to Abu Dis, an estimated one-third of its tens of thousands of Palestinian residents (who carry Jerusalem IDs) have chosen to reside in this area. One reason is the severe housing shortage facing them inside the parts of EJ that are officially part of the JM.

A fourth example is the village of Sheikh Saed, which, by virtue of the Wall's route, has remained on the 'Palestinian side' of the structure.[156] Its inhabitants

151 The village of Sheikh Saed serves as a good illustration. Israeli authorities decided to construct a section of the Wall in the Jerusalem area (1.3 km long) inside the JM, thereby cutting off the village from the rest of Jerusalem. When its residents appealed the land confiscation orders to the appeals committee, the committee concluded that even though Sheikh Saed is, officially speaking, outside the JMB, it has been de facto recognized as part of Jabal Al Mukabir. According to the committee, routing the Wall along the JMB, completely disregarded the urban reality and 'fabric of life' of its residents. It then ruled that the land confiscation order is invalid on grounds that it was disproportionate. Government authorities appealed the decision. (HCJ 7337/05) [2010] *Mohamed Naif Shakir et al. v. IDF Commander of Judea and Samaria*, unofficial English translation by Avichay Sharon (May 2014), on file with author at 2–3 [*Shakir* Judgment]. The petition was dismissed by the HCJ.

152 Such as the areas of Dahiyat Al-Barid, Al-Ram, Bir Nabala, and Beit Hanina.

153 Menachem Klein, 'Old and New Walls in Jerusalem', (2005) 24 Political Geography (2005) 53 at 63.

154 *B'Tselem*, 'The Separation Barrier Surrounding Al-Ram', (updated 1 January 2016), online: *B'Tselem* www.btselem.org/separation_barrier/a-ram.

155 *B'Tselem*, 'A Wall in Jerusalem', *supra* note 141.

156 *Iado* Judgment, *supra* note 98.

predominantly carry Jerusalem IDs.[157] Over the years, the village had formed one contiguous urban area with the EJ neighbourhood of Jabal Al Mukabir (which is part of the JM). The latter constitutes the main source for services and employment for the village residents.[158] Here again, the thousands of Palestinians with Jerusalem IDs living in these suburbs have found themselves facing a daily reality of having to traverse checkpoints and gates in the Wall to access the JM (on the 'Israeli side' of the Wall). Coupled with the increased time needed to reach the city from the suburbs through these checkpoints, the Wall's route has undermined their ability to access employment, education and other social benefits and has augmented their concern about their future ties with their city.[159]

Where the Wall's route in the Jerusalem area runs along the JMB or inside the JM: severing the access by Palestinians with 'West Bank' IDs to EJ

In the case of Palestinians with 'West Bank' IDs, those residing in 'West Bank' communities in close proximity to the JMB are the ones most affected by the Wall's construction.[160] Many of these neighbourhoods have for decades existed as one urban continuum with the EJ Palestinian neighbourhoods of the JM.[161] With a population of more than 100,000, its residents have relied heavily on EJ for services, employment opportunities and social ties.[162]

Although government authorities have argued that the interest of the Palestinian local population would be taken into account when constructing the Wall and its associated regime,[163] this remains doubtful.[164] Of the 16

157 Unlike Jabal El Mukabir, Sheik Saed was never annexed by Israel in 1967 and, therefore, remained part of the 'West Bank'. *B'Tselem*, '5 May 2010: High Court of Justice Approves Separation Barrier near Sheikh Sae'd in Jerusalem Area, Seriously Infringing the Village's Human Rights', (5 May 2010), online: *B'Tselem* www.btselem.org/separation_barrier/20100505_sheikh_saed_ruling. Thus, when Israel annexed part of the 'West Bank' and incorporated it in to the jurisdictional area of the JM, the MB ran through the area, including parts inside the JM (such as Jabal Al Mukabir and Sawahreh Al-Gharbiyeh). Its Palestinian inhabitants were granted Jerusalem IDs. Other parts, such as the majority of Sheikh Saad and Sawahreh Al Sharquiyeh, were not incorporated into the JM. However, a few houses in the north-west corner of the village lie inside that municipality. *B'Tselem*, 'Facing the Abyss: The Isolation of Sheikh Saad Village – Before and After the Separation Barrier', Report (February 2004), online: *B'Tselem* www.btselem.org/publications/summaries/200402_sheikh_saed.

158 *B'Tselem*, 'Facing the Abyss', ibid. Most of its residents work in Jerusalem. *B'Tselem*, '5 May 2010: High Court of Justice Approves Separation Barrier', ibid.

159 Francesco Chiodelli, 'Reshaping Jerusalem', *supra* note 31.

160 *Report of the UN Special Rapporteur of the Commission on Human Rights John Dugard, on the Situation of Human Rights in the Palestinian Territories Occupied by Israel since 1967* ECOSOC E/CN.4/2005/29 (7 December 2004) 3 at 34, online: UN https://documents-dds-ny.un.org/doc/UNDOC/GEN/G04/166/92/PDF/G0416692.pdf [UN Special Rapporteur Report 2004].

161 Such as Al-Ram, Dahiyet Al Bareed, Hizma, Anata, Al-Ezariyah and Abu Dis, Sheikh Saad and Sawahreh Al Sharkiyyeh.

162 OCHA-oPt, 'East Jerusalem: Key Humanitarian Concerns', *supra* note 68.

163 *Bimkom*, 'Between Fences', *supra* note 114.

164 OCHA-oPt, 'East Jerusalem: Key Humanitarian Concerns', *supra* note 68.

functioning Wall-crossing points/checkpoints, only four are accessible to 'West Bank' Palestinians entering EJ.[165] An additional six are only made available to Israeli citizens (including Israeli 'West Bank' settlers), to Palestinians with Jerusalem IDs and to non-Israelis (example: tourists) with valid visas. Palestinians with 'West Bank' IDs have to go through checkpoints that consist of large terminal like structures, and undergo elaborate security checks and procedures, every time they wish to access Jerusalem to and from the 'West Bank', which has resulted in long waiting hours.[166]

In terms of consequences, the village of Sheikh Saed, from which one of the petitions originates, serves as a good demonstration. Up until 2002, village residents were able to enter and leave Jerusalem and the 'West Bank' through a road running through Jabal Al Mukabir. In September 2002, the Israeli military authorities blocked this road with concrete blocks.[167] Those who have managed to receive valid permits to enter 'Israel' have been required to access Jerusalem through another Wall checkpoint instead (the Olive checkpoint), which in turn requires them to commute along a difficult road.[168]

The legality of the route of the Wall in and around Jerusalem: a summary of petitions

All the arguments that have been raised both by petitioners and by respondents were made in an effort to justify their position around one essential element: whether the decision of government and/or military authorities to requisition the land for the construction of sections of the Wall was legal. It must also be recalled that, depending on where the route of the Wall runs, land was either requisitioned under domestic Israeli law, namely the *Emergency Land Regulation Law*, or by way of an Israeli MO. This depended on whether the route of the Wall was to run along the JMB or inside the JM – in which case the former is the main source for the confiscation order, or whether it was to run inside the 'West Bank' beyond annexed EJ – in which case, it is requisitioned by way of the latter.

Procedural issues

As a general rule, the Court does not adjudicate matters if a claimant had recourse to alternative forms of judicial or quasi-judicial remedy.[169] Guided by Israeli administrative law, the Court generally refused to replace the discretion

165 Provided they carry valid permits. UN OCHA-oPt, 'The Humanitarian Impact of the Barrier', update (July 2013), online: OCHA-oPt http://unispal.un.org/pdfs/OCHA_Wall-HumImpact.pdf [OCHA-oPt, Humanitarian Impact 2013].

166 *B'Tselem*, 'Ground to a Halt', *supra* note 145.

167 *B'Tselem*, 'Security Forces Tighten Siege on Sheikh Sa'ed Village', (28 June 2006), online: *B'Tselem* www.btselem.org/separation_barrier/20060628_sheikh_saed.

168 *B'Tselem*, 'Facing the Abyss', *supra* note 157.

169 *Salameh* Judgment, *supra* note 98 at paras 6–18.

of an appeals committee when it reviews the legality of the decision to requisition land by way of an MO (with its own).[170] This applies equally to petitions that have challenged the decisions of the appeals committee established under the *Emergency Land Regulation Law (5710–1949)*.

In the *Abu Ziad* case for example, some land was confiscated under the *Emergency Land Law*, to route the Wall inside the JM. Other land parcels were requisitioned by way of an Israeli MO for the construction in this area of other segments of the Wall that deviated from the JMB into the 'West Bank'. Although the petition appeared to challenge the land requisition for constructing the Wall's 'West Bank' segments, during the proceedings it became clear that what the petition really sought to overturn was the land confiscation orders that were made under the *Emergency Land Regulation Law*. Given that it was the route of the parts of the Wall that ran inside the JM or along the JMB which stood in the way of including the petitioners on the 'Israeli side' of the Wall,[171] and since the petitioners' appeal of the land confiscation order was still pending in front of the appeals committee (at the time that the HCJ was adjudicating the petition), the justices concluded that the Court was not the appropriate forum for deciding the petition and dismissed it.[172]

In other petitions, where Palestinians had challenged the legality of confiscating land under the *Emergency Land Law*, the Court determined that it enjoyed concurrent jurisdiction with the relevant administrative appeals bodies to adjudicate claims challenging the authorities' exercise of their power to confiscate a given piece of land. The Court also ruled that it enjoyed discretion in deciding whether or not it will adjudicate the matter itself.[173] In the *Shakir* judgment, the respondents argued that the HCJ was not entitled to review the decision of the appeals committee. In rejecting this contention, the Court emphasized that nothing prevents the HCJ from reviewing the decision of that committee if the latter had erred in its legal conclusions.[174] In another case, *Salameh*, the Court determined that the focus of the petition was on two issues: the land confiscation order, delivered under the *Emergency Land Regulation Law*, and the access arrangements that had been put in place by the government authorities for the affected residents to move in and out of the JM areas that had remained on the 'Israeli side' of the Wall. In this regard, the justices explained that a determination of the legality of the land confiscation order was bound to be influenced by the determination of the extent to which the impact

170 Eyal Benvenisti, *The International Law of Belligerent Occupation*, *supra* note 4.

171 The Wall's route had left the petitioners outside the Wall on the 'Palestinian side'. See *Abu Ziad* Judgment, *supra* note 98 at 3.

172 Under these circumstances the court found that there are no grounds for judicial intervention in regards to the 'West Bank' land confiscation orders. *Abu Ziad* Judgment, *supra* note 98 at 3.

173 The Court relied on article 15(c) of the *Basic Law: Judiciary*. For the law see *Knesset*, Basic Law: *Judiciary*, online: *Knesset* www.knesset.gov.il/laws/special/eng/basic8_eng.htm. *Salameh* Judgment, *supra* note 98 at paras 6–18.

174 As opposed to factual findings. *Shakir* Judgment, *supra* note 151 at paras 15–35.

of the access/crossing arrangement, put in place by government authorities, was proportionate. Hence, the Court held that it had a wider jurisdiction than the appeals committees to review both issues and decided to examine the aforementioned petition.[175]

The petitioners' arguments

Palestinians on both sides of the Wall have for decades lived as part of an intertwined community. Hence, a common denominator is that the Wall has seriously undermined the 'fabric of life' of both population groups in a manner that cannot be justified by the alleged security objectives and needs of government authorities. Yet, a by-product of the Wall's construction has been the enforcement of the legal distinctions that authorities have set up since 1967, between Palestinians who are considered 'Israeli permanent residents' and/or who live inside the JM, and those who are not. Hence, to better understand the arguments made by the petitioners, these arguments have been grouped together in two categories: those raised by Palestinians with Jerusalem IDs and those raised by West Bank' Palestinians.

Points raised by Palestinian petitioners carrying Jerusalem IDs

Palestinians with Jerusalem IDs have challenged the route of the Wall on several grounds. Some have questioned the authority of the government to build the Wall in the Jerusalem area, alleging that political considerations and not legitimate security concerns were the driving force behind it, thereby rendering this construction illegal under international law. One of these political considerations is the desire to consolidate the political objective of cementing Israel's *de jure* annexation of EJ. This was the situation in the *Al-Ram Local Council* case.[176] In this case, petitioners argued that, by running the route of some segments of the Wall along the JMB, authorities were seeking to consolidate Israel's physical control of the annexed territory in violation of international law.[177]

Another set of political considerations that petitioners claimed were driving the government decision to build the Wall along the designated route were demographic in nature. They argued that it included the desire to exclude as many Palestinians as possible from being included inside the Wall. Again, this was a point raised by petitioners in the *Al-Ram Local Council* case, in which petitioners argued that the route of the Wall left an estimated 60,000 residents – the majority

175 This was the conclusion of the Court even though it concurred with the State that there was a subjective and objective delay in submitting the petition. See *Salameh* Judgment, *supra* note 98 at paras 6–18.

176 *Al-Ram Village Council* Judgment, *supra* note 27. The Court jointly examined the three petitions in this case (HCJ 5488/04) (HCJ 6080/04) and (HCJ 3648/05).

177 That is, despite the illegality of the acquisition of territory by force. *Al-Ram Village Council* Judgment, *supra* note 27 at paras 23–30.

of whom are Palestinians with Jerusalem IDs – on the 'Palestinian side' of the Wall.[178] They also argued that these authorities were using the Wall as a tool for making 'border' adjustments to include as few Palestinians as possible on its 'sovereign' territory.[179] This was also the position of petitioners in the *Abu Ziad* case. Here, petitioners residing in the Sheikh Saed village, had their places of residence excluded by the route of the Wall to remain on the 'Palestinian side' of the structure,[180] a decision that was motivated by 'demographic considerations'.[181]

In another case, *Ras Khamis Residents Committee*,[182] Palestinian residents of the EJ neighbourhood of the Shu'afat ridge[183] submitted a petition to the HCJ demanding that the route of the Wall, which separated them from the rest of the city, be moved further east of the JMB, so that they could remain on the 'Israeli side' of the Wall.[184] By separating the ridge from the nearby Israeli settlements of Pisgat Zeev, the French Hill and Ramat Shlomo, the route of the Wall also surrounded the ridge from three directions (north, west and south). This left the ridge and its residents on the 'Palestinian side' while the aforementioned settlements were included on the 'Israeli side'.[185] Petitioners also argued that the real motive behind the route is to de facto cut off the Palestinian residents in those neighbourhoods from the JM as a way of maintaining a Jewish majority in the city.[186] Similar points were also advanced by Palestinians with Jerusalem IDs in petitions that challenged the decision of the Israeli government not to include their 'West Bank' neighbourhoods of Jerusalem on the 'Israeli side'. Again in the *Al-Ram Local Village Council* case, petitioners argued that their neighbourhoods were part and parcel of EJ. In their view, the desire of the respondents to exclude them was also motivated by demographic considerations, and disregarded the geopolitical reality of the West Bank and the 'fabric of life' of the EJ Palestinian communities that had emerged on both sides of the municipal divide.[187]

A second set of arguments that were raised by the petitioners is that, even if the route of the Wall can be justified on security grounds, it remains unlawful because of the disproportionate harm on the residents in the area and on their

178 *Al-Ram Village Council* Judgment, *supra* note 27 at 4.

179 *Iado* Judgment, *supra* note 98 at para 4.

180 *Abu Ziad* Judgment, *supra* note 98 at 2.

181 Ibid. at 1–2.

182 (HCJ 6193/05) [2008] *Ras Khamis Residents Committee v. the Authorized Administrator under the Land Emergency Law*, unofficial English translation by Avichay Sharon (April 2014), on file with author [*Ras Khamis Residents Committee* Judgment]. The petition was dismissed by the HCJ.

183 Consisting of the neighbourhoods of Ras Khamis, the Shu'afat Refugee Camp and the Dahiyet Al-Salaam neighbourhood of Anata. *Ras Khamis Residents Committee* Judgment, *supra* note 182 at paras 1–7.

184 *Ras Khamis Residents Committee* Judgment, *supra* note 182 at paras 1–7.

185 Ibid. at paras 1–7.

186 Ibid. at paras 8–10.

187 *Al-Ram Local Village Council* Judgment, *supra* note 27 at paras 23–30.

ability to enjoy some of their Israeli constitutionally protected rights.[188] In the case of Palestinians with Jerusalem IDs, petitioners have pointed out that the disproportionate impact of the route of the Wall in the Jerusalem area is particularly evident in two situations. The first is how Palestinian neighbourhoods of EJ, which constitute an official part of the JM, have been left on the 'Palestinian side' of the Wall.[189] One petition that highlighted this resulting disproportionate impact is the *Abu El Tir* petition.[190] In this case, Palestinians with Jerusalem IDs, from the villages of Zur Baher and Um Tuba (both of which are officially part of the JM),[191] contested the route of the Wall in the area because it separated them from residential buildings and other property that they own a few metres beyond the JMB, on the 'Palestinian side' of the Wall.[192] This was also the situation in the *Abu Ziad*, *Iado* and *Salameh* cases, where petitioners had found themselves on the 'Palestinian side' of the Wall even though they resided in areas that were officially part of the JM.[193] The harm they suffered to their property rights was twofold: it resulted in the confiscation of their land (under the *Emergency Land Regulation Law*) for the purpose of constructing the Wall; and it left their property outside the Wall, thereby contributing to a sharp drop in the value of their property.[194]

The second situation where the disproportionate impact was also alleged by Palestinians with Jerusalem IDs was in instances in which Israeli authorities had decided to route the Wall along the JMB, thereby excluding 'West Bank' suburbs and neighbourhoods of EJ on the 'Palestinian side' of the structure. This argument was made in the *Al-Ram Local Village Council* case. By placing the western section of the Wall's current route along the JMB, petitioners claimed that the route had effectively split through the traditional road that Palestinians with Jerusalem IDs use to access the JM (route 60). Addressing the decision of the government to re-direct all the commute to and from the JM through the Qalandia checkpoint, they underscored that this checkpoint would not effectively address the large influx of individuals who need to travel to and from Jerusalem on a daily basis for work, educational, religious, social and other reasons.[195]

In the same case, the route of the southern section of the Wall, which made incursions inside the 'West Bank' beyond the JMB, was also challenged for its disproportionate impact. After reiterating that the route is not consistent with

188 Most notably, the right to freedom of movement, property rights and religious rights. *Salameh* Judgment, *supra* note 98 at paras 6–18. See also *Al-Ram Village Council* Judgment, *supra* note 27 at 8.

189 *Ras Khamis Residents Committee* Judgment, *supra* note 182 at paras 8–10.

190 (HCJ 940/04) [2004] *Abdel Rahman Abu El Tir et al. v. IDF Commander in Judea and Samaria*, unofficial English translation by Avichay Sharon (April 2004), on file with author [*Abu El Tir* Judgment]. The petition was dismissed by the HCJ.

191 *Bimkom*, 'Survey of Palestinian Neighbourhoods in East Jerusalem: Sur Baher', at 1, online: *Bimkom* http://bimkom.org/eng/wp-content/uploads/3.4_sur-baher-w.pdf.

192 *Abu El Tir* Judgment, *supra* note 190 at 1.

193 *Abu Ziad* Judgment, *supra* note 98 at 2. See also *Iado* Judgment, *supra* note 98 at para 4.

194 *Abu Ziad* Judgment, *supra* note 98 at 2.

195 *Al-Ram Local Village Council* Judgment, *supra* note 27 at 4 and 8.

the *Beit Sourik* and *Mara'abe* judgments, petitioners explained that the section, which ran through the Dahiyet El Bareed neighbourhood of the village (splitting it into two on each side of the Wall), ensured that Palestinians with Jerusalem IDs who found themselves on the 'Palestinian side' of the Wall had no access to essential social services available on the 'Israeli side'.[196]

In the *Shakir* case, Palestinians from the 'West Bank' village of Sheikh Saed had been separated from Jerusalem by the Wall. With an estimated half of its residents carrying Jerusalem IDs, petitioners argued that the decision of government authorities to construct a road that would improve the connection of their village towards the east (i.e. West Bank), in the direction of Sawahreh Al Sharqiyeh,[197] constitutes an effort by those authorities to disconnect the village from its traditional reliance on the nearby EJ neighbourhood of Jabal Al Mukabir (on the 'Israeli side') and to create a false perception of a separate 'centre of life' for the Sheikh Saed residents away from Jerusalem.[198]

Several petitions with Jerusalem IDs have also expressed concern that the decision to leave them on the 'Palestinian side' of the Wall would, in the long run, undermine their ability to receive the municipal services that they are entitled to as 'Israeli' residents.[199] Often the only way for them to commute to or from the JM that remains on the 'Israeli side' is to take a long detour around the 'West Bank', and to cross into the city through one of the designated checkpoints inside the Wall.[200] This has made the task of demonstrating to Israeli authorities that Jerusalem remains their 'centre of life' very demanding. Many expressed fear that this would increase the risk of getting stripped of their 'Israeli' residency rights in the future.[201]

In court, petitioners and their counsel have also proposed alternative routes to the Wall. The first alternative that has been highlighted is one that ensures that they remain on the 'Israeli side' of the structure.[202] Some even argued that

196 This was the petition 3648/05 which the HCJ examined jointly with the other *Al-Ram Village Council* petitions (HCJ 5488/04), challenging the western sections, and (HCJ 6080/04), challenging the southern sections. Although, initially, authorities sought to keep the whole of the Dahiyet El Bareed neighbourhood on the 'Palestinian side', they decided against this move, on the ground that the harm caused to the school children would have been greater than the harm that is currently being inflicted on the confined families. *Al-Ram Local Village Council* Judgment, *supra* note 27.at 4.

197 *Shakir* Judgment, *supra* note 151 at 2.

198 Ibid. at paras 1–9.

199 Such as in the case of Palestinians with Jerusalem IDs who live in the Abu Ma'er neighbourhood of EJ. The route of the Wall inside the JM left parts of the neighbourhood where the petitioners lived, which constituted officially part of the JM on the 'Palestinian side' of the Wall. *Salameh* Judgment, *supra* note 98 at 1.

200 *Abu Ziad* Judgment, *supra* note 98 at 2. *Iado* Judgment, *supra* note 98 at para 4.

201 *Abu Ziad* Judgment *supra* note 98 at 2. See also *Al-Ram Local Village Council* Judgment, *supra* note 27 at 8; *Iado* Judgment, *supra* note 98 at para 4.

202 *Salameh* Judgment, *supra* note 98 at para 3; *Iado* Judgment, *supra* note 98 at para 4; *Ras Khamis Residents Committee* Judgment, *supra* note 182 at paras 8–10; *Al-Ram Local Village Council* Judgment, *supra* note 27 at paras 23–30.

they have historically been considered part of Jerusalem.[203] Second, they proposed that government authorities make available Wall-crossing arrangements in the vicinity of their homes or that they improve the operation of existing crossings, so as to reduce the daily hardship resulting from their commute to and from Jerusalem. For example, in the *Iado* judgment, petitioners demanded that a Wall gate closer to their homes be made available, one that they can access by foot or in their vehicles.[204] In the *Salameh* judgment, petitioners proposed that, at the very least, the opening time of the Wall gates near their homes be extended to 24 hours a day.[205]

Issues raised by Palestinian petitioners carrying 'West Bank' IDs

Palestinians with 'West Bank' IDs have also challenged the argument of Israeli military authorities that the Wall's route in their area has primarily been spearheaded by security considerations. This was the situation in the *Al-Eizariyah Village Council* case.[206] In this case, they argued that, by including parts of their land on the 'Israeli side', authorities were seeking to annex land that belongs to the village, with the Israeli settlement of Ma'ale Adumim, thereby underscoring that security-based objectives, were not the primary consideration.[207] Similarly in the *Beit Sahour Municipality* case,[208] petitioners from the village of *Beit Sahour* in the 'West Bank'[209] challenged the decision of military authorities to confiscate privately owned land for the construction of a section of the Wall, which left some of the village's land and the nearby Israeli settlement of Har Homa on the 'Israeli side' of the Wall.[210] Here, as well, petitioners argued that the MC's decision was based on political considerations of annexing the land that has been trapped in the Seam Zone, to allow for the settlement's expansion.[211]

In a third case, *Halawa*, the route of the Wall in the area included a hill belonging to the residents of the town of Anata on the 'Israeli side'. Petitioners challenged the allegations by military authorities that this was necessary to

203 *Shakir* Judgment, *supra* note 151 at 3.

204 *Iado* Judgment, *supra* note 98 at paras 1–4.

205 *Salameh* Judgment, *supra* note 98 at para 3.

206 *Al-Eizariyah Village Council* Judgment, *supra* note 28.

207 The petitioners invoked in this regard the ICJ *Wall* Advisory Opinion, *supra* note 45 at paras 5–6.

208 (HCJ 3937/07) [2010] *Beit Sahour Municipality et al. v. Prime Minister et al.*, unofficial English translation by Avichay Sharon (February 2014), on file with author [*Beit Sahour Municipality* Judgment]. The petition was dismissed by the HCJ.

209 Beit Sahour is a Palestinian city located 1.5 km (horizontal distance) east of Bethlehem. A little over 1,000 dunums of the village land was included in the JMB, Applied Research Institute-Jerusalem (ARIJ), 'Beit Sahour City Profile', online: ARIJ http://vprofile.ARIJ.org/bethlehem/pdfs/VP/Beit%20Sahour_cp_en.pdf.

210 Seventy dunums were confiscated for the Wall's construction, while 96 dunums of land remained on the 'Israeli side' of the Wall. *Beit Sahour Municipality* Judgment, *supra* note 208 at paras 1–3.

211 The term is interchangeably used by the Court to refer to the 'Israeli side' of the Wall. *Beit Sahour Municipality* Judgment, *supra* note 208 at para 4.

secure the protection of the residents of the nearby settlements of Pisgat Ze'ev and of Israeli travellers on highway 45, which connected that settlement to the JM.[212] In a fourth case, *Walajeh Village Council*,[213] Palestinian petitioners from Al-Walajeh village, south of the JMB,[214] challenged a land requisition order for the construction of the last section of the southern segment of the Wall in the area. Surrounding the village from three directions, the route of the Wall included the Israeli settlements of Har Gilo[215] and the Gush Etzion bloc on the 'Israeli side', in contrast to the village, which was effectively kept on the 'Palestinian side' of the Wall.[216]

In terms of property rights, many petitioners alleged that the Wall resulted in the requisition and damage to some of their privately owned lands. In the *Walajeh Village Council* case, they highlighted that dozens of dunums of cultivated lands would be damaged and trees uprooted. They also underscored that the Wall's construction along the chosen route would cause severe damage to an old cemetery and a natural spring in the area.[217] In another case, *Al-Ram Local Village Council*, the fact that the route of the Wall ran between houses, splitting the 'West Bank' neighbourhood of Dahiyet El Bareed into two areas (one on each side of the Wall), had resulted in the drop of their property value and the closure of hundreds of shops.[218]

In addition, they highlighted that the Wall's route separated them from land and other property (to remain inside the Seam Zone). For example, in the *Al-Eizariyah Village Council* case, petitioners showed that the route had left a hill inside, on the 'Israeli side' of the Wall. Other than confiscating land for the actual construction of the structure, its route also separated them from an

212 Highway 45 is a 'bypass' road located at the intersection of the Gi'vaat Zeev settlement. *Ma'an* Development Center, 'Apartheid Roads: Promoting Settlements Punishing Palestinians', Report (December 2008) at 15, online: OCHA-Opt https://web.archive.org/web/20160423093009/www.ochaopt.org/documents/opt_prot_maan_apartheid_roads_dec_2008.pdf. See also (HCJ 6451/04) [2006] *Mahmoud Halawa et al. v. Prime Minister et al.*, unofficial English translation by Avichay Sharon (February 2014), on file with author, at para 5 [*Halawa* Judgment]. The petition was dismissed by the HCJ.

213 (HCJ 9516/10) [2011] *Walajeh Village et al. v. Military Commander of the West Bank*, unofficial English translation by Avichay Sharon (March 2013), on file with author [*Walajeh Village Council* Judgment]. The petition was dismissed by the HCJ.

214 Parts of the village are inside the JMB and parts are outside it. *Walajeh Village Council* Judgment, *supra* note 213 at 2.

215 The settlement is 1.8 km from the Green Line. *B'Tselem* '14 November 2010: Separation Barrier Strangles al-Walajah', online: *B'Tselem* www.btselem.org/separation_barrier/20101114_al_walajah_separation_barrier.

216 A fenced road in the direction of Har Gilo, which remains off limits to Palestinians, closes off the fourth side. Karin Laub, 'Security Wall to Encircle Palestinian Village Walajeh', *Jerusalem Post* (13 July 2010).

217 *Walajeh Village Council* Judgment, *supra* note 213 at para 4.

218 *B'Tselem*, 'The Separation Barrier surrounding a-Ram', *supra* note 154. Schools that relied on children of Palestinians with Jerusalem IDs also reported lower registration. *Al-Ram Local Village Council* Judgment, *supra* note 27 at 8.

additional 1,000 dunums of land that constituted an important source of their livelihood.[219] Similar harm to property rights was also alleged in the *Beit Sahour* Municipality case,[220] with farmers highlighting that they were experiencing difficulties in reaching this land and in cultivating it.[221] In the *Halawa* case, Palestinians also argued that the route not only left the nearby Pisgat Zeev and Anatot Almon settlements on the 'Israeli side' but also included a hilltop with an old cemetery (dating back to the Byzantine era) that they still visit and use.[222]

In the *Al-Ram Local Village Council* case, petitioners argued that the decision of authorities to include the land surrounding the village on the 'Israeli side' was motivated by a desire to provide the nearby Israeli settlement of Neeve Yacov with land reserves for its own expansion.[223] Petitioners also claimed that the Wall's route undermined their 'fabric of life' particularly because of the movement restrictions it imposed on those residents wishing to access the JM.[224]

Elsewhere, the main argument has been that the Wall's route has disconnected them from 'West Bank' urban centres on which they depend for vital social services. In the *Al-Ram Local Village Council* case, petitioners also challenged the functioning of the alternative roads that had been constructed by military authorities.[225] In the *Walajeh Village Council* case, they argued that by surrounding them from three sides, the Wall isolated them and restricted their ability to reach the 'West Bank' governorate of Bethlehem, which serves as their natural urban hinterland.[226]

In addition, they identified alternative routes for the Wall which, if adopted by Israeli authorities, would mitigate the harmful impact of the Wall. This was the situation in the *Abu Ziad* case, where they demanded that the Wall's route be moved several hundred metres so that they can be included on the 'Israeli side'. Moreover, they challenged the notion that doing so would result in additional security risks.[227] A similar argument was adopted in the *Halawa* case, where the counsel for the petitioners argued that an alternative route to the Wall could leave the contested hill outside the structure (i.e. on the same side as the petitioners), without undermining the declared security objective of the government.[228] In the *Al-Ram Local Village Council* case, petitioners and their counsel also relied on the input (as amicus curiae) of the *Council for Peace and Security* (CPS), which argued that the route, as determined by the respondents

219 *Al-Eizariyah Village Council* case, *supra* note 28 at paras 2 and 5–6.

220 *Beit Sahour Municipality* Judgment, *supra* note 208 at para 4.

221 *Walajeh Village Council* Judgment, *supra* note 213 at paras 6–17.

222 *Halawa* Judgment, *supra* note 212 at 2.

223 *Al-Ram Local Village Council* case, *supra* note 27 at 5.

224 *Abu El Tir* Judgment, *supra* note 190 at 2–3.

225 *Al-Ram Local Village Council* Judgment, *supra* note 27 at 8.

226 *Ir Amim*, 'Walajeh – A Village under Siege', *supra* note 103.

227 *Abu Ziad* Judgment, *supra* note 98 at 2.

228 This could be achieved if the route encircles a different hill north of one other nearby settlement in the area, *Halawa* Judgment, *supra* note 212 at 2.

(particularly in its western section), was not the most optimal route from a security point of view.[229]

In other petitions, they demanded that the contested section of Wall be re-routed to include them on the 'Israeli side'. This was the situation in the *Walajeh Village Council* case, where petitioners proposed that the route be placed along the JMB (as opposed to inside the 'West Bank') and argued that doing so would not undermine the attainment of the declared security objectives of the respondents.[230] In one other case, *Shakir*, petitioners highlighted that most of the village's Palestinians with 'West Bank' IDs had valid permits to enter Jerusalem. Therefore, including their village on the 'Israeli side' of the structure would not result in disproportionate harm to them.[231]

That there are alternative security-based physical measures that can be resorted to – other than the construction of the Wall – was also put forward in other petitions. For example, in the *Al-Eizariyah Village Council* case, Palestinians proposed that military authorities put in place smaller concrete barriers or that the route of the Wall be moved closer along routes 1 and 417 (connecting Jerusalem, Ma'ale Adumim and the Dead Sea), as this would result in the confiscation of smaller areas of land from them.[232] Palestinians have also challenged security-based measures that are associated with the Wall. For example, in the *Anata Boys High School* case, the high school parents' board and individual Palestinian petitioners from the village of Anata, located north-east of Jerusalem, challenged the decision of the military authorities to place a cement barrier inside the yard of a boys' school, which is located inside the JMB.[233] In this regard, petitioners underscored that the cement barrier is part of the Wall in the Jerusalem area, which military authorities were building, and therefore constituted a deviation from the route of the latter and the land confiscation order issued for that purpose.[234]

The position of the respondents

Israeli authorities have argued that the Wall's construction in and around *Jerusalem* is a legitimate 'self-defence' measure,[235] one that is driven by security/topographic considerations, as a way of preventing infiltration by Palestinian West Bank 'terrorists' into Israel.[236] They also claimed that the fence aims to

229 *Al-Ram Local Village Council* Judgment, *supra* note 27 at 5 and 14.
230 *Walajeh Village Council*, *supra* note 213 at paras 6–17.
231 *Shakir* Judgment, *supra* note 151 at paras 12–14.
232 *Al-Eizariyah Village Council* Judgment, *supra* note 28 at 1 and 3.
233 (HCJ 10043/05) [2005] *Anata Boys High School Parents Board et al., v. Minister of Defense et al.*, unofficial English translation by Avichay Sharon (April 2014), on file with author at 1 [*Anata Boys High School* Judgment]. The petition was dismissed by the HCJ.
234 *Anata Boys High School* Judgment, *supra* note 233.
235 *Al-Ram Local Village Council* Judgment, *supra* note 27 at paras 31–39.
236 Ibid. at paras 1–22. See also *Shakir* Judgment, *supra* note 151 at paras 1–9; *Beit Sahour Municipality* Judgment, *supra* note 208 at paras 5–6.

separate between Jerusalem and the West Bank to provide security for Israeli citizens and the residents of Jerusalem.[237] Another element that they underscored is that the Wall's construction along the route they have chosen was necessary not only to ensure the safety of its military forces patrolling the structure, but also to guarantee the security of the residents of Israeli settlements and that of Israeli travellers on roads connecting parts of Jerusalem with the settlements located in the 'West Bank'.[238]

For example, in the *Halawa* judgment, including the hill on the 'Israeli side' of the Wall was deemed necessary to protect the residents of the settlement of Pisgat Ze'ev and Israeli travellers on road 45 from possible gunfire and to detect any infiltrators into Jerusalem.[239] In another case, *Beit Sahour Municipality*, they explained that the Wall's route was influenced by the desire to prevent shooting into the Har Homa settlement and to provide, topographically speaking, a sufficient range from the settlement's houses, one that would grant the military time respond to infiltration attempts.[240] In the *Walajeh Village Council* case, one of the reasons for choosing the route of the Wall, which was challenged by petitioners, was to safeguard the nearby Jerusalem light rail and its travellers.[241]

However, while government authorities certainly reiterated that the security of Israelis is the primary reason influencing the route of the Wall in the area, it was not necessarily presented as the sole consideration. For example, in the *Al-Ezariyah Village Council* case, they did not rule out that providing space for the expansion of the settlement was a secondary consideration.[242] Similarly, in the *Al-Ram Local Village Council* case, they argued that the route allegedly supports the diplomatic political interests of the State.[243]

Efforts were also made by the respondents to highlight the security-based justifications for implementing measures associated with the Wall. For example, in the *Anata Boys High School* case, they maintained that the small cement wall that had been put in place was not part of the Wall in the Jerusalem area, but was a temporary measure designed to protect Israeli military forces and workers constructing the Wall in the vicinity of the school from stone throwing by Palestinian students.[244]

According to the respondents, the starting point when determining the route of the 'fence' is that all of Jerusalem is part of the State's territory, and that

237 *Walajeh Village Council* Judgment, *supra* note 213. See also *Iado* Judgment, *supra* note 98.

238 *Al-Eizariyah Village Council* Judgment, *supra* note 28 at para 7.

239 *Halawa* Judgment, *supra* note 212 at paras 6–8.

240 *Beit Sahour Municipality* Judgment, *supra* note 208 at paras 5–6.

241 *Walajeh Village Council* Judgment, *supra* note 213 at paras 6–17.

242 *Al-Eizariyah Village Council* Judgment, *supra* note 28 at para 7.

243 The CPS had suggested that the Wall's route separates Palestinian neighbourhoods and Jewish settlements in EJ. The respondents argued that this would leave large areas of annexed EJ on the 'Palestinian side' of the Wall, which would have 'far reaching diplomatic consequences'. See *Al-Ram Local Village Council* Judgment, *supra* note 27 at 9.

244 Respondents pointed out that an estimated 30 metres of the school yard lies on 'state land', (on which the school has 'trespassed'). *Anata Boys High School* Judgment, *supra* note 233 at 1–2.

therefore, it took into consideration the JMB, which separates Jerusalem from the 'West Bank'.[245] Only if there was a pressing security/topographic consideration, or a desire to minimize the harm inflicted on local residents, did the Wall's route diverge from that border.[246] Where petitioners had challenged the decision of authorities to route the Wall along the JMB, thereby leaving 'West Bank' neighbourhoods of EJ on the 'Palestinian side' of the Wall, government authorities said that they would not be able to do so without violating international law: in the absence of considerations for topography, security or the interest of the local residents, accommodating the request of some petitioners to be included on the 'Israeli side' would require them to route the Wall inside the 'West Bank', an occupied territory, as opposed to Israeli sovereign territory. Since this would not constitute a legitimate consideration, this would result in the violation of both Israeli domestic law and of the law of belligerent occupation.[247]

Where petitions challenged the legality of the route of certain Wall segments that run inside the 'West Bank', respondents maintained that this was absolutely essential for security/military and/or topographic considerations.[248] This also accounted for why, in some instances, the route of the Wall had resulted in the inclusion of 'West Bank' Palestinian population centres inside the Seam Zone, or in particularly harsh realities for individual petitioners. While acknowledging that these consequences were severe, respondents argued that they were proportionate.[249]

The same security-based arguments were adopted by government authorities in petitions that left EJ neighbourhoods that are officially part of the JM, on the 'Palestinian side' together with their residents (mostly Palestinians with Jerusalem IDs).[250] For example, in the *Ras Khamis Residents Committee* case, respondents argued that the decision to leave the Shu'afat ridge on that side of the Wall was taken in response to security considerations, namely because the ridge has represented an ongoing source of infiltrators from the 'West Bank' into Jerusalem.[251] They also sought to provide the Court with assurances that leaving those areas and their residents outside the Wall will have no impact on the status of these neighbourhoods as part of the JM, or on the ability of Palestinians with Jerusalem IDs to retain their 'Israeli permanent residency' and/or to access social services provided by the Israeli JM.[252] In addition, they

245 *Al-Ram Local Village Council* Judgment, *supra* note 27 at paras 31–39.

246 In one case they argued that humanitarian considerations of wanting to leave the school inside the Wall are what ultimately prompted them to leave parts of Dahiyet Al Bareed inside the Wall. *Al-Ram Local Village Council* Judgment, *supra* note 27 at 9.

247 *Ras Khamis Residents Committee* Judgment, *supra* note 182 at paras 14–25; *Shakir* Judgment, *supra* note 151 at paras 10–11.

248 *Beit Sahour Municipality* Judgment, *supra* note 208 at paras 5–6. See also *Walajeh Village Council* Judgment, *supra* note 213 at paras 6–17.

249 *Al-Ram Local Village Council* Judgment, *supra* note 27 at 4 and 9; *Beit Sahour Municipality* Judgment, *supra* note 208 at 3.

250 *Salameh* Judgment, *supra* note 98 at paras 4–5.

251 *Ras Khamis Residents Committee* Judgment, *supra* note 182 at paras 11–13.

252 *Salameh* Judgment, *supra* note 98 at paras 4–5.

committed themselves to providing social service points at designated checkpoints/gates in the Wall as a way of demonstrating an effort to reduce the disproportionate impact of the Wall's route on the lives of the inhabitants.

In some instances, certain Palestinian neighbourhoods that are officially part of the JM are also home to Palestinians with 'West Bank' IDs. Consequently, government authorities have argued that deviating from the JMB, was necessary to avoid trapping large numbers of those Palestinians in a Seam Zone-like situation. Such a situation would mean that its 'West Bank' Palestinian residents would not be able to access the JM (for lack of valid permits), and would not be able to reach their destinations in the 'West Bank' without passing through a Wall gate and having to succumb to the requirements of the zone's permit regime.[253] This was the situation in the *Ras Khamis Residents Committee* case, where they pointed out that adopting the alternative route proposed by petitioners would mean that they would have to put in place a checkpoint in the area to control the movement of people in and out of Jerusalem, and that, doing so, would disrupt the 'fabric of life' of residents in a much more significant way.[254]

In other cases, such as *Shakir*, the respondents maintained that they could not fulfil the petitioners' request of running the Wall inside the 'West Bank' to include the Sheikh Saed village on the 'Israeli side' of the Wall. This would not be possible because it would force its residents to live in the Seam Zone, with all its associated movement restrictions that it would entail.[255] Where petitioners had proposed alternative routes to the original Wall route, government representatives rejected those claims on the ground that these alternative routes would not be feasible from a topographic/security point of view.[256]

In terms of the proportionality of harm, respondents maintained that they have exerted a sincere effort to balance the different considerations and to reduce the harm of the Wall on the Palestinian communities on either side of the structure in several ways. The first way is by modifying the original route of some of the contested segments. For example, in the *Abu El Tir* case, the original route of the Wall had left most of the lands of Sur Baher on the 'Israeli side' of the Wall. Subsequently, government authorities declared in court that, following extensive negotiations with the residents, they had re-routed some

253 *Ras Khamis Residents Committee* Judgment, *supra* note 182 at paras 14–25.

254 Ibid. at paras 11–13.

255 *Shakir* Judgment, *supra* note 151 at paras 10–11.

256 Arguments presented include the idea that alternative routes would endanger the military forces manning the Wall because it would reduce the 'buffer zone', or that they would run through heavily dense neighbourhoods or create tensions. *Abu El Tir* Judgment, *supra* note 190 at paras 7–9, ibid. See also *Abu Ziad* Judgment, *supra* note 98 at 2; *Salameh* Judgment, *supra* note 98 at paras 4–5; *Ras Khamis Residents Committee* Judgment, *supra* note 182 at paras 11–13; *Iado* Judgment, *supra* note 98 at para 5; *Al-Ram Local Village Council* Judgment, *supra* note 27 at 9; *Beit Sahour Municipality* Judgment, *supra* note 208 at 3; and *Walajeh Village Council* Judgment, *supra* note 213 at 4.

sections of the Wall in the area a few hundred metres (to the east) in order to maintain some of the buildings of, and land belonging to, the petitioners on the 'Israeli side' of the Wall.[257]

This is not to say, of course, that the respondents have always agreed to modify the geographic route of the Wall to accommodate the petitioners' requests. Where they had refused to modify the route of the Wall, they emphasized that great care was exercised to ensure that the harm inflicted on the petitioners' property was as small as possible. For example, in the *Al-Eizariyah Village Council* case, they highlighted that the route of the Wall ran as close as possible to the roads which it was seeking to protect, thereby confiscating only what was strictly necessary in terms of the petitioners' land for this purpose.[258] In the *Halawa* and the *Walajeh Village Council* case, they stressed that no damage to the property of the petitioners will ensue, should it remain on the 'Israeli side' of the Wall, or that they would leave the property on the 'Palestinian side' of the structure.[259]

The second way is by respondents refuting the allegations made by petitioners that the harm was indeed substantial,[260] or emphasizing that most of the land requisitioned inside the 'West Bank' amounted to 'state land' (as opposed to privately owned land)[261] or rocky/uncultivated land.[262] But for other petitions, including the *Abu El Tir* case, they alleged that changing the route of the Wall in its southern end (as requested by the petitioners) to ensure that their property would remain on the 'Israeli side' of the Wall, would in fact cause substantial harm to other Palestinian residents in the area, or would require sealing off an important road which serviced other 'West Bank' Palestinian residents in the area.[263]

The third way in which military authorities have sought to convince the Court that they have indeed struck a balance between security needs and the human rights of the 'local population' relates to the nature of the crossing arrangements that had been put in place. On the substantive level, for example, they claimed to have put in place arrangements which would minimize the harm incurred by the petitioners as a result of the movement restrictions (to and from

257 This amendment would be made for humanitarian reasons. *Abu El Tir* Judgment, *supra* note 190 at 2–3.

258 *Al-Eizariyah Village Council* Judgment, *supra* note 28 at para 7.

259 *Halawa* Judgment, *supra* note 212 at paras 6–8; *Walajeh Village Council* Judgment, *supra* note 213 at para 5.

260 Respondents argued that the cemetery on the hill kept inside the Wall was not an 'active' cemetery. *Halawa* Judgment, *supra* note 212 at 3.

261 In one case, the respondents alleged that most of the land that was to remain inside the Wall was not cultivated and, therefore, not a significant source of livelihood. *Al-Eizariyah Village Council* Judgment, *supra* note 28 at para 7.

262 *Beit Sahour Municipality* Judgment, *supra* note 208 at 3; *Walajeh Village Council* Judgment, *supra* note 213 at 5.

263 *Abu El Tir* Judgment, *supra* note 190 at paras 7–9; *Beit Sahour Municipality* Judgment, *supra* note 208 at 2.

Jerusalem) associated with the Wall. This was the situation in the *Abu Ziad* case, where government representatives argued that a gate in the Wall would be made available at a distance of only a few kilometres from the petitioners' area of residence,[264] and that it would be open for crossing 24 hours a day.[265] In another case, *Salameh*, the respondents declared in court that they would extend the opening hours of the Wall gate (in line with the request of the petitioners) to allow pedestrian access for Palestinians with Jerusalem IDs 24 hours a day. At a later stage, they also declared their readiness to allow vehicles to cross through the same gate during the daytime.[266] Similarly, in the *Iado* judgment, the respondents stated (again in court) that they would consider allowing some petitioners to access the *Sawahreh* crossing in their vehicles.[267] As for the request by the petitioners to operate Wall crossings closer to their homes or to allow them to access those crossings by vehicles, they would not be able to respond favourably to these requests out of concern for the security of their forces.[268]

In the case of petitions filed by Palestinians with 'West Bank' IDs, the government committed itself to granting permits to the petitioners for access to their properties that have remained on the 'Israeli side' of the Wall[269] and ensuring the petitioners' access through gates in the Wall to the Seam Zone.[270] Where petitioners had alleged that the route of the Wall undermined their ability to reach other parts of the 'West Bank', they expressed readiness to authorize the construction of roads which, in turn, would improve their connectivity to other parts of the 'West Bank'.[271] In petitions by Palestinians who carry Jerusalem IDs, government authorities stated that crossing the Wall at checkpoints is a much easier endeavour for those Palestinians (since they do not require permits). They also committed themselves to allowing them to continue doing so unhindered.[272] In other petitions, the respondents asked the justices to dismiss petitions, claiming that the route of the Wall undermined their right to movement and access to Jerusalem on procedural grounds.[273]

264 *Abu Ziad* Judgment, *supra* note 98 at 3; *Halawa* Judgment, *supra* note 212 at paras 6–8.

265 *Ras Khamis Residents Committee* Judgment, *supra* note 182 at paras 11–13.

266 Until the first hour after sunset. *Salameh* Judgment, *supra* note 98 at paras 4–5 and at paras 6–18.

267 As opposed to only on foot. *Iado* Judgment, *supra* note 98 at para 5.

268 *Iado* Judgment, *supra* note 98.

269 *Halawa* Judgment, *supra* note 212 at paras 6–8.

270 *Walajeh Village Council* Judgment, *supra* note 213 at para 5. In another case, they committed themselves to issuing permits so that the petitioners can access the Wall to their property through a nearby checkpoint. *Halawa* Judgment, *supra* note 212 at paras 6–8.

271 *Al-Ram Local Village Council* Judgment, *supra* note 27 at 4–5.

272 *Walajeh Village Council* Judgment, *supra* note 213 at 6.

273 For example, petitioners were accused of violating the statute of limitations, because the former had not joined the earlier negotiations regarding the original route. *Abu El Tir* Judgment, *supra* note 190 at 3. For other procedural ground reasons, see *Abu Ziad* Judgment, *supra* note 98 at 2; *Beit Sahour Municipality supra* note 208 at paras 5–6; *Salameh* Judgment, *supra* note 98 at paras 4–5; *Iado* Judgment, *supra* note 98 at para 5.

The HCJ's adjudication of petitions challenging the legality of the Wall in the Jerusalem area

In referring to EJ, the Court has consistently regarded EJ as a territory that is separate and distinct from the 'West Bank'. In some judgments, however, it did not pronounce itself explicitly on whether or not it considers EJ to be part of Israeli territory or part of the occupied territory.[274] In other judgments, the Court refers to it interchangeably as 'Jerusalem', 'Israel' or 'Israeli territory'.[275] For example, in the *Halawa* judgment, when explaining the primary reason for the route of the Wall in the area, the justices identified the objective as the need to prevent terrorists from infiltrating what they referred to as Israel (especially Jerusalem) from 'Judea and Samaria'.[276] In the *Al-Ram Village Council* case, Justice Barak offered a clearer position when, in addressing the issue of the annexation of East Jerusalem, he opined that, according to Israeli law, the application of Israeli law and administration on the whole of Jerusalem has been grounded in a Basic Law and an administrative order and therefore Jerusalem is part of Israeli territory.[277]

However, the Court's efforts to draw a distinction between Jerusalem (considered part of Israel proper), and 'Judea and Samaria' (deemed occupied territory) become evident when examining the legal framework that the Court applies to its analysis of the Wall's route, both in terms of its reasonableness and the proportionality of the harm inflicted on the surrounding communities. Again, the aforementioned *Al-Ram Local Village Council* case offers a good illustration. In this case, the south and south-east sections of the Wall that were the subject of the petition were identified by the Court as segments that run inside the 'West Bank'. By contrast, the justices determined that the route of the Wall's western sections runs inside the JM. In light of this, the justices explained that they examine sections of the 'fence' running inside Israel proper and the sections running through occupied territory.[278]

One other element that influenced the Court's choice regarding the applicable legal framework is the category of individuals affected by the route. Thus, in the aforementioned case, it underscored that 'authorities must account for and consider the effects of the fence on [the] rights and needs of all [those] who will be affected by it'.[279] These are Israelis living in Israel; Israeli settlers in the 'West Bank'; Palestinians with Jerusalem IDs (whose rights are constitutionally protected); and Palestinians with 'West Bank' IDs (who constitute 'protected persons' under the Fourth Geneva Convention).[280] The consideration of the

274 *Shakir* Judgment, *supra* note 151 at paras 15–35.
275 *Ras Khamis* Judgment, *supra* note 182 at paras 14–25.
276 *Halawa* Judgment, *supra* note 212 at paras 9–18.
277 *Al-Ram Local Village Council* Judgment, *supra* note 27 at paras 40–60.
278 Ibid. at paras 40–60.
279 Ibid. at paras 40–60.
280 Ibid. at paras 40–60. *Salameh* Judgment, *supra* note 98 at paras 6–18.

rights afforded to the members of each of these groups is different because the normative regimes for these groups are different.[281]

Adjudicating the legality of the Wall in the Jerusalem area running inside the JM or along the JMB

The applicable legal framework

Where the route runs along the JMB or inside the JM, the justices have considered it to run entirely on Israeli territory.[282] Once this was established, the Court concluded that the scope of authority and discretion of the government in building the Wall must be determined in light of the principles and rules governing Israeli law,[283] most notably, Israeli administrative and constitutional law. Hence, it reiterated that, in determining the route of the 'fence' in Israel, it is consistent with the principles of reasonableness and proportionality, and that where the fence entails necessary infringement of individual rights, the infringement must meet the conditions set out in the limitation provision in the Basic Laws relating to human rights.[284] The Court also identified the provisions of Israeli domestic law that are relevant to the decision by Israeli authorities of confiscating the land for the Wall's construction. These include provisions from the *British Defence Regulations of 1945*,[285] which, to date have remained part of local laws that are in effect in Israel.[286]

According to the Court, where the route of the Wall affected Palestinians with 'West Bank' IDs, the law of belligerent occupation may also be deemed relevant.[287] For example, in the *Salameh* judgment, given that the route of the Wall had significantly impacted Palestinians (with 'West Bank' IDs) living on the 'Palestinian side' of the Wall, (despite the Wall running inside the JM), the impact of the Wall's route on their rights must also be assessed. Here, it is important to underscore that the manner in which the Court articulated itself on this indicates that it does not consider Palestinians with Jerusalem IDs to be part of the 'protected persons' category, as per the Fourth Geneva Convention.[288]

It then examined the orders authorizing the confiscation of land under Israeli domestic law, for the purpose of the Wall's construction. Where the Court examined the legality of the land confiscation order under the aforementioned

281 *Al-Ram Local Village Council* Judgment, *supra* note 27 at paras 40–60.
282 *Ras Khamis* Judgment, *supra* note 182 at paras 14–25.
283 Ibid. at paras 14–25.
284 *Al-Ram Local Village Council* Judgment, *supra* note 27; *Shakir* Judgment, *supra* note 151.
285 These regulations were first enacted by the British authorities during their mandate of Palestine (1922–1947). Uri Shoham, 'The Principle of Legality and the Israeli Military Government in the Territories', (1996) 153 Mil L Rev, 245.
286 Emanuel Gross, 'Democracy in the War against Terrorism: The Israeli Experience', (2002) 35 Loy LA L Rev 1161.
287 *Al-Ram Local Village Council* Judgment, *supra* note 27 at paras 40–60.
288 Ibid. at paras 40–60. See also *Salameh* Judgment, *supra* note 98 at paras 6–18.

Emergency Land Regulation Law, it concluded that the Wall's construction fulfilled one of the legitimate purposes of the *Emergency Land Regulation Law*. It subsequently examined whether this order satisfies the limitation clause in the Basic Law: *Human Dignity and Liberty*.[289]

The legality of the route of the Wall: the Court's examination of substantive issues

Petitioners had argued that Israeli authorities had no right to establish parts of the Wall along a specific route inside annexed EJ (because it remains occupied territory under international law). The justices dismissed the argument, noting instead that 'Jerusalem', according to the borders that have been defined by the state, is part of the territory of the State of Israel.[290] Subsequently, they examined the question of whether or not government authorities had properly exercised their discretion when building the Wall along the particular route they had chosen. Where the Wall's route ran inside the JM or along the JMB, allegedly affecting the rights of Palestinians with Jerusalem IDs, the Court noted that by virtue of being 'Israeli' permanent residents, any infringements on their constitutionally protected rights must, accordingly, meet the requirements of the limitations clause in the Basic Law: *Human Dignity and Liberty*.[291]

Given that the Court does not consider EJ Palestinians to be 'protected persons' under the Fourth Geneva Convention,[292] the emphasis on the protections they are afforded under domestic law become apparent. It then proceeded to examine whether or not the route's alleged violation of the petitioners' individual constitutional rights was consistent with the limitation provisions of the aforementioned Basic Law and which are:[293] that the challenged measure is based on express legal authority; that it has been implemented for a proper purpose and that it is consistent with the principles of reasonableness and proportionality. In deciding the route of the 'fence' the state had struck a balance between the security considerations and objectives and the considerations regarding the protection of the human rights that will be violated by the route of the 'fence'.[294]

In examining the first requirement, the justices examined whether the part of the Wall's route running inside the JM or along the JMB fulfilled a proper purpose as provided for under the *Emergency Land Regulation Law*. In some

289 *Ras Khamis Residents Committee* Judgment, *supra* note 182 at paras 14–25.
290 *Al-Ram Local Village Council* Judgment, *supra* note 27 at 13.
291 Ibid. at paras 40–60.
292 Ibid. at paras 1–22.
293 *Knesset*, Basic Law: *Human Dignity and Liberty* (1992), online: *Knesset* www.knesset.gov.il/laws/special/eng/basic3_eng.htm.
294 *Ras Khamis Local Residents Committee* Judgment, *supra* note 182 at paras 14–25. See also *Salameh* Judgment, *supra* note 98 at paras 6–18; *Al-Ram Local Village Council* Judgment, *supra* note 27 at paras 40–60.

petitions, Palestinians had claimed that the military and government authorities lacked the authority to build the sections of the Wall along the proposed route on the ground that it was motivated by illegal political considerations, and not by legitimate security reasons. However, the Court was quick in rejecting those arguments explaining that the mere fact that the route of the 'fence' separates between 'Jewish and Arab neighbourhoods' does not necessarily lead to the conclusion that illegitimate security considerations were at play. Instead, it seeks to separate between 'Judea and Samaria' on the one hand, and Jerusalem on the other hand, including its 'Jewish and Arab neighbourhoods'.[295] It also concurred with the respondents' position that, as a matter of policy, the route in the area tries to follow the JMB and only diverges from it for security and/or topographic considerations.[296] Since the Court deemed the construction of the Wall, in and around Jerusalem, to constitute a legitimate security tool for preventing infiltration from the 'West Bank' into Israel more generally, and into Jerusalem in particular, the confiscation of the land was generally deemed to fulfil one of the legitimate purposes expressly provided by the *Emergency Land Regulation Law*. These include security reasons or consideration for 'public safety,[297] as stipulated by article 3(b) of that law.[298]

Subsequently, the justices examined whether or not the authority was exercised reasonably and proportionately. When it comes to assessing the government's discretion in exercising its authority for the route of the Wall under Israeli law, the proportionality test proved central[299] It is also very similar (if not identical) to the proportionality test employed by the Court to examine the legality of the Wall's route inside the 'West Bank'. In fact, the justices attached similar importance to the two tests, concluding in the *Al-Ram Local Village Council* judgment that it will hold all of the sections to the same strict test similar to that which is used for examining a breach of Basic Laws.[300]

Afterwards, the Court assessed the proportionality of the Wall's route by resorting to the well-established three-pronged proportionality doctrine used in Israeli administrative law. Examining whether the route of the Wall fulfilled the first proportionality sub-test (rational link), the HCJ held that this was indeed the case because the Wall's route sought to prevent infiltration into Israel (including Jerusalem) in response to a real security threat and, therefore, ensures a separation between terrorism and Israel.[301] The Court upheld this conclusion, even where the route of the Wall had deviated from the JM in some areas to exclude EJ Palestinian neighbourhoods on the 'Palestinian side' of the Wall. To

295 *Ras Khamis Residents Committee* Judgment, *supra* note 182 at paras 14–25. See also *Al-Ram Local Village Council* Judgment, *supra* note 27 at paras 40–60.

296 *Ras Khamis Residents Committee* Judgment, *supra* note 182 at paras 14–25.

297 Ibid. at paras 14–25. See also *Salameh* Judgment, *supra* note 98 at paras 6–18.

298 *Shakir* Judgment, *supra* note 151 at paras 15–35.

299 *Al-Ram Local Village Council* Judgment, *supra* note 27 at paras 40–60.

300 Ibid.

301 Ibid. See also *Shakir* Judgment, *supra* note 151 at paras 15–35.

support its conclusion, the justices expressed their satisfaction that the evidence presented by government authorities demonstrated a real need for the Wall in the area. In another case, the *Ras Khamis Residents Committee* judgment, the Court upheld the respondent's argument that leaving the Shu'afat refugee camp (that is part of the JM) outside the Wall was necessary given the existence of what respondents had described as a 'terrorist infrastructure' in the camp. Another reason justifying the decision was the presence of thousands of Palestinians with 'West Bank' IDs residing in the area illegally, a situation calling for required measures to be adopted by government authorities that would enable supervision and control over the entry into Israel.[302]

In the case of the second proportionality sub-test (minimal impairment), the Court explained that two elements needed to be considered here. The first was the proportionality of the actual (physical) route of the Wall. The second one was the proportionality of the access regime, which authorities had put in place to allegedly reduce the harsh impact of that route on the freedom of movement of Palestinians with Jerusalem IDs and other Israeli citizens (in reference to the Arab Palestinian citizens of Israel) living in communities on both sides of the structure. For the first element, the Court acknowledged that an alternative route as proposed by petitioners would indeed reduce the harm incurred by them. However, it still upheld the respondents' argument that this alternative route would undermine efforts to attain the declared security objectives.[303] This was the situation in the *Al-Ram Local Village Council* judgment. Here, the justices conceded that the alternative route of the Wall in the area, proposed by the CPS, would reduce the distance or buffer zone between 'Israeli neighbourhoods' (i.e. settlements) and Palestinian EJ neighbourhoods,[304] and lessen the harmful consequences of the Wall's construction for the petitioners. Nevertheless, they were not convinced that such a route would have achieved the security objectives identified by the respondents. Adopting the alternative route suggested by the petitioners, they argued, may result in more harm to other residents (mostly Israelis or 'Israeli' permanent residents trying to access Jerusalem).[305]

This was also the Court's position in petitions that challenged the deviation of the Wall's route from the JMB, thereby excluding Palestinian neighbourhoods of the JM.[306] According to the justices, petitioners had not succeeded in providing enough evidence to challenge the security assessment provided by the

302 *Ras Khamis Residents Committee* Judgment, *supra* note 182 at paras 14–25.

303 *Iado* Judgment, *supra* note 98 at paras 6–7. See also *Salameh* Judgment, *supra* note 98 at paras 6–18; *Ras Khamis Residents Committee* Judgment, *supra* note 182 at paras 14–25.

304 *Al-Ram Local Village Council* Judgment, *supra* note 27 at 15.

305 Here, the Court was referring especially to the proposal by petitioners challenging the route of the southern section of the Wall in the Dahiyet Al Bareed neighbourhood. This proposal demanded that all of the neighbourhood remain on the 'Palestinian side' of the Wall. Government authorities had changed the route in response to requests by Christian religious institutions. *Al-Ram Local Village Council* Judgment, *supra* note 27 at paras 23–30.

306 *Salameh* Judgment, *supra* note 98 at paras 6–18.

government.[307] Thus, in petitions in which Palestinians demanded that the Wall be re-routed along the JMB (so that their neighbourhoods are included on the 'Israeli side' of the Wall), the Court rejected the feasibility of this proposal.

One main reason is that the justices have accepted the respondents' position that doing so would result in including a substantial number of Palestinians with 'West Bank' IDs on the 'Israeli side' of the Wall. This was the situation in the *Salameh* judgment, where the justices underlined that such a situation would be unacceptable and should be avoided whenever possible because it would leave Palestinians in a Seam Zone-like situation (i.e. between the Wall and the JM), unable to enjoy unrestricted movement in the direction of either the JM or the 'West Bank'.[308] A similar conclusion was reached by the Court in the *Ras Khamis Residents Committee* judgment. Here, the justices concurred with the respondents' position that moving the Wall's route closer to the JMB would not be feasible for two reasons. The first one is that it would, once again, compromise the buffer zone deemed necessary to provide the military forces with enough time to respond to any infiltration attempts. Second, adopting the alternative route would require the construction of a checkpoint at the entrance of the Shu'afat refugee camp (home to the petitioners) in order to screen travellers in the direction of the JM. This would result in far more harm to the residents and would require the confiscation of lands inside the 'West Bank' for reasons not absolutely justified for military/security reasons.[309]

In a second case, the *Shakir* judgment, the residents of the Sheikh Saed village demanded that the Wall in the area be re-routed so that, instead of running inside the JM, it would run inside the 'West Bank' as a way of including them on the 'Israeli side' of the Wall. This would be necessary, so that they may be able to maintain their historic attachment to the EJ neighbourhood of Jabal Mukabir (the latter is part of the JM). In dismissing the petition, Chief Justice Beinisch explained that if the appeals committee's decision of invalidating the route of the Wall inside Jerusalem were to stand it would entail even greater harm to the residents of the neighbourhood since it would mean that they would find themselves enclaved between 'fences' both on the east and the west – in a Seam Zone regime. The result of such a determination would mean that the Sheikh Saed residents would live under the Seam Zone regime surrounded by fences and under movement restrictions that would require permits and passing through crossings and checkpoints every time they left the neighbourhood – both in the direction of the West Bank and Jerusalem.[310]

307 *Iado* Judgment, *supra* note 98 at paras 8–13; *Ras Khamis Residents Committee* Judgment, *supra* note 182 at paras 14–25.

308 They would still need Israeli-issued valid permits to enter Jerusalem across the JMB. *Salameh* Judgment, *supra* note 98 at paras 6–18.

309 *Ras Khamis Residents Committee* Judgment, *supra* note 182 at paras 14–24.

310 *Shakir* Judgment, *supra* note 151 at paras 15–35.

In that judgment, the Court also addressed the appeals committee's decision to invalidate the land confiscation order for the construction of the Wall inside the JM on the ground that an alternative route (one that includes the village of Sheikh Saed inside the Wall) would have been more proportionate. Here, the Court was quick to invalidate the committee's decision, agreeing with authorities that to do so, would amount to re-routing the Wall inside the 'West Bank' to include the village. This would then force government authorities to build the Wall inside the occupied territory (or 'Area'), as opposed to Israeli territory. Moreover, in the absence of security reasons justifying such a move, they appeared to share the respondents' position that this would violate both Israeli and public international law. The justices then proceeded to explain that, on the face of it, this reason alone would be enough to lead to the conclusion that the security fence should not be built on an alternative route.[311]

When considering the proportionality of the Wall's route, the Court generally took into account a second element, namely that government authorities committed themselves to putting in place a number of measures that would seek to improve the ability of both Palestinians with Jerusalem IDs, and those with 'West Bank' IDs (carrying valid permits to access the JM). These measures, allegedly sought to improve their commute through the Wall to and from Jerusalem or to and from their areas of residence to other parts of the 'West Bank'. Authorities had also promised in court that they would improve the existing crossing arrangements instead of re-routing the Wall in the area. The value accorded by the Court to the promises by government authorities was substantial and enough to let the Court conclude that, therefore, the impact of the Wall's route on the petitioners was proportional.[312] For example, in the *Ras Khamis Residents Committee* judgment, the Court appears to acknowledge that the current route of the Wall significantly undermined the ability of Palestinians with Jerusalem IDs (left on the 'Palestinian side' of the Wall) to access social services inside the JM, acknowledging that the fence burdens the residents of Shuafat ridge neighbourhoods, including permanent residents, in going to and from work, accessing daily services, education and social and also municipality services which are located, for the most part, in the other parts of Jerusalem, including to schools, health clinics and hospitals and other facilities.[313]

Concerning the second element (the proportionality of the access regime) the justices expressed their satisfaction with government commitments that were made in Court that an additional crossing in the western section of the Wall would be built and made functional.[314] They also took into account the pledge by government and military authorities to provide governmental, municipal and

311 Ibid. at paras 15–35.

312 Ibid. at paras 15–35.

313 *Ras Khamis Residents Committee* Judgment, *supra* note 182 at paras 14–25.

314 The promise by government authorities was in response to the judgment rendered by the appeals committee, which had examined and upheld the legality of the land confiscation order. *Ras Khamis Residents Committee* Judgment, *supra* note 182 at paras 14–25.

postal services at a designated Wall crossing/gate, as a way of ensuring that the residents with Jerusalem IDs would not be prevented from accessing them in the future.[315] The respondents' assurances as to the smooth operation of the crossings were an important element rendering the route of the Wall proportional. In another case, the *Salameh* case, the Court highlighted the willingness of the respondents to allow vehicles to cross through a given Wall gate (during daytime), even though passage through these gates had originally been reserved for the exclusive use of pedestrian Palestinians with Jerusalem IDs.[316] Similarly, in the *Al-Ram Local Village Council* judgment, the Court took note of the government's assurances that it would streamline the movement of people across the Qalandia checkpoint, to reduce waiting time and delays, and that it would provide social services at the checkpoint for Palestinians with Jerusalem IDs remaining on the 'Palestinian side' of the Wall. By doing so, the respondents fulfilled their obligation of minimizing the overall harm incurred by the petitioners.[317] Should these arrangements turn out to be unsatisfactory, the petitioners would be able to 'return to this court'.[318] Where the respondents had noted that they would not be able to 'operationalize' a Wall crossing closer to the homes of petitioners, or that only pedestrians would be allowed to access a certain crossing, the justices have also accepted the security justifications for the respondents' decision.[319] In light of these two elements, the Court has generally concluded that, despite the burden incurred by Palestinian commuters as a result of long detours, movement restrictions and crossing arrangements, the Wall's route fulfilled the second proportionality sub-test (the least harmful measure).[320]

Moving on to the assessment of the third requirement that must be fulfilled by the measure to meet the conditions set out by the third proportionality sub-test (narrow proportionality),[321] the justices acknowledged that the harm rendered to the petitioners and their rights due to the Wall's route in the area has been significant. At the same time, they concluded that it is not so severe as to render the route of the challenged segment of the Wall disproportionate. This, they argued, is because the 'fence' achieves an extremely important security purpose of preventing terrorists from freely crossing into Israel,[322] and of protecting the lives of Israeli citizens and residents of Jerusalem.[323] Simultaneously, the justices pointed out that reaching this conclusion hinged on the respondent's

315 *Ras Khamis Residents Committee* Judgment, *supra* note 182 at paras 14–25.

316 *Salameh* Judgment, *supra* note 98 at paras 6–18. See also *Iado* Judgment, *supra* note 98 at paras 6–7.

317 *Al-Ram Local Village Council* Judgment, *supra* note 27 at paras 40–60.

318 Ibid. at paras 40–60.

319 *Iado* Judgment, *supra* note 98 at paras 6–7.

320 Ibid. at paras 6–7.

321 *Ras Khamis Residents Committee* Judgment, *supra* note 182 at paras 14–25.

322 Ibid. at paras 14–25.

323 *Salameh* Judgment, *supra* note 98 at paras 6–18; *Al-Ram Local Village Council supra* note 27 at 17.

ability to implement the measures they had committed themselves to as a way of ameliorating the experience of commuting through the Wall crossings for the Palestinians.[324]

In making this assessment, the Court underscored that a distinction must be drawn between the manner in which the Wall's route affects the right to movement of Palestinians with Jerusalem IDs on one hand, and that of Palestinians with 'West Bank' IDs on the other. This was the case because the members of the latter population group did not enjoy a right to enter or reside on 'Israeli' territory (including the JM) unless they had received valid permits issued by the CA to enter Jerusalem. Hence, two consequences flow from this. First, that the extent of harm to the rights of 'West Bank' Palestinians is not the same as that of Palestinians with Jerusalem IDs. This is because only the latter are entitled to enter Jerusalem (without restrictions) and to receive its services (by virtue of being considered 'Israeli' residents). Second, the Court points out that, in the case of Palestinians with 'West Bank' IDs residing 'illegally' inside the JM (such as in the case of the Shu'afat ridge), the security assessment by government authorities indicates that the probability for persons to conduct 'terrorist attacks' is allegedly much higher among those Palestinians. Consequently, while those 'illegal' residents will no doubt be harmed by the route of a 'physical barrier' (the Wall) restricting their movements into Jerusalem, it is a proportionate harm.[325]

Analysis

An assessment of the HCJ's judicial decisions discussed here displays a number of trends which, when viewed together, have made the task of challenging the legality of the construction of the Wall in the Jerusalem area or its security rationale a daunting task indeed for petitioners.

The first one is the Court's views regarding the government's declared position that EJ is part and parcel of Israeli territory. Although the justices fall short of stating explicitly that EJ has been *de jure* annexed, the terminology that they employed and how they chose to refer to it, suggests that, for all practical purposes, they do consider EJ to be part of Israel or at the very least have taken it for granted. Following the promulgation of the Basic Law: *Jerusalem*, the Court's judgments have reflected a more straightforward position not challenging the executive on this point.

The second trend is the HCJ's continued reliance on domestic provisions and sources of Israeli domestic law for adjudicating the legality of land confiscation orders for the Wall's construction and for assessing the reasonability and proportionality of its route, specifically of those segments that are inside the JM or along the JMB. A third trend is the absence of any reference by the Court to

324 *Iado* Judgment, *supra* note 98 at paras 6–7.
325 *Ras Khamis Residents Committee* Judgment, *supra* note 182 at paras 14–25.

the principles of public international law more generally, or to the principles of the law of belligerent occupation, and international human rights law in particular, when examining the legality of the Wall's route inside or along the JMB. This stands in contrast to cases where the Court refers to the rights of Palestinians with 'West Bank' IDs (who have been affected by the route of the Wall inside the JM or along the JMB) as 'protected persons'. It is also a clear demonstration of the Court's acceptance of the notion that EJ is not occupied. The Court's point of departure ensures that any discussion regarding the authority of the government to build the Wall or to determine its route (inside the JM or along the JMB) is addressed within the confines of Israeli constitutional and administrative law. When assessing the legality of the construction through a domestic prism, the issue for the Court is not that of determining whether or not the government had the authority to construct the Wall inside EJ, or whether the objectives amount to lawful considerations (under international law). Rather, the focus of its adjudication is on examining whether the Wall's construction meets the requirements of the limitation's clause under the Israeli Basic Law*: Human Dignity and Liberty.* Viewing the conflicting interests through the lens of domestic law, it is not surprising that the Court refers to the Israeli settlements in EJ as 'neighbourhoods' of the JM, despite their illegality under international law. Entrenching the discussion in a domestic legal framework also allows the Court to avoid addressing the question of the status of settlements under the Fourth Geneva Convention.

A fourth trend that emerges is that the government's decision to build the Wall in Jerusalem is framed by the justices as a lawful security measure, built by Israel on its 'own' territory, to counter serious security threats' emanating from 'Judea and Samaria'. As with judgments discussed elsewhere in this research, the Court displays great deference to the security-based assessment of government authorities, both in terms of the reasonableness of the Wall's construction in the first place and its specific route. This, in turn, has important implications for the outcome of the constitutional balancing that the Court undertakes. In a domestic setting, a government enjoys a wider discretion in implementing measures on its own territory. This would explain why the Court did not pay much attention to claims raised by petitioners that political considerations may also be influencing the decision to build the Wall.[326] After all, if a sovereign state cannot implement politically motivated measures on its own territory where else would it be able to do so? As long as the security reasons for the construction of the Wall fulfil the requirements as stipulated by the provisions of domestic law (*Emergency Land Regulations* and the Basic Law: *Human Dignity and Liberty*), its route has been deemed by the Court to be proportional; as far as the justices are concerned, the 'domestic' Rule of Law (RoL) requirements have been fulfilled.

Had the Court considered EJ to be occupied territory, this would not have been possible. Under the law of belligerent occupation, an Occupying Power's ability to implement certain measures in the occupied territory, which result in

326 *Al-Ram Local Village Council* Judgment, *supra* note 27 at paras 40–60.

restricting some of the most fundamental rights of the occupied population (such as freedom of movement) must meet stringent conditions. Israeli authorities would have had to demonstrate, for example, that measures implemented in the occupied territory were in response to legitimate security/military needs or for the benefit of the 'local population'. They would also have had to demonstrate that the construction of the Wall does not seek to entrench the wider political or economic interests of the occupier in the occupied territory.[327]

Fifth, in a setting of regular formal sovereignty (i.e. within a country's own territory), the debate regarding the legality of a certain measure is different than in an occupied territory. It becomes one that concerns itself with the margin of appreciation that should be afforded to national authorities, the particular nature of the interference that they seek to implement for the alleged purpose of protecting national security and the extent to which it interferes with the rights of the affected individuals, who are predominantly citizens or 'permanent residents' of the State. In short, 'the issue becomes a factual context for balancing everybody's rights which the turn to proportionality by the High Court achieves'.[328] This wider margin of appreciation is enthusiastically granted by the Court to government authorities as it accepts the assurances of the latter that it would implement measures to reduce the hardships of access for the affected Palestinians with Jerusalem IDs. Not questioning those commitments allows the Court in turn to rule that the Wall's impact was indeed proportionate.[329] This takes place even though, to date, some of these promised measures have not been implemented, and while the effectiveness of other measures continues to be disputed by the domestic and international human rights community.

Sixth, the Court's approach strips the petitions of their political context. Reading the decisions, it is easy to forget that EJ is and remains an occupied territory under international law or that it has been annexed in violation of international law. It is even easier to lose sight of the fact that Palestinians with Jerusalem IDs are still, from the perspective of international law, considered 'protected persons' under the Fourth Geneva Convention. This negates the duty of the Occupying Power under the international law of belligerent occupation to safeguard some of their most fundamental rights and to ensure that they '[…] shall be treated […] by the Party to the conflict in whose power they are, without any adverse distinction based, in particular, on race, religion or political opinion'.[330]

327 This includes consolidating the *de jure* annexation of parts of the occupied territory. This is because occupation is supposed to be temporary in nature.

328 Martti Koskenniemi, 'Occupied Zone', *supra* note 12 at 38. Although this argument is made with respect to the Court's adjudication of Wall-related case law as it pertains to the 'West Bank' it offers a useful point of departure for analysing the Court's adjudication of the Wall, in and around Jerusalem, using Israeli law.

329 By 2014, the service centre and administrative office – including Social Security and MoI offices and a branch of the Israeli Post Office – which the government had promised in the *Ras Khamis* Judgment had not been built. *Ir Amim* Response 2014, *supra* note 26.

330 Article 27 of the Fourth Geneva Convention, *supra* note 12.

Instead, the context that emerges from reading the Court's reasoning is one of a domestic court seeking to manage competing interests that may well arise in the context of domestic or even municipal politics, and to examine petitions which challenge the distribution of resources to one social group or the other. The discussion that appears to be taking place is one that focuses on how best to manage the access of the petitioners to social services, which traditionally have been tied to their ability to demonstrate their continued residence in 'Israel' and to prove that Jerusalem is their 'centre of life'. At best, within the parameters of such a domestic human rights discourse employed by the Court, any determination that the national government has fallen short of its obligations would (at best) rise to the level of discrimination.

Moreover, this approach ignores the political dimension that is common to these petitions, in terms of an Occupying Power and an occupied population. It also views the Wall's construction in isolation from other policies that have been implemented by the government in relation to EJ, which have been criticized for promoting a particular Israeli political and demographic agenda that is detrimental to the rights of the occupied Palestinian population. In this regard, the justices skilfully avoid granting any consideration to this criticism by focusing their analysis on the effect of the Wall at the micro-level. For example, it dissects the Wall's route depending on where it runs (JM v. 'West Bank'), who it affects (Palestinians with Jerusalem IDs v. Palestinians with 'West Bank' IDs); how access to and from the JM on the 'Israeli side' of the Wall can be improved as well as how the services that are provided by the JM at a particular checkpoint or Wall gate can be ameliorated. In short, the bigger picture of ongoing occupation gets lost in the details. Needless to say the notion that certain illegal acts committed by the Occupying Power inside an occupied territory could amount under international law to war crimes, thereby invoking individual criminal responsibility and an obligation of reparation by the violating State, becomes irrelevant.[331]

Furthermore, where the route of the Wall has, in some areas, run inside the JM, and in some other parts in areas of the 'West Bank', the Court has decided to analyse the Wall's route in terms of the proportionality doctrine and its three subtests, as applied within the framework of Israeli administrative law and to invoke references to Israeli constitutional law. On a more positive note, one could argue that the Court's decision to judge the route of the Wall in its entirety by standards of Israeli constitutional and administrative law reflects a desire to improve the protection afforded to the affected Palestinian communities under domestic law. This would not be the first time the Court has chosen to address the rights of Palestinians, even those with 'West Bank' IDs, as rights that are constitutionally protected. However, it has already been demonstrated elsewhere in this research

331 ICRC, 'Rule 156: Definition of War Crimes', in J.M. Henckaerts and Louise Doswald-Beck, eds, *Customary International Humanitarian Law* (Cambridge: Cambridge University Press, 2005) at 462–463, online: ICRC www.icrc.org/customary-ihl/eng/docs/v1_cha_chapter44_rule156. See also an interview with Charles Shamas by author via Skype (21 November 2014, Ramallah) [*Shamas* Interview].

that such an approach dilutes the protection afforded to Palestinians under international law and is consequently ill-suited to a situation of occupation. This conclusion remains relevant to the situation of Palestinians with 'West Bank' IDs affected by the Wall in the Jerusalem area.

Adjudicating the legality of the route of the Wall in the Jerusalem area deviating from the JMB into the 'West Bank'

The applicable legal framework

In some parts, the route of the Wall in the Jerusalem area has made incursions into the occupied 'West Bank'. The manner in which the Court examines the legality of the construction and route of the Wall, in petitions that challenge those segments, reflects very much the same approach it adopted when examining the legality of the Wall segments. Since the HCJ acknowledges that this is indeed occupied territory, the Court's point of departure here changes or, as a matter of fact, reverts back to an approach that is based on international law. In fact, upon examining the relevant petitions challenging the decision of the MC to route the Wall inside that territory, the justices have explicitly reiterated the relevance of the legal framework which the Court had established in the *Beit Sourik* and *Mara'abe* judgments, as well as other landmark 'West Bank' Wall-related judgments.[332]

One landmark petition is the one that was filed by residents of nine Palestinian village councils challenging this route north-west of Jerusalem. The petition was submitted to challenge the new route resulting from modifications by Israeli authorities in compliance with the *Beit Sourik* ruling. The overview also shows how the approach that the Court adopts varies depending on whether it views the territory as occupied or not, as well as on whether the affected population are 'Israeli' permanent residents and/or citizens or not.

The Biddu Village Council *case*

Following the *Beit Sourik* judgment, Israeli authorities decided to modify the route of the 26km-long section of the Wall in the area. Both Palestinian and Israeli petitioners challenged the decision. In the case of the former, Palestinians argued that the modified route still caused harm to their property rights, as well as to their ability to commute to EJ and to other parts of the 'West Bank',[333] on

332 *Al-Eizariyah Village Council* Judgment, *supra* note 28 at paras 8–17; *Halawa* Judgment, *supra* note 212 at paras 9–18. See also *Al-Ram Local Village Council* Judgment, *supra* note 27 at 12.

333 (HCJ 426/2005) was a principled petition filed by five Palestinian village councils against the legality of constructing the Wall as a whole on this route. Four other petitions (HCJ 2223/05) (8264/05) (8266/05) and (8265/05) were submitted by individual Palestinians whose private property has been affected by this route. *Biddu Village Council* Judgment, *supra* note 121 at paras 6–7.

which they relied for daily public services.[334] They also alleged that the Wall's route, which left a major road (road 436) servicing near the Israeli settlement of Pisgat Ze'ev and others on the 'Israeli side' of the Wall, should be re-routed even more closely to the Green Line, because of its disproportionately harmful impact on their 'fabric of life'.[335]

In the case of the latter, the Israeli settlement council of Har Adar and residents of the Israeli town of Mevasseret Tzion (inside Israel proper) had also challenged the newly modified route.[336] This is because the route edged closer to their line of houses and left strategic hilltops overlooking major roads on the 'Palestinian side' of the Wall. This, they argued, undermined the MC's ability to protect them against any security threats.[337] They also objected to the decision of the MC to leave land that was part of the settlement's jurisdiction on the 'Palestinian side' of the structure.[338]

The respondents, for their part, reiterated the security-based rationale of the Wall.[339] Where the route intruded inside 'West Bank' territory and thus trapped Palestinian communities in a Seam Zone, they argued that this was necessary for protecting the Israeli settlements around Jerusalem.[340] In explaining why they deem the harm resulting from the Wall to be proportionate,[341] the respondents pointed out a number of elements. One of these elements is that they have decided to modify the route even further in some areas so that some of the petitioners and their villages would remain on the 'Palestinian side' of the Wall. They also decided to construct a new 'fabric of life' road, as a way of ensuring that petitioners access major nearby 'West Bank' towns relatively unhindered.[342] Moreover, they noted that reverting to the original route of the Wall would entail a disproportionate harm to the lands of other Palestinian villages. As for leaving the hilltop on the 'Palestinian side' of the Wall, they claimed that any security threats would be effectively addressed by other means.[343] Finally,

334 *Biddu Village Council* Judgment, *supra* note 121 at paras 6–7.

335 Particularly on the 'fabric of life' of the residents of Al-Nabi Samuel. See *Biddu Village Council* Judgment, *supra* note 121 at paras 6–7.

336 (HCJ 2056/04) [2004] *Beit Sourik Village Council v. Government of Israel* (2005), official English translation, online: HCJ https://supremedecisions.court.gov.il/Home/Download?path=EnglishVerdicts\04\560\020\A28&fileName=04020560_a28.txt&type=4 [*Beit Sourik* Judgment]. The petition was upheld partially by the HCJ.

337 *Biddu Village Council* Judgment, *supra* note 121 at paras 6–7.

338 Those were petitions (HCJ 1767/05) and (HCJ 11409/05) See (HCJ 426/2005). *Biddu Village Council* Judgment, *supra* note 121 at 4.

339 That of protecting Israelis in Israel proper and the settlements, including commuters on the roads to and from those settlements. *Biddu Village Council* Judgment, *supra* note 121 at paras 8–9.

340 *Biddu Village Council* Judgment, *supra* note 121 at paras 8–9.

341 Addressing the particular situation of Al-Nabi Samuel, they argued that, since it is located on a hilltop that overlooks road 436 and the northern houses in the EJ settlement of Ramot Alon, including it on the 'Israeli side' of the Wall constitutes 'an essential security need'. *Biddu Village Council* Judgment, *supra* note 121 at paras 8–9.

342 *Biddu Village Council* Judgment, *supra* note 121 at paras 8–9.

343 Ibid. at paras 8–9.

regarding the complaint by the Israeli petitioners that some of the land constituting part of the settlement jurisdiction needed for its expansion would be left on the 'Palestinian side' of the Wall, they argued that this does not constitute a legitimate consideration that can guide the Wall's route in the area.[344]

In the judgment, the Court reiterated the idea that the objective behind the Wall's construction is to protect Israeli settlers; hence, it constitutes a legitimate response to pressing security needs. This, according to the Court, authorizes the MC under the law of belligerent occupation, to requisition land for its construction.[345] In determining whether the route chosen by the MC has adequately balanced between the different considerations that can lawfully guide his actions in the occupied territory, the Court once again insisted on the importance of resorting to the proportionality doctrine.[346] It also reiterated that the MC is the one that determines where the 'fence' should pass.[347] After listing the factors that have led it to conclude that the challenged sections of the 'fence' are proportional in their effect on the petitioners,[348] the Court upheld the respondents' argument that there was no alternative route capable of achieving the same security objective.[349]

Subsequently, the Court addressed the concerns of the Israeli petitioners. While acknowledging that the added security value provided by the Wall's modified route is inferior to the added security value provided by the structure's original route in the area, it expressed confidence in the ability of the MC to protect Israeli petitioners through other means. It also endorsed the respondents' position that amending the route of the Wall would entail harm (that is more severe in nature) to other communities. The Court then concluded that a proper balance has been struck between the conflicting considerations, and dismissed the petition.[350]

The Court's adjudication of petitions challenging the route of the Wall in the Jerusalem area running inside the 'West Bank'

In examining other petitions discussed here, where the route of the Wall made incursions into the 'West Bank', the Court confirmed that the MC is entitled to requisition land for this purpose if it is in response to genuine security/military

344 Ibid. at paras 8–9.
345 Ibid. at paras 10–15.
346 Ibid. at paras 10–15.
347 Ibid. at paras 10–15.
348 These elements are: that the land confiscated for the Wall's construction and the land which has been trapped in the Seam Zone was significantly reduced after the Wall had been re-routed following the *Beit Sourik* ruling; that agricultural gates would be put into place to enable Palestinians to access their property in that zone; that compensation would be offered; that a 'fabric of life' road would be constructed; and that movement restrictions that had been imposed on the Bir Nabala residents would be eased. *Biddu Village Council* Judgment, *supra* note 121 at paras 10–15.
349 Those who still feel harmed by the permit system and access through the Wall gates will have the opportunity to re-petition the Court. *Biddu Village Council* Judgment, *supra* note 121 at paras 10–15.
350 If, in the future, military authorities conclude that this route fails to provide the needed level of security, it will be re-examined. *Biddu Village Council* Judgment, *supra* note 121 at paras 10–15.

considerations.[351] In this regard, the justices reiterated that similar to the findings in the *Beit Sourik* judgment, the decision to construct the 'fence' in this area was driven by security concerns after September 2000,[352] as a way of preventing the infiltration by Palestinians into 'Israel' (including EJ),[353] and by the need to protect Israeli settlers and commuters. For example, in the *Beit Sahour Municipality* judgment, the Court explained that the Wall's deviation from the Green Line is necessary to include (the settlement of) Har Homa, which is located on the southern edge of Jerusalem, only a few hundred metres from the JMB, as a way of securing its residents.[354]

The justices again emphasized that expansive deference will be granted to the expertise of military authorities[355] and that the safety of the Israeli settler population and of Israeli travellers is part of the MC's legitimate security-based considerations under international law, even if they are not considered 'protected persons'. For example, in the *Halawa* judgment, the Court endorsed the respondents' position that the MC enjoyed this authority because the Wall bolstered the security of the Israeli settlement of Pisgat Ze'ev and of Israeli travellers on road 45.[356] Finally, the justices also held that the MC had the authority to establish security-based measures that have been put in place in association with the Wall,[357] and to requisition land for this purpose.

Once this was established, the justices then examined the question of whether the MC had properly exercised his discretion to route the Wall along the particular route that he had chosen. Here, they stated that their own role is limited to determining whether the MC had acted within the scope of his discretion.[358] In exercising this authority, the Court recalled that the MC must balance between the following considerations: the security and the need to maintain order in the area under his control, including the security of the

351 *Biddu Village Council* Judgment, *supra* note 121 at paras 10–15; *Al-Eizariyah Village Council* Judgment, *supra* note 28 at paras 8–17. The Court cited article 52 of the Hague Regulations, *supra* note 8 and article 53 of the Fourth Geneva Conventions, *supra* note 12 as authorizing the MC to do so. *Halawa* Judgment, *supra* note 212 at paras 9–18; *Abu El Tir* Judgment, *supra* note 190 at paras 10–21; *Al-Ram Local Village Council* Judgment, *supra* note 27 at 12.

352 *Al-Eizariyah Village Council* Judgment, *supra* note 28 at paras 8–17.

353 *Halawa* Judgment, *supra* note 212 at 3–4.

354 The Court also stressed the fact that the route of the Wall does not change the municipal boundaries between Jerusalem and Beit Sahour. *Beit Sahour Municipality* Judgment, *supra* note 208 at paras 7–18.

355 *Ras Khamis Residents Committee* Judgment, *supra* note 182 at paras 14–25; *Al-Ram Local Village Council* Judgment, *supra* note 27 at 12; *Iado* Judgment, *supra* note 98 at paras 6–7.

356 *Halawa* Judgment, *supra* note 212 at paras 9–18. *Al-Ram Local Village Council* Judgment, *supra* note 27 at 3; *Al-Ezariyah Local Village Council* Judgment, *supra* note 28 at 2. See also *Iado* Judgment, *supra* note 98 at paras 8–17.

357 In one judgment, the Court was satisfied that the cement wall built by government authorities on the schoolyard was a temporary security measure, the sole purpose of which was to protect the individuals working on the Wall in and around Jerusalem, and dismissed the petition. *Anata Boys High School* Judgment, *supra* note 233 at 2.

358 *Al-Ram Local Village Council* Judgment, *supra* note 27 at paras 40–60.

armed forces; the well-being of the local 'Arab population',[359] who are considered 'protected persons';[360] and the security and the human rights of Israeli citizens,[361] which, under both international and Israeli domestic law, the MC is obliged to protect.[362]

Addressing the third consideration, the Court explains that although it has traditionally been invoked in relation to Israeli settlers, it is also relevant in situations where the rights and interests of the Arab citizens of Israel or 'Israeli' permanent residents are at stake.[363] At the same time, the rights of both Palestinians with 'West Bank' IDs and those of the 'Israelis' were not absolute. Therefore, in order to determine whether the route chosen by the government authorities fell within the 'range of proportionality', the proportionality doctrine with its three sub-tests must be invoked.[364]

In the case of the first sub-test (rational link), the Court upheld the conclusion that the route of the Wall advances security objectives in the area.[365] Since the Wall separates between the 'West Bank' and Israel, it is synonymous with creating 'a barrier between terror and Israelis'.[366] The Court then rejected the allegation by petitioners that the Wall in and around Jerusalem had been built to secure political objectives as opposed to legitimate security-based considerations.[367] Underscoring that the structure replaces military offensive operations to prevent this infiltration into 'Israel' from the 'West Bank',[368] it concluded that the Wall fulfilled the requirements of the first sub-test.[369]

In regard to the second proportionality sub-test (the least harmful test), the Court explained that, while there is no doubt that this route would be less harmful to the petitioners, it could not conclude with certainty that it would be an effective means to achieve the security objectives.[370] To establish whether the conditions of the second sub-test were met, it was necessary to consider two elements: the geographic route of the Wall and the permit and movement regime in place.[371] In examining which physical route of the Wall is the least harmful yet still achieves the desirable security-based objectives, the justices generally deferred to the MC's assessment that the alternative routes (proposed

359 *Abu El Tir* Judgment, *supra* note 190 at paras 10–21; *Al-Eizariyah Village Council* Judgment, *supra* note 28 at para 17.
360 *Al-Ram Local Village Council* Judgment, *supra* note 27 at 12–13.
361 *Al-Eizariyah Village Council* Judgment, *supra* note 28 at paras 8–17; *Halawa* Judgment, *supra* note 212 at paras 9–18.
362 *Al-Ram Local Village Council* Judgment, *supra* note 27 at 12–13.
363 Ibid. at 12–13.
364 Ibid. at 13. *Abu El Tir* Judgment, *supra* note 190 at paras 10–21; *Al-Eizariyah Village Council* Judgment, *supra* note 28 at paras 8–17, and *Halawa* Judgment, *supra* note 212 at paras 9–18.
365 *Al-Eizariyah Village Council* Judgment, *supra* note 28 at paras 8–17.
366 *Halawa* Judgment, *supra* note 212 at paras 9–18.
367 *Al-Ram Local Village Council* Judgment, *supra* note 27 at paras 40–60.
368 Ibid. at 14 and 15.
369 *Beit Sahour Municipality* Judgment, *supra* note 208 at paras 7–18.
370 Ibid. at 5.
371 *Halawa* Judgment, *supra* note 212 at paras 9–18.

by petitioners) would not fulfil those objectives,[372] and pointed out that they cannot prefer the security analysis of experts supporting the position of the petitioners over that of the MC who is responsible for the security in the area.[373]

As for the movement and permit regime, the justices noted that the measures put in place by the respondents, or which they committed themselves to implementing, would ameliorate the impact of the Wall on the petitioners' rights. This was the situation in the *Halawa* judgment where the Court explained that since a Wall gate was made available to petitioners at a 2.5 km distance from their houses and was rendered operational 24 hours a day, the harm suffered by the petitioners was significantly reduced. Hence, the Wall's route fulfilled the second sub-test.[374] In another case, *Shakir*, the justices rejected the petitioners' argument that the decision of military authorities to construct a 'fabric of life' road would connect their villages eastward to the rest of the 'West Bank' at the expense of the historic links that Sheikh Said enjoyed with EJ. After underscoring the authority of the MC to plan and build roads in the occupied territory if these roads served the interest of the 'local population',[375] the justices rejected that this road would create a new/different reality for the social, family or other links with Jerusalem.[376] Similarly in the *Iado* judgment, the promises by military authorities that they would allow petitioners to be added to a list of individuals who can use the Sawahreh crossing, and to enable them access with their vehicles was considered by the Court a reasonable and effective solution[377] that would help minimize the harm incurred by the residents. The Court then concluded that the measures fulfilled the second proportionality sub-test.

In the case of the third proportionality sub-test (proportionality in the narrow sense), the Court emphasized once again that the Wall constitutes an essential element in the overall Israeli fight against Palestinian attacks and in saving lives.[378] Moreover, it rejected alternative routes proposed by petitioners on the ground that, if adopted, it would decrease the accrued security benefits.[379] In reaching the

372 Including that of protecting residents of Israeli Settlements. *Halawa* Judgment, *supra* note 212 at paras 9–18; *Al-Eizariyah Village Council* Judgment, *supra* note 28 at para 17; *Beit Sahour Municipality* Judgment, *supra* note 208 at paras 7–18.

373 *Halawa* Judgment, *supra* note 212 at paras 9–18. See also *Beit Sahour Municipality* Judgment, *supra* note 208 at paras 7–18; *Walajeh Village Council* Judgment, *supra* note 213 at 5.

374 *Halawa* Judgment, *supra* note 212 at paras 9–18. See also *Abu El Tir* Judgment, *supra* note 190 at 8. Elsewhere, the Court took note of the fact that respondents had promised to make two Wall gates operational for the crossing of petitioners, which would allow petitioners to also secure the access of tractors and other agricultural vehicles. *Walajeh Village Council* Judgment, *supra* note 213 at 6.

375 *Shakir* Judgment, *supra* note 151 at paras 15–35.

376 Ibid. at paras 15–35.

377 *Iado* Judgment, *supra* note 98 at 5.

378 *Al-Eizariyah Village Council* Judgment, *supra* note 28 at paras 8–17; *Halawa* Judgment, *supra* note 212 at paras 9–18; *Beit Sahour Municipality* Judgment, *supra* note 208 at paras 7–18; *Walajeh Village Council* Judgment, *supra* note 213 at 5; *Shakir* Judgment, *supra* note 151 at paras 15–35.

379 *Halawa* Judgment, *supra* note 212 at paras 9–18; *Al-Eizariyah Village Council* Judgment, *supra* note 28 at paras 8–17.

conclusion that the challenged route fulfilled the third sub-test, it considered a number of elements that contributed towards a substantial reduction of the harm resulting from the Wall's route. In the *Halawa* judgment, for example, the Court explained what these elements were. The first is that, by surrounding the hill allegedly belonging to petitioners, the Wall's route prevented any damage to the graves on top of it. The second is that the route did not enclave cultivated land or interfere with any sources of livelihood. The third is that it did not trap people in the Seam Zone or cut off residents from access to daily services.[380] The Court also upheld the argument of the respondents that adopting an alternative route for the Wall in the area would result in the violation of rights of other local Palestinian residents and, therefore, would not minimize the overall harm caused to the local Palestinian residents in the area.[381]

Similarly, in the *Al-Eizariyah Village Council* judgment, the justices noted that leaving the hills on the 'Palestinian side' of the Wall would reduce the harm incurred by the Palestinian petitioners (with 'West Bank' IDs)[382] and that this was sufficient to render the route of the Wall proportionate under the third sub-test.[383] In reaching this conclusion, the Court accepted the guarantees made by the respondents that most of the land requisitioned for the Wall's construction is 'state land' or uncultivated and that, accordingly, the harm resulting from the Wall's route was not as significant as petitioners claimed.[384] Other elements which the Court took into account before deciding that there was no ground to intervene in the decision of the MC are as follows: including the hill inside the Wall did not undermine access of the petitioners to routes that connect between the villages and any other villages/cities in the area; that no residents will be trapped in the Seam Zone; and that the route would not cut off petitioners from essential services, or sources of livelihood.[385]

In the *Beit Sahour Municipality* judgment, after acknowledging that the Wall and its access regime has disrupted the petitioners' daily lives, the justices pointed out that the promise by respondents to put in place a seasonal agricultural gate allows the former to access their land inside the Seam Zone. In addition, since the Wall did not undermine their access of Palestinian cities to other parts of the 'West Bank', its impact was deemed proportional.[386]

In another judgment, *Shakir*, the Court noted that its decision regarding the proportionality of the Wall was contingent upon the respondents making the necessary adjustments and arrangements for the operation of a permanent Wall

380 The justices also took into account the assurances by the government that it would compensate the petitioners with an alternative plot of land elsewhere. *Halawa* Judgment, *supra* note 212 at paras 9–18.

381 Ibid. at paras 9–18.

382 *Al-Eizariyah Village Council* Judgment, *supra* note 28 at paras 8–17.

383 Ibid. at paras 8–17.

384 Ibid. at paras 8–17. *Walajeh Village Council* Judgment, *supra* note 213 at 5.

385 *Al-Eizariyah Village Council* Judgment, *supra* note 28 at paras 8–17.

386 Such as nearby Bethlehem. *Beit Sahour Municipality* Judgment, *supra* note 208 at paras 7–18.

gate at the entrance of the petitioners' neighbourhood and upon them making sure that it is operational for those with Jerusalem IDs or valid entry permits to access it 24 hours a day.[387]

Assessment

All of the elements that have traditionally characterized the HCJ's approach in petitions challenging the legality of the Wall's route inside the West Bank remain relevant to the Court's analysis of the legality for the sections of the Wall, which have deviated from the JMB into the 'West Bank'. These elements include the irrelevance of the legality/illegality of the settlements under international law to an assessment of the legality of the Wall's construction along the route chosen by government authorities; the idea that the MC is responsible for the security of the Israeli settlers, even if they are not 'protected persons'; and the proposition that the Wall's route in the settlements' vicinity, which has included them on the 'Israeli side' is a lawful security response. The Court also endorsed (except when clear and unambiguous evidence had arisen) the security assessments of the MC as to which route best achieves this objective and maintained its heavy reliance on the proportionality doctrine in order to regulate the impact of the Wall in the area, not the very authority of the MC to construct it.

However, the fact that the HCJ does not deem EJ to constitute part of that occupied territory has predetermined the outcome of the Court's judicial reasoning into whether the harm resulting from the 'West Bank' sections of the Jerusalem Wall on nearby 'West Bank' Palestinian communities was proportionate. Unlike its approach on segments of the Wall that run inside the JM or along the JMB, the Court's point of departure is that the 'West Bank' is an occupied territory that, accordingly, is regulated by the principles of the law of belligerent occupation. Hence, there is once again extensive reference and discussion of provisions to the Hague Regulations and to the Fourth Geneva Convention. Reference to Israeli constitutional law only takes place to the extent that it underscores the rights that are afforded under the Basic Law: *Human Dignity and Liberty* to Israeli citizens (Israeli settlers, Arab Palestinian Citizens of Israel) and to 'Israeli' permanent residents (Palestinians with Jerusalem IDs) who are living beyond the Green Line.

For example, when discussing the proportionality of the impact of the Wall's route, the justices endorsed the efforts of the government to improve the access of Palestinians with 'West Bank' IDs to other parts of that 'Area' even if this would, practically speaking, amount to re-orienting their communities away from their traditional reliance on Palestinian neighbourhoods of EJ. Without going into much detail as to why it rejected the petitioners' claims that these measures (such as constructing 'by-pass' roads or installing Wall gates that facilitate their access to the 'West Bank' but not to Jerusalem) seek to consolidate

387 *Shakir* Judgment, *supra* note 151 at paras 15–35.

objectives other than ameliorating the petitioners' 'fabric of life', the Court dismisses those allegations. In this regard, the Court's acceptance that EJ is part of Israeli 'sovereign' territory also explains why it refuses to consider that Palestinians with 'West Bank' IDs should enjoy an inherent right of access to EJ, or right to free movement between it and the rest of the West Bank.[388]

Unlike Palestinians with Jerusalem IDs, 'West Bank' Palestinians are not deemed to have a right to the conferment of government services and other economic rights.[389] This explains how the Court was able to reach the conclusion that military authorities sufficiently reduced the harsh impact of the Wall by implementing measures that facilitate the access of members of the affected communities to other parts of the 'West Bank'. Moreover, the Court's formalistic approach does not take into account the bigger picture, one in which the social and economic fabric of the Palestinian communities on both sides of the JMB are linked.

Closing remarks

The manner in which the HCJ has adjudicated the legality of the Wall in and around Jerusalem has offered Palestinian petitioners a venue for challenging some of the disproportionate impacts of its construction. This has primarily been achieved through its heavy reliance on the proportionality doctrine and its three sub-tests. At the level of individual petitions, the fact that the legality of a given measure is being reviewed by the Court has forced the respondents in several petitions to make changes to the route of the Wall, as a way of reducing their harmful measures on the Palestinians.

However, a number of elements explain why the Court's ability to provide a venue for effective remedy remains limited. To begin with, the steps that government authorities have taken to *de jure* annex parts of the occupied territory (i.e. EJ), has considerably reduced the Court's manoeuvring space. Second, the nature of the Israeli legal system has allowed the justices to avoid dealing with the illegality of the annexation under international law. Third, the Court's own sensitivity to the domestic backlash that it could face at the Israeli domestic level (both from other branches of government and Jewish Israeli public opinion), should it choose to question Israel's control or right to EJ, may be a less obvious but equally important factor.

Fourth, the Court's inability and/or unwillingness to question the security-based assessment of government authorities (unless unequivocal evidence requires this), has diluted the justices' capacity to question and to challenge the idea that those measures had indeed been implemented in response to genuine security considerations. In this regard, the Court's ability to act as a safety valve

388 *Ras Khamis Residents Committee* Judgment, *supra* note 182 at 8.

389 (HCJ 114/78) *Burken v. Corporation for Reconstruction and Development of the Jewish Quarter in the Old City of Jerusalem LTD* (1980) 20 Isr YB Hum Rts 374.

against abuses by military authorities is already far from perfect. This is especially the case given the limited capacity of the Court to question the security-based assessment of these authorities. Arguably, when it comes to scrutinizing the measures implemented by them in a territory that they consider part of the 'sovereign' territory, the Court's ability to prevent political considerations from influencing those measures, is diminished further. This approach, while leading to improvements at the micro-level, does little to change the impact of a government security-based policy at the macro-level.

While part of this is due to institutional constraints, it is also due to the legal framework the Court has deemed relevant to its adjudication of competing interests. By grounding its analysis in Israeli constitutional and administrative law, and by avoiding the invocation of principles of international law when examining segments of the Wall that have been built inside the JM, the Court has skilfully predetermined the outcome of its adjudication, an outcome that evades any necessity to address the continued status of EJ as an occupied territory, or the legality of its annexation. This approach has also allowed the justices to address the claims against the Wall's route and its impact as an issue of mundane government and to reduce the conversation to nothing more than the management of complex social issues among antagonistic groups.[390] The lack of reference to the law of belligerent occupation when discussing the impact of the Wall on Palestinians with Jerusalem IDs means that the rights which they are afforded as 'protected persons' are not just diluted (as is the case with the rights of Palestinians with 'West Bank' IDs), they do not exist altogether. Consequently, the larger picture that has emerged is one in which the heavy price extracted from Palestinian communities on both sides of the Wall in social, human rights and humanitarian terms has essentially been upheld as lawful. As for the segments of the Wall that run inside the 'West Bank', including around Jerusalem, the Court's approach to the interpretation of international law and Israeli administrative law is essentially the same as the one that it has adopted in Wall-related petitions more generally.

If the contribution of the Wall's route towards the two sets of considerations (physical control and demographic objective of securing a Jewish majority) is viewed in tandem, the emerging picture is that of an effort by government authorities to create a greater 'Israeli Jewish Metropolitan Jerusalem' and to substitute the Green Line for the Wall's route as its new municipal border.[391] When decisions regarding the route of the Wall inside the JM are analysed together with decisions regarding the Wall's route inside the 'West Bank', it has been argued that the Court has legalized (knowingly or unknowingly), the government's efforts to reconfigure the territory and demographic make-up of the JM. This is because its judicial approach has not been able to challenge the de

390 Martti Koskenniemi, 'Occupied Zone', *supra* note 12.

391 Anne B. Shlay and Gillad Rosen, 'Making Place: The Shifting Green Line and the Development of "Greater Metropolitan Jerusalem"', (2010) 9:4 City Community 358.

facto annexation of areas around Jerusalem where the largest settlement blocs are located[392] or the *de jure* annexation of EJ. Seen as the latest in a series of measures which seek to consolidate social and demographic relations of the Israeli settler population with Jerusalem, and to redefine those relations for 'West Bank' Palestinians away from the city, the Wall has no doubt fractured the relation of EJ with the rest of the occupied territory, and strengthened Israel's control of it.[393] The Court has not challenged this. Arguably, the only thing that still needs to be done in order to formalize the status of the borders of the JM that are being redrawn by Israeli authorities, is for these authorities to issue an executive decision or legal enactment to endorse the contours of the metropolitan Jerusalem that is being consolidated.[394]

The HCJ appears to have also internalized the reasoning of government authorities that the Wall's main function is to separate between the 'West Bank' (as the alleged source of terrorism) and Israel (which, it does not challenge, includes EJ). Moreover, it is aware of the consensus among the Israeli public, stating that the larger Israeli settlement blocs around Jerusalem must remain part of Israel in any final status settlement with the Palestinians or as part of a unilateral Israeli decision to delineate its borders.[395] The interpretation by the Court of international law and domestic law has provided the legal endorsement for the emerging situation and the preferences of the Israeli general public.

In the meantime, Israeli organizations documenting the impact of the Wall have warned that the structure's very presence in the Jerusalem area is likely to be a contributing factor to more social, economic and political discontent and resentment emerging among EJ Palestinians.[396] By compounding the violations of the rights of the Palestinian residents of EJ, it is argued that the Wall is reducing 'the stake of [Palestinian] residents in a stable Jerusalem'.[397] Slowly but surely, the Wall and its associated policies in the Jerusalem area have increased the risks of turning Jerusalem (once more) into a 'powder keg', thereby undermining the very purpose for which it was allegedly built: enhancing Israeli security.[398]

392 The extension of the protective functions of Israeli law to them (via the MC), coupled with the extension of Israeli jurisdiction *in personam*, blurs the formal status of these settlements, and undermines the distinction between sovereignty and occupation. Martti Koskenniemi, 'Occupied Zone', *supra* note 12.

393 Youssef Courbage, 'Les enjeux démographiques en palestine après le retrait de gaza', (2006) No. 31 Critique Int'l 2: 23.

394 David Newman, 'La frontière israël-palestine', (2004) 4/No. 9 Outre Terre, 131 at 28.

395 Cédric Auzat, 'D'un mur a l'autre: la séparation vue par les israéliens (2002–2010)', (Hiver 2010) 4 Politique Etrangère 743.

396 Israel Kimhi, 'Introduction', in Israel Kimhi, ed, *The Security Fence around Jerusalem: Implications for the City and its Residents* (Jerusalem Institute for Israel Studies (JIIS), 2006) 9 at 10, online: JIIS www.jiis.org/.upload/the%20security%20fence%20around%20jerusalem.pdf.

397 *Ir Amim*, 'Beyond the Wall', *supra* note 37 at 13.

398 ICG, 'The Jerusalem Powder Keg', *supra* note 108.

5 The HCJ and 'unauthorized outposts'

> [...] I must emphasize: an unauthorized outpost is not a 'semi legal' outpost. Unauthorized is illegal.[1]
>
> – Attorney Talia Sasson, former special legal advisor to the Israeli Government

Introduction

'Unauthorized outposts' is a term that refers to Israeli settlements that were built without approval from the Israeli political echelon,[2] but which nevertheless have been constructed with the involvement, assistance and funding of various government ministries, public authorities, and military bodies, including the Civil Administration (CA).[3] Hence, they were established 'not only in grave breach of international law, but also in violation of [Israeli] domestic law'.[4]

Following the landmark *Elon Moreh* judgment by the Israeli High Court of Justice (HCJ),[5] the official position of successive governments was that land that is privately owned by Palestinians should not be seized for military purposes as a way of establishing new settlements.[6] However, despite the ruling, the State has

1 MoFA, Prime Minister's Office, 'Summary of the Opinion Concerning Unauthorized Outposts', (10 March 2005), online: MoFA www.mfa.gov.il/mfa/aboutisrael/state/law/pages/summary%20of%20opinion%20concerning%20unauthorized%20outposts%20-%20talya%20sason%20adv.aspx [Sasson Report]. All links in this chapter have been last accessed on 19 June 2018.

2 Although calling them outposts helps distinguish them from settlements that have been built and/or expanded with government approval, all settlements are illegal under international law. Michael Sfard, *The Wall and the Gate: Israel, Palestine and the Legal Battle for Human Rights* (New York: Metropolitan Books, 2018).

3 These include the Ministry of Construction & Housing; the Settlement Division of the World Zionist Organization; and the Ministry of Interior Affairs. Sasson Report, *supra* note 1.

4 Michael Sfard, 'Regularization Law', in Orna Ben-Naftali, Michael Sfard and Hedi Viterbo, eds, *The ABC of the OPT: A Legal Lexicon of the Israeli control over the Occupied Palestinian Territory* (Cambridge: Cambridge University Press, 2018) 362 at 362.

5 The Israeli Information Center for Human Rights (*B'Tselem*), 'Seizure for Military Needs and the Elon Moreh Ruling', (13 March 2013), online: *B'Tselem* www.btselem.org/settlements/seizure_of_land_for_military_purposes.

6 *Peace Now*, 'Methods of Confiscation – How does Israel Justify and Legalize Confiscation of Lands', (1 January 2009), online: *Peace Now* http://peacenow.org.il/en/methods-of-confiscation-how-does-israel-justify-and-legalize-confiscation-of-lands.

continued to initiate and allow the construction of settlements and of new neighbourhoods of established settlements, on property that was known to be privately owned by Palestinians.[7]

The phenomenon of the construction of 'illegal outposts' began in the 1990s following an Israeli government decision that new settlements could only be built if they had obtained unanimous government approval as well as the Minister of Defence's authorization for various planning stages.[8] In 2004, the government-commissioned Sasson Report underscored that for settlements to be legal (under Israeli domestic law) their building and expansion must fulfil certain criteria:[9] that there is an official government resolution authorizing the construction of the settlement; that the land on which it is built is one that has been declared 'state land',[10] or has been purchased by Israelis and registered in the land registry;[11] that it is built according to a master plan (pursuant to which building permits may be issued); and that its jurisdictional borders were approved by the regional military commander.[12] In principle, any illegal construction underway becomes the subject of a stop-work order or a demolition order by the Enforcement Unit of the CA.[13] At the same time, the Sasson Report underscored that 'law enforcement authorities in the West Bank systematically avoid the enforcement of planning and building laws on Israeli settlers in case of misconduct,[14] and that '[t]he failure to execute delimiting orders gives a good example of the lack of enforcement coming from the political echelon'.[15]

7 *B'Tselem*, 'By Hook or by Crook: Israeli Settlement Policy in the West Bank', Report (July 2010), online: *B'Tselem* www.btselem.org/download/201007_by_hook_and_by_crook_eng.pdf.

8 Yesh Din: Volunteers for Human Rights. *Yesh Din*, 'Under the Radar: Israel's Silent Policy of Transforming Unauthorized Outposts into Official Settlements', (March 2015), online: *Yesh Din* http://files.yesh-din.org/userfiles/Yesh%20Din_Under%20The%20Radar%20-%20English_WEB(3).pdf.

9 *B'Tselem*, 'The Ofra Settlement: An Unauthorized Outpost', (December 2008), online: *B'Tselem* www.btselem.org/sites/default/files/sites/default/files2/publication/200812_ofra_eng.pdf.

10 Sasson Report, *supra* note 1.

11 *B'Tselem*, 'The Ofra Settlement: An Unauthorized Outpost', *supra* note 9.

12 Sasson Report, *supra* note 1.

13 Land allocation, building and planning processes in Area C must be authorized by the CA. Its enforcement unit oversees the application of building and planning laws on both Palestinians and settlers in Area C. Yesh Din, 'Through the Lens of Israel's Interests: The Civil Administration in the West Bank', Position Paper (December 2017), online: *Yesh Din* https://s3-eu-west-1.amazonaws.com/files.yesh-din.org/Minhal+Ezrahi/YeshDin+-+Haminhal+-+English.pdf.

14 *Yesh Din*, 'Land Takeover Practices Employed by Israel in the West Bank: Summary of Legal Proceedings with which Yesh Din Assisted 2006–2016', Report (September 2016) at 6, online: *Yesh Din* https://s3-eu-west-1.amazonaws.com/files.yesh-din.org/פרקטיקות+/Land+Takeover+Practices+-++English.pdf.

15 Sasson Report, *supra* note 1. In addition, law enforcement officials systematically fail to indict and punish those Israelis involved in the illegal construction. *Yesh Din*, 'Crime without Punishment: Law Enforcement in Cases of Illegal Construction and Violation of Judicial and Administrative Orders by Israelis in the West Bank', (January 2017), online: https://s3-eu-west-1.amazonaws.com/files.yesh-din.org/חטא+בלי+עונש/crime+without+punishment_english.pdf.

Thus 'illegal outposts' were built without obtaining the necessary approvals in violation of Israeli domestic requirements. For example, many were established on land that the government had not allocated for them,[16] or lacked building plans or jurisdictional borders that were not approved by the regional military commander.[17] In addition, they came to be constructed entirely or partially on private Palestinian land,[18] or on 'survey land'.[19] This comes despite the fact that previous HCJ rulings have underscored that the right to private property, including that of the Palestinians, is a constitutional right.[20] In this regard, the Court has ruled that the right to property, as stipulated by the Basic Law: *Human Dignity and Liberty*, applies to all persons[21] including the Palestinian inhabitants of the occupied West Bank:

> In our legal system, property rights are protected as a constitutional human right (s. 3 of the Basic Law: Human Dignity and Liberty). This right is of course also recognized in public international law [...]. Therefore, the residents in the territories held under belligerent occupation have a protected right to their property.[22]

Currently, there are two categories of private Palestinian land: the first one is land which Palestinians have managed to have registered in the land registry operated by Israel in the West Bank. The second one is unregistered private land, which has been held and farmed by its Palestinian owners, but which has not been registered.[23] By 2015,[24] an estimated 2,000 structures in settlements and outposts had been built on land that is privately owned by Palestinians.[25] Current projections indicate that there are approximately 100 outposts.

This brief chapter will review some key trends regarding the position of government authorities as well as key aspects of the judgments rendered by the

16 *B'Tselem*, 'By Hook or by Crook', *supra* note 7.

17 Ibid.

18 *Yesh Din*, 'Glossary of Terms: Settlements and Outposts in the West Bank', (20 June 2017), online: *Yesh Din* https://web.archive.org/web/20180413222311/www.yesh-din.org/en/glossary-terms-settlements-outposts-west-bank/.

19 'Survey Land' is land about which there is doubt as to private ownership. Israeli authorities have initiated land survey procedures aimed at determining its status. *Yesh Din*, 'Glossary of Terms', supra note 18.

20 Sasson Report, *supra* note 1.

21 Article 3 of Basic Law: *Human Dignity and Liberty* (Isr), online: *Knesset* website as amended by Basic Law: *Human Dignity and Liberty – Amendment*, 1994, online: *Knesset* http://knesset.gov.il/laws/special/eng/BasicLawLiberty.pdf.

22 (HCJ 9593/04) [2004] *Rashad Morar et al. v. IDF Commander in Judaea and Samaria et al.* (2006) at para 14, official English translation, online: HCJ https://supremedecisions.court.gov.il/Home/Download?path=EnglishVerdicts\04\930\095\n21&fileName=04095930_n21.txt&type=4.

23 *Yesh Din*, 'Glossary of Terms', *supra* note 18.

24 There are no official government figures regarding the number of outposts in the West Bank or the number of Israeli settlers living in them. *Yesh Din*, 'Under the Radar', *supra* note 8.

25 Chaim Levinson, '2,026 Settlement Homes Built on Private Palestinian Land, Right-wing Study Finds', *Haaretz* (3 May 2015).

HCJ when adjudicating petitions that have challenged the construction of 'unauthorized outposts' on land that is privately owned by Palestinians.

Hence, while there have been numerous petitions filed to challenge the legality of constructing 'unauthorized' outposts on what Israeli government authorities consider to be 'state land', these petitions will not be discussed. The reason is that, together with two other elements characterizing these petitions, namely that they are challenging the construction of settlements which fail to meet the requirements and criteria under Israeli domestic law (as opposed to only international law) and that there is no security-based dimension to the policy being challenged, they will illustrate why the HCJ has been able to adopt much more forceful positions vis-à-vis government and military authorities acting as respondents. The petitions also shed light on why the Court has been able to adopt a much more investigative approach vis-à-vis the alleged facts and feeling less pressured to defer to the assessment by these authorities. At the same time, various aspects of the Court's adjudication can still be criticized for granting government authorities repeated time extensions to implement the rulings, many of which were requested by the State at the last minute.

The state's practice and the Court's position: some trends

The respondent commits to desisting from practice following the petition's submission

Documentation by Israeli organizations indicates that several petitions were filed to request the State to implement demolition orders and stopwork orders that had been issued against illegal construction on land that is privately owned by Palestinians.[26] In some petitions, government authorities committed themselves to taking action, such as restoring the Palestinian landowners' rights before a judicial decision was handed down by the HCJ, as a way of avoiding a decision.[27] Consequently, petitions were rendered moot in the early stages of the proceedings after the State executed the demolition orders. While this can be construed as an attempt to avoid a situation in which 'a rule or precedent is set with respect to the issue of principle addressed in the petition',[28] the legal battles have resulted in the decline in the construction on privately owned land.[29]

26 *Yesh Din*, 'Tailwind: Non-Enforcement of Judicial Orders, Foot Dragging and the Retroactive Legalization of Illegal Construction in the Occupied Palestinian Territories', (October 2011), online: *Yesh Din* https://s3-eu-west-1.amazonaws.com/files.yesh-din.org/תיבג+חור/חור+תיבג+חודה+אלמה+EN.pdf.

27 *Yesh Din*, 'Land Takeover Practices', *supra* note 14.

28 Ibid. at 8.

29 Michael Sfard, *The Wall and the Gate*, *supra* note 2. Examples include (HCJ 10016/06) [2007] *Ibrahim Rashid Ahmed v. Commander of IDF Forces in the West Bank*; (HCJ 1486/12) [2014] *Izzat As'ad Rasheed Sawan v. the Minister of Defense*; (HCJ 4341/13) [2016] *Muhamed Ibrahim Ahmed Abu Rahme v. the Minister of Defense*; (HCJ 9419/10) [2015] *Ahmad Sha'aban Ahmed Nafa v. the Minister of Defense* cited in *Yesh Din*, 'Land Takeover Practices', *supra* note 14.

Retroactive authorization/legalization by the state

In its June 2012 report, the Levy Commission made a number of recommendations with implications for 'unauthorized outposts'. These include the suggestion to retroactively authorize these outposts[30] as a way of dispelling 'any ambiguity concerning their legal status, and consequently their fate'.[31] It also recommended the establishment of a land tribunal that would have jurisdiction over land disputes (and whether they are privately owned or 'state land') instead of the HCJ.[32] With regards to Palestinian ownership, even where it is proven that the land over which the outpost neighbourhood has been established is privately owned, this, according to the Committee, should not necessarily result in the return of the land to its owners. Instead, other solutions, such as compensating the owner, should be prioritized over evacuation and demolition.[33]

And although Israeli government authorities did not officially adopt the findings of the report, their subsequent practice indicates that they have in effect endorsed the findings. Recently, there has been a surge in retroactive authorization of 'unauthorized outposts' and existing illegal construction in settlements.[34] The State has made the case that it will be retroactively legalizing many of the outposts on Israeli declared 'state land', the construction of which was being challenged in front of the HCJ, for failure to fulfil some of the other criteria (such as being undertaken without building permits or without a valid master plan.).[35] By 2016, an estimated one-third of all outposts were retroactively authorized or were in the process of receiving authorization.[36]

The shift in position of government authorities vis-à-vis outposts preceded the Levy Commission's recommendations. In 2008, during proceedings in front

30 Retroactively authorizing outposts includes, inter alia, determining an area of jurisdiction, changing the status of the land and promoting zoning plans. *Yesh Din*, 'Glossary of Terms', *supra* note 18.

31 *Yesh Din*, 'From Occupation to Annexation: The Silent Adoption of the Levy Report on Retroactive Authorization of Illegal Construction in the West Bank', Position Paper (February 2016) at 7, online: *Yesh Din* https://s3-eu-west-1.amazonaws.com/files.yesh-din.org/חופיסל+שוביכמ/From+Occupation+to+Annexation+English+Yesh+Din.pdf.

32 Ibid.

33 Ibid.

34 B'Tselem, 'Retroactive "Laundering" of Itamar, Shvut Rachel, Sansana and Yaqir part of Government Policy to Annex Palestinian land to State of Israel', (22 November 2015), online: www.btselem.org/settlements/20151122_retroactive_laundering_of_settlements.

35 For example in 2009, *Peace Now* petitioned the HCJ to instruct the Ministry of Defense to immediately halt illegal construction activities in the settlement of Halamish-Neve Tzuf (north-west of Ramallah) on Israeli-declared 'state land'. (HCJ 3899/09) *Peace Now – S.A.L. Educational Enterprises v. Minister of Defense et al.*, unofficial English translation by Avichay Sharon. The Court issues an interim order to stop the construction on at least 10 permanent structures. Aviad Glickman, 'High Court orders Freeze of Construction at Settlement', *Ynet* News (31 May 2009). In 2011, the Israeli Defense Ministry approved a plan to authorize those structures retroactively. *Peace Now*, 'Defense Minister Ehud Barak Approves Plans to Legalize over 20 Illegal Structures in the West Bank', (8 February 2011), online: *Peace Now* http://peacenow.org.il/en/defense-minister-ehud-barak-approves-plans-to-legalize-over-20-illegal-structures-in-the-west-bank.

36 Isabel Kershner, 'Israel Quietly Legalizes Pirate Outposts in the West Bank', *New York Times* (30 August 2016).

of the HCJ, Israeli government officials presented a document with the list of priorities according to which demolition of illegal construction would be carried out.[37] In 2011, State representatives acting as respondents began arguing that only illegal structures on land that is privately owned by Palestinians would be demolished while construction on Israeli declared 'state land' would be considered for approval.[38]

In some instances, government authorities narrowed further the range of illegally constructed structures that they would commit themselves to removing. In the petition by *Peace Now* in 2005, against nine permanent structures in Amona, the State was asked to enforce the demolition order that had been issued by the CA.[39] While the respondents announced their readiness to evacuate the outpost

37 State response from 28 October 2008 as part of petition *HCJ 9051/05 Peace Now – S.A.L. Educational Enterprises et al. v. Minister of Defense et al.* concerning the construction in the outposts of Hayovel and Haersha (near the settlements of Eli and Talmon) cited in *Yesh Din*, 'Tailwind: Non-Enforcement of Judicial Orders', *supra* note 26. 'A Performance-Based Roadmap to a Permanent Two-State Solution to the Israeli–Palestinian Conflict', (30 April 2003), online: Global Policy Forum www.globalpolicy.org/images/pdfs/roadmap122002.pdf. In a position elaborated by the State during the proceedings of a petition challenging the illegal construction in the Haresha and HaYovel outposts, the State listed its demolition priorities as the following: demolition orders in response to a judicial decision; against structures in their early stages of construction; against structures on land that is privately owned and registered by Palestinians; against structures on unregistered land which has not been declared 'state land'; against outposts built after March 2001; against outposts built before that date; and finally against structures located outside the parameters of detailed and approved building plans and then other buildings. '(HCJ 7891/07) *Peace Now Shaal Educational Enterprises v. Minister of Defense et al.* [2013]: Complimentary Response Affidavit on Behalf of Respondent 1–2', at para 6, unofficial English translation, online: *Peace Now* http://peacenow.org.il/wp-content/uploads/2011/10/state_response_070311.pdf.

38 Chaim Levinson and Barak Ravid, 'Israel Vows to Raze All Illegal Outposts built on Private Palestinian Land', *Haaretz* (1 March 2011).

39 The initial petition was (HCJ 6375/05) [2006] *Peace Now v. Minister of Defense et al.*, and sought an order nisi against the State for failing to enforce stop work orders and implement demolition orders that had been issued regarding nine structures built in the outpost of Amona on land that is privately owned by Palestinians. The HCJ issued an interim injunction. In 2006, settlers filed a petition asking the Court to dismiss the original *Peace Now* petition. When the State declared its intention to demolish buildings in question, the Court vacated the original petition. In 2006, settlers filed another petition to stop the demolition, which was rejected. *Americans for Peace Now*, 'Settlements in Focs – Vol 2, Issue 3: Amona Redux', (20 February 2006), online: *Peace Now* http://archive.peacenow.org/entries/archive2237. This last petition is (HCJ 851/06) [2016] *Amona Farmer's Cooperative for communal settlements Ltd. v. Minister of Defense* cited in Michael Sfard, 'Regularization Law', *supra* note 4. In 2008, Palestinian landowners filed a petition to demand the enforcement of the demolition orders issued by the state for all the structures that were built on their privately owned land in the outpost of Amona. The petition is HCJ 9949/08 *Maryam Hassan Abd al-Kareem Hamad v. the Minister of Defense* discussed in *Yesh Din*, 'Petition to Remove the Unauthorized Outpost of Amona', (25 November 2008), online: *Yesh Din* https://web.archive.org/web/20180414010713/www.yesh-din.org/en/petition-to-remove-the-unauthorized-outpost-of-amona/. The petition was upheld by the Court in a decision rendered in 2014. *Yesh Din*, 'Why is Amona being Evacuated?', (1 February 2017) https://web.archive.org/web/20180413232437/www.yesh-din.org/en/why-is-amona-being-evacuated.

that was on land that is privately owned by Palestinians, they subsequently modified their position to indicate that it would only demolish structures that were built on the specific plots of the Palestinians who had petitioned the HCJ, and would refrain from enforcing the law on the illegal construction of landowners who had not done so.[40] This move, however, was rejected by the Court, which requested the evacuation of the whole outpost, and which underscored that measures to prevent the violation of the right to ownership creates 'an obligation to actively work to protect the rights to private property of the protected residents, which includes protecting them from unlawful construction on their land and seizure of it'.[41]

In response to another petition, in which five residents of the village of Ein Yabrud, together with *Yesh Din* and *B'Tselem* demanded the enforcement of demolition orders against illegal construction taking place on their privately owned land in the Ofra settlement, north-east of Ramallah,[42] respondents claimed that the petition 'raises "a sensitive matter that includes enforcement, planning, security, diplomacy and social considerations" '.[43]

Attempts at delaying their obligation to uphold the HCJ judgments

In the case of petitions challenging the illegal construction on land that is privately owned by Palestinians, respondents have generally conceded in Court that this is illegal (per Israeli domestic legal requirements). However, this has not prevented them from attempts to delay the enforcement of the Court's judgments with regard to the demolition of illegal structures and evacuating its residents. An overview of some of the more recent high profile judgments best illustrates the point. One notable example is the *Migron* case, which involved a petition filed in 2006 by residents of the Palestinian villages of Burqa and Deir Diwan, demanding that the HCJ enforces an order issued by the CA to evacuate the illegal outpost of Migron and to demolish existing structures built on the petitioners' privately owned land.[44]

40 *Yesh Din*, 'Land Takeover Practices', *supra* note 14.

41 (HCJ 1308/17) *Silwad Municipality et al. v. Knesset et al.*, at para 57, unofficial English translation, online: The Legal Center for Arab Minority Rights in Israel (*Adalah*) www.adalah.org/uploads/uploads/PDF_Final_English_translation_Settlements_Regularization_Petition_May_2017.pdf [thereafter *Adalah et al* – Petition].

42 (HCJ 5023/08) [2015] *Said Zahdi Muhammad Shehadeh v. the Minister of Defense* cited in *Yesh Din*, 'Petition to Remove Nine Illegal Structures in the Settlement of Ofra', (4 June 2008), online: *Yesh Din* https://web.archive.org/web/20180414073134/www.yesh-din.org/en/petition-to-remove-nine-illegal-structures-in-the-settlement-of-ofra/ [thereafter *Ofra* Judgment – Overview].

43 Ibid. In March 2009, the HCJ issued an order nisi instructing the State to explain why the demolition orders had not been implemented.

44 '(HCJ 8887/06) *Yousif Musa' abdel Razek el-Nabut et al. v. Minister of Defense et al. – Petition*' at paras 3, 21–25 and 33, unofficial English translation, online: *Peace Now* http://peacenow.org.il/wp-content/uploads/2006/10/Migron_Petition_Eng_Oct2006.pdf [*Migron* petition].

While respondents admitted that Migron was an 'illegal outpost', they requested more than one extension before implementing the aforementioned orders, primarily on the ground that they needed time to complete talks with the settler residents regarding their voluntary evacuation and to develop a plan of relocating them to another West Bank settlement.[45] In February 2008, respondents committed themselves to evacuating the outpost in six months. A year later, this was followed by a declaration that they made stating that they intended to construct a new neighbourhood in the existing settlement of Adam to house the evacuees.[46]

In August 2011, the HCJ finally rendered a decision, obligating government and military authorities to evacuate the outpost by March 2012.[47] In its judgment, the Court was highly critical of the authorities' conduct, noting that, despite their repeated declarations attesting to the illegality of the outpost and that it fits within the list of priorities slated for demolishing, five years had passed since the petition was filed.[48] Moreover, while the Court was mindful of the respondents' efforts to vacate the outposts without resorting to force, it underscored that authorities should have enforced the law from the very onset.[49] Furthermore, and given that any further delay in implementing the demolition order would have serious consequences for the rule of law and for the rights of the petitioners, the justices concluded that there was no reason to justify the granting of more extensions.[50] Migron became 'the first time that the Supreme Court has ordered the evacuation of an outpost [given that] [s]o far the Court has refrained from issuing rulings, instead deliberately waiting for the State to evacuate the illegal outposts'.[51]

In another judgment, the Court addressed a petition by residents of the Palestinian village of Dura-a-Kara, challenging the construction of 10 buildings near the settlement of Beit El, on a site known as Givat ha-Ulpana (Ulpana Hills/Jabal Atris) on land that is privately owned by Palestinians.[52] Petitioners

45 In February and May 2007, the respondents requested 60 days' extension, while in November 2007, they requested another 90 days to submit their position to the Court, and to devise an evacuation plan and complete talks with the Yesha Council and the residents. *Peace Now*, 'The Migron Petition', (1 October 2006), online: *Peace Now* http://peacenow.org.il/en/the-migron-petition.

46 *Peace Now*, 'The Migron Petition', *supra* note 45.

47 (HCJ 8887/06) [2011] *Yousif Musa' abdel Razek el-Nabut et al. v. Minister of Defense et al.* at para 16, unofficial Arabic translation, online: *Peace Now* http://peacenow.org.il/wp-content/uploads/2015/02/court_ruling_migron_ARABIC020811.pdf [*Migron case*, Judgment].

48 Ibid. at para 14.

49 Ibid.

50 This came in response to another request by government authorities for an additional 16 months. *Peace Now*, 'The Migron Petition', *supra* note 45.

51 *Peace Now*, 'The Migron Petition', *supra* note 45.

52 (HCJ 9060/08) [2012] *Khaled Abdullah Abd al-Ghani Yassin et al. v. Minister of Defense et al.* at para 1, unofficial English translation, online: Versa: Opinions of the Supreme Court of Israel http://versa.cardozo.yu.edu/opinions/yassin-v-minister-defense [*Ulpana Hill* Judgment]. See also Raphael Ahren et al., 'High Court Insists on Demolition of Homes in Ulpana Neighborhood by July 1', *Times of Israel* (7 May 2012).

had demanded the Court to order the execution of demolition orders and stop-work orders that had been issued against these buildings by the CA, to which the Court responded positively in 2011.[53] In May 2011, the respondents committed themselves to removing the buildings that were the subject of the petition within one year.[54] A few months later, the Court rendered a judgment that adopted the State's notification, and deemed the petition to have been exhausted and the proceedings to have been completed.[55] However, a few days before the date by which the demolitions should have been undertaken, the respondents requested a renewal of the discussions of the petition.[56] Subsequently, they requested another delay of 90 days for the consolidation of the position, arguing that 'any decision made regarding the Buildings discussed in the petition is liable to influence other construction in Beit El and in other communities that were also constructed on private Palestinian land'.[57]

In 2012, the Court rendered its final judgment in which it underscored three elements: first, that there was no ground for reopening the hearing on the petition; second, it noted that the principal of *res judicata* does not allow the opening of an already completed proceeding,[58] ('certainly not on claims that were resolved in the judgment'[59]); and third, that by requesting the reopening of the case, the respondents were undermining the basic principle of fulfilment of judgments which ensures that judicial proceedings are executed within the time period prescribed by the court.[60] However, it did grant government authorities 60 more days to meet its obligation (up until July 2012).[61]

In a third decision, the *Ofra* judgment of February 2015, the HCJ ruled that the nine houses must be demolished, and granted the State two years to enforce the demolition order.[62] In response to a request by settler residents for a three-month delay in enforcing the order, the Court granted them one month to allow security forces enough time to enforce the ruling.[63] While acknowledging the difficult consequences that demolition and evacuation will have for residents of these structures, the Court also underscored that they do not justify the retroactive

53 The State had rejected claims of the Beit El Yeshiva Center that the land had been purchased, noting that if the transaction had taken place, it is invalid. *Ulpana Hill* Judgment, *supra* note 52 at para 1.

54 *Ulpana Hill* Judgment, *supra* note 52 at para 2.

55 Ibid. at para 3.

56 It noted that the buildings slated for demolition are inhabited and that claims of purchase have been made. This is despite the fact that respondents acknowledged that those claims had been rejected by the CA. *Ulpana Hill* Judgment, *supra* note 52 at para 3.

57 *Ulpana Hill* Judgment, *supra* note 52 at para 4.

58 Ibid. at para 5.

59 Ibid. at para 6.

60 Ibid. at para 9.

61 Ibid. at para 12.

62 Ibid.

63 Elisha Ben-Kimon and Rotem Elizera, 'High Court Postpones Ofra Evacuation by a Month', *Ynet* News (5 February 2017).

authorization of illegal construction on private property or authorize the failure by the respondents to enforce the law, according to the policy it had set out for itself.[64] Furthermore, the justices underscored that dismissing the petition would result in great harm to the rights of the petitioners in the area and to the rule of law, both of which would be unacceptable.[65] In 2016, the houses were demolished amid efforts by hundreds of settlers to resist the evacuation.[66]

A year later in 2017, Israeli security forces evacuated the illegal outpost of Amona as a way of implementing the HCJ judgment in 2014 and which had been pushed back repeatedly.[67] Although the Court had granted government authorities an initial two years to carry out the demolition order (up until 25 December 2016), it eventually acceded to the former's request to extend the deadline for evacuation to another 45 days.[68] At the same time, the Court underscored that this would be the last and final extension and that its implementation would not be conditional on whether or not authorities succeed in finding alternative housing for the evacuees.[69]

Closing remarks

The reviewed HCJ decisions shed light on some of the trends characterizing both the government's policies and position (as respondents) vis-à-vis petitions that have challenged the legality of construction in violation of Israeli domestic legal requirements and of the right to private property that is strongly enshrined in Israeli constitutional law. And while the Court has repeatedly granted respondents time delays and extensions before having to implement the judgments, the justices have stood firm on the need to demolish illegal structures and/or evacuate 'illegal outposts'.

Often, what has facilitated the ability of the Court to adopt a more robust position vis-à-vis those petitions is also the fact that, in court proceedings, government authorities had acknowledged that the construction that was being challenged is illegal in Israeli law. Hence, while they may have tried to stall on the date and means of implementing the Court's orders, at no point in time was there a question about the former, especially when constructed on land that is privately owned by Palestinians. Unlike its attitude with regards to petitions challenging the construction or expansion of other Israeli settlements (illegal under international law but fulfilling Israeli domestic legal requirements), the

64 Ofra Judgment – Overview, *supra* note 42.

65 Ibid.

66 Toi Staff, 'Ofra Settlement Homes Bulldozed after Final Protesters Evacuated', *Times of Israel* (1 March 2017).

67 *Haaretz*, 'Amona Live Updates: After Years of Delay, Israel Evacuates Illegal West Bank Outpost', *Haaretz* (2 February 2017).

68 Yotam Berger, 'Israeli Court Agrees to Postpone Evacuation of Illegal Outpost of Amona', *Haaretz* (22 December 2016).

69 Ibid.

Court has refused to treat the issue of 'illegal outposts' on land that is privately owned by Palestinians as a political issue.

Each of these evacuations brought about a political storm in Israel's strong pro-settlement lobby that campaigned against those evacuations.[70] Arguably, it is as a result of these legal battles, and the Court's approach, that in February 2017 the *Knesset* passed the *Settlements Regularization Law*.[71] Its purpose is to 'regularize settlement in Judea and Samaria, and to enable it to continue to strengthen and develop'.[72] Moreover, it allows Israeli authorities to appropriate the rights to use and hold land on which a settlement was built 'in good faith on lands that require regularization or received the state's consent for its construction'.[73] This includes land that is privately owned by Palestinians, both registered and unregistered.[74] It also instructs authorities to register the land as government property (where it is privately owned but not registered) or pass it on to the CA's Custodian Unit Section (where land is both privately owned and registered), and to complete planning procedures that would allow for the retroactive approval of existing construction on this land.[75] Furthermore, it establishes a moratorium on all enforcement proceedings against illegal construction taking place on the land affected by it, pending the completion of planning procedures.[76]

As a result of the law, it is estimated that the law will result in the legalization of 3,921 housing units by expropriating 8,183 dunums of private Palestinian lands in settlements and outposts,[77] as well as legalizing 55 illegal outposts built either partly or entirely on private Palestinian lands.[78]

Petitions have been filed to demand that the Court declare it unconstitutional.[79] The petitioners argued that by passing the law, the *Knesset* has exceeded its

70 Michael Sfard, 'Regularization Law', *supra* note 4.

71 *Law for the Regularization of Settlement in Judea and Samaria, 5777–2017*, Unofficial English translation, online: *Adalah* www.adalah.org/uploads/uploads/Settlement_Regularization_Law_English_FINAL_05032017.pdf [thereafter Regularization Law].

72 Ibid. at article 1.

73 Ibid. at article 3. State consent has been defined very broadly to refer to 'explicit or implicit, in advance or after the fact, including assistance in laying infrastructure, granting incentives, making plans, issuing publications aimed at encouraging construction or development or participation in cash or in kind'. Regularization Law, *supra* note 71 at article 2.

74 Regularization Law, *supra* note 71 at article 3.

75 Ibid. at article 6. Landowners are offered the choice of compensation. Regularization Law, *supra* note 71 at articles 8–10.

76 Regularization Law, *supra* note 71 at article 7(a).

77 *Peace Now*, 'The Grand Land Robbery: Another Step toward Annexation', (November 2016), online: *Peace Now* http://peacenow.org.il/wp-content/uploads/2016/11/regulation-law-report.pdf.

78 Ibid.

79 (HCJ 2055/17) *Head of Ein Yabrud Council et al. v. the Knesset* cited in *Yesh Din*, 'Petition to Annul the Bill to expropriate private Palestinian land (the Regularization Bill)', (5 March 2017), online: *Yesh Din* https://web.archive.org/web/20170415011342/www.yesh-din.org/en/petition-annul-bill-expropriate-private-palestinian-land-regulation-bill/. In August 2017, the Court issued a temporary injunction against the law. See also *Adalah*, '17 West Bank Palestinian municipalities, 3 human rights groups petition Supreme Court against Settlements Law', (10 February 2017) at 2, online: *Adalah* www.adalah.org/en/content/view/9030.

authority: the land to which it will apply is 'outside of the sovereignty and the jurisdiction of the State of Israel, and is expropriated from persons who are not citizens or residents of Israel, and therefore not represented in the legislative process which they are victims of'.[80] It has also been criticized for violating numerous provisions of international law, and for facilitating the commission of war crimes,[81] and violating the Palestinians' right to private property.[82]

80 Association for Civil Rights in Israel (ACRI), 'ACRI, Peace Now and Yesh Din Petition the High Court against the Expropriation Law', (5 March 2017), online: www.acri.org.il/en/2017/03/05/acri-peace-now-and-yesh-din-petition-the-high-court-against-the-expropriation-law/.

81 Michael Sfard, 'Regularization Law', *supra* note 4.

82 Yaël Ronen and Yuval Shany, 'Israel's Settlement Regulation Bill Violates International Law', (20 December 2016), online: Just Security www.justsecurity.org/35743/israels-settlement-regulation-bill-violates-international-law/.

Conclusion

> [...] it is essential, if man is not to be compelled to have recourse, as a last resort, to rebellion against tyranny and oppression, that human rights should be protected by the rule of law.[1]
>
> – Preamble of the Universal Declaration of Human Rights

Overview

By subjecting the actions of Israeli military authorities to judicial review in 'real time'[2] the Israeli High Court of Justice (HCJ) has demonstrated that Palestinians stand a real chance of compelling Israeli officials to reconsider the effects of their proposed measures and the rights and interests of affected individuals. Often, the mere possibility of 'going to court' to challenge these measures, has ensured that Israeli government and military authorities are aware they are acting 'in the shadow' of the potential judicial decisions of the HCJ,[3] and that they may be required to defend their actions in court, including on the basis of the norms of international law.[4]

The book sought to offer a roadmap of the elements that have heavily influenced the manner in which the HCJ has adjudicated security-based measures in relation to the security of settlements and settlers, as a way of understanding why its adjudication of petitions by Palestinians challenged the legality of such measures. If one excludes out-of-court settlements, the HCJ's adjudication of those petitions has provided a limited domestic judicial venue for Palestinian petitioners to effectively challenge alleged violations of their rights, which are first and foremost protected under international law. The typology of elements

1 Preamble III of the *Universal Declaration of Human Rights*, G.A. res. 217A (III), U.N. Doc A/810 at 71 (12 December 1948) reprinted in (Supp. 1949) 43 AJIL 127.

2 Amichai Cohen 'Legal Operational Advice in the Israeli Defense Forces: The International Law Department and the Changing Nature of International Humanitarian Law', (Spring 2011) 26:2 Conn J Int'l L 367.

3 Daphne Barak-Erez, 'Broadening the Scope of Judicial Review in Israel: Between Activism and Restraint', (2009) Indian J Const L 118.

4 David Kretzmer, 'The Law of Belligerent Occupation in the Supreme Court of Israel', (Spring 2012) 94: 885 Int'l Rev Red Cross 207.

explains two other consequences of the Court's adjudication: first, that despite its declared commitment to promoting the international rule of law (RoL), it has only promoted the formal aspects of that RoL. This is evident from its position on the Hague Regulations' applicability and the relevance of the Geneva Conventions and some international human rights treaties. In terms of its commitment to the formal and substantive aspects of the domestic RoL, the extent to which it has upheld it hinged on whose interests or rights were at stake (Israeli v. Palestinians), what they were and whether the challenged measure had a security-based rationale to it.

One element that has significantly influenced the outcome of the HCJ's adjudication is the deference afforded to government and military authorities. Given that the justices would only question these justifications when evidence (presented in court) suggested beyond a reasonable doubt that political considerations and not security were at play, they have generally upheld the good faith nature of those arguments. Even where petitioners sought to bolster their position by resorting to the security-based assessment of former Israeli military officers, the Court has usually deferred to the opinion of the latter. This suggests that 'the chance of getting remedy [in those cases] is a chance of a miracle'.[5]

The Court appears to have adopted the government authorities' position that the situation in the West Bank continues to be that of 'an armed conflict short of war'. This explains why the Court has not challenged the position of military authorities that the security-based measures are necessary from a 'military point of view', and puts in context the Court's approach to the MC's considerations under article 43 of the Hague Regulations. In the majority of cases, the justices have not questioned the notion that the policies implemented by military authorities were necessary responses to genuine security concerns or that they were taken for security reasons or for the benefit of the 'local population' even when strong indications to the contrary were present.

A second influential element is the HCJ's position vis-à-vis the applicability of the major instruments of the law of belligerent occupation and of IHR law. In this regard, there is no doubt that the Court has substantially invoked rules and principles of 'humanity law' to frame some of the broader aspects of its judicial reasoning. For example, it has consistently reiterated that the Hague Regulations (1907) are reflective of customary international law and therefore, that they are applicable to the occupied West Bank, and have invoked the Fourth Geneva Convention as a reference point for adjudicating the legality of many of the Israeli security-based measures.

At the same time, it has not challenged the Israeli government's refusal to recognize the *de jure* applicability of major IHR and IHL conventions and treaties. Where the Court does refer to the Fourth Geneva Convention and to

5 Interview of Israeli Attorney Michael Sfard, by author via Skype (21 October 2014, Tel Aviv) [*Sfard* Second Interview].

IHR treaties and conventions, it appears as if the weight granted to them by the Court is that of a source of persuasive authority as opposed to a source of positive legal obligations.[6] This has undermined the purpose and object of these treaties: to safeguard rights and ensure humane treatment to civilians in all circumstances. The Fourth Geneva Convention remains 'a humanitarian convention par excellence [...] that has as its principle object and purpose the protection of the civilian population of occupied territories'.[7] While Israel's dualistic legal system (in relation to constitutive treaty law) allows it to determine which parts of international law it wants to receive into domestic law through legislative implementation,[8] the selective approach to international law, particularly insofar as its position with regards to the Fourth Geneva Convention is concerned, undermines 'the principle of *pacta sunt servanda* [which] means that treaties are binding on states that have ratified them as a matter of law, not of discretion, and that treaties are binding in whole, not in part'.[9] Furthermore, since Palestinians of the occupied West Bank are not citizens of Israel, they cannot weigh in on public policy formulation: they are not part of the constituency that can influence legislative efforts to promote and ensure the adoption of implementing legislation. This is despite the fact that the actions of the executive have affected every facet of their lives for decades. Consequently, and rather ironically, the HCJ has been described as the one government branch where Palestinians still have a voice at the 'domestic' level.[10]

A third influential element is the meaning and content afforded by the HCJ to legal rules, principles and notions of the international law of belligerent occupation. On one hand, the Court has reiterated that, by definition, an occupation is a temporary state of affairs; that the actions of the MC in the occupied territory to be lawful under international law must be guided by lawful considerations (in conformity with article 43 of the Hague Regulations); and that Palestinians, with the exception of those carrying East Jerusalem IDs, are 'protected persons'.

However, the Court has not ensured the faithful application of the relevant provisions of the law of occupation. This can be discerned from its analysis of what constitutes legitimate considerations that can lawfully guide the actions of the MC under article 43 of the Hague Regulations, and which has significantly expanded the scope of considerations to include the security and well-being of

6 Barak Medina, 'Domestic Human Rights Adjudication in the Shadow of International Law: The Status of Human Rights Conventions in Israel', (2017) 50:3 Isr LR 331.

7 Theodor Meron, 'The West Bank and International Humanitarian Law on the Eve of the Fiftieth Anniversary of the Six-Day War', (April 2017) 11:2 AJIL 357.

8 Armand de Mestral and Evan Fox-Decent, 'Rethinking the Relationship between International and Domestic Law', (2008) 53 McGill LJ 573 at 581–582.

9 Theodor Meron, 'The West Bank and International Humanitarian Law', *supra* note 3.

10 Interview of Israeli Attorney Michael Sfard, by Avichay Sharon on behalf of author (10 July 2014, Jerusalem), [*Sfard* First Interview]. Another lawyer said it gives voice to critical Israeli resistance. Interview with Attorney *Netta Amar-Shiff* by Avichay Sharon (24 August 2014, Jerusalem) on file with author [*Amar-Shiff* Interview].

Israeli citizens, both those residing in Israel proper and in the occupied territory. Another example is the Court's expansion of the notion of 'local population' to include the Israeli settler population, and which has bestowed legality upon actions by the MC that have effected far-reaching and long-term changes in the occupied territory, arguably beyond what is permissible under that body of law. Even if one assumes that the law of belligerent occupation has not provided clear-cut answers to some of the challenges arising from the long-term nature of the Israeli occupation, the Court's interpretation of this body of law has favoured the interests of the government authorities and their citizens, at the expense of the Palestinian occupied population. A third example is its interpretation of the notion of 'protected persons'. While it has conceded that Palestinians with Bank IDs qualify as 'protected persons', it has excluded Palestinians with East Jerusalem IDs from that definition. And while it sought to regulate the impact that the security-based measures has had on them, by enshrining the balancing of competing interests in a constitutional law framework, the conflict of interest between Israeli settlers and Palestinian East Jerusalemites is framed at best as a clash of interests between different social groups. It also does little to question the legality of the Israeli security-based measures under international law.

A fourth influential element is the manner in which the HCJ has invoked domestic forms of judicial interpretation, and more specifically, the manner in which the justices have balanced between the following rights and interests, particularly through the proportionality doctrine and its three sub-tests. In the case of the first group of judicial decisions relating to the legality of the construction of the Wall, the Seam Zone and the SSZs in the occupied West Bank (other than EJ), the Court has generally imported the proportionality doctrine from Israeli administrative law. Concerning the second group of petitions relating to the legality of measures restricting the movement and access of Palestinians for the alleged sake of guaranteeing the security of Israeli settlers and settlements, the HCJ has sometimes evaluated the legality of the measures through Israeli administrative law. In other instances, it has affected a constitutional balance between the rights of the Palestinians and those of Israeli settlers. Here, it must be recalled that while the Court has explained that several rights, which the Palestinian population enjoys, are constitutionally protected, to date it has refused to rule on the *de jure* applicability of the Basic Law: *Human Dignity and Liberty* to them. In the third group of cases, relating to the legality of constructing the Wall in and around EJ, the Court has oscillated between grounding the proportionality-based analysis in administrative law or in constitutional law, depending on whether the sections of the Wall examined run inside the JMB or inside the 'West Bank', and whether the rights which may be infringed are rights of Palestinians with Jerusalem IDs, or Palestinians with 'West Bank' IDs.

On a positive note, the HCJ has sought to ensure that Israeli actions in the occupied West Bank fulfil certain minimal levels and aspects of the domestic RoL. In fact the Court's approach can be viewed as that of a sliding scale: in constitutional balancing more substantive aspects of domestic RoL are taken into consideration; in balancing that is grounded in administrative law, more procedural aspects of that RoL are considered by the Court. Given the great importance that Israeli authorities have traditionally attached to portraying their military rule in the occupied territory as one that adheres to fundamental notions of the domestic RoL in its formal aspect, this is understandable.[11] The findings also underscore how the proportionality analyses and its three sub-tests, have allowed the Court to uphold certain petitions filed by Palestinians, on the ground that certain measures have had a disproportionate impact, either under the second or third sub-tests, or both. Thus, by invoking the Israeli administrative or constitutional law-based definition of proportionality, the Court has been able to regulate some of the harsher impacts of certain government-led policies on the Palestinians.

Even if one readily assumes for a moment that the judges invoked the proportionality doctrine in order to improve the level of protections afforded to Palestinians under Israeli law, this approach is ill-suited to a situation of occupation. In this regard, it is no accident that the notion of the domestic RoL has often been highlighted as a feature of democratic systems of government (and vice versa). In other words, it is most effective in promoting the rights of citizens (i.e. Israeli citizens), as opposed to the Palestinians, whom the Court has denied a clear authoritative source for their rights under international or domestic law. Hence, embedding the conversation into a domestic legal framework, one that relies on the balancing exercise, is likely to render the rights or interests of the Palestinians as a secondary consideration when balanced against the rights afforded to the Israeli settlers, or against the security considerations of government and/or military authorities.

In the case of the proportionality analysis that was grounded by the Court in Israeli administrative law as the first sub-test ('rational means' test), the judges failed to examine whether the connection between the means and the objective is also a fair one (i.e. suited to achieving the objective).[12] Nor have they required relevant authorities to demonstrate that the measures they have chosen to implement, do indeed promote the very core of the declared objective (i.e. security), as opposed to only certain peripheral aspects of it.[13] This has consolidated the 'unassailable' nature of the security-based measures purported by authorities, thereby making it very difficult for petitioners to challenge them, and explains why the judges have rarely declared any security-based measures to fall short of fulfilling the first proportionality sub-test.[14]

11 *Amar-Shiff* Interview, *supra* note 9. According to Attorney Sfard, this is why it has invested a lot of energy 'into making sure that they have legal formal backing for many of its policies and practices in the occupied territory'. He also opined that Israeli authorities are only fulfilling the requirement of the RoL in the sense that 'the only thing that the government is allowed to do, is what is entrusted to it by law'. See *Sfard* Second Interview, *supra* note 5.

12 Mordechai Kremnitzer, 'Constitutional Proportionality: (Appropriate Guidelines)', in Gideon Sapir, Daphne Barak-Erez and Aharon Barak, eds, *Israeli Constitutional Law in the Making* (Portland, OR: Hart, 2013) 225.

13 Ibid.

14 Aeyal Gross, 'Human Proportions: Are Human Rights the Emperor's New Clothes of the International Law of Occupation?', (2007) 18:1 EJIL 1.

In the case of the second sub-test (the 'least injurious means' test), by insisting that any less harmful measures must have an identical effect to that of the measure that is being challenged, the judges have narrowed the spectrum of measures proposed by the petitioners and their counsel that can be entertained as perfectly legitimate alternatives to those proposed by the government. Under the third sub-test (the 'proportionality in the narrow sense' test), the Court enjoys broad discretion in determining the significance that should be accorded to the competing values.[15]

In the case of the proportionality analysis that was grounded by the Court in Israeli constitutional law, a number of elements render this particular balancing approach of limited suitability for a number of reasons: the first, is that the Israeli Basic Laws, most notably the Basic Law: *Human Dignity and Liberty*, were deemed to apply *in personae* to Israeli settlers, but not to Palestinians living in the same territory. The second is that, when the constitutional right of Israeli settlers to 'safety of life' is balanced against the 'constitutional rights' of the Palestinians, and given the nature of the values that are at stake, the Court has tended to grant the right of the former a higher constitutional value than the rights of the latter. This proportionality analysis places both the occupier and the occupied on a purportedly equal plane, thereby distorting the real imbalance of power between the two population groups in a situation of occupation, as it wipes out the exceptional nature of the occupation itself.[16] It also puts the occupier and occupied on an equal footing in terms of the rights they are afforded, when the main source of the protection of the rights of the Palestinians is the law of belligerent occupation and IHR law as opposed to Israeli constitutional law. By grounding its adjudication in Israeli domestic law, coupled with its approach of refusing to rule on the *de jure* applicability of the Basic Laws, the Fourth Geneva Convention and major IHR law treaties, the Court has effectively ensured that the fundamental rights of the Palestinians have no clear domestic or international source for grounding positive obligations by the State towards them.

Even when the judges have upheld certain petitions on the basis that the challenged security-based measure failed to fulfil one or more of the sub-tests, these instances are scarce: justices have traditionally accepted promises by the military or government authorities to alleviate the otherwise disproportionate impact of security-based measures on the Palestinians' 'fabric of life' and rights. This has diminished the manoeuvring space available to the petitioners to challenge their legality – if only on the ground of the lack of proportionality.

Furthermore, the judges have often adopted a compartmentalized approach. For example, they have preferred to review the legality of the Wall in a section-by-section approach; to analyse the impact of movement restrictions for Palestinians in a checkpoint-by-checkpoint fashion; and to examine the consequences of the Wall in Jerusalem for access by Palestinian East Jerusalemites on a gate-by-gate basis.

15 Mordechai Kremnitzer, 'Constitutional Proportionality', *supra* note 12.

16 Martti Koskenniemi, 'Occupied Zone – "A Zone of Reasonableness"?', (October 2008) 12:8 Isr LR 13.

One major consequence has been that the judges' role has been reduced to regulating the impact of the occupation and its multifaceted security-based measures, and of fine-tuning the procedural aspects of the functioning of the Israeli system of control. It does little, however, to assess their legality under international law. Moreover, it has limited the potential of petitioners to demand restitution, as opposed to compensation.

A fifth influential factor is the primacy granted by the Court to domestic legislation, especially when it clashes with provisions of customary law, in which case the former prevails. This has consolidated domestic legitimacy of the annexation of EJ. This also confirms that the HCJ is not the best venue for challenging measures that seek to legalize control by Israel over the parts of the territory that they have *de jure* annexed.[17] Closely related to this is a sixth influencing factor, namely the manner in which the Court has invoked the political question doctrine to maintain the non-justiciability of the legality of Israel's settlement policy. While the institutional constraints facing the HCJ cannot be taken lightly, the Court could have done more in terms of underlining the prohibition of settlement activity under international law,[18] reflective of customary international law,[19] and 'to maintain the relevance of IHL on this issue'.[20] Had the Court done so, it would have restricted the scope of legislative and administrative actions that the MC can lawfully undertake under international law in response to the security needs of the Israeli settlers.

In terms of the seventh element, the HCJ's relations with other branches of government, courts remain sensitive to national interests,[21] and to public opinion.[22]

17 Gad Barzilai, 'Between the Rule of Law and the Laws of the Ruler: The Supreme Court in Israeli Legal Culture', (June 1997) 49: 152 Int'l Soc Sci J 193.

18 *Amar-Shiff* Interview, *supra* note 8. Given the near unanimous position that this provision reflects customary international law, the Court could have done so on its own accord, without having to urge *Knesset* to issue an implementing legislation. Interview with Israeli Attorney A-04 by Avichay Sharon, in English) (10 July 2014, Jerusalem) [Attorney *A-04* interview].

19 Had the Court adopted a firm stance regarding the prohibition on settlement activity in the early days of the occupation, when the Israeli public was less favourable to the settlement enterprise, it 'would have really saved the country'. However:

> [T]hen the government might not have listened to it, and it would have been ineffective, and I think the Court [judges] argue often, maybe not in decisions but when they are lecturing when they retire, that in order to be effective, the Court has to be attentive to what is possible and feasible and doable and to reflect sort of the will of the people. But is this a way a Court should function? I think not. It does not absolve the Court from its responsibility to apply international law in a manner that does not undermine the very principles on which it rests.
>
> Interview with Raja Shehadeh (2 October 2014, Ramallah), by author via Skype, [*Shehadeh* interview]

20 Attorney *Sfard*, Second Interview, *supra* note 5.

21 Eyal Benvenisti, 'Judicial Misgivings Regarding the Application of International Law: An Analysis of Attitudes of National Courts', (1993) 4 EJIL 159.

22 Daphne Barak-Erez, 'Collective Memory and Judicial Legitimacy: The Historical Narrative of the Israeli Supreme Court', (2001) 16:1 CJLS 93.

This, at times, prevents courts from generating international law-compliant decisions, particularly in times of crisis.[23] It shares the narrative and language used by the executive branch for the origins and features of the conflict.[24] And while the HCJ is not the bastion of left-wing elitism or the interventionist ultra-left court that it is made out to be,[25] recent legislative initiatives seeking to further restrict the authority of the HCJ,[26] to strip it of its jurisdiction to hear some petitions by Palestinians from the West Bank,[27] and to change the judicial selection process have all made strides in the *Knesset.*[28]

As for the eighth element, of the total number of petitions filed by Palestinians, of the 40 petitions, the Court dismissed an estimated 31, that is, 77.5 per cent of all petitions. In the case of petitions with implications for the first normative principle (that occupation is temporary), from the 19 judicial decisions that have been analysed, the Court has upheld the petitions only in 5 cases or an estimated 26 per cent of the petitions. In the case of petitions with implications for the second normative framework (that occupation is a form of 'trust'), from a total of 9 judicial decisions examined, the Court upheld the petition only in 4 cases. This represents a 44.4 per cent success rate for petitioners and their counsels. As for petitions challenging the legality of measures with the implication for the third normative framework (that occupation does not bestow sovereignty), the HCJ has upheld none of the 12 petitions (0 per cent success rate).

The impact of the HCJ's adjudication for the three normative principles of the law of belligerent occupation

According to Michael Sfard, there is little doubt that Israeli policies have undermined all three pillars of the normative framework of the law of belligerent occupation:

> [...] especially when it comes to the colonization of the West Bank: all aim at creating permanent, not temporary domination, breach fundamental

23 Felice Morgenstern, 'Judicial Practice and the Supremacy of International Law', (1950) 27 Brit YB Int'l L 42.

24 Daphne Barak-Erez, 'Collective Memory and Judicial Legitimacy', *supra* note 22 at 101.

25 Sharon Pulwer, 'Israel Taps Four New Supreme Court Justices, Shifting Balance of Power to the Right', *Haaretz* (23 February 2018).

26 The Ministerial Committee for Legislation, backed legislation which would enable a majority of 61 MKs to overturn Supreme Court decisions that have struck down *Knesset* legislation as unconstitutional. Raoul Wootliff, 'Opposition Skewers Bill to Reign in High Court; Kahlon Vows to Block It', *Times of Israel* (30 May 2018).

27 The legislation backed by the aforementioned ministerial committee, would see the cases transferred to the Jerusalem District Court, including claims of land ownership. Jonathan Lis, 'Ministers Back Bill Barring Palestinians from Petitioning High Court', *Haaretz* (25 February 2018).

28 Marissa Newman, 'Chief Justice Slams Minister over Bid to Change Selection Process for Judges', *Times of Israel* (3 November 2016).

> pillars/rules of usufruct and advances step by step to narrow the gap between an occupier and a sovereign. The main thing that creates all of this is the settlements. Not only having your own nationals/community [but also] imposing your own laws and creating settlements that by definition are not temporary. The demographic change and the immense way in which the territory is changed (handled and built) and [the] refusal to advance to an end of the occupation shows all pillars are under attack.[29]

This book sought to demonstrate how the Court's adjudication has demonstrated a weak commitment to the substantive aspects of the international RoL, thereby undermining the aforementioned normative pillars. It has refused to question the legality of measures that have consolidated the *de jure* annexation of EJ; the de facto control of other parts of the West Bank (most notably the Seam Zone); the extension of *in personae* jurisdiction to an estimated half a million Israeli settlers; and the implementation of policies that have brought about long-term changes that alter the physical and legal status of the occupied territory in a manner that is contrary to the interests of the occupied population. It has also condoned the existence of two separate and unequal legal systems applying in relation to Israeli settlers and Palestinians who live in one and the same territory, which has been described as an effort to reconcile a 'schizophrenic legal system'.[30] The Court has sought to extend the liberal Israeli legal system, one in which the substantive aspects of the domestic RoL are strong, to its citizens in the West Bank as a way of shielding them from the hardship of living under a military government while granting Palestinians some level of protection under Israeli administrative and constitutional law, all the while diluting the relevance of the international legal framework that is the main source of their rights (humanity's law) and distorting the interpretation of key aspects of the law of belligerent occupation.

Reflecting on the reasons why the Court avoids intervening in core disputes of the Israeli–Palestinian conflict, such as the settlements, and what is deeply problematic with its approach, Sfard notes that:

> It comes from the justices' intuitive feeling that the separation of powers draws a line between judicial review over 'ordinary' policy, which does come under the court's purview and is justiciable, and criticism of the very foundation of the regime, which should be left for 'politics'. [...] My criticism of this approach is [...] [i]t ignores the mixed character of the Israeli arena: it is not really a democracy when only one segment of the people affected by the decisions the court cedes to politics participates in the political process – the occupiers. The occupied are excluded from the decision-making process which makes the democratic argument false, even

29 *Sfard* First Interview, *supra* note 10.

30 David Kretzmer, 'The Law of Belligerent Occupation as a System of Control', *supra* note 4 at 52.

dangerous. The court's refusal to address these crucial questions leaves the least powerful, those who have no civil rights or representation in any governmental authority, defenceless. Yet this is the approach taken by the justices who consider themselves part of the democratic side of the mixed arena and adjudicate as if there were no other darker side.[31]

The end result is that the Court has contributed its fair share to distorting the logic on which this body of law is built, namely that there is equilibrium between military necessity and humanity and that the occupant is not entitled to benefit from its occupation. At the very least, its approach has helped to promote the legal indeterminacy that is characterizing the actions of Israeli military and government authorities in the occupied territory:

> Israel acts in the territory as a sovereign insofar as it settles its citizens there and extends to them its laws on a personal and on a mixed personal/territorial basis, yet insofar as the territory has not been formally annexed and insofar as this exercise of sovereignty falls short of giving the Palestinian residents citizenship rights, Israel is not acting as a sovereign. In this manner, Israel enjoys both the powers of an occupant and of a sovereign in the oPt, while Palestinians enjoy neither the rights of an occupied people nor the rights of citizenship. This indeterminacy allows Israel to avoid accountability in the international community for having illegally annexed the territories, while pursuing the policies of 'greater Israel' in the West Bank without jeopardizing its Jewish majority.[32]

Given the wider implications that a review by the HCJ of their petitions can have, Palestinians and their supporters have underscored the moral dilemmas that the human rights lawyer faces when petitioning the Court, and the possibility that their work is contributing 'to the ***workability*** of the Israeli domination and thus to the ***durability*** of the occupation'.[33] In describing a second disadvantage, one other Israeli lawyer noted that even though the litigation cannot stop settlement activity, judicial access also allows one to pay 'lip service to Israeli human rights and democracy'.[34] A third explained that 'when sometimes you win, it [also] gives the appearance of a fair trial and a fair judicial review'.[35]

Asked whether the disadvantages outweigh the advantages to such an extent that it requires Palestinians to stop litigating in front of the HCJ, it was noted that '[i]t is up to us, litigating in front of the court to understand and to

31 Michael Sfard, *The Wall and the Gate: Israel, Palestine and the Legal Battle for Human Rights* (New York: Metropolitan Books, 2018) at 442–443.

32 Orna Ben-Naftali, Aeyal Gross and Keren Michaeli, 'Illegal Occupation: Framing the Occupied Palestinian Territory', (2005) 23 Berkeley J Int'l L 551 at 610–611.

33 Michael Sfard, 'The Human Rights Lawyer's Existential Dilemma', (2005) 3:3 Isr LR 154 at 67.

34 *Amar-Shiff* Interview, *supra* note 10.

35 Attorney *A-04* Interview, *supra* note 18.

evaluate the advantages and to make a considered decision when it would be wise or not and basically the decision must be of the Palestinians'.[36] Another underscored the same idea by noting that this must be conducted on issues of principles: where the Court is likely to uphold a government policy which is likely to have wider negative consequences for the Palestinians' effort, petitioning the Court should be avoided. In the end, however:

> The One who decides this is the Palestinian who comes to us. If he thinks that appealing the High Court could save his house (and give his children a roof over their heads) for one extra year, and since no one is going to help him if his house is demolished, neither Israel, you, I or the Palestinian Authority can make this decision on his behalf.[37]

In the meantime, the need to provide effective judicial remedy goes hand in hand with the need to ensure accountability for wrongful acts committed by or on behalf of State organs. Together, they constitute a central requirement for satisfactory adherence to the international RoL, including in situations of occupation. As the 'gatekeeper' straddling the interface between international and domestic law, the HCJ must not lose sight of those requirements … all the while it still can.

36 Ibid.
37 Interview with Palestinian–Israeli Attorney *Quamar Mishriqi* by Avichay Sharon on behalf of author (26 June 2014, Jerusalem) [*Mishriqi* Interview].

Index